Gods *of* War

Gods *of* War

History's Greatest
Military Rivals

James Lacey AND
Williamson Murray

BANTAM BOOKS | NEW YORK

Published in the United States by Bantam Books, an imprint of
Random House, a division of Penguin Random House LLC, New York.

BANTAM BOOKS and the HOUSE colophon are registered trademarks of
Penguin Random House LLC.

Hardback ISBN 978-0-345-54755-2
Ebook ISBN 978-0-345-54756-9

Printed in the United States of America on acid-free paper

randomhousebooks.com

2 4 6 8 9 7 5 3 1

First Edition

Book design by Andrea Lau

To Mrs. Jordan Horner Saunders and Mrs. Charlene Marshall
For their years of generous support for the
Marine Corps University Foundation

Contents

Introduction

The genesis of this book was a series of conversations we had with other historians after the publication of our previous work, *Moment of Battle: The Twenty Clashes That Changed the World*. Someone suggested that we write a book based on history's great captains, starting with Alexander. We both liked the idea, but we also wanted to do something different, to get beyond a mere retelling of well-known historical narratives. Plus, doing justice to every great captain from Alexander the Great to the present day would yield a book much too long to publish. And if *Moment of Battle* taught us anything, it was that readers would not stand for you leaving out their favorite battles—or captains.

So we seized on the idea of writing about only those military geniuses who had fought a general of equal caliber. There were certainly not many of these instances in history, which helped with our length problem. Some readers may be upset that generals like Alexander and Gustavus Adolphus did not make the list, but while they and many others may have been great commanders, we cannot be so sure that a mediocre general would not have also defeated Darius, Tilly, or Wallenstein.

More crucially, we wanted to make sure our readers really learned something about warfare. We took as our guide both of our experiences learning to play chess. There is only so much you can learn by playing someone inferior to you or by revisiting the games of neo-phytes. There is, however, much to absorb, think about, and learn from studying games that pitted one grandmaster against another. Similarly, anyone wishing to learn about the conduct of war would gain much from studying those few occasions when true masters of the military art engaged each other.

Before getting to the six case studies in this work, we open with a rather sweeping historical examination of the changing character of warfare. This serves two purposes. First, it will familiarize readers with the various time periods we cover in this volume. Second, the military commanders at the center of this book did not fight in a vacuum. They were all products of their time. As such, how they thought about war and executed military operations was driven by the societies they fought for, the military culture of the period, and the technologies available to them. This initial chapter lays out how changes in these elements affected the choices of each of our great captains.

We were loath to end this book with a final case study, as we both believe that history is best used when it can help one make sense of the present and hopefully guide decisions impacting the future. With that in mind, we conclude with a piece aimed at exploring the role of military genius in the modern era, and whether there will be a place for such a genius in future conflicts.

Gods *of* War

A Framework for War

At the end of *On War*, Prussian general Carl von Clausewitz makes a supremely ironic comment: "No one starts a war—or rather, no one in his senses ought to do so—without being clear in his mind what he intends to achieve by that war and how he intends to conduct it." And that is precisely the point; rarely if ever do statesmen, their advisers, or their military leaders think through the consequences of what will transpire after they have launched their military forces into war. Even when fought for the noblest of reasons, war and the battles that result from its conduct represent the darkest of human impulses. As the Duke of Wellington aptly commented, "Nothing except a battle lost can be half so melancholy as a battle won." War is the great destroyer, leaving in its wake a path of wanton destruction, rapine, and death, with the bodies and minds of those who survive broken by its savagery. Yet men have pursued its tarnished glory throughout the ages, beginning in our written history with Achilles choosing a young and glorious death in battle against the Trojans over the possibility of a long and comfortable life.

Sometimes these wars are fought by men of talent, but not often, as military genius is a rare commodity. The context and circumstances of the political, military, and social milieu must be right for military genius to emerge in full flower. Had Napoléon been born fifty years earlier, he would have retired as a captain of artillery in an army dominated by the great nobles of France. Similarly, had the Civil War happened ten years earlier or later, it is hard to imagine Grant emerging as a major figure. That said, it is perhaps a good thing that military genius has been so rare in history. Unfortunately, those few who have possessed its attributes too often have found themselves driven by a restive impulse to employ their talents in search of conquest and personal glory. In effect, that search has led them to ignore Clausewitz's dictum "that war is . . . a continuation of political activity by other means" in pursuit of their own dreams. Thus, they have pursued their own personal glory instead of the larger needs of not only their soldiers but their societies as a whole.

All great generals, no matter how noble their cause and their persona, must in the end possess a certain ruthlessness. For some the pursuit of military genius, driven by their demons, has turned into a hardness that knows no bounds. Walking over the desolate landscape of the Battle of Eylau, Napoléon commented to one of his marshals as he kicked over the frozen bodies of his dead soldiers, "Small change." Marshal Ney's comment when he saw that same terrible battlefield, in which the eminent historian David Chandler estimated the French may have lost as many as twenty-five thousand men killed or wounded with their enemies losing a further fifteen thousand casualties, was, *"Quel massacre! Et sans resultat."*—"What a massacre! And without result."

One also must note that the pursuit of glory by military genius has in many cases brought little benefit to mankind. Rather, it has all too often led emperors, kings, and generals to attempt to emulate the glory of those who have gone before them. Genghis Khan and his successors wrecked much of China and western Asia all the way to eastern Europe, setting Russian civilization back by at least two centuries and permanently scarring the psyche of Russia's people. But in the end the Mongolian invaders left little in their wake except massive destruction and death, only the pyramid of skulls they built in Baghdad in A.D. 1258 as a monument to their military genius. Alexander the Great destroyed the great Persian Empire, but his own empire blew away with the sands of Mesopotamia. As he lay dying, his one possibility of saving it disappeared, when he replied to the query of his generals as to who was to succeed him: "To the strongest." The result was nearly two centuries of interminable wars that lasted until the Romans brought their concept of political order to the Eastern Mediterranean.

Napoléon's record in terms of reforming France's legal and administrative system suggests talents that lay far beyond those of war making. Nevertheless, he had already brought France the bulk of those reforms before he embarked on his great wars of conquest in 1805. Certainly, the French people as a whole were sick of the wars of revolutionary France by the time Napoléon's coup d'état in November 1799 placed him at the pinnacle of political power, initially as first consul and then as emperor. But all of Napoléon's achievements pale before the ravaging of Europe and the death and destruction that were the main result of his battles.

Similarly, Caesar's conquest of Gaul had enormous impact over the centuries. For one, it brought Gaul into the greater Mediterranean civilization, resulting in a French language directly descended from the Latin the Romans imposed on the conquered. His conquest of Gaul also brought Rome strategic depth and frontiers. The survival of much of Greco-Roman civilization and its transmission to the West depended on that depth when the great waves of barbarians began to wash over the lands surrounding the Mediterranean in the fourth century A.D. Yet, for all of his sophistication and literary abilities, Caesar demonstrated little concern over Rome's welfare. He conquered Gaul not to create a strategic buffer but to further his own glory, as the new Alexander. His brilliant political and military campaigns aimed only at making himself "the first man in Rome." And when Rome found a champion to oppose him—Pompey—Caesar's ruthless drive for power brought the Roman Republic to ruin.

Of course, there have been great captains throughout history who have been harnessed to a good cause. General Ulysses S. Grant, for instance, preserved the union of the United States and, through his military victories, brought an end to the evils of slavery on the North American continent. And it should go without saying that General George Patton and Field Marshal Bernard Montgomery employed their military talents for governments set on destroying one of the vilest régimes in world history. But for every great captain who has used his sword in the service of a noble cause there are at least an equal number of military leaders—Robert E. Lee and Erwin Rommel—who are more than willing to serve even the most abhorrent government's causes.

Acknowledging the misery caused by many of history's military geniuses, it is surely a good thing that there have been so few of them. The fact that military genius has been so rare and yet destructive warfare so prevalent suggests that there are other factors at work. The point is not to show how rarely they have arisen, but to demonstrate that many states throughout history have produced enviable military records without ever having the benefits of a battlefield genius to lead their armies.

The Greeks

Why? One might suggest that society and politics play a major role in both dampening the ruthless pursuit of power and producing military systems capable of winning victories despite having generals who display only average levels of military competence. The nature of Greek city-states is an interesting case in point. Sparta may well be the most militaristic state that human beings have developed over the twenty-five hundred years of Western history. Everything in Spartan society aimed at preparing its warrior class for combat. A servile, thoroughly cowed group of helots supported the city-state economically. There was little trade with the external world. The coinage in Lacedemonia consisted of chunks of iron; Spartan men drilled constantly or exercised, while their women focused on bearing—but not raising—healthy babies, whose task was to serve the state's military needs. The result was that for nearly three hundred years the fierce, red-cloaked Spartan hoplites crushed every army that threatened the security of their state. They did so without ever producing a military genius of any historical note.

In fact, the Spartan constitution aimed at maintaining a government that made it nearly impossible for a single person to dominate it. The system consisted of two kings, five powerful ephors who shared power with the kings, and an assembly that voted on laws. It was a conservative form of governance aimed above all at ensuring the status quo. Anyone who dared to step outside the bounds of what the Spartans regarded as their changeless system soon found themselves on the outside looking in. Pausanias, the Spartan general who crushed the Persians at Platea in 478 B.C., was shortly thereafter walled up and starved to death in the temple of Athena in Sparta for his supposed treasonous efforts to betray the Greeks. In Sparta, kings commanded the armies but were given no opportunity to rise far above their peers or even to lead the Spartan army in anything more than a tactical sense. As the British pundit Basil Liddell Hart has noted, Sparta's military leaders were little more than sergeants.

In one famous example in Thucydides's account of the Peloponnesian War, the Spartans shipped their most capable general, Brasidas, to Thessaly in command of an army made up of helots who had every reason to deeply hate their commanding general. Thus, the Spartans achieved a twofer: They eliminated a dangerous general and moved ambitious helots out of the Peloponnesus. Astonishingly, Brasidas led an extraordinarily successful campaign that undermined Athenian power in the northwestern Aegean, but fortunately from the perspective of the Athenians—and probably the Spartan leaders as well—he perished in the battle of Amphipolis.

The Spartans' great opponents, the Athenians, proved to be their polar opposites in almost every respect. They did manage to bring forth from their population one of the great military and political geniuses in history, Themistocles. Thucydides deemed the Athenian politician the most outstanding statesman and general-admiral of his time. Unlike most of his countrymen, he identified continuing danger from Persia even after the victory at Marathon. He played a major role in the creation of Athenian democracy, persuaded his countrymen to use the proceeds of a newly found seam at the Athenian silver mines in Laurium to fund a large fleet of triremes, developed a strategy to deal with the Persian invasion, convinced the other Greek city-states to follow the Athenian lead, led the Greeks to victory at the great naval battle at Salamis, swayed the Athenians to fortify their city, and then created the alliance of Greek naval powers that established Athens as the other superpower in Greece. It was an extraordinary record. As Thucydides notes:

> Indeed Themistocles was a man who showed an unmistakable natural genius; in this respect he was quite exceptional, and beyond all others deserves our admiration. Without studying a subject in advance or deliberating over it later, but using simply the intelligence that was his by nature, he had the power to reach the right conclusion in matters that have to be settled on the spur of the moment and do not admit to long discussions, and in estimating what was likely to happen, his forecasts of the future were always more reliable than those of others. . . . To sum him up in a few words it may be said that through force of genius and by rapidity of action this man was supreme at doing precisely the right thing at precisely the right moment.

Yet in spite of his accomplishments—perhaps because of them—the Athenian people used one of the safeguards of their new democracy and ostracized Themistocles. It appears that a majority of the Athenians had grown jealous of his successes and drove their most effective strategist and general into exile. Later in the war, they would drive out the highly competent general Alcibiades, as well. He then explained to both the Spartans and later the Persians how to defeat their Athenian enemy.

The Romans

In many respects, the Romans were like the Spartans. They, too, had a double executive, in this case two consuls, who more often than not stood in sharp opposition to each other. They also had an assembly that played virtually no role in the making of policy; major decisions were made by the Senate, which consisted of those who had held office previously. And they rested their society on a fierce warrior ethos. Like the Spartans, their goal was to keep their polity firmly anchored in conservative principles. While the Romans aimed at creating an immensely competitive polity, they ensured that no one would remain at the top of the greasy flagpole for long. Buried in the midst of Rome's myth was a deep fear that their city-state would find itself ruled again by kings, who had established their polity in its earliest days but whom the Romans had overthrown because they had become tyrannical.

Unlike Sparta, Rome was an expansionist power, a city-state built on conquest. The myth of the rape of the Sabine women by Romans eager to acquire wives says a great deal about their value system. They also displayed exceptional skill in either incorporating their former enemies directly into their political system or making them allies. Everyone understood that once the conquered had joined, they would suffer the most terrible of punishments should they ever attempt to sever their connection to the "Senate and People of Rome." Thus, over the centuries, Rome's control slowly but steadily expanded, first into central Italy and then gradually to the south and north. The Roman political and military culture was intensely competitive, but the two consuls—who commanded the legionary forces Rome deployed against its enemies—served for only one year, ensuring that those who reached the pinnacle, the consulship, did not remain at the top for a long enough period to disturb the conservative political framework.

This meant that during the early and middle periods of the republic, great generalship was simply not a factor in the equation of Roman success. Yet Rome was almost always at war. As Plutarch notes, "Janus also has a temple at Rome with double doors, which they call the gates of war; for the temple always stands open in time of war but is closed when peace has come. The latter was a difficult matter, and it rarely happened." How, then, to explain Rome's success in launching a series of military conquests that built and sustained the ancient world's greatest empire for seven hundred years? First, like the Spartans, the Romans were a fiercely militaristic people. Their legions, from the earliest days, were highly disciplined and "willing to bear any burden and pay any price" in the pursuit of victory over their enemies. Tactically, they adapted to create the most effective military organization in the ancient world. And, perhaps most important with a conservative government, the republic never overreached its capabilities. The Romans eventually did create a military genius in Scipio and allowed him to hold offices and commands that had not been allowed to any individual up to that point. But only a desperate military situation, with the survival of the republic at stake, led them to compromise their deeply held principles.

Scipio's career was shaped by the strict framework of Roman politics within which he was operating. Although he had amply repaid the trust the Romans had shown him, significant elements in the Senate—mostly older senators wary of the young upstart—remained his fierce enemies, despite his having saved the republic. Even after he had conducted a successful war against Antiochus III at Magnesia in Asia Minor, he found himself prosecuted for supposed peculation of funds that should have gone into the republic's coffers. But Scipio, rather in the manner of the myth of the Roman soldier-farmer Cincinnatus, decided he had enough of politics and retired to his estates along the coast of Campania. His enemies, content to see him depart from the political fray, did not pursue him further. Supposedly the inscription on his tombstone read "Ungrateful fatherland, you will not even have my bones." His treatment underlines the Roman fear of the great general who would overthrow the republic due to his success and ambition.

The ability of the Roman constitution to control its successful generals by sending them out to pasture or mitigating their ability to influence Rome's political and military systems began to break down toward the end of the second century B.C. First, the immense riches won in Rome's wars throughout the Mediterranean created severe tensions between rich and poor. Equally debilitating was the fact that Rome's government was sufficient to run the affairs of a medium city-state at best, and the expansion of its domains into an empire made governance almost unmanageable. Moreover, Roman armies began deploying on campaigns to the far reaches of the Mediterranean for years rather than months. The result was that the republic lost control of its armies, which now gave their loyalties to their generals, the men who paid them and led them for substantial periods of time. The crisis came to a head with the invasion of the great German tribes—the Teutons and Cimbri—that threatened Rome's existence. To meet this threat, Rome put aside the constitutional strictures that had checked the power of ambitious generals, and allowed victorious generals such as Marius and Sulla to hold multiple consulships and even dictatorial power, which was enforced by legions who put their loyalty in their generals rather than in Rome. The consequences were disastrous. The ensuing contest between Marius and Sulla led to half a century of civil wars that only ended with Octavius's triumph over Antony at Actium.

Octavius, eventually to become Augustus, managed to do what Caesar failed to: create a stable political system in which he appeared to be only the "first among equals." But he ruthlessly removed his rivals in a fashion that Caesar had not been willing to, leaving only the army to deal with. How to maintain its loyalty? Augustus first professionalized the army, deploying it to guard the empire's frontiers and then making it clear that he and his successor were the paymasters of the legionaries. In addition, the provinces that possessed legions had governors appointed by Augustus—largely drawn out of his family or immediate circle.

Thus, for most of the next two centuries, Augustus and his successors ensured that no general gained enough power to challenge the emperor's position in Rome. Military competence replaced the wild anarchy of the civil wars, which had produced military geniuses (Marius, Sulla, Pompey, and Caesar) to the general detriment of the Roman-Mediterranean world. The Romans still conducted major campaigns during the period of the empire's heyday, such as the conquests of Britain and Dacia (modern Romania), but the reigning emperor—no matter his capacity as a military commander—was always present to keep any of his more ambitious generals from reaching out for political power. Sometimes the emperor was just a figurehead—Claudius with the conquest of Britain. Other times he acted as the actual commanding general—Trajan, the great emperor and general during the Dacian wars. In other circumstances, where there were particularly large concentrations of troops, the emperors were present but allowed their generals to command, as did Hadrian with the Bar Kokhba revolt in Judea in A.D. 132 and Marcus Aurelius with the German invasions of the late second century A.D.

With Nero's suicide in A.D. 69, which ended the Julio-Claudian line, three separate power centers contested the empire: The praetorians in Rome, the Rhine legions, and the army deployed to Judea to put down the first great Jewish revolt. The latter under Vespasian triumphed and made its general emperor, but only after a terrible civil war that threatened the empire's fabric and stability. Afterward, the great Roman historian Tacitus commented that the frontier legions had discovered the secret of the empire—that they could make and unmake emperors.

Still, for the next hundred years the empire maintained a stable balance between the frontier legions and the great expanse of the Mediterranean Greco-Roman civilization they were protecting, to the great advantage of both. That stability depended on the emperor ensuring that his generals became neither too famous nor too powerful. But in the third century A.D. the army came apart. Soldiers, generals, and legions contested for control of the empire, contributing to the eventual collapse of the western half of the empire. Despite this, the creation and maintenance by Augustus and his successors of a system that aimed at military competence in the field, without imposing on civilians the enormous costs involved in conquests waged by military geniuses, must rank as one of the higher points of human history.

What accounts for this? The answer lies in examining what Rome had created—a "system of genius" that ensured there were always capable leaders, supported by quality staffs, and backed by an institutional infrastructure second to none in the ancient world. With such a system, Romans could win wars, even if they suffered periodic battlefield disasters, without ever relying on the rise of a battlefield genius. Scipio may have won the final victory against the great Hannibal, but Rome found it could keep him contained—and simultaneously defeat other Carthaginian commanders—with generals who were rated as merely capable. A flash of military brilliance was always welcome, but hardly a necessary ingredient for victory. For centuries the Roman military system was infused with sufficient resilience that, until the end of the empire, it could sustain repeated disasters and after each one rapidly return to the struggle. In the case of Scipio, his talents likely hastened the end of the Second Punic War, but as long as Rome's will to continue the contest remained solid, the eventual outcome was in little doubt.

Military Genius and the Emergence of the Modern World

After the collapse of the Roman Empire in the west, a group of warring tribes contested over a dreary landscape of the remains of a great civilization. That tribal, feudal world eventually coalesced into political entities that had one thing in common: the pursuit of violence and glory. Some first-rate captains appeared from time to time, but none could rank among the great military geniuses of history. Nevertheless, even more than the Greece of the fifth and fourth centuries B.C., the Europe of the Middle Ages was a place of violence. Ironically, its commitment to Christianity had virtually no effect on the actions of its leaders or followers. Jean Froissart, chronicler of the early part of the Hundred Years War, described Edward III's soldiers taking the sacrament in the morning and then in the afternoon murdering and looting the citizens of Caen. Included in their activities was the wholesale raping of the city's nuns. There was no romance in the great victories of Edward III and Henry V, so celebrated by Shakespeare; instead murderous nobles and their thugs contended for power. After his victory at Agincourt,

Henry V refused to allow his archers to enter the English-controlled town of Calais: such was their reputation for criminal behavior that their king did not trust them.

But in the seventeenth century two great changes occurred: the creation of the centrally administered state and the formation of full-time professional military forces. They were undoubtedly linked, but the details of their relationship remain unclear. The more important of these was the creation of the modern state in a nascent bureaucratic form. Included in that administrative establishment were war offices and admiralties that could now manage armies and navies in an efficient and effective manner. There was clearly a symbiotic relationship between the emerging modern states and their military, the most obvious of which was the enormous increases in the size and capabilities of armies and navies. By the beginning of the eighteenth century the army of Louis XIV numbered close to four hundred thousand soldiers, while at the start of the seventeenth century the French could barely put one hundred thousand men in the field. But the real change lay in the fact that these armies consisted of full-time soldiers, clothed and equipped with weapons by a central controlling government. They no longer ravaged the countryside except when at the bidding of their masters to crush rebellions and ensure that the provinces paid their taxes.

Of military geniuses there were few. The most obvious were the Swedish king and military leader Gustavus Adolphus in the first half of the seventeenth century and the Duke of Marlborough in the first decades of the eighteenth. The former came close to breaking Catholic power in Central Europe before he was killed in battle. The latter, while a brilliant strategist and battlefield commander, maintained a strict obedience to the dictates of Queen Anne. Thus, in no respect was he a political threat to the British constitutional system. And with the coming to power of a government that aimed at making peace at any price, Marlborough gave up his positions. For the most part, the wars of the eighteenth century were conflicts that had no religious or ideological aspects to their conduct. They were fought for territory and colonies but had relatively little impact on the populations of the countries involved. Even generals as competent as Frederick the Great had no illusions of being in a position to conquer their neighbors, much less Europe.

The simple reality was that despite the consolidation of state power, the huge increase in wealth, and the development of state and military administrative systems, no western state yet had the power or wherewithal that would allow a military genius to decisively change Europe's overall political arrangement. Moreover, even those generals who showed some promise were kept well in hand by their governments, who showed no reluctance to humble any general who stepped outside of his defined boundaries. It is remarkable that some states managed their military affairs extremely well without rising up a military genius. Britain, for instance, built a global empire during the Seven Years' War without a general of much historical note, though it was greatly aided by the genius of Prime Minister William Pitt.

All of that changed with the arrival of Napoléon and the French Revolution. It was the latter that created the circumstances that allowed Napoléon to flourish—and created the myths that have distorted our understanding of the nature of military genius since he abdicated his throne after his disastrous defeat at Waterloo. But before dealing with Napoléon and his myths, one must examine the two great revolutions that shook Europe to its heart and made possible the terrible wars that devastated Europe for nearly a quarter of a century. These revolutions were, in effect, as important as the creation of the modern state and its military organizations in changing the character of European war. Interestingly, they occurred concurrently, yet had little direct effect on each other.

The first of these great perturbations, the French Revolution, was political in nature, but the resultant capacity to enact the *levée en masse* put the entire population and resources of the French nation at the disposal of the revolutionaries in Paris, as they fended off the invading Austrian and Prussian armies. As Clausewitz noted in his classic study *On War:*

> But in 1793 a force appeared that beggared all imagination. Suddenly war again became the business of the people. . . . The people became a participant in war; instead of governments and armies as heretofore, the full weight of the nation was thrown into the balance. The resources and efforts now available for use surpassed all conventional limits; nothing now impeded the vigor with which war could be waged, and consequently the opponents of France faced the utmost peril. . . . Under these conditions the war was waged with a very different degree of vigor. . . . War, untrammeled by any conventional restraints, had broken loose in all its elemental fury.

It took the major European powers nearly two full decades before they were willing to mobilize their populations and resources to the point where they could match the efforts of the French. Here the financial resources of Britain were essential in enabling allies, with weaker economic infrastructure, to finance the burdens of repeatedly raising huge forces to defeat Napoléon.

The essential component in that financial support was the second of Europe's great revolutions—the Industrial Revolution—which had its initial start in the last decades of the eighteenth century and until the mid-nineteenth century remained largely confined to the British Isles. Napoléon once characterized the British as a nation of shopkeepers, but in fact the French were shopkeepers; the British were a nation of entrepreneurs. As the inventor Matthew Boulton, who with James Watt designed and then produced a far more effective steam engine, declared to John Boswell, "I sell here, sir, what the world desires to have—POWER!" The rapidly growing British economy, fueled by individuals like Watt and Boulton, along with

Britain's control of global trade, resulted in an explosion of wealth in Britain. It also allowed the British to mount an impressive military effort, using the Royal Navy to control the world's oceans and blockade the French and their allies. At the same time, Britain supported a major military campaign on the Iberian peninsula under the Duke of Wellington, and it provided the essential financial support that undergirded the massive military effort to break Napoléon's control of Central Europe and defeat him in the campaigns of 1813 and 1814.

Napoléon Versus the Rest of Europe: The Search for Decisive Victory

When Napoléon seized power in December 1799, not only were the other major European powers exhausted by the fighting that came immediately after the French Revolution but France was as well. Only the appearance of Napoléon and his extraordinary genius—and goals that bordered on the megalomaniacal—kept Europe at war for another fifteen years. With a nearly endless supply of manpower provided by France's *levée en masse* and an officer corps honed by a decade of war, Napoléon went to war with Europe. In October 1805 he destroyed the Austrians at Ulm before the Russian armies could arrive. Two months later he destroyed the combined allied armies of Austria and Russia at Austerlitz. That was enough for the Austrians, who quickly made peace, while the Russians, badly wounded, retreated into their lairs in eastern Europe. On hearing the news of Austerlitz, British prime minister William Pitt commented: "Roll up the map of Europe, it will not be wanted these ten years." He could not have been more prophetic. One year later, the Grande Armée destroyed the Prussian Army at the double battle of Jena–Auerstädt, thus removing the Prussians from the European chessboard. Napoléon's cavalry general, Murat, reported that his pursuit of the beaten Prussians had ended for a lack of any Prussians left.

But as Napoléon's victories swelled the emperor's ego, his opponents began to learn his ways. His self-induced disaster of an invasion in Russia in 1812 gave them their opportunity. As the remnants of Napoléon's invading forces retreated, Russian armies moved into Poland and toward Central Europe, while the Prussians decided to switch sides and join the Russians against the French. In the spring of 1813, with a cobbled-together army that consisted of new conscripts, veterans, and soldiers pulled from Spain and occupation duties throughout Europe, Napoléon came close to destroying the Prussians and Russians at the Battles of Bautzen and Lutzen. But his victories were not sufficient to persuade the two powers to quit. After an armistice that lasted for much of the summer, Napoléon now found himself confronting the Austrians as well. Again, Napoléon was able to win an impressive victory at Dresden, where he destroyed a substantial portion of the Austrian army. But the emperor could not be everywhere, and where he was absent the allies advanced. Eventually in mid-October 1813 the allies cornered Napoléon and his army at Leipzig. Displaying extraordinary incompetence in tactics, but enjoying greatly superior numbers, the allied armies crushed the French. Yet the Battle of Leipzig was not decisive. Six more months of hard fighting occurred before Napoléon abdicated his throne. In 1813 and 1814 there had been no decisive victory.

In stark contrast to Napoléon, Wellington never sought a decisive victory over the French. For the first years of his time in Portugal and Spain, his main problem was just surviving, given the extent of the French threat and London's unwillingness to support him with sufficient resources. But even after he had broken out into Spain for the last time, he still had to be careful not to take too many risks. Given the constraints under which he and his army were operating, there could be no such thing as a decisive battle over his French opponents. Part of the reason was undoubtedly that Wellington did not have a blank check from the British government in terms of manpower or resources as did Napoléon. The cabinet in London was simply incapable of supplying him beyond a bare minimum, given its many other commitments. Thus, the Iron Duke learned to husband his troops and their lives, not necessarily because he felt any deep commitment to them in a personal sense, but out of necessity. When his troops had engaged in a looting expedition after the Battle of Vitoria, he commented, "We have in the service the scum of the earth as common soldiers." He was eventually to achieve a great victory at Waterloo, but it proved decisive not just because of the battlefield victory, but also because the French people were sick of the Napoleonic adventure and its endless casualties.

Napoléon cynically commented after he sailed off to exile at St. Helena that God had been on the side of the big battalions. He was right, but he failed to draw the correct conclusion. Victory, after 1812, was no longer a matter of winning brilliant battles; it was a matter of assembling the greatest amount of resources and putting together an effective alliance system to overwhelm one's opponents. Outstanding generalship did matter, but it was no longer enough.

What should have been clear, even toward the end of the Napoleonic era, was that the age of decisive battles—where a war could be decided in an afternoon—was ending. The regenerative capacity of the nation-state, already formidable in the eighteenth century, hugely increased as the Industrial Revolution spread and gathered steam. While battles remained the focus of war, what truly mattered was the larger political, strategic, and economic framework in which these battles were fought. In the future, as long as a great state could sustain its political cohesion and economic strength, it could recover from any number of lost battles. Yet, the focus of military theorists, historians, and pundits in the period after the Napoleonic Wars remained fixated on brilliant battlefield maneuvers. In fact, one still can feel the tremors that the legend of Napoléon created reverberating in the staff and war colleges of most of the military organizations in the world today. It is, however, well past time to get over the idea that wars can be won with one quick battle. If one great state wants to defeat another, it must accept that the combat will be drawn out and bloody.

The End of Decisive Battle:
The American Civil War and World War I

The impacts of the French Revolution, with its ability to mobilize the people and resources of the state, and the Industrial Revolution, with its capacity to provide lethal technology improvements and provision armies of previously unimagined size, only began to reveal themselves during the Napoleonic Wars. Comprehending the rapidly changing character of war demands that one follow these two themes through the great bloodlettings of the late nineteenth and early twentieth centuries. And to them one must add the crucial importance of a coherent and effective strategy—far more important than brilliance in generalship. In effect, a national entity with an effective strategy can redeem whatever weaknesses its military organizations might possess at the operational and tactical levels. But brilliant performance at the operational and tactical levels will rarely, if ever, redeem a fundamentally flawed strategy.

The American Civil War witnessed the consummation of the marriage of the French Revolution and the Industrial Revolution. That deadly combination contributed directly to the length of the war, as the former made possible the mobilization of resources and popular support for a conflict fought over continental distances, while the latter provided the weapons and means—steamboats and railroads—to project Northern military power into the Confederacy's heartland. With one hundred thousand factories at work in the North, the Union was able to mobilize, equip, and logistically support an army of one million men with six hundred thousand in the field out of a population of barely twenty-three million. Even as its factories were supporting this massive military effort, the North was also producing no less than 233,000 reapers, while immigrants and easterners moving to the lands on the other side of the Mississippi River created 430,000 new farms.

The result was a war the Confederacy could not win if it lasted any considerable period of time. The great generals who determined its outcome, Robert E. Lee and Ulysses S. Grant, represented the two sides of the coin of war: the past and its future. Lee would spend his time in command of the Army of Northern Virginia vainly searching for the decisive Napoleonic victory. Thus, in the Seven Days Battles, he would mercilessly pursue George McClellan's Army of the Potomac. He did win a series of tactical victories, but McClellan was defeated, as his victories made no strategic impact on the capacity of the Union to carry on the war. Lee would then move north and, with his invasion of Maryland in September 1862, attempt to destroy the Army of the Potomac. That attempt was abruptly concluded at the Battle of Antietam, in which it was the Army of Northern Virginia that came perilously close to destruction. Only McClellan's pusillanimity saved Lee from a catastrophic defeat.

Even after gaining his greatest victory at Chancellorsville in 1863, Lee showed himself incapable of grasping the war's larger strategic picture. Rather than employ portions of the Army of Northern Virginia to prop up the deteriorating situation along the vital Mississippi River, he opted to continue his quest for a war-winning decisive battle by launching a great invasion of Maryland and Pennsylvania. In doing so he doomed Vicksburg, the army protecting it, and the final hopes of the Confederacy. In 1864, Lee was able to fend off Grant in a series of costly battles, but only in the Wilderness was he able to take the initiative, and then only for a short time. Thereafter, he was constantly on the defensive, as the Army of the Potomac, supported by the Union's full industrial might, pounded at its Confederate enemies. In the end Grant held Lee, while Sherman rampaged through the Confederacy's heartland, ripping out its vital productive capacity.

Like Lee, Grant admitted that at the beginning of the war, he had felt that one major victory would achieve total victory for the Union. In his early triumph at Forts Henry and Donelson, where he captured an entire Confederate army, he believed that he had achieved such a victory. But the terrible killing battle of Shiloh that followed disabused him of that notion. Grant would achieve two more extraordinary victories in 1863: the capture of Vicksburg with its entire army and then Chattanooga, where the Union armies under his command thoroughly wrecked Braxton Bragg's Army of Tennessee. But in no sense did Grant see those successes as decisive victories in and of themselves. In 1864, upon taking over the direction of the Army of the Potomac, Grant understood that, with its incompetent senior leadership, his new army was incapable of achieving the kind of successes that his armies in the West had achieved. But that hardly mattered, as the terrible battles of attrition upon which Grant embarked robbed the Confederacy of its ability to outlast the North. In the end, the numbers of the Army of the Potomac broke the Confederacy, but it was Lee's search for a decisive victory and the losses he incurred in doing so that ensured the Confederacy would not have the wherewithal to withstand Grant's final onslaught.

The Union's victory was a result of Lincoln finally finding a crop of generals—Grant, Sherman, Sheridan—able to break from the grip of the Napoleonic vision and adopt a doctrine of near-total war aimed at the South's economic base and the strategic will of its population. The campaigns of 1865 were so decisive because Grant, by locking the Army of Northern Virginia in a vise grip, denied Lee's forces the time to recuperate that they had become accustomed to. Simultaneously, Confederate forces were losing access to men and matériel reinforcement, as Sherman tore out the South's supporting sinews and the Union blockade enforced its stranglehold on Southern commerce.

This was a new kind of war, one fought by huge military forces on a continental scale. While battlefield confrontations remained important, from early 1864 to the end, the Union coupled them with a deliberate strategy of destroying the political and economic structure that sustained their opponent. Grant understood that in a "People's War," it was the "people" who had to be conquered, and more than that, they had to know they had been defeated. This became the true "American Way of War." It was not, as too many historians have defined it, the use of overwhelming matériel superiority to crush a weaker opponent, though a large matériel advantage often eased the path to victory. Rather, it was the relentless use of force to wear down enemy field armies while, whenever possible, also reducing the capacity—and the will—of an enemy to continue the struggle.

In this regard, Grant is still referred to by too many as a butcher who won only because he had sufficient matériel and manpower to wear down his opponents, but only by accepting horrendous losses. To maintain this argument, one must overlook many inconvenient facts. First, prior to coming east, Grant, through brilliant maneuver, had captured two entire Confederate field armies at Forts Donelson and Vicksburg, and then destroyed a third at Chattanooga. There is no doubt that he pushed his matériel advantage to the fullest in 1864, but this must be seen as only one part of his grander plan to strike throughout the breadth and depth of the South. His 1864 campaign plans should also be weighed against the dismal record of the Army of the Potomac prior to his arrival, where it had fought an average of two or three bloody battles a year without making any appreciable strategic gain. Moreover, throughout the 1864 Overland Campaign, Grant continually sought to win advantages through maneuver rather than battle. Unfortunately, the enemy gets a vote, and when pitted against a general like Lee—who almost always sought battle—hard fighting could not be avoided.

If one can overlook localized periodic flare-ups—the Crimean War and the wars of German unification—the years after the Civil War were a rare period in which the world's great states maintained a general peace with one another. This should have given European armies time to absorb the lessons of the American Civil War, but evidence demonstrates that they learned little from the American experience. For the most part, those on the Continent regarded the conduct of that war as nothing more than the mass slaughter of ill-trained militia, led by generals who had no qualifications for the post they held. The British accepted the white Southern narrative of noble Confederate cavaliers and yeomen farmers fighting off hordes of Union numbers in a romantic effort to gain their freedom. Both views were nonsensical, reflecting a general lack of understanding of the extent and ferociousness of the conflict. The wars in Europe in the 1860s and 1870s had remained relatively short, mostly because of the almost criminal incompetence of Austrian and French generals who allowed their armies to be encircled and destroyed before their states had time to mobilize for total war. And because they were brief, the changes in the character of war engendered by the French and Industrial Revolutions had no time to manifest.

Ironically, the Europeans had come close to replicating the course of the American Civil War. In 1870, with the outbreak of the Franco-Prussian War, Prussian chancellor Otto von Bismarck had unleashed Prussian and German nationalistic feeling against the French, who had replied in kind. But the stunning initial victories by the great Prussian field marshal Helmuth von Moltke allowed the Prusso-German forces to capture virtually the entire French field army, which meant the French had no trained cadres on which to fall back. The result was that the Prussian armies were able to slaughter the untrained French levies called up by the republic's efforts to declare a *levée en masse*. The war was over in nine months. Yet, the extent of the Prusso-German success rested largely on Bismarck's strategic genius, which manipulated the other great states of Europe so as to isolate Prussia's military targets. On the basis of the wars of 1866 and 1870–1871, most European military pundits estimated that future wars between the major European powers would last no more than a year. Moltke disagreed, and when he retired in 1888 at the age of eighty-seven, he warned that the next European war could last thirty years. If one believes, as some historians do, that World War I and World War II were part of the same struggle—Germany's efforts to create a hegemony in Europe—then he was spot on.

If the American Civil War was a cautionary tale about the irrelevancy of seeking decisive victory, then World War I represented the fulfillment of that warning. Tragically, the generals who conducted the Great War continued to seek the grail of decisive victory. The German Army's opening move, the Schlieffen Plan, a massive outflanking maneuver through the Low Countries, aimed to achieve a decisive victory over France in the first month of the war. But the

Germans paid no attention to the strategic consequences of such a move: the violation of the neutrality of the Low Countries guaranteed Britain's entrance into the war at the outset of hostilities. Because of the Royal Navy's superiority and Britain's geographic position, British participation in the war would cut the German economy off from the global economy. When the Schlieffen Plan failed, the Reich found itself involved in a conflict that, as early as November 1914, the chief of the German general staff, General Erich von Falkenhayn, admitted Germany could not win.

In fact, the intertwining of the French and Industrial Revolutions made anything other than a terrible war of attrition impossible. Caught in a web of nationalistic demands for victory, both sides proved capable of mobilizing seemingly endless numbers of soldiers and supplying them with weapons and munitions. That, however, did little to stop the generals in their efforts to achieve a decisive victory. In the terrible Battle of the Somme, Field Marshal Douglas Haig sought to achieve a rupture of the German line that would allow the British cavalry to charge through and massacre the supposedly fleeing Germans. He would have the same grandiose vision of decisive victory in the Passchendaele offensive of the summer and fall of 1917, a horrendous battle in which wounded soldiers often drowned in the mud. Yet, Haig still had the cavalry ready to charge through the breach that the infantry and artillery were supposedly going to make.

Nevertheless, at the strategic level the British waged a truly effective war. By portraying the extraordinarily bad behavior of German troops in their march through Belgium and France—they shot six thousand civilians as hostages—as even worse than it was, British propaganda won the war for the narrative in the first months of the conflict. Thereafter, Britain continued its efforts to persuade the neutrals to support the war economically against "the Hun," as the British termed the Germans, and eventually to join the war. Britain was helped by the extraordinary strategic ineptness of the German leadership, who, by disregarding the neutral powers, brought the United States into the war and sealed their doom.

The Germans, too, were looking for a decisive victory. The German Navy not once but twice persuaded the government to declare unrestricted submarine warfare against the British Isles and the commerce that supported Britain's war effort. Supposedly, the U-boat campaign was going to bring about the collapse of the British economy by choking off the flow of commerce, a decisive blow that would end the war. It was an ironic reflection of how important the economic calculus had become in the waging of war, but the German strategy rested on entirely faulty calculations. Moreover, the Germans undertook this effort despite knowing that it would inevitably draw the United States into the conflict, throwing the weight of its economic power and its military potential onto the scales. By the summer of 1918, two hundred thousand American troops were arriving every month, and the American Expeditionary Force would play a major role in Germany's defeat. The decision to launch unrestricted submarine warfare was undoubtedly the greatest strategic mistake the Germans made in the war.

What ensured Germany's defeat in the fall of 1918, however, were the desperate offensives launched in the spring of that year under the command of Field Marshal Paul von Hindenburg and General Erich Ludendorff. The German offensive operations again flirted with the hope of achieving a decisive victory, in this case through the use of imaginative tactical innovations. But beyond effective new tactics, the Germans did not even possess operational goals, much less a strategic objective. Ludendorff commented to one of the senior German generals when asked what the operations were supposed to achieve: "We will punch a hole in their front, for the rest we shall see." For the first time on the western front, an attacker managed to break through an enemy defensive line and out into the open, but with no means to exploit their breakthrough and no coherent operational goal, the German offensives, like the attacks Lee launched in 1864, added to an immense casualty bill the Germans could not afford. Thus, bereft of any sense of strategy, the Germans ran out of soldiers, food to feed their people, and resources to continue the war against the immense superiority of the Allied powers.

Hugely contributing to Allied victory was the performance of the American army, led by General John Pershing. In a similar fashion to Grant, Pershing often comes under attack for his apparently attrition-based approach during World War I's Meuse-Argonne offensive. But this kind of analysis misses many of the larger points of the American campaign. First, a frontal or attritional approach was the only battlefield option in 1918, where the German trenches extended from Switzerland to the English Channel. Furthermore, though the American offensive stumbled at the start, Pershing soon brought it up short, retrained all the assault divisions, and then launched an attack that smashed the German line asunder. And this is the linchpin of Pershing's strategic thought. His plan never envisioned winning the war through attrition. Rather, as with Grant, hard fighting through the Argonne was necessary so that Pershing could get astride the German communications lines and then transition from trench fighting to a war of maneuver. Pershing also understood that the American offensive was part of a vaster scheme where French and British divisions attacked all along the front. By holding in place and then decimating more than three dozen German divisions, Pershing made possible the great Allied offensives of 1918 that finally brought the Germans to their knees.

By any measure, the American performance in World War I was truly spectacular. When the war started, the U.S. Army was barely one hundred thousand strong, with just over one hundred thousand more in the National Guard. This force, only a twentieth the size of the standing German Army, was scattered in small pockets and rarely conducted maneuvers greater than a brigade in size. In 1916, U.S. resources were stretched just to pursue a Mexican bandit force. But within eighteen months of entering the war this force had expanded to more than four million, of which two million were overseas, one million of those already on the front line. In World War II the United States repeated this performance but on a much vaster scale, leading Prime Minister Churchill to comment: "It remains to me a mystery as yet unexplained how the very small staffs which the United States kept during the years of peace were able not only to build up the armies . . . but also to find the leaders [to guide] those armies on a scale incomparably greater than anything that was prepared for or even dreamed of."

Strategy über alles: The Fate of Generalship After 1918

The lessons of the Great War should have been clear, just as those of the American Civil War should have been. Grand strategy, economic power, and the ability to efficiently mobilize men and resources would be key to the next war—which the Germans certainly intended to launch. Not surprisingly, statesmen and military organizations largely focused on what had been effective for them before. For the Germans, that was combined arms tactics and finely honed tactical skill, which would result in the Wehrmacht's initial victories in the Second World War. But the Germans paid relatively little attention to the strategic lessons of the last war, and so they also repeated every major strategic mistake they had made. After its second disastrous defeat, the German military complained that Hitler was responsible for these strategic mistakes. That was nonsense. In fact, the army and Luftwaffe generals had welcomed the decision to invade the Soviet Union with enthusiasm and accepted without question the führer's assumption that the Soviets would collapse like a house of cards. Nor was there any serious doubt about Hitler's decision to declare war on the Americans in the immediate aftermath of the bombing of Pearl Harbor. The supposedly "decisive" victory over the French in the spring of 1940 was as much a result of the gross ineptitude of French generals as of German operational brilliance. But as to what the next strategic step should be, the Germans were largely at a loss. The effort to bludgeon Britain into submission proved a costly failure, and at that point the only solution Hitler and his generals could come up with was to invade the Soviet Union, planning for which began as early as July 1940, initiated by the army's leaders before they had even received instructions from Hitler.

The contrast between German strategic decision making and

that in Britain and the United States during this period exemplifies why the Allies won the war. Churchill's greatest moment came between May 10, 1940, when he assumed the position as Britain's prime minister, and July 3, 1940, when he ordered the Royal Navy to attack the French fleet anchored at the naval base at Mers-el-Kébir. In that period of fifty-four days the new prime minister fought off a substantial group of Tory politicians who wanted to make peace with the Germans, desperately attempted to stave off a French surrender, prepared the British people with his great speeches for the coming onslaught the Luftwaffe would launch in the Battle of Britain, and reached out to President Franklin Roosevelt and the United States. For Churchill understood one crucial strategic factor—that the United States and the Soviet Union would decide the war. Churchill believed that the Americans could not possibly allow the Germans to crush the United Kingdom from a strategic point of view. He assumed the same held true of the Soviets, and that in the latter case an eventual clash between the Soviets and Nazis was inevitable.

For his part, Roosevelt recognized that it was in the interests of the United States to become involved in the conflict, but a substantial portion of the American population remained strongly against any kind of military commitment to the defense of the British Isles. Roosevelt confronted that conundrum up until the Japanese attack on Pearl Harbor united the American people in their commitment to the war. In the intervening period between the summer of 1940 and December 1941, Roosevelt had his military planners consider the strategic situation. The contrast between his strategic understanding and theirs is worth noting. When the president proposed sending arms from American military stocks after they had been declared surplus, he ran into substantial opposition from the army's chief of staff, General George C. Marshall. The general was undoubtedly a great man, but he was not a grand strategist, at least in the summer of 1940. Like most of his colleagues, he believed that the Germans would overwhelm the British and commitment of scarce U.S. arms made no sense. He was wrong.

The following June, when Hitler launched Operation Barbarossa, the invasion of the Soviet Union, military leaders including both Marshall and Field Marshal Alan Brooke, Britain's chief of the Imperial General Staff, argued that the German conquest of Russia would be a relatively swift process. Again, the so-called military experts were wrong. Roosevelt and Churchill knew better. With their sense of history and knowledge of geographic realities, they understood instinctively that the Soviets were not going to be a pushover for the Nazis.

In the conduct of the war, the Anglo-American political leaders proved to be masters of strategy, in stark contrast to their Axis opponents. Helped by the warning that the French collapse had given the Western powers in the spring of 1940, both the prime minister and the president pushed for the massive mobilization of their nations' manpower, industry, and other resources. In percentage terms, the British were the most successful in squeezing the lemons until the pips squeaked. But Roosevelt utilized the enormous latent economic potential of the United States to its fullest extent, given the political constraints. The efforts of the two countries yet again reflected a marriage of the French and Industrial Revolutions.

It was not that Allied strategy managed to get everything right. General Marshall's enthusiasm for a second front in northern Europe, initially supported by Roosevelt, in either 1942 or 1943 would have resulted in a disaster for Allied arms. On the other hand, when it was clear to the president that a second front on the coast of France in 1942 was not going to happen, he forced his senior military advisers—against their strong opposition—to support Operation Torch, the landing in French North Africa, the only possibility open to Allied ground forces in Europe. That decision resulted in the destruction of a major Axis army in Tunisia in May 1943. Churchill also made strategic miscalculations on a rather regular basis, although, unlike Roosevelt, he never overruled his military advisers. The prime minister's desire to put off Operation Overlord in favor of further operations in the Mediterranean was certainly wrongheaded, but by 1944 the Americans held a position of overwhelming power in the alliance, and they forced the decision to invade Normandy in June 1944.

So where does this leave generalship? There were certainly no decisive battles in the conduct of the war. The defeat of France in May 1940 only opened the door for the Germans to fight a sustained long war, but one in which, from this point on, their opponents would possess strategic depth and far superior manpower and resources. They did not fully understand the nature of the dangers that confronted them until the roof quite literally began to collapse around them in the spring of 1943, when the RAF Bomber Command began to inflict terrible damage to the German war economy with its assault on the Ruhr. Thus, in the largest sense one cannot speak of decisive battles. At best one can speak of decisive campaigns. But the fact that perhaps the most important of these, the Battle of the Atlantic, lasted from Britain's declaration of war on September 3, 1939, through to the war's end suggests how irrelevant the word "decisive" is.

Nevertheless, generalship and military leadership do matter. The success of Allied strategy over the course of the war depended on the capabilities and performance of the generals and admirals at the top. The admirals who ran Western Approaches command in the Battle of the Atlantic did manage to limit the ability of the U-boats to damage the commerce on which the air and ground campaigns against Germany depended. But the victory rested not on a single individual but on a host of ship captains, intelligence officers, code breakers, and, of course, the immense ability of U.S. shipyards to turn out merchant vessels and their escorts by the thousands.

And what of Rommel, Patton, and Montgomery? Their generalship was important, but no longer was it decisive. Of the three, Rommel had the instinctive sense of a great captain. In the breakthrough of May 1940 by German panzers that sealed the defeat of the French Army, as the foremost historian of that campaign has pointed out, Rommel's 7th Panzer Division achieved the key success. After his defeat at El Alamein and even before Operation Torch, he understood that the Axis forces needed to abandon the shores of

North Africa. Similarly, had he been given a free hand to defend the coast of France, he might well have placed the Americans in an extraordinarily dangerous situation in their landing at Omaha Beach. Would Germany have won the war as a result? No. It would only have prolonged the catastrophe, with the end result that the Americans would likely have dropped the first atomic bomb on Germany rather than Japan. As for Patton and Montgomery, they never fought a truly decisive battle, but they did shorten the war. Moreover, their competence saved the lives of innumerable Allied soldiers under their command. Ironically, the true modern general in the war against Germany was Dwight D. Eisenhower, who, with his skillful diplomacy and understanding of the larger strategic framework, was able to keep Allied forces in the West running effectively *together*.

Overall, the advent of the Industrial Age has assuredly limited the scope for the kind of military genius that streaks across the firmament for a brief moment of history. It has not, however, done away with the need for thoughtful generalship, for, as George Santayana reminds us, "Only the dead have seen the end of war." While no one, particularly those who have experienced the horrors and destructive consequences of combat, would ever wish for war, statesmen, strategists, and soldiers must always be cognizant of the Roman proverb *"Si vis pacem, para bellum"*—"If you want peace, prepare for war."

For many, imagining such preparation congers up images of multitudes of ships, tanks, and aircraft assembled to do battle against a similarly equipped foe. But for military professionals, the preparations for war are mostly mental, gained only through experience or through deep historical study of previous conflicts. Though the ages have witnessed unceasing changes in the character of war, its nature has remained immutable, leaving many strategic and operational lessons from which to draw. The best lessons unquestionably come from those who both mastered the art of war in their own time and had their mastery tested against a general of equal caliber. The case studies that follow represent an effort—the first of its kind—to examine those few times in history when generals at the pinnacle of their powers met each other in battle.

Hannibal and Scipio

In 1914, German armies implemented the Schlieffen Plan, which launched their forces deep into Belgium in a great turning movement to encircle and annihilate the Allied armies. The plan's designer, Field Marshal Alfred von Schlieffen, used for his inspiration Hannibal's great victory at the Battle of Cannae, fought more than two thousand years before. To assist in the planning effort, he had the general staff's historical section prepare a series of "Cannae Studies" for his planning staff to reference. Such is the hold Hannibal has had on the imagination of military strategists for two millennia. In a series of brilliant strokes, Hannibal came within a hairbreadth of bringing Rome to its knees. No other army would approach the walls of Rome for six hundred years. In the end, though, Hannibal was bested by a young commander, Scipio, whom the historian B. H. Liddell Hart considered the best of history's many great captains.

From what we know of the personalities of these two great captains, they were very much alike, at least in their approach to war. Hannibal learned how to conduct a campaign at the foot of his father, Hamilcar Barca, Carthage's greatest military commander prior to his son's ascendency. As a teenager Scipio accompanied his father on only a single minor campaign. He learned the art of war from Hannibal himself, having been a junior officer on the losing side of several of Hannibal's greatest victories. Both were brilliant at operations, and when they finally met at the Battle of Zama, each had known nothing but victory as commanders. But Scipio differentiated himself in one crucial way—he was the better strategic thinker. For, despite all of his glorious battlefield victories, Hannibal never formulated a war-winning strategy. Noting his failing, one of his senior commanders remonstrated, "You, Hannibal, know how to gain a victory; you do not know how to use it."

Scipio, on the other hand, never lost sight of his strategic goal— the defeat of Hannibal's army and the total subjugation of Carthage. That he was able to complete his design against one of the greatest generals in history is testament to Scipio's genius. Still, it is Hannibal's brilliant battlefield performance at Cannae that is most remembered and has become an exemplar of masterful maneuver. Even today, generals continue to study the Battle of Cannae and dream of one day emulating the masterstroke that annihilated two of Rome's consular armies in an afternoon. The dream of decisive battle is never far from the military mind, but today's military leaders would be better off studying Scipio's campaigns more closely, as he was the one who best understood how to use battles in masterful combinations to actually win wars.

Background

After seeing off a series of existential threats, by the start of the third century B.C., Rome ruled all of central and southern Italy and had forced peace terms on the Gauls in the north. Only a short-lived invasion by Pyrrhus of Epirus threatened the city's hold on power. Pyrrhus, the self-styled protector of the Greeks in southern Italy, landed in Italy in 280 B.C. and thrice pitted his superbly trained and equipped soldiers against the raw levies of Rome. He won two victories at Heraclea and Asculum before Rome fought him to a bloody draw at Beneventum. Such victories gained Pyrrhus nothing, as after each battle, Rome, tapping a seemingly inexhaustible pool of manpower, replenished its army and renewed the contest. Pyrrhus, who had few matériel or manpower resources on which to fall back, saw his military power dwindling, while Rome, despite its battlefield defeats, appeared unaffected. As he surveyed the carnage after the Battle of Asculum, Pyrrhus clearly understood his dilemma, stating, "If we are victorious in one more battle with the Romans, we shall be utterly ruined."

When Pyrrhus finally gave up the fight and sailed for home, he reputedly commented: "What a wrestling ground we are leaving, my friends, for the Carthaginians and the Romans." As Plutarch notes, "This conjecture was soon afterwards confirmed." It was Carthage's misfortune not to have learned the single most important lesson of Rome's war with Pyrrhus—the Romans were insensitive to defeats. Rome could and did lose entire armies during its rise to power in Italy. But what continually astounded its enemies was the city's capacity to generate new armies and restore battered ones. This was much the story of the First Punic War, 264–241 B.C., where the Romans opted to cripple their finances by building successive fleets until the Carthaginians could no longer stay the course.

Rome's greatest test came just over two decades after the First Punic War's end, when a series of defeats brought the city's fortunes to a nadir not repeated for more than six hundred years. Its adversary this time was Hannibal, the greatest battlefield commander Rome had ever faced. Over sixteen years Hannibal humiliated a long list of Roman generals, until he finally met a commander worthy of him—Publius Cornelius Scipio, who, except for Julius Caesar, surely ranks as the greatest of all Roman generals.

Hannibal

Exhausted by more than two decades of conflict, Carthage ended the First Punic War by ceding Sicily to Roman control and agreeing to pay 3,200 silver talents as a war indemnity over twenty years. Because of this huge indemnity, Carthage lacked the funds to pay off the mercenaries it had employed to fight the war. When the mercenaries revolted, Carthage was forced into two years of further con-

flict that nearly brought the city to ruin. It was saved by the genius
of Hamilcar Barca, the general who had fought the Romans to a
standstill in Sicily. Soon after the Mercenary War concluded, Carthage began casting about for ways to rebuild its fortune. With expansion to the north and east closed off by the Romans, who had
gratuitously seized Corsica and Sardinia after the First Punic War
ended, the city's rulers turned to Iberia (Spain) where they had already established several colonies—Gadir (Cadiz), Malkah (Málaga),
and New Carthage (Cartagena).

Bust of Hannibal
(© 1932 by Phaidon Verlag [Wien-Leipzig])

In 237 B.C. Hamilcar and his three sons, Hasdrubal, Mago, and
the ten-year-old Hannibal, landed in Iberia. Over the next eight
years Hamilcar defeated a series of inland tribes and greatly expanded
Carthage's new empire. But Carthage's dominion was one in name
only, as Iberia increasingly became the private domain of the Barca
family rather than a province of Carthage. When Hamilcar died in
229 B.C., his more politically attuned son-in-law, Hasdrubal the
Fair, assumed command of Spain, while continuing to expand Car-

thage's holdings through diplomacy and political marriages. Hannibal himself was married off to an Iberian princess, but not much else is known about him during this period. According to Livy, while still a boy, Hannibal was taken by his father to an altar and forced to swear an oath of undying enmity to Rome. And, although it is not recorded, he must also have spent much of his time with the army on campaign, since when Hasdrubal was murdered in 221 B.C., the soldiers elected the twenty-six-year-old Hannibal as their leader.

The following year Hannibal launched a successful attack deep into Iberia, capturing Salamanca and subduing central Iberia. This success was followed in 219 B.C. by the Siege of Saguntum, the only major port on Iberia's Mediterranean coast not controlled by Carthage. Historians still debate whether Saguntum's relationship with Rome was as a friend or as an ally, but there is little doubt that Rome considered the city part of its sphere of control in the western Mediterranean. As such, Hannibal must have known that his attack would be viewed by Rome as an act of war. The siege was a hard one, during which Hannibal was severely wounded by a spear or arrow bolt in his thigh and his army came close to disintegration. When, after nine months, Saguntum fell, Hannibal set his soldiers free to sack the city. Remarkably, the Romans made no attempts to assist the city, either because they were otherwise occupied—they were fighting a major war in Illyria—or because they wanted to use the city's fall as a casus belli.

When Carthage refused demands to return the city and hand over Hannibal to Roman justice, Rome declared war. Not surprisingly, Rome had little idea of the dangerous path on which it had embarked, while the young Carthaginian general had learned the lessons of the First Punic War well. As Carthage could never hope to match Rome's resources, particularly in terms of Rome's inexhaustible supply of young, tough soldiers, Hannibal would not wait to fight on Rome's terms. He would bring the war directly to Rome's doorstep.

Hannibal understood that Rome was certain to win a war of attrition. Moreover, it had the naval capacity to wreck Carthaginian trade and cut off Carthage's communications with Spain. This over-whelming naval superiority also allowed Rome to sustain armies on multiple fronts: Spain, Sicily, Africa, and, if necessary, Italy itself. Consequently, Hannibal's one hope of altering the strategic balance was to invade Italy. Only in Italy could he win quick and possibly decisive victories that would force Rome to negotiate. Even if Rome fought on, such victories held the promise of bringing many of the towns and cities recently absorbed into Rome's polity over to the Carthaginian cause. As such, Hannibal planned to portray himself as a liberator of Italy from Roman tyranny, hoping to deprive Rome of its one great advantage—Italian manpower.

In 218 B.C. Hannibal set out from New Carthage with his well-trained veterans. According to the historian Polybius, he began his march with ninety thousand infantry and twelve thousand cavalry. Appian's account adds thirty-seven elephants. After crossing the Ebro, the traditional dividing line between Roman and Carthaginian interests, Hannibal was obliged to fight his way through the fierce mountain tribes that made the Pyrenees their home. Their continuing antagonism induced him to leave a sizable force behind to secure his supply lines through this newly "pacified" region. But that was not the end of his travails. To his further dismay, the fighting in the Pyrenees revealed that a sizable portion of his army could not be relied on outside their native territories, and eleven thousand of these unreliable soldiers were sent home. Pressing on with fifty thousand infantry and nine thousand cavalry, Hannibal evaded a small Roman army commanded by Scipio's father, Publius Cornelius Scipio, and crossed the Rhône. After a torturous march through the Alps, Hannibal led the much reduced and exhausted Carthaginian army—twenty thousand infantry and six thousand cavalry remained—onto the plains of northern Italy. Through accidents, sickness, and the resistance of tribes in both Gaul and the Alps, Hannibal's grand army was reduced by three-quarters and had yet to face a Roman army in the field.

After resting his soldiers, Hannibal led them in storming the main town of the Taurini, one of the few northern plains tribes not to welcome him. Other local tribes then provided him with his first small reinforcements. Although a large number of other Gaelic tribes had announced their readiness to join his cause, most remained on the fence until the Carthaginians had demonstrated they could beat the Romans in battle. By this time, C. Scipio, after sending most of his army to Spain, arrived in Italy to assume command of the small Roman force gathered in the north. True to the Roman playbook, where aggression almost always took the place of strategic thinking, C. Scipio marched his force to intercept Hannibal.

The two armies met at the Battle of Ticinus. In reality this battle was no more than a cavalry action, as Hannibal's infantry never entered the fray and Rome's three legions were still forming when the Carthaginian attack began. The Romans never had a chance. Scipio had sent his *velites,* or Roman skirmishers, forward to screen his mostly Gaelic cavalry, but Hannibal's cavalry routed them almost before they could throw a single javelin. The exposed Gaelic cavalry fought hard until Hannibal's Numidians, at the time the finest light cavalry in the world, swept in on both flanks and put the Roman allies to flight.

During the fighting, C. Scipio found himself surrounded by enemy cavalry. His son and namesake, Scipio—then only seventeen and on his first campaign—saw his father's predicament and ordered a cavalry squadron assigned to his protection to charge. Overawed by the enemy's numbers, they refused, causing Scipio to rush at the enemy alone. Seeing their commander recklessly expose himself to the enemy shamed the squadron into following. Their sudden assault shocked the Numidians, and Scipio's small band cut a path through to their fallen commander. Such was young Scipio's first taste of combat. The Romans had lost the battle, but he proved his own bravery. Polybius claimed the young Scipio's actions demonstrated his "clear head." Scipio's clearheadedness did become apparent later in his career, but it surely was not apparent in this reckless act.

Hannibal's victory was a small one, but it rallied the majority of the Gauls to his cause and the Carthaginian army swelled to forty thousand men. In the meantime, forces transferred from Sicily and commanded by Tiberius Sempronius Longus had reinforced Scipio's army. Sempronius was eager to fight a battle before the elder Scipio recovered from his wounds and before the election of the new consuls. Hannibal, worried about the capricious nature of the Celts and wanting to get at the Romans before their raw recruits were battle-hardened, was willing to oblige him. He selected a piece of flat ground perfectly suited for the Roman style of war and enticed his foe forward. Unbeknownst to the Romans, Hannibal had sent his brother with eleven hundred handpicked infantry and eleven hundred cavalry to conceal themselves in the folds and bushes that dotted the seemingly flat plain.

Battle of the Trebia

Hannibal started the engagement by sending his Numidian cavalry across the Trebia River to harass the Roman camp. Sempronius took the bait and dispatched his own cavalry and six thousand *velites* to drive the Carthaginians off and cover the main Roman army as it formed. The wise move—which Scipio apparently recommended—would have been to stand on the defensive along the Trebia and force Hannibal to attack the Roman army in its strong defensive position. This would have given the Romans a significant advantage on the battlefield as well as a fortified camp to retreat into if the battle went against them. But Sempronius, in a rush to win glory, ordered the army forward.

Hannibal probably could not believe his luck. His men were rested and well fed and had spent the morning rubbing themselves down with olive oil to ward off the December cold. Before them stood a Roman army that had forgone breakfast and had already been standing in full armor for several hours before beginning its advance. Roman spirits further evaporated as they marched through the freezing breast-high waters of the flooded Trebia, arriving on the far bank in "a wretched state from the cold and want of food." Hannibal sent out his cavalry to harass the Romans, but he waited until his opponents were fully across the river before ordering his main force to extinguish their fires and form for battle, throwing out a screen of almost eight thousand spearmen and slingers to engage the Roman *velites*. A ferocious hand-to-hand fight developed, but the Roman screen was eventually thrown back in disarray, as they had already been "on hard service ever since daybreak and had expended most of their weapons in the engagement with the Numidian [cavalry]."

As the Roman heavy infantry advanced, Hannibal sent his cavalry on each wing forward. In a pattern that was to become all too familiar, the Roman cavalry proved unequal to the Carthaginian onslaught. They buckled and then ran away, leaving the flanks of the infantry exposed. Doggedly, Sempronius's four legions pushed forward, as their Italian allies on each flank tried to maintain the advance while protecting their flanks from the swarming Carthaginian cavalry. Despite the trying conditions, Sempronius's confidence was, for a time, justified, as the legionaries began pushing through Hannibal's center.

It was at this point that disaster struck. Hannibal's subordinate, Mago, saw the Roman rear march past his hidden troops and noted that the forward Roman ranks were fully engaged, and so he chose that moment to launch a surprise assault directly into the rear of the Roman center. The seasoned Roman veterans, always at the rear of their battle formations, took the attack in stride and faced about, while the center ranks filled in on the flanks. The resulting tactical deployment created a hollow square that kept moving forward, killing large numbers of Carthaginian infantry as it advanced. But the shock of Mago's assault was too much for the hard-pressed infantry on the flanks, mostly Rome's Italian allies, who broke in a disordered panic. At the river's edge the Carthaginians massacred the allied forces trying to escape. At the same time, the core of the army, four Roman legions, managed to cut its way through the Carthaginian center. Believing there was nothing they could do to help the rest of the army, Sempronius ordered the legions to march off to the protection of the town of Placentia. The wreckage of the rest of the army streamed into the Roman camp, and that night a still-ailing

Scipio led them out to join the rest of the army at Placentia. It was a devastating defeat. Rome had lost at least twenty thousand troops and control of Cisalpine Gaul (northern Italy). Hannibal's losses had also been heavy, but it was mostly Celts who had fallen, leaving the core of his Spanish and African veterans unscathed. And these losses were soon made good, as Celts now swarmed to his banner—swelling his army to sixty thousand soldiers.

Battle of Lake Trasimene

In the spring of 217 B.C., after a long winter of retraining his veterans and exercising his new Gaelic recruits, Hannibal roused his army for a new campaign. This time he surprised the Romans by traversing the Apennines and entering Etruria, present-day Tuscany. Though caught flat-footed, the Romans, as always, reacted quickly. A new consul, Gaius Flaminius, took over Sempronius's army and followed Hannibal into Etruria. Hannibal made a careful study of his opponent and, after discovering that the Roman general was a "mere mob-orator and demagogue with no ability in the conduct of military affairs," Hannibal realized that he could easily pull Flaminius into a trap. If he ravaged the rich Etrurian countryside, Hannibal calculated, Flaminius's concern for his reputation would result in the Roman commander rashly pursuing the Carthaginians until Hannibal could turn on him at the place of his choosing.

As Hannibal marched away from Flaminius, he destroyed everything along his path until he reached Lake Trasimene. Hannibal's line of march had the added benefit of interposing his army between Flaminius and Rome. While Flaminius might not have cared a wit about the destruction of much of Etruria, he could not tolerate a Carthaginian army sitting astride his line of communications. When Hannibal learned that Flaminius was marching hard in pursuit, he took his army through a narrow defile that ran between the lake and some forested low hills. Here, he found terrain suitable for an ambush on a scale vast enough to swallow an entire Roman army. At the end of the defile Hannibal posted his Spanish and African veterans on a hill that was all but invulnerable to a frontal assault. Hidden in the forest along the hills, his light troops sat in extended order, while behind the hills and near the opening of the defile, his cavalry was in such a position that they could sweep in behind the Romans and cut off any attempt they might make to flee the trap.

Convinced that Hannibal was at least a day's march ahead of him, Flaminius marched into the defile with approximately twenty-one thousand legionnaires on the morning of June 21 or 22. Desiring glory and contemptuous of their Carthaginian opponents, the Romans were not expecting an engagement and had not taken even the most rudimentary precautions. They had sent no scouts forward, nor had they positioned any light troops to cover the flanks. These oversights were compounded by the weather, it being an unusually misty morning. Expecting a hot day, almost all of the troops along the strung-out column had piled their arms and armor into carts and were marching in loose order, nearly defenseless, into a deadly trap.

As the lead maniples approached the end of the defile, Hannibal gave the signal to attack. Reeling in shock as the thousands of bolts, spears, and arrows flew out of the mist, finding unprotected flesh, the Roman column convulsed in panic. Roman centurions, unable to make out what was happening, had great difficulty rallying any troops to their standards, as thousands made a mad dash to the carts to grab their weapons and don at least some armor before the Carthaginian force was upon them. But for most it was already too late. Hard on the heels of the slings and arrows came Hannibal's light troops, shouting their hideous war cries as they crashed into the unformed Roman maniples. At the same time the Romans could hear the well-known Gallic shouts in the rear as Hannibal's cavalry swept forward to seal off the Roman escape route. At some point, probably where the *triarri*—the most veteran soldiers in the legion—stood, the Romans managed to form and fight. As the fighting continued in some spots for nearly three hours, one can assume that a few Roman units recovered from the shock and stood to their standards until finally overwhelmed. In fact, six thousand legionnaires managed to cut their way through the Carthaginian line and escape. They were later trapped by Hannibal's leading general, Maharbal, and surrendered on the promise that the Carthaginians would spare their lives. Most of the army was not so fortunate; "most of them were cut down in the order of march, without being able to defend themselves: exactly as though they had been actually given up to slaughter by the folly of their leader." Flaminius paid the ultimate cost for his folly, dying sword in hand after being run through by a spear.

After the battle Hannibal released all of his non-Roman prisoners, telling them that he had not come to fight Italians, but on their behalf against Rome. Despite Maharbal's promise, the Roman prisoners were executed. Hannibal had lost fifteen hundred men in the battle, again most of them Celts. As for Rome, in two great battles separated by a mere six months, it had lost more than fifty-five thousand men. For any other Mediterranean state these would have been catastrophic losses. But the Romans just dug deeper into their manpower reserves, which Polybius estimated at better than seven hundred thousand men of military age, and reconstituted their armies. As the Romans formed and trained up these new legions, they appointed a dictator, Quintus Fabius Maximus, to command the war effort and the city's strategic approach to the Hannibal problem. In taking over as dictator, Fabius eschewed the Roman predilection for seeking a decisive battle at the earliest opportunity. Instead, he instituted a policy of harrying Hannibal at every opportunity, but always avoiding a pitched battle. Under Fabius thirty thousand Roman troops shadowed Hannibal's every move and conducted numerous small engagements aimed at hindering the Carthaginian's plans. This went on for several months, as Hannibal marched where he wished, and Fabius followed with an army that stayed safely in the hills and was ever mindful of traps. Neither the legionaries nor the Roman population appreciated what became known as "Fabian tactics," and Fabius soon gained the nickname "the *Cunctator*"—the delayer.

At one point Fabius almost trapped Hannibal, maneuvering the Carthaginian into a corner where the Romans had constructed fortified positions on three sides, with the ocean on the fourth. As Hannibal had already laid waste to the local area, his booty-laden army could not winter where it was. Only one escape route remained, a pass guarded by a legion behind strong fortifications, while the rest of the army was encamped in nearby hills. To escape, Hannibal reached deep into his bag of tricks. He ordered torches strapped to two thousand captured oxen and, after dark, forced the panicked beasts up and over the ridgeline. The four thousand Romans guarding the pass, seeing the torches making their way across the ridge above them, assumed that Hannibal was making his escape. Coming upon the flaming oxen and the light troops Hannibal had sent with them, the legionaries, unable to comprehend what was happening, moved to a nearby hill to await the clarity of dawn. In the meantime, Hannibal used the now-unguarded pass to make good his army's escape, along with its collected booty.

Hannibal's escape fueled criticism of Fabius and his methods. Desiring a more aggressive policy, the Romans gave his second in command, Minucius, equal power to that of the dictator's. Moreover, they decided to split the army between the two, with the generals tasked to coordinate their operations. Then, without much if any coordination, Minucius prodded the bear and nearly had his army annihilated. Only the timely arrival of the alert Fabius with his legions salvaged the day and saved the Romans from disaster. A chastened Minucius was wise enough to admit his folly and once again placed himself under Fabius's command.

The Battle of Cannae

At the end of his six-month term as dictator, Fabius laid down his magistracy, making room for the newly elected consuls, Lucius Aemilius Paullus and Gaius Terentius Varro, to assume command of the armies. Historians of the time have little good to say of Varro, as one would expect of a man who would lead to destruction the largest army Rome had ever assembled. At the time of his election as consul, Varro was considered a new man, popular with the people but disliked by the Roman aristocracy. The son of a butcher, he must have been a man of rare talents to have risen as high as he did in the rigid structure of Roman politics. Unfortunately, as we will see, generalship did not number among his talents.

For some time after the election nothing much happened on the combat front, as proconsuls Servilius and Regulus commanded the army in accordance with methods Fabius had laid out. This quiet period ended when Hannibal, short on supplies and needing to feed his army, attacked and seized a major Roman supply depot at Cannae on the Apulian Plain. Rome's reaction was immediate and overwhelming. Putting the defeats at Trebia and Lake Trasimene aside, the Roman population and leaders resolved to finish off Hannibal once and for all. They authorized the consuls to raise twice the number of legions as in any year in Roman history. Each consular army would consist of four Roman legions and an equal number of allied legions. This was a huge army, numbering as many as eighty thousand legionaries, but many of the legions were newly raised and consisted of a large number of barely trained recruits about to see battle for the first time. Moreover, the Roman defeats of the past several years had undoubtedly cut into the number of centurions available to train up the new legions.

The two consular armies marched toward Cannae with Paullus and Varro alternating command of the combined force on successive days. Despite Rome's numerical advantage, if Polybius is to be believed, Paullus was firmly against meeting Hannibal on open ground, particularly given Hannibal's overwhelming superiority in cavalry. Varro, on the other hand, was anxious for a fight wherever Hannibal would offer the Romans the opportunity.

Just after dawn on August 2, Varro, as the consul in command of the Roman army, ordered the legionaries to march out of their camps and form for battle. Opposite them, Hannibal issued similar orders. The Roman right and the Carthaginian left both rested on the Aufidus River, which was little more than a shallow stream by this point in the summer. The Romans left approximately ten to fifteen thousand men to guard their camps, so they had approximately seventy thousand men on the field. They stationed their cavalry on the right, near the river, with their infantry aligned alongside reaching far into the plain. Unusually, Varro had changed the formation of the maniples to give them more depth than was usually the case. This had the effect of narrowing the Roman front, packing the legionaries close together and limiting the number of swords at the point of impact. It appears that Varro believed the extra weight provided by such depth would quickly smash through Hannibal's line. It was not a forlorn hope, as Roman troops had broken through Hannibal's lines in each of their previous defeats. What Varro neglected was that those troops had cut their way through by hard fighting, not by the press of numbers. The cavalry of the allied contingents was on the left wing, with a strong line of *velites* to the front.

Hannibal had also adopted a unique formation. As usual, he placed his Balearic slingers and spearmen to the front as skirmishers. On the left wing were the Celtic and Iberian cavalry under Hasdrubal and next to them approximately half the Libyan heavy infantry. Beside them stood the Iberian and Celtic infantry in the center, with the other half of the Libyan heavy infantry under Hanno on the right. Hannibal thereby placed his most unreliable troops in the center of his line, where he expected the strongest Roman assault. But this was not all, as he also advanced his center ahead of the solid Libyan infantry on the flanks. Hannibal's intent was to make the Roman center fight a considerable distance before they engaged the Libyans. His hope appears to have been that such a placement would take the impetus out of the Roman charge, while providing his cavalry more time to defeat their opponents. Because of Varro's unusually deep formation, coupled with the inexperience of many of his legionaries, Hannibal's plan worked better than he could possibly have foreseen.

For those Romans fighting in their first battle, the sight before them must have been terrifying. The alternating companies of naked Celts, many painted blue, and Iberians in short tunics with purple stripes, appeared strange and grotesque. Moreover, the Libyans had suited up as if they were in the legions, equipped as they were with the armor and weapons the Carthaginians had taken from Romans killed in earlier battles. This was coupled with the loud and—to the Romans—fiendish war cries of the Celts, along with the dust billowing from where Hannibal's ten thousand never-before-beaten cavalry stood. The battle opened in the usual way, with each side's skirmishers fighting as the cavalry tried to gain an advantage, or at least hold their own.

Hannibal first hurled his cavalry on the left wing against the Romans. Because of the river there was little room to maneuver. Thus, the attack turned into a hard fight, with many of the Carthaginian troops dismounting and fighting on foot. Polybius notes:

> As soon as the Iberian and Celtic cavalry got at the Romans, the battle began in earnest, and in the true barbaric fashion: for there was none of the usual formal advance and retreat; but when they once got to close quarters, they grappled man to man, and, dismounting from their horses, fought on foot. But when the Carthaginians had got the upper hand in this encounter and killed most of their opponents on the ground—because the Romans all maintained the fight with spirit and determination—they began chasing the remainder along the river, slaying as they went along and giving no quarter.

By now the steadily advancing Roman infantry had smashed into the center of the Carthaginian line with its Celtic-Iberian troops, which Hannibal had pushed out ahead of his Libyan infantry on the wings. The Romans slowly began to hack their way forward. Polybius again:

> For a short time, the Iberian and Celtic lines stood their ground and fought gallantly; but, presently overpowered by the weight of the heavy-armed [Roman] lines, they gave way and retired to the rear, thus breaking up the crescent. The Roman maniples

followed with spirit, and easily cut their way through the ene-my's line.

Now the Romans' inexperience showed. The legionaries began crowding toward the center, where they could see the Carthaginian line being torn asunder. As they did so, Hannibal's heavy Libyan infantry on each flank were left unmolested. As the Romans pushed through the center, these veteran troops respectively wheeled to their right and left, redressed their ranks, and charged into the flanks of the confused and tightly packed Romans. It was a nearly perfect double envelopment, a tactical apotheosis that lesser generals have been trying to replicate for two thousand years. Within moments Roman organization collapsed, but "still they fought, though no longer in line, yet singly, or in maniples, which faced to meet those who charged them on the flanks." Seeing the desperate plight of the army, Paullus rushed into the heaviest fighting, but he could not restore order before Carthaginian infantry cut him down.

While the Roman legionaries fought for their lives, Hasdrubal crushed the Roman cavalry to his front and then swept along the rear of the Roman line to attack the Roman cavalry on the other flank, which was already heavily engaged with Hanno's Numidians. The Roman cavalry, seeing Hasdrubal's approach, broke and fled. Hasdrubal sent the Numidians in pursuit, while he gathered his own cavalry and brought them into the rear of the Romans' main battle. Polybius noted: "By charging the Roman legions on the rear and harassing them by hurling squadron after squadron upon them at many points at once, he raised the spirits of the Libyans, and dismayed and depressed that of the Romans."

As the Carthaginian lines closed in, the Roman formations were compressed close together, making it difficult for the legionnaires to wield their swords. Still they kept fighting to the bitter end. "As long as the Romans could keep an unbroken front, to turn first in one direction and then in another to meet the assaults of the enemy, they held out; but the outer files of the circle continually falling, and the circle becoming more and more contracted, they at last were all killed on the field."

With no quarter asked or given, the Romans were slaughtered where they stood. The final tally of Romans killed is much disputed. The pack of legionaries soon became so tight that many could no longer breathe and suffocated where they stood. What the sources do tell us is that only 14,450 rallied to Varro, who had fled the field when disaster was certain, at Canusium. For all practical purposes the Carthaginians had crushed the greatest army Rome had ever fielded and killed the great majority on the plains of Cannae. The wreckage of survivors made its way back to a panicked Rome, where the leaders prepared for a last desperate defense of the city. But Hannibal's losses had also been great—at least fifty-five hundred infantry, fifteen hundred of them from his reliable and almost irreplaceable Libyan veterans, along with several hundred cavalry.

In the wake of the fight Hannibal's subordinates urged him to launch an immediate attack on Rome. He demurred. The Carthaginians lacked a siege train, and without one Rome's walls were impregnable. Even had he possessed the equipment necessary to besiege Rome, such a military effort represented an imposing proposition. Moreover, Rome still had legions in Italy, Sicily, and abroad. Its leaders would have recalled all of these to defend the city. Hannibal also remembered that it had taken nine months for his army to overcome the insignificant city of Saguntum. In the process he had been severely wounded and his army nearly destroyed. And in an age without antibiotics or any concept of proper sewage, sieges were always the great killers of armies.

Moreover, there are no indications that Hannibal entered Italy to eradicate Rome in the first place. From the beginning his plan was to strip it of allies and force the Romans to negotiate. By all the precedents of Mediterranean warfare, after such a disastrous defeat as Cannae had been, Rome would negotiate. Only later did Hannibal learn that in this regard Rome was different from all other states. When he announced his decision not to attack Rome, one of his generals, Maharbal, lamented, "You know how to win a victory, Hannibal, but you do not know how to use it."

Hannibal Counting Rings of Roman Dead after the Battle of Cannae (*Louvre Museum*)

After the Battle of Cannae, Hannibal was able to secure allies and establish a base in southern Italy and an independent kingdom of Gauls in the north. In a blow to Rome almost as great as Cannae, Italy's second-largest city, Capua, came over to the Carthaginians. The Capuans were unable to resist the temptation to become Italy's leading city, which seemed an inevitable consequence of so many Roman disasters. But they came with a price, which included forbidding Hannibal to recruit or levy their population for his army. Other Greek cities came over to Hannibal but never as many as he hoped, while no Latin cities changed allegiance, undoubtedly discouraged by the punishments the Romans inflicted on those who betrayed their alliance to the city.

Besides bonds of loyalty, the Latin cities, even after Cannae, were not sure Rome would lose. In its moment of greatest extremis, Rome raised new armies, recalled Fabius, and returned to the strategy of harry and delay. Hannibal could call on a city to surrender or join him, but that was rarely a possibility when everyone in the city could see the light of thousands of campfires in the hills. When Hannibal and his army departed a region, as they always did, to forage for desperately needed supplies, the Romans would inevitably come down from the hills. If a city had gone over to Hannibal or offered him solace of any kind, Roman retribution would be terrible.

In fact, even powerful Capua would pay a terrible price for its treachery at Rome's most dire hour. Two full Roman armies eventually moved to besiege the city. Hannibal marched to the relief of the beleaguered Capua, but he failed to entice the Romans from their entrenchments. With time running out, Hannibal marched on Rome, hoping to compel the Romans to lift the siege in order to defend their own city. He camped his army at the walls of Rome, laid waste to the surrounding countryside, and even rode about the walls, taunting the defenders. But the armies at Capua were set on their task and refused to budge. As he could not lay siege or storm the walls of Rome, Hannibal eventually departed, leaving Capua to its fate. When the Romans finally retook the city in 211, its chief citizens were crucified along the Appian Way, while the Romans sold the remainder into slavery.

In short, after Cannae, Hannibal was, for a time, able to gather allies. But as Rome continued to field new armies, each larger than Hannibal's own, protecting these new allies became nearly impossible. Moreover, the need to garrison each city whittled down Hannibal's effective force. Over succeeding years, Rome's armies and a growing number of fortified chokepoints progressively limited the area in which the Carthaginians could operate. Hannibal fought more battles over the next several years and even won a few against careless or overconfident Roman commanders. But those victories were never decisive enough to change the military dynamic, as Rome shrugged off its losses and patiently stuck to its strategy—hem in Hannibal and win the war overseas.

Carthage's only chance to reverse its fortunes in Italy was to send a large reinforcement of men and treasure to Hannibal. As Rome controlled the seas, Carthage could only accomplish this task by sending another army across the Alps. In 207 B.C., Hannibal's brother, Hasdrubal Barca, made the attempt and led a new army out of Spain and into northern Italy. Unlike his brother, Hasdrubal did not find inexperienced Roman armies made up of new levies of raw recruits. Rather, after ten years of war, Rome's legions had become seasoned forces filled with combat-hardened veterans and tough centurions. Upon notice of Hasdrubal's arrival in Italy, Gaius Claudius Nero, the consul charged with keeping watch of Hannibal's army, led a handpicked force of six thousand infantry and one thousand cavalry away from Hannibal's army and force-marched it north to join the army of the consul, Marcus Livius Salinator. Riders went ahead of the march route to order local farmers to set provisions along the road, so that the army could feed without having to stop.

Hasdrubal offered battle at Metaurus without at first recognizing that he was facing a consular army that had been reinforced with the best legionaries of Rome's second field army. Together Nero and Livius annihilated Hasdrubal's army, killing Hasdrubal in the process. The night after the battle Nero began a second forced march back to Hannibal's encampment, arriving in its original defensive position before Hannibal was aware of its departure. In fact, the first word Hannibal had of his brother's fate came when a Roman cavalryman flung Hasdrubal's head into the Carthaginian camp. Recognizing his brother, Hannibal supposedly commented: "I perceive the evil destiny of Carthage." After this setback there was a lengthy lull in war activities in Italy. As Livy reports: "No action was fought with Hannibal this year, for after the blow which had fallen upon him and upon his country, he made no forward movement, nor did the Romans care to disturb him, such was their impression of the powers which that single general possessed, even while his cause was everywhere round him crumbling into ruin." Hannibal remained in Italy until 203 B.C. when the Carthaginian Senate recalled him to Africa to defend the city against the army of Publius Cornelius Scipio, whom we first met in northern Italy as a seventeen-year-old. Throughout that period Hannibal accomplished little besides maintaining a toehold presence on Italy's southern boot.

Scipio

Scipio received an education in war in the hardest and bloodiest of all schools—on the battlefield against Hannibal. He had accompanied his father into northern Italy and took part in the Roman defeat at the Battle of Ticinus. Though this was the first of Rome's many defeats at Hannibal's hands, Scipio personally distinguished himself by charging a superior force of Carthaginian cavalry to save his father's life. Though the ancient historians are mostly silent about Scipio's early military experiences, we know that he was a tribune at the Battle of Cannae and probably gained the experience required to achieve tribune status by fighting at the battles of Trebia and Lake Trasimene.

Scipio was certainly at Cannae, and at the end of the battle he was one of the survivors who had cut their way through the Carthaginian center and were trying to reorganize themselves at Canusium. In the makeshift camp Scipio learned about a group of young Roman patricians planning to desert the army and Rome. Twenty-year-old Scipio burst upon them with his sword drawn and forced each of the waivers to swear an oath never to desert Rome. Not satisfied, he then exacted a second oath that they would kill anyone of their number who broke his first oath, as well as any other Roman who tried to desert. Scipio was performing exactly as expected of a Roman patrician. Only in the greatest extreme were Roman commanders expected to die leading their troops in a forlorn hope. Instead, a defeated leader's supreme duty was to rally his remaining forces and see them safely off for reconstitution and to fight another day. For Romans of the upper classes, those with political connections, there was little shame in defeat, only in giving up.

Bust of Scipio
(Naples National Archaeological Museum)

But what gave young Scipio his chance was the strategic foresight of the Roman Senate, which even in the wake of Cannae never lost sight of the bigger picture. The Senate wisely dispatched many of its best legions to fight overseas. Legions campaigning in Sicily and Spain ensured that the resources and manpower of these locations were never available to reinforce Hannibal, and they also deprived Carthage of allies and ports from which it could have contested Roman naval superiority. Rome made its supreme effort in Spain, where Hannibal drew his true strength. If the legions could strip Spain from Carthage, Hannibal would find himself sundered from the mines that financed his army as well as from the possibility of reinforcements, such as those Hasdrubal had attempted to bring to his brother.

Understanding that Spain was the key to Carthage's strength, the Roman Senate committed a powerful army, commanded by Scipio's father and uncle, in northern Spain. That force made considerable progress for more than a half-dozen years following Cannae. As a result, the Carthaginians were forced to expend huge resources defending Spain that otherwise would have gone to Hannibal. But in 211 B.C. Rome's Spanish allies deserted them for the Carthaginians, wiping out these successes. The resulting battle nearly exterminated Roman power in Spain and left both Scipio's father and uncle dead. Only a few remnants of the army gathered on the northern side of the Ebro, where they grimly held on until C. Claudius Nero brought ten to fifteen thousand reinforcements late in the autumn of 211. Nero managed to stabilize the situation enough so that the Romans possessed a secure base from which to renew the offensive as soon as reinforcements and a new commander could arrive.

But when the Senate called for a new general, none came forward. Many senior politicians believed it would take years to ready Roman forces in Spain for a renewed offensive. At the same time, Spain was a distant theater and far from Hannibal. As potential generals undoubtedly would have seen, the place to find glory was in Italy, facing Carthage's greatest general. It is likely that many leaders in the Senate did not want to ask for the job, preferring instead for the Senate to beg them to take command and salvage Rome's prestige. This is what occurred with Fabius after Cannae, and were not these other Roman generals as great as he? Short of easy options, the Senate called an assembly of the people to elect a proconsul who would be "honored" to take the position. As Livy relates, "they [the Roman voters] looked round at the countenances of their most eminent men, who were earnestly gazing at each other, and murmured bitterly that their affairs were in so ruinous a state and the condition of the commonwealth so desperate that no one dared take command in Spain." Scipio alone stepped forward to declare himself a candidate, though he was only twenty-four years of age and not legally qualified to hold such a position. Despite the legalities of the matter, he found himself elected by overwhelming popular acclaim and confirmed by the Senate.

Scipio arrived in Spain with ten thousand infantry reinforcements and some cavalry, bringing the total Roman and Italian forces at his disposal to somewhat more than thirty thousand men. Greeting him were three Carthaginian armies, each of them larger than his own, but operating widely dispersed from one another. Scipio learned that the three Carthaginian commanders were quarreling and that many of their Spanish allies—their subjects—were unhappy with their rule. And although Scipio probably counted on Roman discipline and tactical skill to defeat any single Carthaginian army, an aggressive strategy entailed many risks, for there was a strong likelihood that the Carthaginians would put aside their squabbles to concentrate and defeat him.

Scipio eventually seized on the idea of striking at the key Punic base in Spain—New Carthage. The Punic commanders believed the city's strong fortifications could be defended by only one thousand soldiers—a ridiculously small number considering that the nearest relieving army was almost two weeks distant. The key to Scipio's offensive was to keep his intentions secret. Thus, he spent the winter months preparing his army and instilling in it a new sense of confidence, but he shared his plans with only one trusted subordinate, Gaius Laelius.

When he finally marched in the early spring, neither the army nor its senior commanders had any idea of his plans. Pushing his legionaries forty miles a day, Scipio's twenty-five thousand infantry and twenty-five hundred cavalry arrived before the walls of New Carthage in less than a week. Laelius then arrived with thirty-five Roman war galleys to begin blockading operations, and Scipio began his siege. The city's stunned defenders began doing what they could to shore up the defenses, including drafting two thousand of the city's strongest citizens into a militia to supplement the thousand soldiers. Though New Carthage was a natural strongpoint, surrounded on three sides by water, the defenders knew they needed time to prepare better defenses, but Scipio was determined not to let them have it.

At the start of the Roman third hour (about 7:00 A.M.), Scipio prepared two thousand of his eager legionaries to throw against the walls, promising a golden crown and other honors to the first man to reach the top. To stop them, New Carthage's commander, Mago, ordered his two thousand militia citizens to sally from the gates and assault the slowly advancing Romans. Scipio halted the advance and drew his men back toward the Roman camp. This both shortened the distance his reinforcements needed to march when called forward and added approximately a quarter mile to the distance the Punic force had to travel. His obvious intention was to trap the Carthaginians outside the city and annihilate the better part of them, "knowing that if he destroyed those who were so to speak the steel edge of the population of the town he would cause universal dejection, and none of those inside would venture out of the gate." The Carthaginians made up the extra distance quickly. With no other choice Scipio's men met the charge, and for a considerable time the outcome remained in doubt. But as reinforcements in the camp donned their armor, organized into battle formation, and marched into the contest, Roman discipline turned the tide. As Mago must have anticipated, his citizens, untrained to the exertions of close combat, soon tired. Then the stolid Roman veterans began their grim work on the exhausted and nearly helpless foe. The centurions and legates fed the battle-hardened men of the *triarii,* the veteran troops in a Roman legion, into the fight. It was too much for the Carthaginians, who collapsed and ran: "Many of them fell in the actual battle or in the retreat but the greater number were trodden down by each other in entering the gate."

In rapid pursuit, the Romans nearly forced the gates before the defenders could close them. Without pause the legionaries assaulted the walls with ladders, but here they encountered the Punic mercenaries who still had fight left in them. By mid-afternoon, Scipio saw that the attack was faltering and ordered his soldiers back to camp to rest. The exalted defenders did not have long to rejoice; when dusk fell the legionaries advanced again. It was time for Scipio's master-stroke. Alerted by local fishermen that the ebbing tide reduced the water levels in the lagoon to fordable levels, Scipio sent five hundred chosen men to scale an undefended section of the wall. "They entered the city without meeting any opposition, and at once marched at full speed to the gate around which much of the fighting had gathered. The defenders had focused their attention on the strug-gle . . . so riveted on the fighting that not a single man was aware that the city behind him was captured until the missiles began to fall upon them from the rear."

By this time those Romans attacking the main gate had made substantial progress, as the defenders ran out of missiles. Learning of the progress of the force in the lagoon, Roman "courage . . . re-doubled, and under cover of their shields they forced their way in dense order to the gate and began to cut down the doors with axes and hatchets." As Livy relates:

> Now that they had the enemy in front and rear they gave up the defense, the walls were seized, the gate was battered from both sides, smashed to pieces, and carried out of the way to allow a free passage to the troops. A large number surmounted the walls and inflicted heavy slaughter on the townsmen, but those who entered through the gate marched in unbroken ranks through the heart of the city into the forum.

Scipio ordered his legionaries to kill everyone they encountered. Polybius referred to this as a "Roman custom" and explained its reasons: "They do this, I think, to inspire terror, so that when towns are taken by the Romans one may often see not only the corpses of human beings, but dogs cut in half, and the dismembered limbs of other animals, and on this occasion such scenes were very many owing to the numbers of those in the place." Such carnage went on throughout the city until Mago surrendered the citadel. Once he did, Scipio gave a signal to put an end to the slaughter, so that the city could be given over to pillage.

Only a week had gone by since Scipio undertook his first military campaign and he had already overthrown the entire defensive edifice of Carthaginian Spain. He had deprived the Carthaginians of their main supply base, captured almost enough war galleys to double the Roman fleet, and seized the entire Carthaginian treasury. Just as important, he discovered and released three hundred noble hostages whom the Carthaginians had taken from Spain's most powerful tribes. Despite the fact that many of these men came from tribes that had betrayed his father, Scipio's honorable treatment of them made a deep impression on them. Coupled with his proven ability to win startling victories, his wise political choices brought increasing numbers of Spanish allies into the Roman camp. Scipio used them, but he was never so foolish as to trust them.

In a single campaign Scipio marked himself as a commander of unusual ability. In just a few months he had rallied a beaten army, marched it through 280 miles of hostile territory in the face of three Punic armies that greatly outnumbered his own, and led that army in a successful assault of the greatest and best-defended city in Spain. But Scipio wisely decided not to press his temporary advantage. Instead, he consolidated his position and then put his army through an intensive training regimen. It was at this point that he demonstrated one of the greatest traits of military genius: the capacity to learn and adapt. Remember that Scipio had witnessed most, if not all, of the disasters Hannibal had inflicted on Roman arms. He therefore knew firsthand what was wrong with the Roman methods of war, and that summer he went about fixing them. His major tactical reforms added maneuverability to the army. In the past, the three lines of the Roman army had each reinforced each other, one coming forward as the previous line tired. There was no procedure to maneuver maniples independently of the line, or for a line to do anything but move forward. This made a Roman army nearly defenseless if struck from the flank or rear, as happened at Cannae. Scipio corrected these deficiencies and, in the following campaigning season, brought into the field an army that was not only superbly skilled and conditioned, but also trained to maneuver and fight in a manner unlike any previous Roman army.

Scipio led his legions—rested and with their training complete—against the Carthaginian army commanded by Hannibal's brother, Hasdrubal. To entice him into a fight, Scipio camped his army beside the silver mines at Baecula. As Hasdrubal occupied a strong position, both armies appeared content to spend two days staring at each other. But on the third day Scipio, wary of the approach of the armies of Mago and Hasdrubal Gisco, dispatched two cohorts to guard the approaches and prepared the rest of the army to attack. Scipio sent forward his skirmishers with a picked force of infantry to press Hasdrubal's screening force of light troops. When Hasdrubal moved to support his hard-pressed forward troops, Scipio sent about half of his remaining force under Laelius around one flank, while he took the remaining force around the other flank. By moving along concealed routes, each of the flanking columns escaped Hasdrubal's notice until they struck his exposed flanks. The legions tore the inferior Carthaginian troops to their front to pieces, before turning on the better-trained forces in the center. But Hasdrubal, having had no Roman troops attacking his center to pin him in place, was able to move his remaining forces out of harm's way before the twin pincers could close.

Scipio won a confidence-building but, in the end, minor victory at the Battle of Baecula. Hasdrubal had extricated his best troops and soon left Spain on his march into Italy to reinforce his brother, where, as we saw above, his army was destroyed by Nero at Metaurus. But Scipio learned a valuable lesson; maneuverability might be decisive, but he would also have to send sizable forces to pin the enemy's main body in order to prevent its escape.

With Hasdrubal on his way to Italy, Scipio had only two armies to contend with in Spain, but they were now concentrated to meet him. In 206 B.C., with about forty-five thousand men, less than half of them well-disciplined legionnaires, Scipio marched against a Punic army nearly double the size of his own force, led by Hasdrubal Gisgo and another brother of Hannibal, Mago. The two armies met near Ilipa, and for the next few days both sides left their camps each day and formed up facing each other, but neither army was willing to bring on a general engagement. Each day Scipio would lead his troops out of camp only after the Punic force had formed up. Each time Scipio put his best troops—his Roman legions and Latin allies—in the center, while his Spanish allies held the flanks. Likewise, the Carthaginian commanders put their best African troops in the center and their own Spanish allies on the flank.

After several days of this Scipio suddenly changed his entire deployment scheme. He ordered his troops to eat early and form up on the plain before the Carthaginians, who had to skip their morning meal in the rush to meet the sudden Roman approach. To perplex the enemy further, Scipio placed his legions on the flanks and the Spaniards in the center. By the time Hasdrubal and Mago were aware that they were facing a different deployment from what they had seen on previous days, there was little they could do. With Scipio's Spanish allies massed in front of the Punic center, the Carthaginians could not adjust their formation without falling into a dangerous disorder. Scipio pressed his flanks forward at a quick march, while the Spaniards were told to advance more slowly. In effect, he was creating the reverse of Hannibal's formation at Cannae, but one that would have the same effect. Scipio advanced in column, allowing him to close the distance with the Carthaginians at a speed they must have thought incomprehensible. Only at the last moment did the legions wheel into line and smash into Carthaginian flanks. It was a masterpiece of maneuver that no army since Alexander's could even contemplate undertaking.

Though the Carthaginians initially put up spirited resistance, they eventually broke under the relentless Roman attack. Scipio pressed his advantage, as both flanks closed on the center of the Carthaginian line, just as Scipio's Spanish allies pinned them in place by pressing hard against the front of the remaining Punic units. Pressed on three sides and with Scipio's light troops and cavalry beginning to move into their rear, the usually reliable African mercenaries broke and ran for their camp. Only a providential downpour, or what Polybius referred to as the interposition of a deity, saved the Punic army from complete ruin. During the night, Hasdrubal's Spanish allies deserted, and what was left of the Carthaginian army tried to escape under cover of darkness and a storm, but was virtually annihilated by a relentless Roman pursuit.

Spain was now secure, and Scipio returned to Rome, where he entered into a bitter political battle with jealous rivals. In the end, the Roman people eventually elected him consul with the direction that he would lead a Roman army into Africa to attack the heart of Carthaginian power. An unhappy Senate, upset over Scipio's popularity with the masses, refused him permission to recruit for this expedition and limited his force to the two legions already in Sicily. However, they could not stop him from enrolling volunteers, who flocked to his banner as soon as word spread that he was raising a new army. That allowed Scipio to enroll seven thousand veteran volunteers and take them with him when he left Italy. One suspects the lure of plunder in the rich and unspoiled cities of northern Africa was at least as much of a draw as the opportunity to fight for Rome under Scipio.

These volunteers joined the legions already in Sicily. The Senate had created these legions from the survivors of Cannae, who were then exiled to Sicily. These men keenly felt the stain of dishonor, and every year they petitioned the Senate to allow them to return to Italy and prove their valor in battle against Hannibal. The senators ignored them. But Scipio understood these men and their desires. To him, they were not men beaten at Cannae, but legionaries who had refused to panic and, through sheer hard fighting, had cut their way through the Carthaginians and then re-formed to protect Rome. Adopting the same techniques he had used when he joined the demoralized army in Spain, Scipio praised their performance and honored their service. In return, a dispirited army that had initially viewed him as another stranger sent to humiliate them gave Scipio its undying devotion. If he asked, these men would have followed him into hell. He asked, and they did.

Despite the veteran status of his new legions and most of his volunteers, Scipio spent the next year drilling them in the movement and combat techniques that had served him so well in Spain, as well as preparing the logistical infrastructure required to support an invasion of Carthage's home territories. As his army trained, Scipio launched a daring sea raid against the North African coast. Thirty warships, commanded by Gaius Laelius, sailed almost unmolested along the African coast and laid waste to whatever they saw. The fleet also made contact with Masinissa, who, with his Numidian cavalry, had previously served the Carthaginian cause in Spain. He was now locked in a civil war against a Numidian rival, Syphax, and was willing to transfer his loyalty to Rome, if Scipio would promise Roman support against his Numidian enemies. This was an easy promise to make, as it divided the loyalty of an army on which the Carthaginians had come to rely. Moreover, it provided Scipio with the one element Roman armies were always lacking: a numerous and effective cavalry force.

In early 204 B.C., Scipio judged that all was ready, and a Roman invasion fleet of four hundred transports and approximately forty warships, carrying approximately sixteen thousand infantry and sixteen hundred cavalry, left for North Africa. After a small skirmish with Carthaginian cavalry, the Romans firmly established themselves near Utica. There Masinissa joined them with a paltry unit of two hundred Numidian cavalry. Scipio had likely expected far more, but he made do. Taking advantage of the chaos the landing had caused among the Carthaginians, he moved rapidly to lay siege to the Punic stronghold of Utica. He found the city strongly defended and awaiting the arrival of a promised Carthaginian relief force, thus unwilling to surrender.

Some historians have criticized Scipio for opting to besiege Utica over a direct march and assault on Carthage. But given the time and effort expended before Utica fell, one wonders how he would have done better in attacking the great fortifications defending Carthage. Moreover, any failure before the walls protecting the Punic capital would have left Scipio with a demoralized army and no safe base into which to retreat. His methodical approach may have disappointed some in Rome who remembered his lightning assaults in Spain and were expecting a quick victory in Africa. But in this case, slow and steady was not only the safe course—it was also the most certain.

It took time, but the Carthaginians eventually succeeded in assembling a large army, and after placing it under the joint command of Hasdrubal and the Numidian king Syphax, they dispatched to lift the siege of Utica. Hasdrubal proved an unfortunate choice as commander. With vivid memories of his superior numbers exterminated at the Battle of Ilipa, he was reluctant to attack despite an overwhelming Carthaginian military superiority. Not willing to risk their mostly raw recruits against Scipio's veterans, Syphax and Hasdrubal were content to stay in their fortified camps and wait for Scipio's army to starve.

Scipio took full advantage of the Carthaginian generals' lack of aggression to suggest peace talks, an offer that they eagerly accepted. Over the next several days, Roman emissaries, accompanied by centurions pretending to be slaves, made their way to the two enemy camps. Several of these centurions, proud veterans of decades of hard fighting as well as "men of tried courage and sagacity," allowed themselves to be beaten and otherwise degraded in order to sell the illusion that they were slaves and therefore not worthy of attention. As the emissaries negotiated, the "slaves" wandered the camps, taking keen notice of their layout and defensive works.

Having men so familiar with the enemy camps emboldened Scipio to conduct the most dangerous of military operations: a nighttime assault on a fortified enemy position. Armies in the ancient world could contemplate night operations only if they possessed highly disciplined troops, and even Alexander refrained from trying it with his Macedonians on the eve of his greatest battle at Gaugamela.

After allowing Syphax to believe he had accepted the peace overtures, Scipio tightened his siege lines around Utica and summoned his tribunes to a war council to present his plans. Every day just after sunset the Roman bugles blared forth, signaling the end of the day's activities and calling the troops to dinner. That night, however, the Romans ate early, and upon the call of the bugles they sallied out of the camp. Unobserved, Scipio's two columns, one under his command and the other commanded by Laelius, joined by Masinissa, advanced on the two enemy camps. Under cover of darkness, Laelius attacked first, taking Syphax's camp by surprise.

Scipio assigned a portion of his force, including Masinissa and his Numidians, to Laelius with instructions to attack Syphax and fire his camp. Then he took Laelius and Masinissa apart and appealed to them each separately to make up by extra care and diligence for the confusion inseparable from a night attack. He told them that he should attack Hasdrubal and the Carthaginian camp, but would wait until he saw the king's camp on fire. He had not to wait long, for when the fire was cast on the nearest huts it very soon caught the next ones and then running along in all directions spread over the whole camp. Such an extensive fire breaking out at night naturally produced alarm and confusion, but Syphax's men thinking it was due to accident and not to the enemy rushed out without arms to try and extinguish it. They found themselves at once confronted by an armed foe, mainly Numidians whom Masinissa, thoroughly acquainted with the arrangement of the camp, had posted in places where they could block all the avenues. Some were caught by the flames, whilst half asleep in their beds, numbers who had fled precipitately, scrambling over one another were trampled to death in the camp gates. The Carthaginians in the second camp, a little over a mile distant, witnessed the conflagration, but discerned no sign of fighting. Believing therefore that the fire was accidental, many of Hasdrubal's men rushed to assist their allies in fighting the inferno. Like the Numidians, many were cut down by cohorts Scipio had placed between the two camps. As for the remainder: "All the rest hurried outside their own camp unarmed, and stood there gazing in astonishment at the spectacle. Everything having thus succeeded to his best wishes, Scipio fell upon these men outside their camp, and either put them to the sword, or, driving them back into the camp, set fire to their huts." In their panic, Hasdrubal's men could offer only feeble resistance to the Roman assault. "For the fire spread with great rapidity, and soon covered the whole area of the camp, the passages of which were full of horses, mules, and men, some half-dead and consumed by the flames, and some frenzied and beside themselves, so that even those ready to make a bold effort were prevented by these obstacles, and owing to the confusion and disturbance there was no hope of safety."

Hasdrubal, realizing that the situation was beyond saving, did not attempt to rally his forces or save the doomed camps. Rather, joined by Syphax, he fled with fewer than twenty-five hundred survivors to the fortified town of Anda. From there he went on to Carthage, hoping to put some steel into the post-debacle deliberations in the Carthaginian Senate, while Syphax built a new fortified camp some eight miles distant at Abba. For the Romans the battle had been an overwhelming success. They had destroyed an army of more than forty thousand men, including the capture of five thousand soldiers, a large number of whom were Carthaginian nobles, all for a trifling cost.

After its horrific loss, much of Carthage was in a state of panic, but the city's Senate acted with the same resolution the Romans had displayed in the wake of the disaster at Cannae. Within thirty days, Carthage fielded an army of thirty thousand troops and remarkably positioned them so as to once again threaten Scipio's ongoing siege of Utica. However, no army so hastily raised and organized was a match for the fierce battle discipline of the legions, who made short work of this force of ill-trained recruits. After Masinissa had seen off the Punic cavalry, which broke on the first charge, the legions advanced in their standard formation with the maniples of the *hastati* leading, followed by the *principes* and finally the grizzled veterans of the *triarri*. Rather than feed in each line in succession, Scipio waited until the *hastati* had pinned Carthage's Spanish mercenaries in place and then, in a maneuver no Roman army could have contemplated before his tactical reforms, marched the other two lines to the left and right. On signal, the Roman columns crashed into the flank and rear of the enemy, cutting the Carthaginians down almost to a man. But once again Hasdrubal and Syphax made good their escape.

Still believing that Carthage was too tough to attack directly, even without a covering army, Scipio sent Laelius and Masinissa into the Numidian heartland to destroy Syphax and place Masinissa on the Numidian throne. Scipio took the rest of the army to demonstrate against Carthage itself. It did not last long, as he soon had to force-march back to Utica to save the Roman fleet from disaster. In the meantime, Laelius and Masinissa marched fifteen days into the heart of Syphax's territory, where they defeated and captured him. With Syphax's fall, Masinissa became the king, and the greater portion of Numidia, along with its cavalry force, went over to the Romans.

Zama: The Final Battle

Carthage had embarked on peace negotiations with Scipio, who was driving a hard bargain, when Hannibal and his veteran army returned to African soil. The Carthaginians immediately broke off negotiations, and Scipio prepared for one final battle, this time against Rome's great nemesis, Hannibal. The Romans renewed the war with a vengeance. "[Scipio] went round the towns, no longer receiving the submission of those which offered to surrender, but taking them all by assault and selling the inhabitants as slaves." Carthage's hinterlands now felt the full brunt of the Roman style of war, and the terrified population screamed for Hannibal to march out against the Romans. This was obviously Scipio's intent, though he refused to offer battle until Masinissa had rejoined him with his Numidian cavalry. Likewise, Hannibal ignored the rising clamor to take the field until his army had received cavalry reinforcements.

When a close relative of Syphax, Tychaeus, arrived with two thousand Numidian horsemen, Hannibal could delay no longer. As he advanced, the Carthaginian general sent out spies to locate and assess Scipio's strength. The Romans captured three of these agents, but rather than execute them, Scipio ordered that they be given a tour of the Roman camp and then sent back to Hannibal. This was quite a ruse, as Scipio by this time knew that Masinissa and his thousands of Numidian cavalry were nearby. The spies, however, saw no trace of the Numidians, and so reported their absence to Hannibal. The knowledge that Scipio was without a cavalry force undoubtedly cheered Hannibal, who learned too late that Masinissa had ridden into the Roman camp the day after the spies departed.

Hoping to take advantage of his apparent position of strength, Hannibal advanced west from Zama and established a camp four miles from Scipio. He chose his camp poorly, as there was no water nearby, and the Carthaginians "suffered considerable hardship because of this." As Hannibal's troops suffered, he sought a meeting with Scipio, either to get the measure of his opponent or to secure better peace terms while he still had an unbroken army at his back. If making peace was Hannibal's intention, he failed miserably. "No understanding was arrived at and the commanders rejoined their armies. Both reported that the discussion had been fruitless, and that the matter must be decided by arms, and the result left to the gods." Polybius described the day after the meeting:

> At daybreak they led out their armies and opened the battle, the Carthaginians fighting for their own safety and the dominion of Africa, and the Romans for the empire of the world. . . . It would be impossible to find more valiant soldiers, or generals who had been more successful and were more thoroughly exercised in the art of war, nor indeed had Fortune ever offered to contending armies a more splendid prize of victory, since the conquerors would not be masters of Africa and Europe alone, but of all those parts of the world which now hold a place in history; as indeed they very shortly were.

Scipio drew up his army with the *hastati* in the lead and the *principes* behind them, as was standard Roman practice. But rather than place the maniples of the *principes* behind the gaps between the maniples of the front line, he placed them directly behind the latter, "owing to the large number of the enemy's elephants." Last of all he placed the *triarii*. His plan was to use these tested veterans for their appointed role late in the battle. Following recent Roman procedures the *triarii* were permitted to loiter as they wished, donning their armor and forming up only when it was time for the final effort. At such times it was common for a general, if asked how the battle was going, to reply: "It is in the hands of the *triarii*." And capable hands they were. Scipio completed his formation by placing Laelius with the Italian cavalry on his left and Masinissa with the whole of his four thousand Numidian cavalry on the right. In front of the Roman army and stationed in the gaps between the maniples was a swarm of light infantry skirmishers—the *velites*. It was their job to disrupt the Carthaginian attack by driving Hannibal's ele-

Battle of Zama *(public domain)*

phants mad and hopefully back onto the Punic lines, though the
Romans had made special preparations to meet any of the great
beasts that charged their lines. With his legions formed, Scipio ha-
rangued his troops:

> Keep before your eyes that if you overcome your enemies you
> will be unquestioned masters of Africa, but also you will gain for
> yourselves and your country the undisputed command and sov-
> ereignty of the rest of the world. But if the result of the battle
> be otherwise, those of you who have fallen bravely in the fight
> will lie forever shrouded in the glory of dying thus for their
> country, while those who save themselves by flight will spend
> the remainder of their lives in misery and disgrace.

As Scipio shouted to make himself heard, the greatest commander of the era arranged his own forces. Hannibal also formed his
army in three great lines. He placed all eighty of his elephants to the
front, and behind them were his twelve thousand mercenaries, composed of Ligurians, Celts, Balearic Islanders, and Moors. These were
veteran troops, but they had never been part of Hannibal's army in
Italy, so their loyalty and quality were uncertain. Behind them he
placed the native Libyans and Carthaginians. These citizens were
mostly raw recruits. They would fight hard, as defeat meant the loss
of everything they held dear, but they were by no means ready to
face a tested Roman army in the field. In the final line was the core
of Hannibal's army, which he had brought over from Italy. Hannibal
stationed these troops over a stade (an eighth of a mile) from the
front, and one can assume they were resting in a fashion similar to
the *triarii*. Sources do not provide an exact number for this core
force, but it was nearly as strong as the entire force of Roman infantry. That would place their number well above fifteen thousand soldiers, most of whom were outfitted in captured Roman armor and
equipped with Roman weapons. Hannibal finished his deployments
by placing his cavalry on the wings, with the Numidians on the left

and the Carthaginian cavalry on the right. He then ordered his commanders to address their troops, while he went among his veterans in the third line, asking them:

> Cast their eyes on the ranks of the enemy. They were scarcely a fraction of the forces that had formerly faced them, and for courage they were not to be compared with those. For then their adversaries were men whose strength was unbroken and who had never suffered defeat, but those of today were some of them the children of the former and some the wretched remnant of the legions he had so often vanquished and put to flight in Italy. Therefore he urged them not to destroy the glorious record of themselves and their general, but, fighting bravely, to confirm their reputation for invincibility.

Hannibal was a seasoned commander, and his discerning eye could not help but note that he was facing a force qualitatively superior to any he had faced before. He must also have had some sense that he was facing a far more competent Roman general than he had confronted in the past. As such, he did away with subtlety and stratagems in favor of a massed assault by his eighty elephants, with his first line of infantry close behind. He obviously calculated that once the elephants had disorganized the first Roman line (the *hastati*), his mercenaries would complete the slaughter. With the *hastati* annihilated, Hannibal probably meant to feed his force in Roman style— a few at a time—wearing down the legions, before he committed his Italian veterans. Such a plan could work only if Scipio committed and exhausted the *triarii* before Hannibal ordered his tested veterans into the fight. As for his cavalry, the best Hannibal could hope for was that it would hold its own until his infantry had defeated the Roman legionaries. This was a far cry from previous battles where his cavalry was the dominant force on the field. Scipio, on the other hand, was counting on his infantry to hold the line long enough for his overwhelmingly superior cavalry to win its respective battles on each flank and then come to the aid of the hard-pressed infantry.

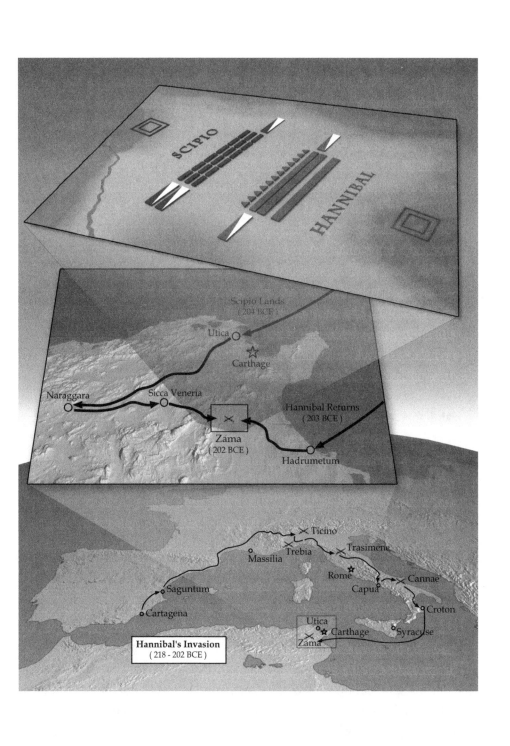

SCIPIO

HANNIBAL

Scipio Lands
(204 BCE)

Utica

Carthage

Naraggara

Sicca Veneria

Zama
(202 BCE)

Hannibal Returns
(203 BCE)

Hadrumetum

Ticino

Massilia

Trebia

Trasimene

Rome

Capua

Cannae

Saguntum

Cartagena

Croton

Utica

Carthage

Syracuse

Zama

Hannibal's Invasion
(218 - 202 BCE)

After ineffectual cavalry skirmishing between the Numidian forces of each side, Hannibal gave the order for the elephants to charge. It was a most unfortunate order, as the elephants proved careless in selecting who they considered an enemy. As they began to advance, Scipio ordered his trumpeters to sound a loud call. "When the trumpets and bugles sounded shrilly from all sides, many of the animals took fright and turned tail and rushed back upon the Numidians who had come up to help the Carthaginians." Masinissa did not miss the opportunity. His own four thousand Numidians charged and drove off Hannibal's Numidian cavalry. Taking the bit between the teeth, Masinissa led his troops off in wild pursuit. The rest of the elephants, Polybius tells us, fell on the Roman *velites* who both inflicted and suffered much loss, until finally, "in their terror many of the elephants escaped through the gaps in the Roman line which Scipio's foresight had provided, so that the Romans suffered no injury, while others fled towards the right and, received by the cavalry with showers of javelins, at length escaped out of the field." It was at this moment that Laelius, availing himself of the disturbance created by the elephants, charged the Carthaginian cavalry and forced them into headlong flight. He, like Masinissa, closely pursued the fleeing Carthaginian horses.

In the meantime, both "phalanxes slowly and in imposing array advanced on each other, except the troops which Hannibal had brought back from Italy, who remained in their original position." The Romans advanced clanging their spears against their shields until they were within throwing range. They then loosed their javelins, raised their blood-chilling war cry, and fell upon their foes. At first, as a result of their courage and skill, the Punic mercenaries held their own, wounding many of the Romans, but the latter continued their advance, relying on the superiority of their arms and their admirable order to push fresh troops to the front. As they fought, the *hastati* could hear the *principes* directly behind them, cheering them on. But the second rank of the Carthaginian force, Polybius tells us, "behaved like cowards, never coming near their mercenaries nor attempting to back them up." As a result, when the first line of the

Punic force gave way, they turned on the Carthaginian citizens, evidently believing they had been left in the lurch by their own side. They "fell upon those whom they encountered in their retreat and began to kill them."

Polybius viewed this turn of events as a good thing for the Carthaginian character, as it "compelled many of the Carthaginians to die like men; for as they were being butchered by their own mercenaries they were obliged against their will to fight both against these and against the Romans." For a barely trained and untested force, the city's citizens acquitted themselves well: "Showing a frantic and extraordinary courage, they killed a considerable number of both their mercenaries and of the Romans." As a result, the cohorts of the *hastati* were thrown into confusion. Seeing this, the centurions of the *principes* brought up their ranks to reinforce the faltering attack.

These fresh troops immediately turned the tide. Advancing in ordered ranks, with their iron swords loudly clanging off their shields, they made a fearsome spectacle as they closed on men who only weeks before had been bakers, weavers, and carpenters. Never having expected to fight in a battle and having no frame of reference to comprehend the horrifying events enveloping them, the Punic second line buckled. It is not difficult to imagine the dread the average Carthaginian merchant must have felt as armor-encased killers, brandishing bloody swords and screaming murderous war cries, slowly closed upon him, intent on only one thing: slaughter. That the men ran should have been expected; that they stood at all, if but a few moments, was a miracle.

At this point, the "greater number of the Carthaginians and their mercenaries were cut to pieces where they stood, either by themselves or by the *hastati*." Even though the *principes* had begun their advance, the bulk of the fighting and killing was still being done by the *hastati*. That was a bad omen for Hannibal, who must have known his only hope of victory was ebbing away, as he had hoped that his core force would face an exhausted Roman army, not one in which two of its three lines remained fresh. This is probably one of the reasons Hannibal refused to allow the survivors of the first two lines to move through the third. Instead, he had the front ranks of veterans level their spears, thus forcing those retreating citizens and mercenaries to flow toward the wings and the open ground beyond. This was a ruthless measure, but Hannibal could not afford any dis-ordering of his third rank if he were to retain hope of stopping the advancing Romans.

The space between the two armies had become a mass of blood and slaughter. So great was the bloodletting that Scipio and his le-gionaries had great difficulty traversing the wretched field. "Every-thing was calculated to make an advance in order difficult,—the ground slippery with gore, the corpses lying piled up in bloody heaps, and with the corpses' arms flung about in every direction."

The fact that the *hastati,* with their bloodlust up, had become a disorganized mob as they pursued the broken Punic line, intent on killing as many Carthaginians as possible, compounded Scipio's problem. But he could still count on legionary discipline. After or-dering the Roman wounded to be conveyed to the rear, he recalled by bugle those *hastati* still pursuing the enemy. As the *hastati* re-formed, Scipio ordered the *principes* to move to one flank and the *triarii* to move to the other, creating a solid line of Roman infantry. Doing so after a hard fight, in the face of a still-undefeated foe of Hannibal's caliber, demonstrates a brilliant coolness under pressure that characterized Roman discipline. Still, such a mid-battle reorga-nization, even if conducted with consummate skill, was a dangerous maneuver and could not have occurred without some initial disrup-tion of the legions' order. This was probably Hannibal's best chance to launch a counterblow, but he inexplicably let it pass, allowing the Romans to re-form their ranks unmolested. Moreover, all of this took time, and that was time Hannibal could ill afford to lose, as every moment's delay in reaching an outcome increased the chance the Roman cavalry would return to the battlefield.

When Scipio had finished aligning his soldiers, both sides "closed with the greatest eagerness and ardor." And as they were "nearly equal in numbers as well as in spirit and bravery, and were equally well armed, the contest was for long doubtful." One could only imagine the terrible carnage of two similarly equipped veteran armies standing toe-to-toe, neither side giving or asking quarter. Men fell where they stood, only to be replaced by the next man in the file. In the compressed ranks, a regular rotation of fresh men to the front likely became impossible, and so the soldiers at the front of each line fought until killed. This was truly a test of determination, will, and discipline. In this contest, generalship counted for little; the side that could stand the gut-wrenching fear the longest would win.

The battle could still have gone either way when Massanissa and Laelius returned from their pursuit of the cavalry and fell upon Hannibal's army from the rear. The Punic army, cut down from front and rear, began to break. Most died in their ranks, and the few who took flight got but little distance, as the Roman and Numidian cavalry were quick and the country flat. When the battle was over, twenty thousand Carthaginian dead littered the battlefield, while a similar number were prisoners. Scipio had annihilated the last great Punic army at a cost of fifteen hundred Roman lives. Hannibal, joined by a few horsemen, made good his escape: "For there are times when chance thwarts the plans of the brave; and there are others again, when a man though great and brave has met a greater still." The latter, we might say, was the "case with Hannibal on this occasion."

Scipio imposed a harsh peace on the prostrate Carthage. He deprived the city of its fleet except for ten triremes. According to Livy, as many as five hundred warships sailed out of Carthage's harbor to be burned. Moreover, Carthage had to pay an indemnity of 10,000 talents over a fifty-year period. The greatest indignity Carthage endured was that it was forbidden to wage war against anyone without Rome's permission. While the city could still govern itself internally according to its own laws and customs, the Romans now determined Carthage's foreign policy.

Conclusion

Scipio returned to Rome and spent a number of years beset by his political enemies. Fortunately, he was shielded from their unrelenting attacks by his tremendous popularity among the mass of Romans. Eventually tiring of the political squabbling, he retired to his villa at Liternum on the Campanian coast. As Livy notes, Scipio was a man of the camp, and not suited to peace:

> He was an extraordinary man, more distinguished, however in the arts of war than in those of peace. The earlier part of his life was more brilliant than the later; as a young man he was constantly engaged in war; with advancing years the glory of his achievements faded, and there was nothing to call forth his genius. . . . Still, he alone won the unique glory of bringing the war with Carthage to a close, the greatest and most serious war that the Romans have ever waged.

During his self-imposed exile Scipio spent a considerable amount of effort magnanimously trying to protect Hannibal—a man he had come to respect—from the wrath of the Roman Senate. Scipio was an ill man for his final years and greatly embittered by the churlish way Rome's political elites treated him and his family. As he neared death, he demanded that his body be buried at Liternum and his tombstone engraved with: *"Ingrata patria, ne ossa quidem habebis"*— "Ungrateful fatherland, you will not even have my bones."

Rome's treatment of its most victorious general was not lost on future successful commanders such as Marius, Sulla, and Caesar. For them the overriding lesson of Scipio's political debasement was that if you wanted to rule, you needed to return home with your legions at your back.

Hannibal was, for a few years, the leading magistrate in Carthage and led a rapid economic revival. An alarmed Roman Senate demanded Hannibal's surrender, whereupon the general fled the city and became an adviser to several eastern rulers who were readying themselves for war with Rome. He typically advised them not to be so foolish, but they rarely listened to him. Throughout his travels the Romans hounded him and demanded his surrender. When one eastern ruler agreed to hand him over to the Romans, Hannibal thwarted his designs by swallowing poison that he kept in a ring for just such an emergency.

And so, within a year of each other, both Hannibal and Scipio were dead. Their memory, however, has endured for two thousand years. Of the two, it is Hannibal's story that still fires the imagination. In the military schools of dozens of nations, Hannibal's great victory at Cannae is still upheld as the exemplar of battlefield genius. But for all his operational and tactical brilliance, Hannibal never put together the formula for ultimate success. This is the consequence of neglecting a dictum that Clausewitz later put into words: "The first, the supreme, the most far-reaching act of judgment that the statesman and commander have to make is to establish . . . the kind of war on which they are embarking." Hannibal appears to have considered Roman politics and society a mirror image of Carthage's, where one or two great victories would bring Rome to the negotiating table, and a settlement favorable to Carthage's interests could easily be obtained. He overlooked two key qualities about how Romans thought about war. First, Rome had a long history of never negotiating while a threatening army remained on Italian soil. As a consequence, the only way to achieve a permanent settlement was for Carthage to destroy Rome, or at least permanently eliminate its warmaking potential. This Hannibal proved either incapable of doing or unwilling to do. Second, Rome had only one way of dealing with perceived existential threats—to exterminate them. While Hannibal went to war with Rome in pursuit of a political settlement that would allow both to coexist in the western Mediterranean, Rome's goal was to so completely destroy Carthage that it could never rise again. This it achieved in the Third Punic War, in an orgy of destruction that has left us the term "Carthaginian peace." As Tacitus later wrote: *"Auferre, trucidare, rapere, falsis nominibus imperium; atque, ubi solitudinem faciunt, pacem appellant"*—"To ravage, to slaughter, to usurp under false titles, they call empire; and where they make a desert, they call it peace."

Scipio, on the other hand, firmly understood the kind of war he had embarked on. As such, he never campaigned in Italy to defeat

Hannibal. Rather, he first went to Spain to deprive Carthage of revenue from the Spanish mines, and of Spanish recruits, which made up a sizable part of Carthage's armies. When Carthage was successfully weakened, he took the war into Africa, where he refused to hurl his legions against the virtually impregnable walls of the city, opting instead to ravage the countryside, so as to further undermine the Carthaginian economy. When Carthage could no longer endure the pain, it recalled Hannibal and his veteran troops, as Scipio knew it must eventually do. By never losing track of his strategic aims, Scipio could weather reverses, while always maintaining the initiative. From the moment he assumed command of Rome's legions in Spain, Carthage was forced to dance to a tune of Scipio's devising.

So, who was the greater general? As with the remainder of the studies in this book, the ultimate victor is always the general who fights his battles with an achievable strategic purpose in mind. That was never true of Hannibal, but always true of Scipio. Hannibal's brilliance on the battlefield is not diminished by recognizing that Scipio had the better grasp of war's nature, and the capacity to turn his own brilliant battlefield achievements into ultimate victory. Without—in modern parlance—an ultimate theory of victory, Hannibal embarked on a venture that he was never capable of winning. The ultimate cost in blood and treasure finally doomed the state for which he was fighting, while Rome went on to conquer an empire that, in the west, lasted another seven hundred years.

Caesar and Pompey

For a period of nearly forty years between approximately 80 and 44 B.C., Gaius Julius Caesar and Gnaeus Pompeius Magnus dominated Roman politics and military affairs—two areas that were much more closely intertwined than they are today. For much of the period Pompey appeared to be the greater general, while Caesar established himself as a ruthless and effective demagogue. Yet, when their lives were over, it was Caesar who had gained the reputation as one of the greatest generals in history, burnished by his performance as a politician, propagandist, and author of a masterpiece of Latin and military literature. Caesar and Pompey's contest for power in Rome heralded the end of the republic and created the foundation on which Caesar's nephew, Octavian, built the Roman Empire, a political edifice that dominated the Mediterranean world and much of western Europe for over four centuries.

In terms of personality, Pompey and Caesar were quite different. Both possessed enormous self-confidence. Caesar believed in his *fortuna* and thus as a general was willing to take extraordinary chances. At times, his willingness to take risks led him and his soldiers into serious trouble, but invariably, he was able to extract them from their difficulties. That willingness also allowed him to catch his opponents at a significant disadvantage. Caesar's belief in both his destiny and his reputation also made it possible for him to display surprising mercy to his opponents in the civil war that finally brought an end to the republic.

Pompey was less willing to take risks but could be equally aggressive when the situation called for it. Like Caesar, he, too, valued his reputation as a general and a statesman, but it is clear that he did not possess his rival's political sense or capacity as an orator and writer. He arrived at precisely the right time to tie his fate to that of Cornelius Sulla's victory in the first of three great civil wars in the early decades of the first century B.C. Thereafter, his military campaigns— except that against Sertorius, who led Iberia in a revolt against Sulla in 80 B.C.—involved less-than-impressive personalities. His political tin ear cost him dearly when the clash came with Caesar. He listened too much to the *optimates,* the conservative senators who were violent opponents of Caesar, causing him to opt for civil war rather than accommodation.

In the end, both men were great generals. In the campaign that led to the climactic Battle of Pharsalus, a battle that determined the future of Rome, Caesar might well have used the comment the Duke of Wellington made after Waterloo: It had been a "damn close-run thing."

Background

Rome, the body politic over which these two generals contested, had reached a turning point by the first decade of the first century B.C. In Rome's Second Punic War against Hannibal in the late third century B.C., the city had established itself as the dominant power in the Mediterranean. Following that great war, the Romans extended their rule to include much of North Africa, Spain, Macedonia, and Greece. Yet the political framework that governed this great expanse of territory remained that of a small city-state, landlocked on the Italian peninsula. Rome had won the great wars against the Carthaginians largely thanks to amateur generals and conscripted peasants, whom it called annually to the colors. Only the ruthless tactical discipline that Romans brought to their legions turned the tough manpower of Italy into soldiers who were willing to "bear any burden and pay any price" to achieve victory over the enemies of Rome.

But the winning of new domains and the wars against the city's enemies in Greece, Macedonia, and Asia changed the nature of Rome's armies, as well as the political stability of the republic. A political framework designed to run a relatively small city-state proved less and less capable of governing as Rome's *imperium* grew into a full-fledged empire.

Moreover, instead of generals who served the state out of patriotism and loyalty, as Scipio had against Hannibal, senior commanders now focused on the wealth that foreign wars could bring them. They received extended commissions to conduct faraway campaigns in North Africa, Greece, and Spain, where their soldiers waged Rome's ruthless approach to war. Common soldiers, finding themselves committed to service in lengthy and distant campaigns, often transferred their loyalty from the weakened republic to the generals who led them. These Roman military leaders, all drawn from the upper classes, used the wars not only to gain a loyal army but also to achieve unheard-of wealth by plundering foes' riches. As the disparity in wealth between those at the top and those at the lower rungs of the republic's pecking order steadily grew, Rome's internal political stability collapsed.

At the turn of the second and first centuries B.C., two great generals, Gaius Marius and Lucius Cornelius Sulla, commanded Rome's armies. But in the aftermath of their victory over a massive invasion of Italy by German tribes, the Teutons and the Cimbri, their contest over political power nearly destroyed the republic. Marius and Sulla charted a path that Pompey and Caesar were delighted to follow.

Marius, with Sulla as his senior subordinate, emerged as a significant military figure in 107–106 B.C. in the war against the North African king Jurgurtha, who caused the Romans no end of embarrassment with his outright bribery of senior Roman politicians. During this period Marius carried out a number of crucial military reforms that transformed the organizational framework of the Roman Army. Politically, he changed the recruitment laws so that a vast number of poorer Romans now became eligible for service in the legions. As a result, the great majority of Roman soldiers became professional, long-term fighters. Too poor to see any future at home, they realized that only a successful army career would allow them to retire on a plot of land—which they counted on their generals to secure from the Senate. This small step blazed the path that would soon see Pompey's and Caesar's legions swearing oaths to their leaders rather than to the Senate or the republic.

Marius also instituted fundamental tactical reforms, including one that created the basic legionary formation that both Pompey and Caesar used with great effect in their wars. This new tactical framework would bring the Romans military superiority over their enemies for the next three centuries.

Before Marius and Sulla destroyed the German tribes, their predecessors had met with disastrous defeats. At Arausio in Gaul, two consuls had refused to cooperate and led their troops into a disaster that saw the Germans slaughter eighty thousand legionaries, a defeat equal to Cannae. The Germans then turned toward Italy, threatening the very security of Rome.

The problem lay in the fact that the legion rested on the tactical basis of a maniple of two centuries, approximately 160 soldiers. In that form, the legions, consisting of maniples, provided the flexibility that had allowed the Romans to defeat Hannibal and outmaneuver the Macedonian phalanxes of Alexander's successors. Nevertheless, the manipular system lacked the staying power to hold for very long against the ferocious rush of the Germans' northern barbarians—the *furor Teutonicus*. Marius created a new unit, the cohort, consisting of six centuries of approximately 480 soldiers. The legion would now consist of ten cohorts, the first of which was of double strength, and could at full strength deploy approximately fifty-five hundred men. Thus, it combined flexibility with staying power on the battlefield.

The equipment of the Roman soldiers was simple: helmet, protective armor on the chest, a shield to cover the left shoulder, a short sword (the gladius), and a throwing spear (the pilum). The pilum weighed between four and eleven pounds; with a hard sharp tip supported by soft iron and its throwing end made of wood, its purpose was to pierce an enemy's shield and then bend, making it virtually impossible to pull out. Each legionnaire apparently carried two pila. He would throw both as the enemy approached within twenty yards. Then, with the enemies' shields weighted down by the pila, the legionnaires would attack with their short stabbing swords.

The Romans' greatest advantage over their opponents came from their ruthless regimen of training. Writing in the first century A.D., Flavius Josephus, who had defected from the Jewish rebellion in Judea, described the training of the Roman soldiers of his day in the following terms:

> They do not begin to use their weapons first in time of war, nor do they put their hands first into motion, while they avoided so to do in times of peace, but, as if their weapons did always belong to them, they have never any truce from warlike exercises nor do they stay till times of war admonish them to use them; for their military exercises differ not at all from the real use of their arms, but every soldier is every day exercised, and that with great diligence, as if it were in time of war . . . nor would [an observer] be mistaken that would call these their exercises unbloody battles and their battles bloody exercises.

An observer of Caesar's legions in the Gallic War would have made similar comments. The legions of the last decades of the Roman Republic were professional soldiers in every sense of the modern word, except in their loyalty to their generals rather than to the republic. They trained and possessed a sense of loyalty to their legion that made them a disciplined and responsive military force. The commands that articulated their movements and maneuvers, both on the march and in battle, are almost the same as those that modern military organizations use in parade—the Dutch prince Maurice of Orange would later copy them from an ancient Latin manuscript to employ in battle during the late sixteenth century.

Roman legions marched to commands in a fashion that allowed them to manipulate their legions on the battlefield in ways their enemies never could.

Caesar's account of the Battle of the Nervii in 57 B.C. underlines the professionalism of Roman soldiers under the pressures of an attack. In this case, the Nervii attack caught Caesar and his legionaries by surprise in the midst of building their evening camp. His soldiers were dispersed when the enemy struck. As the Nervii and their allies surged into the open, crossed the river between them and the Romans, and came into immediate contact with the legionaries, the Romans responded in a fashion that only highly disciplined soldiers could. Caesar recounts their response in the following terms:

> The situation was saved by two things—first, the knowledge and experience of the soldiers, whose training in earlier battles enabled them to decide for themselves what needed doing without being told; secondly, the order which Caesar had issued to all his [legates], not to leave the work, but to stay each with his legion until the camp fortifications were completed. As the enemy was so close and advancing so swiftly, the [legates] did not wait for further orders but on their own responsibility took the measures they thought proper. . . .
>
> The soldiers were so pushed for time by the enemy's eagerness to fight that they could not even take the covers off their shields or put on helmets—not to mention fixing on crests or decorations. Each man, in coming down from his work at the camp, went into action under the first standard he happened to see, so as not to waste time searching for his own unit.
>
> The battlefront was not formed according to the rules of military theory but as necessitated by the emergency and the sloping ground of the hillside.

In evaluating Pompey's and Caesar's generalship, one must remember that their legionaries possessed the same high level of training, discipline, and values. Thus, victory or defeat would turn entirely on the generalship that each would display on the field of battle.

Early Lives

In the Rome in which Pompey and Caesar would embark on their military and political careers, the sureties of the republic and its political institutions were well on the way to collapsing. Rome had established its dominion in the Mediterranean through a political system that encouraged ferocious competition among its leading figures, competition that placed military glory among the highest attributes of what the Romans regarded as *virtu*. Thus, to rise in the city's political system, an individual had to display an ability to lead on the battlefield. As with other ancient city-states, the terms "soldier" and "citizen" were identical. The only road to the top, therefore, lay through success in war, which brought with it wealth and a loyal army. The result was a competitive system that actively encouraged the waging of war, which became a normal feature of Roman public life.

Increasing violence in the political arena also hugely impacted legionnaires, who began to regularly pick sides in the city's political squabbles. Consequently, general/politicians became increasingly willing to use their soldiers against political enemies in the most violent fashion. The denouement came in a fierce contest between Marius and Sulla, as well as their supporters. Sulla returned to Italy with his six most loyal legions after a victorious war in Greece and Asia. Upon landing he marched on Rome and became the first Roman general to enter the city with his army. Marius and the Senate had only armed gladiators to fend off Sulla, and they were quickly vanquished by Sulla's battle-hardened legions. Sulla then employed them in slaughtering his enemies in Rome—Marians.

Thus, Caesar and Pompey were born into a society that was immensely competitive as well as violent, where political defeat often meant proscription, the equivalent to Stalin's purges. But apart from being born within the political elites of Rome, the two men could not have been more different in background. Caesar came from a family of the oldest nobility, supposedly descended from Aeneas, but one that had not particularly distinguished itself in the more recent past. Whatever wealth the family possessed, Sulla confiscated, as the family had strongly supported Marius. Thus, Caesar would have to scramble for money throughout his early career. Moreover, Caesar's aunt had married Marius, an act that, with Sulla triumphant, placed the young Julius in considerable danger. When Sulla demanded that he divorce his wife, Cornelia, Caesar took the extraordinary step of refusing the dictator's demand, a refusal fraught with danger, given Sulla's murderous track record. For a time, Caesar fled Rome and went into hiding, until an unwilling Sulla was persuaded to lift the potential proscription on his life. The dictator did warn his followers that they were mistaken in their leniency toward Caesar, as he saw a potential Marius in the young man.

At that point, with Sulla's distrust hanging over him like the sword of Damocles, Caesar headed off to Greece, where he began his career. He first made a name for himself by winning one of Rome's highest military decorations, the civic crown, awarded to Roman soldiers for saving the life of a fellow soldier. During his travels in the east, he also displayed the sangfroid that would mark him as a politician and general. Captured by pirates in the Aegean, he warned them that after his ransom was paid, he would return and crucify the lot of them, which is precisely what he proceeded to do. With Sulla's death in 78 B.C., Caesar returned to Rome and began his rise to power.

As with nearly all Roman politicians, except for Pompey, Caesar had to follow the *cursus honorum,* the time-honored progression through various jobs by which Romans traditionally reached the se-niormost position in the republic, that of consul. His climb was aided by several advantages: Caesar was a brilliant orator, which played an important role in his electioneering. He also wrote clear, decisive prose, a significant factor given the high degree of literacy among the Roman upper and middle classes. This would also play a major role in burnishing his historical reputation after his death.

Unlike most generals, Caesar was a masterful politician, always in tune with the mood of the populace. As Plutarch, one of the major sources for the lives of great Greeks and Romans, notes: "In his pleadings at Rome, his eloquence soon obtained him great credit and favor, and he won no less upon the affections of the people by the affability of his manners and address, in which he showed a tact and consideration beyond what could have been expected at his age; and the open house he kept, the entertainments he gave, and the general splendor of his manner of life contributed little by little to create and increase his political influence."

Starting out as a military tribune, Caesar then progressed to quaestor, during which time he served in Spain, already exhibiting a capacity for generalship that would mark the remainder of his career. Caesar was also solidly in the camp of those aiming to overthrow most of Sulla's aristocratic reforms that had stripped the plebs, Rome's poor, of what little political power they enjoyed. In so doing, Caesar not only made a considerable number of enemies but acquired a reputation as a demagogue. At the same time, he steadily increased his popularity with the Roman people through the lavishness with which he dispensed favors and supported gladiatorial games.

After holding the position of praetor in 62 B.C., Caesar received command of Hispania Ulterior (southeastern Spain). Ever profligate with money, he had escaped bankruptcy before leaving for Spain by supporting the immensely wealthy Marcus Licinius Crassus in the latter's political contest with Pompey. In return, Crassus paid some of Caesar's debts and served as a guarantor for others. On his journey across the Alps with a small group of friends, Caesar passed a small hamlet. When one of his companions laughingly commented: "Can it be that here too there are ambitious strifes for office, struggles for primacy, and mutual jealousies of powerful men?" Caesar replied: "I would rather be the first man here, than second in Rome." In Spain Caesar was entirely successful, crushing the Calaici and Lusitani, two tribes that had consistently caused the Romans trouble. Proclaimed imperator by his troops, he headed to Rome to claim a triumph, and it was at this point that his interests began converging with those of Pompey and Crassus, causing the three to form one of the most famous political alliances in history—the First Triumvirate.

Pompey's arrival on the Roman political scene was far splashier. His father was a "new man," a rich provincial who had entered Roman politics, where he used his ruthlessness and competence to add immensely to the family fortune. His fortuitous death—after which, according to Plutarch, the Roman people dragged the body from its bier—allowed Pompey to become the head of his family. In 83 B.C., to assist Sulla, who was then commanding Rome's legions against Mithridates in the east, twenty-three-year-old Pompey raised three legions from the area where his father had drawn his political strength and put them at Sulla's disposal. Pompey then led these legions to aid Sulla against Marius, cementing his bond with Rome's new dictator. Although Pompey had held none of the offices that were the basic requirement for general-like qualities, Sulla addressed him as imperator, an indication of the generalship the young Pompey had exhibited. It was, of course, an act that flew in the face of Rome's traditional practices, but then Sulla, who viewed himself as the restorer of the conservative order, was always willing to compromise when it served his self-interest.

Sulla then appointed Pompey as his general, with the task to eliminate pockets of continued support for the popular party outside of the Italian peninsula. In 82 B.C. Pompey led his legions to Sicily, Rome's breadbasket, and brought it under Sulla's control. Here he displayed a ruthless willingness to participate in Sulla's extermination of those whom the dictator regarded as the enemies of the new conservative order, earning the title of "the young butcher" among his enemies. The next year he and his troops moved on to North Africa, where, in a hard-fought campaign, his army defeated the remnants of Marius's popular party as well as the Numidian tribesmen. Pompey then audaciously demanded a triumph, given his success against the Numidians. Sulla at first refused, at which Pompey dangerously suggested to the dictator that his own sun was rising while Sulla's was setting. As Pompey had come back to Rome with his veteran legions at his back, Sulla wisely allowed the triumph, despite the fact that Pompey had not held even the first political post in the *cursus honorum*. The young general decided that he would have his chariot in the triumph drawn by four elephants he had brought from Africa, but the fact that they could not fit through Rome's small gates thwarted his attempt at megalomania.

Not long after Sulla's death, a short revolt sparked by the consul Lepidus aimed to overthrow Sulla's conservative reforms, but Pompey put it down without difficulty. When he asked for *proconsul imperium* to take his army to Spain to crush a revolt led by Quintus Sertorius, a former Roman governor, the Senate at first turned him down cold. They clearly feared Pompey's growing popularity and his personal control over several legions. But it was this control that finally settled the matter. When Pompey refused to disband his legions, the Senate came to see the wisdom in sending the troublesome youth to Spain . . . along with his troops. The struggle there proved a much harder task than his earlier successes in Italy, Sicily, and North Africa.

Sertorius waged a sustained, cautious campaign that rarely sought battle, although he was able to give Pompey's army a thrashing at the Battle of Sucro in 75 B.C., in which Pompey nearly fell into the hands of his enemies. Pompey finally brought the rebel to heel through a vicious and prolonged war of attrition that deprived Sertorius of resources. When one of Sertorius's officers murdered him, resistance in Spain fell apart. Victory earned Pompey another triumph on his return in 71 B.C. It was then that Pompey turned away from the course set by Sulla and took up the causes of the plebs, particularly that of returning veto power over the Senate's laws to the plebian tribunes. In return the plebs put enormous political pressure on the Senate to allow Pompey the honor of running for consul without even having served as a senator. Not surprisingly given his newfound popularity, the people of Rome elected him consul for 70 B.C. to serve with his rival Crassus, the richest man in Rome and conqueror of the slave revolt led by Spartacus in the Third Servile Revolt, 73–71 B.C. Pompey had already made an enemy of

Crassus by arriving with his army just in time to complete the destruction of Spartacus's slaves and claim partial credit for the victory.

Bust of Pompey
(Venice Museo Archeologico Nazionale)

The honors kept piling up for Pompey. Within two years of his consulship he received the assignment to rid Rome of the plague of pirates that had bedeviled Roman commerce in the Mediterranean. Piracy was threatening Rome's grain supply, without which the city would eventually have starved. As Plutarch recorded, the decree "gave him absolute power and authority in all the seas within the Pillars of Hercules (i.e., the Mediterranean) and in the adjacent mainland." Not surprisingly, the decree ran into staunch opposition from many senators, some of whom were jealous of Pompey's successes and some of whom were afraid that the bill would strengthen Pompey too much and he would act to overthrow the republic. Caesar, astutely reading the tea leaves, was not among those in opposition. Within three months Pompey had broken the power of the pirates—at least for the present—in a skillful war that combined force with propaganda. "Besides a great number of other vessels, he took [captured] ninety men-of-war with brazen beaks; and likewise prisoners of war to the number of no less than twenty thousand."

In 66 B.C. Pompey's political power again won him a lucrative position. He replaced Lucius Lucullus in command of the armies fighting one of Rome's perennial enemies in Asia Minor, Mithridates. Matters started off badly, with a furious quarrel between Lucullus and Pompey, the former believing quite rightly that Pompey aimed to steal the glory of destroying a nearly defeated Mithridates from those who suffered most of the hardships. It was a quarrel that was to have a significant political impact when Pompey eventually returned to Rome. The campaign against Mithridates, however, was a swift success.

After crushing Mithridates's army, Pompey then chased the king to the Caucasus, where the Roman army defeated local tribes. With Mithridates now a refugee having no military forces to speak of, Pompey moved on into Syria, where he deposed the last of the Hellenistic kings and a descendent of one of Alexander's generals, Antiochus XIII. Not satisfied with absorbing Syria into Rome's burgeoning eastern empire, Pompey turned toward Judea, where he found the Jewish population once again engaged in a civil war. Roman arms soon returned a semblance of order to the troubled Jewish state and took it into Rome's dominion. With this, Pompey had, in effect, established Roman rule over the eastern Mediterranean and the territories to the east. It would last for seven centuries, until the eruption of Arab tribes under the flag of Islam permanently divided the Mediterranean world.

Pompey returned to Rome in 61 B.C. to celebrate his third triumph, which lasted two days and exceeded his earlier triumphs in every respect. As was true of all Roman conquerors, he used the triumph as propaganda to further solidify his popularity with the common people. At the age of forty-five, he had reached the epitome of success as defined by the Romans. As Plutarch notes: "And well had it been for him had he terminated his life at this date, while he still enjoyed Alexander's fortune, since all his aftertime served only either to bring him prosperity that made him odious, or calamities too great to be retrieved." One of Pompey's first acts upon his return to Italy had been to disband his army, demonstrating that he had learned little from his own experience or that of his mentor, Sulla. With an army at his back he could dictate to the Senate; without one he was a toothless tiger. He could roar but could not intimidate. Pompey believed that the Senate would honor the settlement he had made in the east, which had added vast and taxable territory to Rome's imperium dominions and would also reward his veterans for the sacrifices they had made in defending Rome's interests. It was a serious political mistake, because while he was at war a substantial portion of the Senate had rallied around Lucullus, whom he had replaced and insulted in the east. Motivated by jealousy as well as fear that Pompey was becoming too powerful, the Senate refused to do his bidding. Without an army to make his word law, Pompey needed new allies and was driven by conservative senators into the waiting arms of Caesar and Crassus.

The First Triumvirate and the Destruction of the Republic

At the end of 60 B.C., Caesar had returned from Spain and claimed his right to a triumph. However, the Senate ordered him not to enter Rome until the day the triumph was celebrated. It was a political ploy; unless he entered Rome, he could not stand in the upcoming election for the following year's consuls. In those circumstances Caesar requested the Senate's permission to stand in absentia, but Cato, Caesar's inveterate enemy, persuaded the Senate to turn the request down. Caesar then entered Rome as a private citizen, forgoing his triumph. The senators had also alienated Crassus by interfering with his financial interests, and so the three powerful men found that they had a common interest in combining their strengths to achieve personal goals despite the Senate's opposition: Caesar to achieve the consulship; Pompey to push through his eastern settlement and achieve the rewards he believed his soldiers deserved; and Crassus to achieve the financial authority his tax gathers needed. Caesar brought the skills of a brilliant politician; Pompey the necessary muscle, with soldiers starting to rally to his cause; and Crassus the funding necessary to support the triumvirate's political activities. It was not a marriage made in heaven, but it was one of convenience.

Bust of Caesar—the only one made during his lifetime *(Museo di antichità di Torino)*

The three men did not announce their agreement publicly, but their actions soon made clear their common interests. The *optimates,* the best men, as the conservatives styled themselves, believed they were in a position to thwart any move Caesar made to push popular reforms by electing Marcus Calpurnius Bibulus as Caesar's co-consul. Bibulus intended to thwart Caesar at every turn. In addition, the *optimates* tried to limit Caesar's future power by allotting the woods and pastures of Italy, rather than the governorship of a province, as his military command after his year in office was over.

Believing that they could fence Caesar in with legalisms, Pompey and Crassus had not foreseen or made arrangements to counter the new political alignment that girded Caesar's political power. Caesar's first move was a carefully crafted proposal to redistribute public land for the poor. Bibulus attempted to thwart Caesar's efforts before the Roman assembly by declaring that the omens were unsatisfactory. Accompanied by Cato, he entered the forum, where Pompey's ex-soldiers and a variety of thugs quite literally trashed the two *optimates* and came close to killing them. At the same time Pompey announced his support for Caesar and the new law; the triumvirate was now in the open. Bibulus retreated to his house, where he remained for the rest of his term, while Caesar rammed through the assembly a variety of reforms and laws that were popular with the lower classes and favored the triumvirate.

Caesar's War in Gaul

Perhaps the most crucial of these in retrospect was the overturning of Caesar's allotted province. It would now include Cisalpine Gaul, Illyricum, and Transalpine Gaul. Along with these provinces Caesar secured a five-year tenure in office as proconsul, freedom from potential prosecution by his political enemies while he remained proconsul, and, of crucial importance, four legions, soon to be raised to six by Caesar's extensive recruitment in Cisalpine Gaul. To further cement his connection to the triumvirate, Caesar gave away his daughter, Julia, to Pompey, a political marriage of convenience that turned into one of love in spite of the couple's considerable difference in age. The connection with Pompey and Crassus in Rome protected his political flank, allowing Caesar to focus his efforts on the winning of Gaul, a region that included all of modern-day France, Belgium, and Luxembourg; much of Holland, and the territory on the right bank of the Rhine that is today part of Germany. The war on which he now embarked was nothing less than a war of conquest, waged with all the ruthlessness and effectiveness that the Roman military machine could bring to bear.

Thus far Caesar had had a successful military career, but hardly one that had indicated that he would emerge as one of the greatest generals in military history. Yet, he embarked on the conquest of Gaul without any personal doubt that he would conquer the immense expanse of this territory inhabited by fierce, intractable warriors, thus adding immensely to Rome's wealth as well as its security in the north. Unseen by his allies or enemies and only revealed during his wars in Gaul, Caesar possessed a number of qualities that secure his place on the short list of history's great military captains.

As a general Caesar had an innate ability to judge what his opponents would do; he was rarely caught by surprise, but when he was, he reacted quickly, adapting to the situation as it was rather than as he wished it to be. Above all, he believed in acting with speed; like Napoléon, he understood that time was one quantity that no general could afford to waste. Thus, one finds his commentaries on the Gallic Wars sprinkled with the phrase *quam celerrime:* "as quickly as possible." As Plutarch notes: "Caesar . . . above all men was gifted with the faculty of making the right use of everything in war, and most especially in seizing the right moment." Caesar also had a great facility for getting his soldiers to identify with him, that special bond that leads those in the enlisted rank to act beyond what mighty normally be expected. Again Plutarch:

> There was no danger to which he did not willingly expose himself, no labor from which he pleaded an exemption. His contempt for danger was not so much wondered at by his soldiers because they knew how much he coveted honor. But his enduring so much hardship, which he did to all appearance beyond his natural strength, very much astonished them. For he was a spare man . . . and [was] subject to epilepsy. . . . But he did not make the weakness of his constitution a pretext for his ease, but rather used war as the best physic against his indispositions; whilst by indefatigable journeys, coarse diet, lodging in the field, and continued laborious exercise, he struggled with his diseases and fortified his body against all attacks.

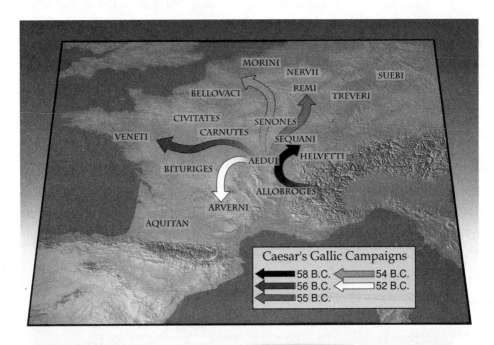

MORINI   NERVII   SUEBI
BELLOVACI   REMI   TREVERI
CIVITATES   SENONES
VENETI   CARNUTES   SEQUANI
BITURIGES   AEDUI   HELVETTI
ALLOBROGES
ARVERNI
AQUITAN

Caesar's Gallic Campaigns

58 B.C.   54 B.C.
56 B.C.   52 B.C.
55 B.C.

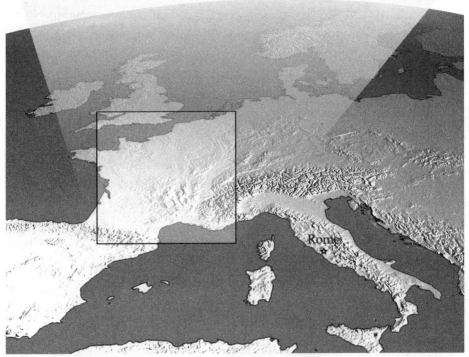

Rome

Of all the campaigns that shaped the ancient world, historians understand Caesar's campaign in Gaul best, thanks especially to his commentaries written in masterful Latin prose. His explanations of his decisions and actions capture the campaigns in a fashion nonexistent for other wars in the ancient world. There are, of course, some caveats: Caesar wrote his commentaries for a number of divergent purposes. It was, of course, a propaganda document aimed at Roman public opinion, to inform the folks back home how the campaign in Gaul was proceeding. It was also meant to guide future generations of soldiers and, as such, has great value in understanding military operations. Only the memoirs of Ulysses S. Grant and William Slim are more honest and useful for the education of future officers.

Caesar chose Gaul in 58 B.C. rather than the seemingly richer provinces in the east because he recognized that the always-unstable situation among the Gallic tribes was unraveling. In particular the Helvetii, who inhabited the mountain valleys of modern-day eastern France and much of Switzerland, had decided to move across Gaul to occupy the richer and far more fertile areas of southwestern France. In addition, a major movement of German tribes across the Rhine seemed imminent. Such vast population movements spelled strategic trouble for the Romans, and Caesar undoubtedly intuited that such troubled political waters offered him considerable opportunities. He was certainly able to justify his initial campaign in Gaul to the Roman people as an effort to protect them against their ancient enemies, the Gauls and the Germans.

In the spring of 58 B.C., the Helvetii moved first, just as Caesar assumed command of his provinces and legions. After gathering sustenance and other supplies necessary to support their long march from eastern to western Gaul, they burned their villages and set out *quam celerrime* to Geneva, where Caesar met delegates from the Helvetii. When they requested that he allow them to cross Roman territory, he delayed responding and asked them to return on April 13. In the meantime, Caesar ordered the one legion at his disposal, the Tenth, to begin a massive engineering work aimed at blocking the route the Helvetii proposed to take. By the time the

Helvetii returned, his legionaries had completed a fortified line that prevented the tribesmen from breaking through. Thwarted, the Helvetii turned to the more northerly route leading down from their Alpine homes to the Rhône River and onto the territory of the Sequani.

While his highly competent legate, Quintus Atius Labienus, held the line at Geneva, Caesar recruited two new legions and brought the three other legions at his disposal forward to meet the Helvetii. At the same time, his officers and centurions were whipping the legions into shape. When his troops were ready, Caesar began his pursuit. He caught the Helvetii after they had moved three-quarters of their numbers across the Saône River. As Caesar recorded: "he set out from the camp with three legions during the third watch, and came up with that division which had not yet crossed the river. Attacking them encumbered with baggage, and not expecting him, he cut to pieces a great part of them; the rest betook themselves to flight, and concealed themselves in the nearest woods."

Caesar's legionnaires then built a bridge across the Saône and took up the pursuit, which continued despite the failure of the Aedui—supposedly friends of Rome—to supply the grain they had promised the Romans. Some of the Aedui leaders were obviously playing a double game.

Caesar's first effort to defeat the Helvetii failed when a staff officer mistakenly reported that Labienus had failed to occupy a key hill. Despite this setback Caesar had the Helvetii almost trapped. Only at the last moment did they recognize the danger and retreat. Eventually Caesar caught up with them; with his two new legions serving as a reserve, he stationed his four veteran legions in the front ranks, in the traditional deployment of four cohorts in each of the first and second lines and the remaining three cohorts in the third line.

Caesar then sent his own horse away, a sign that he would stay with his legionnaires, win or lose. Holding the high ground, the Romans possessed a distinct advantage. The pila served to render most of the Helvetii shields useless, while the charge of the legionnaires quickly drove them back. Threatened by a major Helvetii attack on his right flank, Caesar ordered the Roman third rank to wheel and cover the army's threatened flank. Roman discipline and training to meet the unexpected worked as well in practice as in theory. It was not an easy fight, but as Caesar continued to feed fresh troops into the fight, the Helvetti tired and could no longer stand up to the sustained hammer blows of the legions. Defeated, the Helvetii sued for peace. Caesar's terms were relatively mild: The Helvetii were to return to the lands they had abandoned, since the last thing the Romans needed was a vacuum into which the Germans might move.

That agreement freed Caesar to resolve the problem of the Germans. In the northern portions of Gaul, internecine warfare between the Arverni and Sequani tribes eventually led to invites for German mercenaries from across the Rhine to enter the struggle. Under tribal leader Ariovistus, a torrent of warriors soon dominated the northern Gallic tribes. With no alternative, the Gauls begged Caesar to come to their aid and drive out the German interlopers. Caesar immediately perceived that he could serve both his own ambitions and the strategic interests of the Roman people, since, "the Germans should by degrees become accustomed to cross the Rhine, and that a great body of them should come into Gaul, he saw [would be] dangerous to the Roman people." For their part, happy to get the Romans to do their dirty work, the Gauls entirely overlooked the fact that they were calling on a skilled tiger to eliminate a lion.

Tales of enormous, fearsome German warriors soon spread among not only Caesar's common soldiers but the centurions and legates as well. It took all of Caesar's persuasive powers, recalling among other things the fact that the Helvetii had regularly beaten the Germans, for him to quell a full-scale mutiny and persuade his troops to campaign against the Germans. Only Caesar's announcement that he would take the Tenth alone to go and fight Ariovistus shamed his soldiers into returning to discipline, and the army marched against the Germans.

A considerable time passed after the armies were in contact for the Germans to decide to fight, but eventually they deployed their warriors, but "surrounded their whole army with their chariots and wagons, that no hope might be left in flight. On these they placed their women, who, with disheveled hair and in tears, entreated the soldiers, as they went forward to battle, not to deliver them into slavery to the Romans." Caesar first launched his right wing at what he perceived to be a weak link in the German dispositions and made some progress, as the left flank of the Germans collapsed back on their baggage line. On the Roman left, though, the legionnaires ran into difficulty, until one of the Roman legates, Publius Crassus, saw the danger and led the Roman cavalry in a reckless charge. When the Germans were fully occupied fending off the cavalry, Caesar sent forward the *triarii*. Unable to stand against these grizzled veterans, the German right joined the rest of the army in flight. A mad rout to the Rhine ensued, during which Roman cavalry slaughtered most of the Germans. Thus, for the second time in the year 58 B.C., Caesar had completely destroyed an army of barbarians. For the Gauls, the Roman victory over the Germans was a disaster. They had undoubtedly hoped for a mutual slaughter of Romans and Germans that would leave them to pick up the pieces. Instead, they were left with an all-conquering Caesar, who had every intention of turning his victories over the Helvetii and the Germans to Rome's and his own advantage.

The following year's campaign proved a close-run thing. The fact that the Romans chose to winter in Gaul underlined for many Gallic leaders Caesar's intent to add Gaul to the Roman Empire. The Belgic tribes in northern Gaul were the first to raise the standard of rebellion. Caesar's intelligence suggested they could call up more than three hundred thousand warriors, undoubtedly an exaggeration, but a considerable force that far outnumbered the legionnaires and auxiliaries at Caesar's disposal.

As the horde of tribesmen approached, Caesar took his army across the Aisne River and set up his fortified camp on a hill with the river to his back. Digging two major ditches at a right angle from the hill where he had located his camp, Caesar was then able to deploy six of his legions fully, while he kept two newly recruited legions as a reserve in the camp. His engineers had constructed the two ditches so as to severely limit the number of Gallic warriors who could attack the Romans at one time. Because the Romans had deployed on the hill's slope, the Gauls refused to attack. Instead they attempted to outflank the Romans by crossing the Aisne on fords above the Roman camp. The legate guarding the bridge across the Aisne immediately spied the Gauls and, after informing Caesar what was afoot, launched the cavalry, which caught the small number of Gauls who had crossed. Caesar then arrived with his slingers and archers and heavy infantry behind. A fierce fight ensued, but the Romans had every advantage and the result was a slaughter. Discouraged and almost out of food, most of the Gallic tribes went home. Surprised by the sudden decamping of the enemy, the Romans pursued carefully but soon caught up to the rear guard of Gallic warriors and destroyed them. The others retreated as rapidly as they could.

The next day Caesar moved out to attack the citadel of the Suessiones. After failing to storm the town, the Romans immediately began construction of siege works, including great towers, a sign of determination that prompted the Suessiones to quit the struggle and surrender. Caesar again granted mild terms, as he wanted to move as rapidly as possible against the other Belgic tribes, particularly the Nervii, the toughest of the tribes. As the army moved toward the Sambre, Caesar changed the march order for his legions. Whereas each legion had previously marched with its baggage to its immediate rear, he now had his six veteran legions march with all their baggage concentrated near the rear of the entire army, with the two new legions following at the tail end of the move. Thus, instead of being able to attack separated legions and defeat them in detail, the attack of the Nervii came up against the six veteran legions unencumbered by their baggage. The resulting battle was perhaps the hardest fought of his career, but in the end Roman discipline and training triumphed over the barbarians' bravery and surprise.

But Caesar was not through with the Belgic tribes. Next on his list were the Aduatuci, who had been on the way to support the Nervii when news of the defeat of the latter arrived in their camp. The Aduatuci retreated, followed closely by Caesar, who soon invested their capital and began major siege operations. When the Aduatuci saw the Romans hard at work constructing their siege towers in the distance, they began to mock and taunt the Romans from their wall, unaware that the towers had wheels. Their laughter ceased when the Romans rolled the gigantic towers forward. They immediately sued for peace, which Caesar granted. However, that night after their surrender, they launched a surprise attack, which found the Romans ready and standing to arms. After the slaughter the Romans, on the following morning, broke into the town. Those whom the soldiers did not kill, Caesar—who could be ruthless when he felt he had to send a message—sold to the slave traders, a number he records as fifty-three thousand men, women, and children.

The campaigning season was now over, and Caesar returned to Italy. His report to the Roman people recorded that "the whole of Gaul was pacified." That was certainly an overoptimistic claim, as the events of 56 B.C. would show. Winter had not yet begun when the Twelfth Legion, under the command of Servius Galba in eastern Gaul, came under a major attack by Gallic warriors. Only a desperate sally that caught the Gauls by surprise won the day.

This was only the first of such attacks. Undeterred by that failure, the Veneti, a tribe that dominated the coastal regions of western France, attacked Publius Crassus and his Seventh Legion. In reply Caesar ordered his legates to prepare naval forces to deal with the Veneti, but the initial struggle, which opened the campaigning season of 56 B.C., did not go well for the Romans. Initially, the weapons and tactics the Romans employed in the Mediterranean proved useless against the ships employed by the Veneti. But the Romans adapted quickly. By using their grappling hooks, they disabled the rigging of the Veneti ships' sails, allowing their ships to be taken by storm. Caesar then altered his approach to peace as a warning to the other tribes. He ordered the execution of the entire Veneti Senate and sold the population into slavery.

Caesar returned to Rome to shore up his political flanks and coordinate with the other two members of the triumvirate. Crassus and Pompey had already secured election as consuls for 55 B.C., the former to position himself as the proconsul in Syria from whence he planned to launch a great campaign against the Parthian Empire. Caesar rejoined his troops in Gaul in early spring, after spies had alerted him to a major invasion of Germans, once more summoned by the Gauls but this time to confront the Romans. Driving his legions and auxiliaries in successive force marches toward the left bank of the Rhine, Caesar caught the Germans by surprise. The Romans closed fast "[After an] eight-mile march was so speedily accomplished that Caesar reached the enemy's camp before the Germans could have any inkling of what was happening. They were struck with sudden panic by everything—by the rapidity of our approach, the absence of their own chiefs; and, as no time was given them to think, or to take up arms, they were too much taken aback to decide which was best." When the Germans attempted to do everything at once they succeeded in none. The result was another slaughter with the survivors immediately sold into slavery.

Caesar's immediate response to his victory over the German interlopers was to cross the Rhine and teach the Germans a lesson. The German expedition had as much to do with making a propaganda gesture for those back in Rome, where the memory of the threat posed by the Cimbri and the Teutons—the German tribes that Marius and Sulla had destroyed—remained alive. The surface value of such an advance strengthened Caesar in Rome at a time when Pompey and Crassus, the consuls for the year, were having great difficulty maintaining order against the political assaults of the *optimates* and the increasing resort to violence in the streets by ambitious rabble-rousers.

Having disposed of the Germans as an immediate threat, Caesar decided to embark on a raid against Britain as another source of propaganda. His raid came close to disaster as he took only two legions against a far tougher opponent than Caesar had estimated. But Caesar's luck, as well as the toughness of his troops, allowed the

Roman force to escape and in late September make its way back to Gaul.

Above all, Caesar was a learner. In 54 B.C. he displayed his extraordinary leadership as well as his capacity to move with devastating speed. Since Gaul appeared to be quiescent, he determined to return to Britain with a far larger force. He did not intend to conquer Britain, but rather to make clear to both the Britons and the Gauls that he and his army could move freely and exert their power wherever and whenever they wished. This time Caesar took extensive measures to ensure he would not suffer the fate of the previous year. Three legions made up the heart of the invading force. After defeating the opposition and acquiring enough hostages to ensure the future good behavior of the British tribes, Caesar and his legions returned to Gaul.

A drought over the summer forced Caesar to deploy his legions over a larger area than normal to provide sufficient food from the local population. This meant that the individual Roman camps were too distant to be mutually supporting. One of these bases, consisting of a recently raised legion with five additional cohorts under the command of Quintus Sabinus, came under attack. Sabinus attempted to negotiate with the attacking Eburones and eventually caved in to all of their demands, including that the legion march out of their camp and retire from Gaul. Caught in the open, the Gauls slaughtered them.

The leader of the Eburones, a certain Ambiorix, immediately hastened to spread the word throughout Gaul. The Aduatuci and the remaining Nervii—the latter might have thought better— immediately joined up and attacked a second legionary camp commanded by Quintus Cicero, brother of the orator. Cicero proved more resolute. Immediately on receiving warning, he and his soldiers made extensive efforts to prepare the camp's defenses. To the demand of the Nervii that he surrender, Cicero replied in the tradition of the ancient Romans: "that it is not the custom of the Roman people to accept any condition from an armed enemy: if they are willing to lay down their arms, they may employ him as their advocate and send embassadors to Caesar: that he believed, from his [Caesar's] justice, they would obtain the things which they might request." Subjected to a series of massed attacks, Cicero's legionnaires nevertheless stood their ground and held until relieved. Two centurions, Titus Pullo and Lucius Vorenus—the names given to the soldiers in the HBO series *Rome*—were singled out by Caesar for their bravery.

Cicero sent out a series of anxious messages to inform Caesar of the increasingly desperate situation his embattled force confronted. One messenger finally got through, arriving late in the afternoon to Caesar's camp. Caesar immediately sent a message to Marcus Crassus, son of Caesar's fellow triumvir and commander of the nearest legion, that he was to march at midnight and join up with Caesar. He also alerted two other legionary commanders, including Labienus, to march at their discretion, given the dangerous territory through which they would have to march. Crassus and his legion arrived at approximately nine A.M. after a march of twenty-three miles. Caesar then met up with Fabius and his legion. Thus, with only two legions, Caesar undertook a series of forced marches that penetrated deep into the territory of the Nervii. The Gauls immediately abandoned their siege to turn against Caesar's approaching legions.

But Caesar was warned of their coming. At the precise moment when the Gauls attempted to push their way into the Roman fortified camp: "Then Caesar, making a sally from all the gates, and sending out the cavalry, soon put the enemy to flight, so that no one at all stood his ground with the intention of fighting; and he slew a great number of them, and deprived all of their arms." The relief of Cicero's legion and camp immediately followed, while the Treveri, who were preparing to attack Labienus's camp, immediately fled back to their homes. It was generalship at its best: swift movement and a rapid, merciless attack that broke the enemy in the field.

In the midst of this winter campaign, Caesar's daughter and Pompey's wife, Julia, died in childbirth, thus sundering the familial relationship between the two men. Moreover, Crassus had departed for Syria to begin his disastrous campaign against the Parthians, thus limiting Caesar's room for maneuver on the chessboard of Roman politics. Still, the alliance with Pompey remained sufficiently strong that Pompey allocated to Caesar the legions recruited in Italy for the year. Thus, in the spring Caesar found himself with three new legions, more than enough to make up for those cohorts lost in Sabinus's disaster.

But Caesar's troubles in Gaul were just beginning. The Treveri made extensive overtures to the German tribes across the Rhine. Caesar was informed of the Treveri's plans, as well as the mobilizations of the Nervii, Aduatuci, and Menapii, the Germans on the west side of the Rhine. Threatened on all sides and concerned that the Senones did not assemble according to his command, Caesar attacked. With winter not yet over in 53 B.C., he concentrated the four nearest legions and suddenly moved against the Nervii. Burning their villages, capturing their cattle, and seizing large numbers of their men, the Romans gave the Nervii no choice but to surrender or be eliminated as a people. Caesar then moved with his legions against the Senones before they could assemble their warriors in their towns. Threatened with total destruction of their fields and villages, they, too, caved.

Sending two legions to reinforce Labienus among the Treveri so as to protect the army's baggage train, Caesar moved with five legions and virtually no baggage against the Menapii, who hid in the great primeval swamp immediately south of the Rhine, in modern-day Belgium. Constructing causeways across the swampy terrain, Caesar's legions destroyed everything they came across. The Menapii, too, sued for peace. While Caesar was disposing of the Gauls along the Rhine, the Treveri were attacking Labienus and his three legions. Labienus tricked the Treveri into fighting a major battle in which the Romans slaughtered them.

After the summer and fall's activities in 53 B.C., Caesar felt confident enough of Gaul's stability to return to Italy, where the situation in Rome had further deteriorated after the Parthians destroyed Crassus's army at the Battle of Carrhae. Thus, there were only two great men in Rome, a situation that neither Pompey nor Caesar could tolerate in the long run. And if Caesar thought that the situation in Gaul had stabilized, he was seriously in error. As winter closed in, the restless Gauls were preparing a shock that would rock the foundations of Roman power. A young Gallic aristocrat, Vercingetorix, attracted the loyalty of his peers, and for the first time the Gauls had a single leader of competence in both the military and political spheres. Once Caesar received news of the revolt, he rushed back to Gaul. First, he bolstered the defenses of Roman territory in Cisalpine Gaul. Then, marching his small force over the Cévennes Mountains, Caesar burst on the territory of the Arverni in modern-day south-central France. Caught by surprise, the Arverni panicked and screamed for Vercingetorix to aid them.

Sure that the Gallic leader would reply to their appeals for aid, Caesar left Decimus Brutus—one of Caesar's later assassins—in command of the region and led deeper into Gaul the force he had brought from Italy. Picking up a cavalry force at modern-day Vienne on the Rhône, he rapidly advanced into Aeduan territory where two of his legions were wintering. Toppling Gallic towns with his swiftness, Caesar moved to besiege modern-day Nevers. As the town was surrendering, Gallic cavalry appeared in the distance, and the locals attempted to resume the struggle. But Caesar's cavalry, reinforced by German mercenaries, scattered the Gauls. Caesar allowed the townspeople to sacrifice the "supposed" leaders of the attempted betrayal and surrender, because of his desire to move on.

Vercingetorix hit on a new strategic approach to fighting the Romans that, in current military lingo, would be called "hybrid warfare"; the Gauls would keep their army in the field but refuse to fight the Romans, while their cavalry and raiding parties would attack Roman foraging parties. Because it was March, such tactics caused the Romans severe discomfort, as food became increasingly scarce. In spite of this, and with the Gallic army in the neighborhood, Caesar decided to besiege Bituriges, modern-day Bourges, and eliminate the sizable enemy forces manning the defenses. When his legions finally stormed the town, the legionaries took their fill for what had been a difficult siege. Caesar, perhaps overestimating, calculated the number slaughtered at forty thousand. It was a message that Caesar intended for the Gauls to never forget. In the town, the Romans also discovered a substantial amount of food that relieved Caesar's immediate needs and provided sufficient surplus for him to continue his offensive.

A serious political and military reverse came in his dealings with the Aedui, who had previously been the Romans' staunchest supporter among the Gauls. The Aedui were probably the wealthiest and most politically united of all the Gallic tribes. They also sat along Caesar's communications route to Italy and provided much of the logistical support for the legions in Gaul. They had grown rich by trading with Rome and supplying the Roman war machine. Although Caesar had "protected" them against the Helvetii and others, they had come to resent Rome's presence and overbearing demands. Convinced by Vercingetorix that it was possible for a unified Gaul to defeat the Romans, they deserted the Roman cause.

The training and trust that Caesar had placed in his subordinates now played a crucial role in preventing a spiraling military disaster. He divided his army, with Labienus moving against the tribes in central Gaul. As Labienus pushed his assaults, Caesar moved with six legions against the town of Gergovia. Here, he launched one of his bold strikes, telling his legionaries to capture only the outlying Gallic camps. But only the Tenth Legion, his favorite and best disciplined, halted, while the others disobeyed and attempted to storm the town walls. The result was a severe setback that cost the Romans forty-six centurions and approximately seven hundred soldiers.

In the battles that followed, Vercingetorix made a serious mistake by placing his army in the town of Alesia, which appeared to be a safe haven and too strong to be taken by storm. The Gallic leader underestimated the ability of Caesar's army to sustain a lengthy siege, and despite the fact that Alesia had food for only thirty days, Vercingetorix made the decision to stand a siege. He urged the Gallic tribes to send a massive army to save Alesia before the Romans could starve it into submission. Fully informed of his opponent's intentions and hopes, Caesar laid out a double line of fortifications—one facing toward Alesia to keep Vercingetorix's army in, and the other facing in the opposite direction to keep the relieving army out. It represented a monumental effort, but it underlined not only the engineering capabilities of the army and their general, but the willingness of legionaries to labor under extraordinarily difficult circumstances.

Vercingetorix's hopes that the Gallic tribes would raise a great host were met, but not before Caesar had finished constructing his dual walls. The Gallic host now confronted the task of breaking into Alesia through strong Roman fortifications, while the eighty thousand Gallic warriors on the inside attempted to break out. The ensuing battle proved to be a struggle of Gallic muscle and bravery against Roman discipline and engineering.

The Gauls' first two attempts to break through failed. They then launched a better-organized attack, simultaneously employing both their forces inside Alesia and those outside the Roman fortified walls. Caesar wrote that the attack consisted of sixty thousand of the best Gallic warriors, while the remainder of the enemy army did nothing, allowing the Romans to concentrate on just two areas. The attack from outside the Roman fortified lines came close to breaking through, but seeing that the crisis of the battle was at hand, Caesar sent Labienus with six cohorts to reinforce that portion of the line. Caesar himself went to reinforce the defenders protecting the lines facing Alesia, then under heavy attack from Gauls under Vercingetorix. Once this threat was beaten back, Caesar led a substantial reinforcement to bolster Labienus. Roman morale hugely improved when the legionaries saw Caesar's distinctive red cloak leading determined cohorts to their aid. But it was a cavalry attack unleashed by Caesar that broke the Gauls, who were taken by surprise from the flank and rear. The collapse of the Gallic relief army was sudden and complete, and it doomed the Gauls in Alesia. Vercingetorix had no choice but to surrender and await his death by strangulation at Caesar's triumph. The great rebellion by the Gallic tribes had failed.

The campaign against Vercingetorix displays Caesar's generalship at its best. Under the dangerous threat that the Gauls were uniting against him and Roman rule, he struck in the winter and then continued a campaign of maneuver; the setback at Gergovia, his most serious of the war, did not deflect him from his purpose or resolve. The conduct of the siege at Alesia represented a masterful piece of generalship—one that considered Vercingetorix's attempt at trapping the Roman army by mobilizing all of Gaul to come to the rescue of their fellow tribesmen at Alesia. Caesar then defended his fortified lines by mixing the advantages conveyed by his carefully engineered defenses, the stout resistance of his soldiers, and, at the end, a carefully launched counterattack.

Civil War

Caesar would face continued difficulties over the winter and into the next year. When a particularly tough group of Gauls surrendered after the Siege of Uxellodunum, he ordered his troops to cut off the warriors' hands as a stark warning to the rest of the Gauls not to trifle with him again. His determination to bring the Gauls to heel quickly was driven by political concerns in Rome, where relations with Pompey had steadily deteriorated since the death of his daughter Julia and the destruction of Crassus and his army. In Caesar's account of the Civil War, he paints a picture in which he attempted to meet Pompey halfway. What is certain is that he attempted to split Pompey off from the *optimates,* with whom Pompey was increasingly aligned, even after the Civil War had begun. That said, Caesar's key demand appeared reasonable enough: He wanted to have protection from prosecution by his opponents until he assumed the consulship. For the *optimates,* who were out to destroy him, such a solution was completely unacceptable. Pushed by a desire to maintain his own *dignitas* (reputation), Pompey joined them in their condemnation of Caesar.

But Pompey overestimated the strength of his strategic position as well as the willingness of Caesar to act in direct defiance of the Roman Senate, which had ordered him to disband his army. Neither the *optimates* nor Pompey seem to have taken the military threat that Caesar represented seriously. Pompey announced to his supporters that "whenever I stamp with my foot in any part of Italy there will rise up forces enough in an instant, both horse and foot." There was a dangerous overoptimism among the senatorial party, an optimism that Caesar's chief lieutenant, Labienus, reinforced when he defected with the report that the morale of Caesar's soldiers was low. Consequently, the Senate believed that Caesar could be defeated relatively easily and authorized Pompey to begin levying troops for the coming conflict. They were too late, as there were only a few months left before the fighting began in earnest.

As his last proposal before the war broke out, Caesar suggested that both he and Pompey give up their commands. That was not acceptable to Pompey, and he had the Senate pass a law ordering Caesar to lay down his command and promising, if he failed to do so, to declare him a public enemy. Caesar had deployed his troops at the end of his last campaign in Gaul so that they would not appear threatening, but he retained the Thirteenth Legion in Italy at Ravenna. In early December, as it was apparent that there was little chance that the *optimates* or Pompey would strike a deal, Caesar ordered the Eighth and Twelfth Legions to force-march from Gaul to bolster him in Italy and reinforce the one legion he had at his disposal.

Caesar crossed the Rubicon and, with the legionaries of the Thirteenth, moved rapidly south into Italy. His decision and the rapidity of his march caught the *optimates* and Pompey completely by surprise; in terms of Pompey's responsibility, that surprise must be counted as one of the greatest mistakes of his military career. Full of themselves and their supposed righteousness, the *optimates* had courted the confrontation in the belief that Caesar would prove a pushover. After all, his victories over the Gauls had been against worthless barbarians. Thus, the reports that Caesar had reached Ariminum on November 26, 50 B.C., resulted in panic in Rome. Pompey could do nothing to alleviate it. He was beginning to see that by joining with the *optimates* within the Senate, he had hung an albatross around his neck. Their refusal to name him dictator or commander in chief ensured that he had little control during the crisis. Thus, in late December when he suggested to Lucius Domitius Ahenobarbus that he retreat with his new levies, the latter refused, in the belief that he could stop Caesar. His recruits, however, displayed little confidence in their commander and refused to fight Caesar's veterans. Instead, they ran away.

Caesar's advance into Italy in many respects prefigured Napoléon's return to France in early 1815. In nearly every place he was greeted with acclaim, as those supporting Pompey ran away or kept silent. In fact, the large numbers of young men whom Pompey and the *optimates* had called to the legionary standards merely swelled Caesar's strength. In a panic Pompey and the *optimates* fled. Their flight to Brundisium was both hasty and incompetent. They left the state's treasury in Rome for Caesar to seize and add to his war chest. The haul included fifteen thousand gold bars, thirty thousand silver bars, and thirty million sesterces. An attempt by one of the tribunes in Rome to prevent Caesar from seizing the treasury met Caesar's withering reply that it would be easier to put the tribune to death than to threaten him. Plutarch described the flight of Pompey and his followers in the following terms: "The consuls at once fled, without making the usual sacrifices; so did most of the senators, carrying off their own goods in as much haste as if they were robbing their neighbors." This disgraceful performance displayed none of the courage shown in the past by Rome's aristocratic leadership.

Once at Brundisium, Pompey faced the challenge of where he would retreat: Spain, Africa, or Greece and Asia. Both Spain and Africa offered substantial veteran legions, loyal to Pompey and the *optimates*. Nevertheless, Pompey chose Greece and Macedonia. His previous experience with Sertorius in Spain underlined the weakness of Spain's overall strategic situation. Africa, like Spain, lacked the resources to support a prolonged struggle, and Pompey was already thinking in terms of a long-term war to defeat Caesar, though the supercilious *optimates* were incapable of thinking in such terms.

Once Pompey and his fellows had fled Italy, Caesar had the peninsula firmly in his grasp, while his control of Rome, the political center of the republic, legitimized his control of the government. The question then was whether he should follow Pompey or address the other major territories controlled by his enemies. Caesar apparently calculated that Pompey possessed too few experienced legions to risk an immediate return to Italy. Thus, leaving his subordinates to train the recruits that his enemies had raised, Caesar set off to clear up his rear by destroying Pompey's supporters in Spain before returning to Rome. At the same time he dispatched his legate Scribonius Curio to clean up Africa. But much like Napoléon, Caesar discovered that while his subordinate commanders proved highly competent while they were under his direct supervision, for the most part, that was not true when they received independent commands and had to make decisions on their own. Thus Curio, after some initial successes, was defeated, refused the opportunity to escape, and died with his legionaries in the best traditions of the Roman aristocracy.

Caesar's descent on Spain proved to be no easy matter. Aiming to overwhelm his opponents, he brought nine legions, three from Italy and six from Gaul. On his way there he dropped off three newly raised legions to conduct a siege on the town of Massilia (modern-day Marseilles), whose leaders had calculated on Pompey winning the Civil War. In Spain, Caesar's opponents fielded seven legions against him. The Pompeian generals chose not to fight a battle, but rather intended a drawn-out struggle. That would have trapped Caesar in an untenable situation, far from Rome with Pompey gathering ever-stronger forces in Greece and Asia. It took skillful maneuvering for Caesar's army to cut the Pompeians off from both food and water and force them to surrender in early June 49 B.C. Aiming to grab the political advantage by showing mercy to his opponents, Caesar disbanded the surrendered army and spared the enemy generals, allowing them to return to Pompey. On his return to Italy, he paused at Massilia to conclude the siege.

After returning from Spain and Massaila in the summer of 48 B.C., Caesar turned his attention to Pompey and the center of his ene-

mies' strength in northern Greece and Macedonia. By this time
Pompey had gathered together nine legions, two of which had been
under Caesar's control before he relinquished them to Pompey, supposedly to form the nucleus of an army to attack the Parthians and
avenge Crassus's humiliating defeat. The other legions were of inferior quality, but Pompey had strengthened his forces by acquiring a
large cavalry force, some seven thousand horsemen, and a large
number of slingers and archers. Moreover, Pompey and the *optimates* were growing steadily stronger with an additional two legions
on the march from Syria. Thus, Caesar needed to move with dispatch. By the fall of 48 B.C. Caesar had assembled twelve legions in
Italy. Although all were understrength, they were nearly all veterans
and strongly committed to Caesar, their *imperator,* which height-
ened the danger they posed to Pompey and his allies.

In a major strategic difficulty for Caesar, Pompey controlled the
seas, with a massive fleet of some five hundred ships. The Caesareans
had only sufficient transport in Brundisium to move half the army,
some twenty thousand legionaries at a time, across the Adriatic to
Greece. To attack immediately meant running significant risks: Sailing in the Adriatic in winter risked the possibility that storms would
destroy the fleet, the massive naval superiority of Pompey's fleet
would put much of his army in danger, and the presence of only half
of Caesar's army in Greece would provide Pompey with the opportunity to destroy his army in piecemeal fashion.

But Caesar was a risk taker, and once again he placed himself in
the hands of the goddess Fortuna. On January 4, 48 B.C., he and his
troops embarked, carrying only their basic kit so that Caesar's officers could cram the maximum number of soldiers aboard. Even then
the fleet could bring only seven of his legions. A favorable wind carried them across the Adriatic, while the Pompeian fleet under his old
political enemy Bibulus remained comfortably in harbor. Without
waiting for Antony to take the remaining four legions across to
Greece, Caesar immediately moved to attack the ports that were the
bases for the Pompeian fleet. His troops quickly seized the ports of
Oricum and Apollonis, but the real prize was Dyrrhachium, where

Pompey had stationed much of his supplies. Pompey was no push-over, and he, too, moved with great speed from his training areas in Macedonia to arrive at Dyrrhachium before Caesar's legionaries did. Without Dyrrhachium, Caesar would be in serious trouble. He simply lacked the strength to hazard a battle with Pompey without the three legions stranded in Brundisium, and Antony appeared to be taking his own sweet time in crossing the Adriatic.

Finally, Antony, aided by favorable winds, crossed to the eastern coast. Pompey attempted to catch and then destroy Antony's legions before Caesar could reinforce him, but he failed. With a united army, Caesar immediately set off to attack Dyrrhachium, but at the last moment Pompey arrived, and Caesar could not risk a siege with the enemy army close by. For the next six weeks constant skirmishing took place between the two armies, but Pompey was still unwilling to risk an all-out battle against Caesar's veterans.

At this point, Caesar decided to occupy a number of hills that surrounded Pompey's camp. In so doing he hoped to improve the supply of food for his own forces, block the Pompeian access to fodder for their horses, and, most important, diminish Pompey's prestige as a general. In effect, the two sides were soon constructing elaborate fortified lines as skirmishing continued. But Caesar's strategic situation was anything but favorable: "Caesar was hemming in fresh and unharmed forces with a smaller number of troops. The enemy had plentiful supplies of everything—for every day large numbers of ships were coming in from all directions to bring supplies. . . . Caesar himself, on the other hand, had used up all the corn supplies for a long way around and was suffering extreme shortage."

For a period, the skirmishing continued to go in Caesar's favor. But then two of his auxiliary cavalry officers, both Gallic nobles who had been stealing their troops' pay, defected to the Pompeians. They brought with them a detailed account of the weaknesses in Caesar's overstretched defenses. This setback was compounded by Caesar's own serious error. To regain the advantage after his soldiers, particularly the Ninth Legion, had suffered a rebuff and considerable losses, he led a major raid on a Pompeian position. After an initial success in seizing a portion of the enemy's camp, matters quickly reversed and Caesar was soon on the verge of a disastrous defeat: "Fortune who exerts a powerful influence as well in other matters, as especially in war, effects great changes from trifling causes, as happened at this time."

While Caesar was attacking, Pompey drew five legions from their work on his fortifications and launched a counterattack. As a result, a sudden collapse by the Caesarean legionaries and cavalry threatened to turn into a complete rout. Pompey hesitated to throw the full weight of his forces into the counterattack, but nevertheless the result was a serious setback for the Caesareans. Altogether Caesar lost 960 men killed, including thirty-two military tribunes and centurions. He also lost thirty-two unit standards, which was particularly humiliating, given the prominence that standards enjoyed in Roman armies. In fact, as Caesar's account makes clear, his army had come within a hairbreadth of defeat. The success gave the Pompeians renewed confidence, which explains why Pompey risked a major battle shortly thereafter.

Pharsalus

The serious defeat near Dyrrhachium, which had come close to losing Caesar the war, forced him to revise his strategy. He pulled back from the coast and gave up his efforts to hem Pompey in at Dyrrhachium. He particularly hoped a retreat into Thessaly would restore the morale and confidence of his troops after their setback, as they would find large quantities of food and other necessities in territories untouched by war. As night fell after his defeat at Dyrrhachium, Caesar ordered the baggage and the wounded to begin the retreat with one legion as escort. The remaining legions he ordered to pull out of camp in the late night hours. Unencumbered by their baggage, they were able to move quickly. Caesar described his strategy: "If Pompey took the same route, then, once he [Caesar] had drawn him [Pompey] away from the sea and from those resources he had collected at Dyrrhachium and had cut him off from his supplies

of corn and provisions, he could force him to fight on equal terms."
Pompey did not hesitate to follow, despite having other choices.
Italy appeared attractive to some of his supporters, but Pompey re-
jected that course, as it might look like he was still afraid of facing
Caesar even after his victory. Like most Romans, reputation was ev-
erything to Pompey.

Pompey caught up with Caesar at midday at the latter's old camp
at Asparagium, where the Caesareans had apparently stopped. But
waiting only long enough for the Pompeians to move into fighting
formation, Caesar resumed the march and put eight miles between
his army and that of Pompey, while also joining up with additional
forces under Domitius at Aeginium in Thessaly. Pompey arrived a
few days later. He would have preferred to avoid battle and wait
Caesar out, but he found himself under intense pressure from the
optimates, who had accompanied him like leeches and demanded
that he seek immediate battle with Caesar. Moreover, there was a
chorus of gossip among the senators that Pompey had lost his courage or wished to maintain his position of power by not fighting
Caesar. Caesar wrote of the senior leaders among his opponents:
"Pompey's whole army talked of nothing but the honors or sums of
money which were to be their rewards, or of vengeance on their
enemies; and never considered how they were to defeat their enemies, but in what manner they should use their victory." For Pompey, his reputation may well have been the major factor in his decision
to accept battle.

As the two armies confronted each other, there was an almost immediate series of cavalry skirmishes, most of which went in Caesar's
favor. These successes were largely the result of Caesar having picked
a group of his toughest legionaries and distributed them among the
cavalry. Caesar estimated that he possessed eighty cohorts (each legion possessed ten cohorts) and approximately twenty-two thousand
soldiers, along with approximately ten thousand auxiliaries and eighteen hundred allied cavalry; he claimed that Pompey had forty-five
thousand men (an exaggeration) and 110 cohorts, along with approximately four thousand auxiliaries and well over six thousand cav-

alry. Whatever the accurate numbers, Pompey enjoyed a significant advantage, especially in cavalry.

The geography of the battlefield played a significant role in the relatively straightforward plans that Caesar and Pompey developed. Because there was a stream with steep banks that ran along Pompey's right wing, he deployed virtually all of his cavalry and slingers on his left wing. The two legions that Pompey had acquired from Caesar, which were veterans of the Gallic wars, formed the strength of his left wing; he also stationed the best trained of his recruited legions on the right wing. The main effort was to come from the cavalry on the left, which was to smash the Caesarean cavalry and then attack Caesar's infantry from the rear. In addition, he ordered his infantry to remain in a stationary front and not to advance against the enemy, thus ensuring that they would be fully rested when the Caesarean infantry reached them. He believed that the advance of the Caesareans up the slight slope to the Pompeian position would help tire them out before the close combat began.

Caesar readily recognized what Pompey was going to do. With his weaker cavalry, he confronted a significant problem, but his solution was simple. He took one cohort from the third line of each legion (the *triarii*) and formed them up on the far left wing, behind his own cavalry out of sight of the enemy. He ordered them to attack as the Pompeians struck the Caesarean cavalry, insisting they use their pila to stab at the faces of the enemy. In his words of encouragement to them, he made clear that he believed they would win or lose the battle for him.

It is worth noting that cavalrymen at this time did not possess stirrups, and consequently their seat on their horses was much less secure. Moreover, because only the rich could afford horses, cavalrymen came from the Roman and barbarian upper classes and often lacked the toughness of legionaries. Thus, Caesar calculated that Pompey's cavalrymen would not be able to stomach the enemy's hacking at their faces. As for deployment, Caesar stationed his foremost legion, the Tenth, on the right wing where he believed the crucial fighting would take place. In one other move outside of the

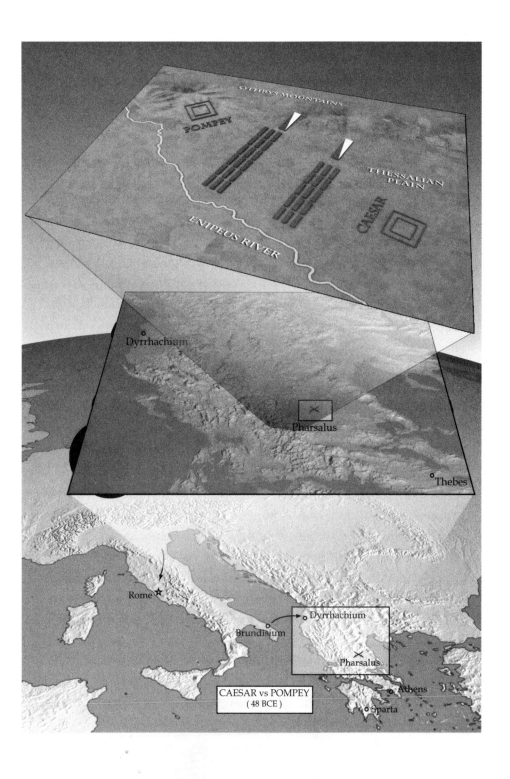

OTHRYS MOUNTAINS

POMPEY

THESSALIAN PLAIN

CAESAR

ENIPEUS RIVER

Dyrrhachium

Pharsalus

Thebes

Rome

Brundisium

Dyrrhachium

Pharsalus

Athens

CAESAR vs POMPEY
(48 BCE)

Sparta

ordinary, he combined the Ninth Legion, which had suffered so heavily at Dyrrhachium, with the Eighth Legion and ordered them to work together.

When Caesar ordered the advance, at first his legions went forward at a trot. But seeing that Pompey's troops were not advancing to meet them, they—without orders—halted, rested, re-formed, and then came on again. That sudden unexpected halt in the face of great danger, performed in the fashion that characterized Caesar's disciplined veterans, undoubtedly added to the fears that beset the Pompeians. After a suitable period of rest, the Caesarean legions charged against the stationary enemy line. Caesar, amazed that Pompey, by keeping his men stationary, had handed him the initiative, commented that "There is a certain impetuosity of spirit and an alacrity implanted by nature in the hearts of all men, which is inflamed by a desire to meet the foe. This a general should endeavor not to repress, but to increase." Both sides then threw their pila and the horrendous slaughter that characterized all ancient battles began.

Initially, the Pompeian infantry, whose formations were very deep, held their own despite the terrifying display of swordplay put on by Caesar's veterans. On the flank, the Pompeian cavalry quickly disposed of Caesar's outnumbered horsemen. But, just as they began to push through the Caesarean cavalry, Caesar sprang his trap, ordering his unobserved infantry to attack. These new and fresh troops advanced rapidly, striking Pompey's cavalry with such force that none of them could hold ground. The Pompeian cavalry fled. At that point Caesar ordered the third line to advance, while at the same time the legionaries who had destroyed Pompey's cavalry found it easy to outflank the enemy's left. As they went they slaughtered the enemy's slingers and archers along their line of march. The collapse on the left infected the entire army with fear, with Pompey among the first to abandon the field, heading straight back to camp.

After the battle and the flight of the Pompeians, Caesar was astonished by what he found in the enemy's camp: "It could readily be judged that they had had no fears for the outcome of the day." Plutarch has left us a graphic account of the overconfidence of Pompey and his followers as they prepared for battle:

> When Caesar's soldiers had taken the camp, they saw clearly the folly and vanity of the enemy; for all their tents and pavilions were richly set out with garlands of myrtle, embroidered carpets and hangings, and tables laid and covered with goblets. There were large bowls of wine ready, and everything prepared and put in array, in the manner rather of people who had offered sacrifice and were going to celebrate a holiday, than of soldiers who had armed themselves to go out to battle, so possessed with the expectation of success and so full of empty confidence had they gone out [to battle] that morning.

It appears to have been a scene quite similar to how Shakespeare would describe the French camp in the night before Agincourt in his great play *Henry V*. Pompey fled to meet his end in Egypt. The pursuit continued after his flight. Trapped on a hill, the remnants of Pompey's army surrendered the next day. The senators trapped with them fled during the night.

Conclusion

The Civil War was not yet over. Pompey's role in it, however, was. Choosing not to go to Asia or Africa, he fled to Egypt in the first ship he could find. There, in a tawdry piece of politics, the locals assassinated him. On Caesar's arrival in Egypt, they presented him with Pompey's head. For their reward, the ruler of Rome ordered those involved with Pompey's assassination executed. Caesar was likely pleased to find that his nemesis was dead, but for non-Romans to have murdered a consul of Rome was beyond the pale. Caesar continued his pursuit of the scattered Pompeian remnants in Egypt, other parts of Africa, and eventually Spain. In the course of those efforts, he would utter the memorable phrase: "*Veni, vedi, vici—*

I came, I saw, I conquered." Victory in the Civil War had not been easy, but even during his greatest trials Caesar kept his balance and escaped the consequences of his rashness through skillful general-ship and leadership.

In the end, "Caesar's daring, his impatience of the long game, and the skill of his opponents brought moments of danger, but the story of the Civil War is the story [of] how his skill and the devotion of his men triumphed over the difficulties." As he had in his war with the Gauls, Caesar relied on speed, imagination, the solid training of his legionaries, and his understanding and calculation of the weak-nesses of his opponents. Arguably he was the greatest general in the ancient world. Moreover, unlike Alexander, whose political inheri-tance rapidly disappeared, Caesar's geopolitical contribution to history—France—still persists.

Had Caesar not been born, or had Sulla meted out to him the treatment that so many others who thwarted his wishes received, Pompey would undoubtedly have remained as the first man in Rome. Nevertheless, he would have faced constant opposition from the *optimates,* and it is probable that eventually the two sides would have clashed. *The Cambridge Ancient History* describes Pompey quite accurately in the following terms:

> It is true that as a politician he was selfish, tortuous in word, ungenerous, greedy of praise. Yet, he cared for good govern-ment and would give the State unswerving service in return for confidence and compliments. Set to a task within the ambit of his powers, he was clear-headed, swift and single-minded. Once the task was done virtue went out of him. . . . An excellent or-ganizer, a skillful tactician, a wary yet bold strategist, he was in the field no unworthy opponent of Caesar himself.

Richard I and Saladin

On June 22, 1187, Richard and his brother John were tenaciously holding the walls of Châteauroux against Philip, king of France, and the feudal host of France. Marching hard to his sons' rescue was Henry II, king of England, who had at his back the full power and might of the Angevin Empire. On the morn, the two great armies faced each other, arrayed for battle. After months of destructive campaigning, both kings appeared set on resolving their struggle in a trial by combat. It was time for God's judgment on who had the right to rule.

For a fortnight the two armies stared each other down across the Indre River, daily massing in full armor despite the sweltering heat. In the end, battle never came, as each king decided that too much was at stake to leave the decision to battle and the fickleness of God. Instead, they permitted the papal legate, Octavian, to persuade them to put aside their quarrel in the interest of uniting Christendom against the common enemy—Islam. Who would rule much of France was a question left for another day.

At almost the same instant, two thousand miles away, King Guy of Lusignan was at Sepphoris, the city where Jesus plied his trade as a carpenter. He was there to inspect the full muster of the crusader force in the Holy Land before it left to meet the Islamic army of Saladin. Unlike the great kings of Europe, the crusaders placed absolute trust in the verdict of God, which explains why they marched to meet an Islamic army 50 percent greater than their own and commanded by the renowned Saladin. Disregarding the long odds, many crusaders, despite a myriad of other interests, still went forth with the words "God wills it" on their lips, few of them doubting that God would see them through to victory. Ranged against them was potentially the largest army the crusaders had yet faced, and the Muslim soldiers also did not lack for certainty that God had already ordained their own victory.

These two widely separate events, in distance if not in time, eventually propelled the two greatest military commanders of the medieval era into war's cruel embrace. For within five years, Richard, by this time king of England, departed Europe at the head of a large army intent on resuscitating crusader fortunes in Palestine and retaking Jerusalem. Waiting for him in Palestine was Saladin, who after vanquishing King Guy's army had reduced the vast crusader dominions in Palestine to a mere rump. Their clash determined the final fate of the Holy Land and set East and West on a historical course that still reverberates today.

Richard

Richard was the third son of one of the most tumultuous and famous couples of the medieval era. His father, Henry II, ruled the Angevin Empire, consisting of England, Ireland, and a substantial portion of what is currently France. Much of the latter territory came to Henry as a result of his marriage to the vivacious Eleanor of Aquitaine. Despite a more than ten-year age difference, their meeting was lust at first sight. At the time, there was much speculation that Henry and Eleanor enjoyed intimate pleasures, although she was still married to Louis, the king of France.

The marriage between Eleanor and King Louis VII was on the rocks almost from the start. Eleanor had brought to the marriage a vivacious love of life, a sharp wit, and steely ambition—all qualities much lacking in her husband. She also brought a gift of inestimable

Richard I
(The Collection of the British Library)

value to the marriage: She was one of France's great magnates, hold-ing vast amounts of land centered on the Duchy of Aquitaine. By marrying Eleanor, Louis more than doubled his own domains in an afternoon. But there was a catch in the marriage agreement. Elea-nor's lands were not to be merged with those of the French king until their first son inherited the throne. Unfortunately for the Ca-petian dynasty the marriage went eight years without issue before producing a daughter, Marie, in April 1145.

The following Christmas, Louis announced that he was taking up Pope Eugene III's request to lead a Crusade to the Holy Land. Not to be outdone, Eleanor insisted on joining the Crusade and even recruited her own Aquitanian army. By this time the royal mar-riage was becoming increasingly estranged and the Crusade only exacerbated the breach between them. At one point, as the French host was crossing Anatolia (modern-day Turkey), a separation in the army caused by one of Eleanor's leading knights led to the rear guard's near annihilation. Louis himself was almost killed, saved only by "bravely" running away. As a contemporary chronicler related:

> The mail clad Franks, now on foot, . . . were separated from one another, spilling the vitals from their defenseless bodies. . . . The king lost his small but renowned royal guard; keeping a stout heart, however, he nimbly and bravely scaled a rock by making use of some tree roots which God had provided him for his safety.

This defeat so early in the Crusade called the king's military leadership into question and did further grievous damage to Eleanor's reputation at court. The rest of the Crusade did nothing to rehabilitate either. Militarily, the Crusade ambled without any apparent strategic direction as the great nobles debated great projects that came and went with startling rapidity. Finally, the crusaders agreed to besiege Damascus, the greatest and most well defended city in Syria. Given the level of leadership displayed to that point, it was perhaps predictable that the crusaders would fail to take the city, and Louis and Eleanor returned home. The Second Crusade, which had begun with such high hopes, had ended in ignominious failure. It would be more than a generation before Europe would find the resolve and resources to try again.

Humiliated by the disaster in Anatolia, Eleanor, for a time, refrained from any further attempts to influence military decisions. But that did not stop idle tongues from wagging. While in the Levant, she had renewed her relationship with her uncle, the Prince of Antioch, Raymond of Poitiers. Though most historians now believe their relationship was platonic and nothing more than a revival of the closeness they enjoyed when Eleanor was a child, those around the king held no such belief. As they saw it, Eleanor and Raymond had entered into an incestuous relationship, and the most reliable chronicler of the period, William of Tyre, flatly states: "Contrary to her royal dignity, she disregarded her marriage vows and was unfaithful to her husband."

After harrowing ordeals, Eleanor and Louis finally arrived in Europe, where Eleanor petitioned Pope Eugene III to annul her marriage on grounds of consanguinity (Eleanor and Louis were fourth cousins once removed). Instead, Eugene tried to reconcile the couple and even went so far as to prepare a special marriage bed for them. The short-lived reconciliation produced another daughter, Alix. But rather than being a joyous occasion, Alix's birth marked the end of the marriage. From Louis's perspective, Eleanor's sixteen-year failure to produce a male heir, her continued unpopularity at court, and the fact that she openly detested him led to a single conclusion: It was time to put his royal influence behind her desire for an annulment. In March 1152, the marriage was duly ended, and the crown returned Eleanor's lands to her.

There was little chance, however, that she would be permitted to retire peacefully to her estates. A rich landed widow or divorcée was not so much an object of desire as she was a target. In fact, during her journey from Paris back to Aquitaine, she just barely escaped two kidnap attempts by covetous nobles. Soon after her arrival in Poitiers, Henry, either by her call or on his own business, entered the city, and the two immediately married with no pomp or fanfare, just eight weeks after her divorce from Louis. Henry was only twenty years old, and Eleanor was around thirty. Henry, who was already Duke of Normandy, now possessed the Duchy of Aquitaine, giving him control of substantially more French territory than the king of France. Two years later, Henry became king of England and Eleanor was once again a queen. In a final note of supreme irony, Eleanor, who had not borne Louis any sons in more than sixteen years, would present Henry with five sons and three daughters in fourteen years.

Louis was enraged. After refusing to recognize Henry's rights to Aquitaine, he formed a coalition and went to war. Henry, who was preparing an army to secure his rights in England, turned furiously on his new foes. In a lightning campaign, demonstrating what would become his trademark way of war, Henry concentrated his force and struck at each foe in succession. Typically, he avoided attacking his opponents' field army, opting instead to take their castles and ravage their lands. Throughout most of the next two decades, Henry confounded his enemies and expanded his domains, mostly at the expense of the French king. Late in life Louis finally stumbled on the key to undoing Henry—sowing discord between him and his now-grown sons. In this, Louis received assistance from Eleanor, who after a long and tempestuous relationship had grown increasingly estranged from Henry.

In 1170, Henry fell ill. Despite his complete recovery, concerns about his own mortality caused Henry to focus on his succession. With four living sons, this was never going to be an easy matter, as each was expecting substantial land as part of his inheritance. But with both the French king and Eleanor working against his interests and fanning the flames of sibling jealousy, it became a near-impossible task. As the third son, Richard likely never expected to succeed to the throne. But he was his mother's clear favorite, and Eleanor pressed hard for his rights and worked assiduously to ensure that Henry willed a significant domain to the young prince. So, when Henry decided to divide his kingdom among his sons while still retaining overall control, Eleanor convinced him that Richard should have Aquitaine. Richard and Eleanor left for Aquitaine in 1171, where Richard was formally invested as ruler of the duchy in the following year. He was not quite fifteen years old.

When Henry tried to provide lands for his youngest son, John, by taking castles from Henry, his eldest son, the interval of family peace abruptly ended. Henry, having been made co-king in 1170 and called "the Young King," was eighteen years old and starting to chafe at his father's restraints. Although his father had nominally given the Young King a crown as well as Duchy of Normandy, he had retained all authority and revenues for himself. When Henry II refused him power and taxing rights, his son raised the banner of revolt. The revolt caught Henry II by surprise, as did the Young King's first move—joining the court of Louis VII along with his brothers Richard and Geoffrey. They had been sent by their mother, who remained in Aquitaine, mobilizing her forces for war. This was an extraordinary decision on her part. Though there are many cases in English history of royal sons revolting against their fathers, Eleanor presents the only case where a wife mobilized and led an army against her husband.

Louis, possibly in coordination with Eleanor, planned well. In addition to the three royal princes in his court, his army was joined by William, king of the Scots, the Counts of Flanders, Boulogne, and Blois, as well as large numbers of Henry's lords only too happy to break free of Henry's strict control. Henry, the Old King, refused to panic. Instead, he sealed up his castles and loosened the purse strings. For two decades, Henry had kept a tight enough rein on government spending to build up a large surplus of funds. Now, in the greatest crisis of his reign, he spent freely, purchasing a huge force of battle-hardened mercenaries—*routiers*—renowned for their prowess on the battlefield. His army assembled, Henry waited to see how his constellation of enemies moved.

Hostilities began when the Counts of Flanders and Boulogne invaded Normandy from the east, while Louis and the Young King pushed slowly into the Vexin—the main invasion route into Normandy from the south. At the same time a large force of Bretons attacked from the west. All of these attacks were aimed at the Norman capital—Rouen—where the combined army expected to meet Henry's army. Each attack foundered.

The Count of Boulogne was killed and, soon after, a crossbow felled the Count of Flanders, who was the brother of Philip. After this the invasion from the east petered out, freeing Henry to turn on Louis and the Young King. Their mostly French army was defeated with heavy loss. As the survivors retreated across the border, Henry sent a large force to destroy the Breton army. As all of this was happening, Henry's surrogates in England crushed the supporters of the Young King at the Battle of Fornham. As winter drew close, the forces arranged against Henry were everywhere destroyed or in retreat. As one knight told the king, "All of your enemies have begun a very bad year."

After peace negotiations at Gisors broke down, the armies took the field again in the spring. This time the rebels were joined by a

Scottish invasion force led by King William. Henry returned to England to face this challenge as well as an invasion of southern England. But before moving to the attack, he did public penance for the murder of Archbishop Thomas Becket, which many in England believed done on his order. Soon thereafter word came that Henry's northern army had defeated the Scots at Alnwick and captured King William. Victory over the Scots combined with his public prostration in atonement for Becket's death did much to restore royal prestige and power, before a renewed assault on his lands by the combined forces of Louis and Philip of Flanders forced Henry to return to Normandy. Henry fell on his foe's combined army at Rouen just as it was preparing for its final assault on the city. Henry routed his enemies and Louis sued for peace.

All of Henry's enemies had quit the field but one: Richard and his small army did not surrender. During lulls in the main theaters in the last two years of the conflict, Henry launched a surprise assault and captured a series of castles, one of which contained his estranged wife, Eleanor. She remained his prisoner until Henry's death. Her capture left the sixteen-year-old Richard in charge of the rebellion in Poitou. He first moved upon La Rochelle, but when that city refused to open its gates he moved his headquarters to Saintes. Henry, after one of the lightning approaches he was famous for, surprised Richard and took the city by storm. Richard only barely escaped and fled to the fortress of Taillebourg. Henry, leaving a small force behind to keep Richard penned in, turned to make sure his other enemies remained quiet.

When Richard learned that all of those who had taken up arms against Henry were dead or surrendered, he threw in the towel and appeared before the king. On September 23, 1174, "Richard, coming with tears, fell on his face upon the ground at the feet of his father, and imploring pardon, was received into his father's bosom." After giving Richard the kiss of peace, Henry brought his sons together and offered them his terms. They gratefully accepted far less than Richard had offered them at Gisors the year before. What they, particularly Richard, had gained was a master's course in warfare conducted by the foremost soldier of the era. The lessons—strategic patience, rapid movement, the use of surprise, and striking hard—served Richard well in the years ahead.

Likely impressed with Richard's capacity as a soldier, Henry sent the eighteen-year-old to Aquitaine in 1175 to smash castles and bring the remaining rebels to heel. Doing so absorbed Richard's time and attention for the next eight years. It was during this period that Richard honed his skills and became expert in the ways of medieval warfare, which always put a premium on the conduct of sieges over battle. Richard demonstrated that he had learned much from his father: When he had selected a target, he moved with great rapidity and often fell upon it before any enemy knew he was in the immediate area. Even when a rebel force managed to slam the gates in his face, he left them no time to prepare for siege or storm and they were therefore rapidly forced to surrender. Richard's greatest triumph came in early 1177, when he undertook a campaign in the depths of winter, when most of his opponents had settled into winter quarters.

By early February he reported to his father that he had crushed the final embers of the great revolt and was releasing his mercenaries. What happened next taught him another important lesson. Out of work and without pay, the mercenaries did what they did best—they fell upon hapless farms and small communities in an orgy of plunder that devastated a substantial portion of the province. Abbott Isambert of Saint Martial eventually stirred the local nobles and peasants to action. Marching behind a crucifix brought from Jerusalem, his "army of peace" fell upon the mercenary force at Malemort and "relieved their outraged feelings in an orgy of slaughter."

The restive barons of Angoumois and Limousin were not as easily settled as Richard had hoped, and in early 1189 he was again on a campaign. His winter assault gained him little, as the enemy was not to be tricked twice. His army was stuck fast before the walls of Pons, which had strengthened its fortifications and stocked sufficient supplies to withstand a long siege. Rather than see his army waste away in a prolonged contest of wills, Richard, leaving just a covering force at Pons, marched on the less well defended Richemont and seized it after only a three-day siege.

Richard now had a choice: return to Pons to continue prosecuting the siege or take a risk and march on the reputedly impregnable Taillebourg fortress, where he had sheltered from his father a few years before. Perched on a steep rock and ringed with impressive walls, Taillebourg appeared so imposing that no one had ever tested it. Richard placed his camp much closer to the wall than was typical, presenting Taillebourg's defenders with a tempting target for a sortie. To push them toward that decision, Richard, even as his siege engines played along Taillebourg's walls, sent troops to lay waste to the countryside. Vines were cut down, villages burned, and wells poisoned, all within site of the fortress.

Enraged by Richard's depredations and, as a result, fearful of facing a winter famine, Taillebourg defenders sortied out. Richard was waiting for them, and the fortress's French defenders were soon reeling backward. Richard was hard on their heels, racing to keep close enough to the retreating French to gain entry to the fortress before the gates were closed. Throughout the brutal struggle at the gate, Richard was constantly exposed to danger as he pressed his men forward. The defenders broke and streamed toward the citadel, from which they surrendered three days later. On hearing the news Pons also surrendered, as did other local fortified towns. After overseeing the dismantling of the walls of those places that had risen against him, Richard released his mercenaries (who promptly wrecked Bordeaux in their quest for pay and plunder) and headed back to England.

By capturing impregnable Taillebourg in just three days, Richard gained a reputation throughout western Europe as a great and brave soldier. Henry demonstrated his pleasure with his son by assigning him the dual titles of Count of Poitou and Duke of Aquitaine. However, before Richard had much time to enjoy his title, he faced a new and—as he would learn in time—a more formidable enemy: Philip II, the son of King Louis VII by his second wife, had succeeded to the throne.

Although Philip was only fifteen when he gained the crown, he was cunning and shrewd. Moreover, he had spent his early years observing how Henry, arguably the shrewdest king ever to mount the English throne, had routinely beaten and humiliated his father. As such, it was Henry rather than Louis who tutored the new French king in the arts of war and statecraft. Louis came to power set on returning France to the greatness it had known during Charlemagne's rule. Achieving this goal meant destroying Plantagenet power in France, and he reasoned the best place to start was supporting the nobles still willing to contest Richard's power. Richard, in the second year of Philip's reign, struck first, marching deep into enemy territory and laying waste to everything in his path. After some initial success his father joined him and deigned to listen to the rebels' grievances. According to the chronicler Roger of Hoveden, Richard was judged a cruel lord: "He carried off his subjects' wives, daughters and kinswomen by force and made them his concubines; when he had sated his own lust on them he handed them down for his soldiers to enjoy." Henry brushed such complaints aside, and he and Richard, soon joined by the Young King, brought a hard war to the Limousin—seizing castles and wrecking the countryside. Faced by such an array of power, and with Philip, who had his own problems, showing little inclination to send an army to their aid, the rebels soon sued for peace.

Together, Henry and his son had demonstrated that they possessed unbeatable might. Unfortunately, their familial bonds were fraying. The Young King, jealous of Richard's growing fame and preeminence, took offense at Richard's building a castle at Clairvaux, which he deemed within his own lands. Henry tried to maintain the peace by taking the castle into his own possession, but the siblings found other causes for war.

This was the opening that King Philip had been looking for, and he and other nobles joined the struggle on the side of the Young King. Richard struck hard, but despite conducting a brilliant campaign, he was in danger of losing Aquitaine to his brother's superior forces. However, fate intervened. In desperate need of funds, young

Henry allowed his army to sustain itself through plunder and ordered the looting of shrines and other holy places. Immediately after looting the famous shrine at Rocamadour, the Young King was struck down in what all were certain was a result of God's fury. Without the Young King as a rallying point, the rebellion collapsed and most of its leading figures returned home.

Rather than end the family squabbles, the death of the Young King opened up a new venue for family warfare. As Richard was now heir to the throne, Henry ordered him to give over Aquitaine to his brother John. When Richard refused, John did what one would expect from any Plantagenet: Encouraged and supported by his brother Geoffrey, he attacked. The fighting consisted mainly of vicious cross-border raiding, and Henry soon called a halt and summoned all three sons to England to force peace upon them.

Peace did not last long. In 1186 Geoffrey died after being trampled during a tournament. His death once again realigned Angevin-Capetian politics. King Philip, taking advantage of the Angevin political crisis, raised a new army and in June marched into Berry. Further progress was arrested by Richard and John's defense at Châteauroux, where they were waiting for Henry to come to their aid with the bulk of the Angevin army. Both kings refused the test of battle, but Philip left that day with something much more important than control of a castle or a county: Richard, believing his father planned to disinherit him in favor of John, deserted his father and joined Philip's camp.

The next two years were filled with nearly unceasing war. At times Richard joined Philip in fighting Henry, while at other times he conducted his own conflict against the always unruly nobles within Aquitaine. Throughout this period coalitions and alliances were made and broken with startling rapidity. Finally, Richard made common cause with Philip against an old and increasingly sickly Henry. Together king and prince drove deep into Angevin territory, their pace hastened when many lords, who realized that Richard would soon be their king and overlord, switched sides. When Tours fell in early July 1189, a sick and demoralized Henry sued for peace and submitted to all of Philip's and Richard's demands. After his surrender, Henry rode to Chinon Castle, where he died on July 6. Richard was crowned king at Westminster Abbey on September 3, 1189.

Richard had taken the cross and agreed to go on a Crusade in 1187, but the constant need to defend his territory and rights delayed his departure. Philip had made his own crusading vow early in 1188 but, for reasons similar to Richard's, had tarried in France. The destruction of the crusader army at the Battle of Hattin and the subsequent fall of Jerusalem gave new impetus to the crusading movement in Europe, and the pressure on both kings to lead their armies to the Holy Land and retrieve Christian losses became irresistible. Still, neither king could leave without the other also going, as neither thought the church's promise to secure their lands sufficient security in their absence. But by the summer of 1190, Angevin-Capetian rivalries were placed aside and preparations completed for the start of the Third Crusade. On August 7, Richard departed Marseille for the ten-month journey to the Holy Land, where a triumphant Saladin awaited him.

Yusuf Ibn Najm al-Din
Ayyub Salah al-din (Saladin)

Saladin, Islam's greatest military leader, showed few early indications that he would become a warrior and general, and fewer still that he would lead the Muslim reconquest of most of Palestine. In fact, if his protests are believable, he was taken much against his will on his first military campaign. It is tempting to view Saladin as the reluctant warrior, forced to take on the mantle of military leadership by circumstances beyond his control and against his deepest wishes. That probably is how he wished himself remembered, and his contemporaneous hagiographic biographers complied to please him. What is certain is that he was far from a military novice when he suddenly burst out of Egypt to claim mastery of many of the Islamic armies contesting the Holy Land with the crusaders. Both

Portrait of Saladin from *Kitab fi ma'arifat al-hiyal al-handisaya*
(*The book of knowledge of ingenious mechanical devices*)
by Ismail al-Jazari *(public domain)*

his father and his uncle were senior commanders under the great
Zengi, and the always observant Saladin must have absorbed much
from them.

Saladin was born in Tikrit in 1138 and is thought to have been a
Kurd, which at the time was more of a tribal distinction than a cul-
tural one. When his uncle, Shirkuh, was accused of murder, the family fled Tirkrit for Mosul, where Saladin's father, Ayyub, and uncle
found employment in the army of Imad Nur ad-Din Zengi. It was
Zengi's capture of the County of Edessa that exposed the Latin
kingdoms to Islamic armies and stirred Europe to launch the disastrous Second Crusade.

By this time the collective wars referred to as the Crusades had
been going on for more than four decades—since Pope Urban II
first summoned Europe's crusading armies in 1095. At its start the
crusading ideal had unified Europe under the papal banner in a
quest to remove Islamic power from the Holy Land and replace it

with a Christian kingdom. That ideal had long since broken down, and by the time of the counterattacks of Zengi and his successor, Nur ad-Din, the Latin kingdom in the east had splintered into a multitude of squabbling petty principalities. The rulers of each owed fealty to the Latin king in Jerusalem, but it was only in moments of crisis that he could gain even nominal control of his powerful nobles. As such, the Latin east was poorly prepared to fend off the great assaults of a unifying Islamic Empire. All Islam needed to turn the tide of war were leaders sufficiently charismatic to hold together their own bickering Arab nobility.

They first found such a leader in Zengi, and then another in Zengi's key lieutenant, Nur ad-Din, who, after Zengi's death, survived a period of turmoil before establishing his supremacy and locating his court at Damascus. Here Saladin lived from 1154 to 1164 in relative luxury, with the honors and opportunities available to the son of the man Nur ad-Din placed in command of the city's military forces. The chroniclers are silent about how Saladin was raised and educated, except to note that, as a youth, he possessed excellent qualities, and Nur ad-Din taught him to "walk the path of righteousness, to act virtuously, and to be zealous in fighting the infidels." One can assume that as he was raised in a Turkish military society, his education was similar to that of other youth of the period, including a good deal of the warrior arts.

Saladin's first opportunity to prove himself came in 1164 when Nur ad-Din sent a military force into Egypt, which had become the region's most important playing card. Nur ad-Din's rise, particularly the capture of Damascus, had established his "kingdom" in Syria as a powerful rival to the kingdom of Jerusalem. As these rivals warily circled each other, it became apparent that Egypt's enfeebled Fatimid Caliphate was the key to securing supremacy. Egypt's viziers, the true power within the country, understood their position and began playing both sides off each other in a delicate balancing game. They overplayed a weak hand.

Nur ad-Din sent two expeditions into Egypt to counter Jerusalem's king, Amalric. The first, in 1164, was commanded by Shirkuh with his nephew Saladin on his staff. The campaign was poorly planned and undersupplied, and Shirkuh's army soon found itself besieged outside of Cairo, saved only when Amalric was forced to break off his assaults to restore his position in the northern portions of his kingdom threatened by Nur ad-Din. A second expedition in 1167, also commanded by Shirkuh with Saladin now second in command, had more of the character of a prolonged raid. Shirkuh, leading two thousand picked Turkoman cavalry, descended on Amalric's crusaders before they were ready and defeated them at al-Babayn—Saladin's first experience in a pitched battle. Shirkuh then split his force, leaving half of it in Alexandria under Saladin while he raided to the south. Saladin was soon trapped by a regrouped crusader army and besieged for three months before a truce was reached and Shirkuh's army returned to Damascus.

Amalric broke the truce in October 1168, when the crusaders once again marched into Egypt. This time they had come not to defend the Fatimids but to conquer. Along the march they sacked Bilbays, where their massacre of the entire population turned a normally quiescent population against the crusaders. As Amalric's army approached Cairo, Nur ad-Din prepared his forces for a major invasion. Once again he appointed the loyal Shirkuh to command. He dispatched two thousand warriors from his own guard and six thousand handpicked Turkmans. This time, however, Saladin, refused to go, saying he never wished to return to Egypt after his experiences in Alexandria. But Shirkuh told Nur ad-Din that Saladin's talents were required, and the emir ordered him to join the expedition. Saladin tried to plead poverty, but Nur ad-Din supplied him with mounts, armor, and sufficient funds for the trip. Left with no honorable choices, Saladin joined Shirkuh for the third invasion of Egypt. As he later said, "It was as though I was being driven to my death, but I went with him and he conquered Egypt."

The campaign of conquest began in December 1168. By early January 1169, Shirkuh, having outmaneuvered the crusader army, joined his forces with the Egyptian army outside Cairo. Heavily outnumbered, the crusaders decided that they would display their valor on another day and retreated back into Palestine, allowing Shirkuh's army to enter Cairo as heroes and liberators. After following the caliph's order to execute the ruling vizier, Shirkuh stepped into that post himself. Within two months he had the "grace to die at the right moment," leaving Saladin in command of the army and the practical ruler of Egypt.

The caliph's other emirs were not pleased by Saladin's assumption of power and so he spent much of the next year consolidating his rule. The greatest threat came when the caliph's Nubian guard revolted. Seeing that his surprised troops were getting the worst of the battle, Saladin, demonstrating that he was as ruthless as he was capable, ordered the barracks housing the Nubians' wives and children set ablaze. When the Nubians broke ranks to rescue their families, Saladin counterattacked and cut down thousands of them from behind as their families perished in the flames. Now secure within Egypt, Saladin turned to confront external threats.

Amalric had paid close attention to developments in Egypt but had not been able to immediately intervene due to threats to other parts of his kingdom. When he eventually attacked he led his force to Damietta and caught Saladin by surprise. Saladin sent troops to reinforce the city and shadow the Crusade force, while he remained in Cairo to stifle political unrest. He also sent with the army one million gold dinars, taken from the caliph, to finance operations. This was a scale of resources the crusaders could not hope to match—precisely why they had feared having one of Nur ad-Din's generals on their flank with complete access to the Egyptian treasury. After Saladin's army was further reinforced by Nur ad-Din, the crusaders, along with the Byzantine fleet sent to support them, gave up the struggle and returned to Palestine. It was their second reversal in Egypt in less than a year and did not bode well for the future.

Over the next several months Saladin slowly but inexorably undermined the Shiite Fatimids, greatly assisted by the sudden terminal illness of the young caliph. Upon the caliph's death Saladin assumed full power in Egypt in name as well as in fact. As he had already laid the groundwork for the change, he swiftly and peacefully converted Shiite Egypt to the Sunni branch of the Islamic faith. This ended two centuries of schism, reuniting Egypt to its neighbors and allowing Saladin to claim the role of champion of Sunni orthodoxy and protector of the faith.

Saladin's growing power and independence soon caused him to run afoul of a suspicious Nur ad-Din. Whether Saladin deliberately failed to cooperate in two expeditions to seize the Transjordan from the crusaders, and thereby open a secure path for Nur ad-Din's armies to descend on Egypt, remains a matter of historical debate. But a pathway to Egypt was not Nur ad-Din's primary concern. Fighting the crusaders and paying to rebuild after a series of devastating earthquakes in 1170 had put tremendous strain on Nur ad-Din's treasury. What he wanted from Egypt was silver and gold, and that was not forthcoming. Saladin was using that treasure to build an army loyal to him, crush pro-Fatimid revolts, and extend his power down the Nile and as far abroad as Yemen.

When Nur ad-Din threatened to lead an expedition to Egypt to crush the upstart, a number of Saladin's advisers suggested that he prepare to resist, but his father offered wiser counsel. Reminding Saladin that time was on his side, he advised that Saladin send an offer of total submission while he continued to stall. Saladin, probably judging that he was not ready for a showdown and having reason to doubt that many of his warriors would fight against Nur ad-Din, replied to his emir: "News has reached us that you intend to lead an expedition to Egypt; but what need is there? My Lord need but send a courtier on a camel to lead me back to Syria by a turban cloth around my neck—not one of my people would attempt to resist him."

By 1174 both sides were mobilizing their forces for a final showdown. Time did indeed prove to be on Saladin's side, as before relations completely ruptured Nur ad-Din died. As Syria plunged into political chaos, dysentery felled the crusader king, Amalric. Saladin saw the opportunity and seized it. Through a combination of brilliant propaganda (appealing to the masses and common soldiers) and fast action, he took control of Syria when Nur ad-Din's eleven-year-old son—as-Salih Ismail al-Malik—was spirited away to Aleppo. The leaders in Damascus, fearing that they would soon be attacked by Aleppo, first appealed to the city of Mosul for help. When they were denied they turned to Saladin, who lost no time coming to their aid; with seven hundred picked men he set out across the Transjordan for Damascus, gathering supporters as he went.

Many were surprised at the small force Saladin had with him, and even more astonished that he had brought little money to use as a bribe. Believing that victory went to the fast and the bold, Saladin had moved with a light force in expectation of a joyous greeting from the Damascenes. He was not disappointed.

More troops and gold came from Egypt, allowing Saladin to extend his control to most of Syria without having to fight. Aleppo, however, proved a difficult nut to crack, and Saladin fought several major campaigns against the city. Most of these revolved around a series of tiresome sieges of castles and small population centers loyal to Aleppo or its new ally—Mosul. The one major battle fought during this period was along the Orontes River on April 13, 1175—the Battle of Hama. A combined force from Aleppo and Mosul challenged Saladin's heavily outnumbered troops. At first Saladin made major concessions, but when they proved insufficient, battle was joined. The hastily assembled recruits from the two cities were no match for Saladin's disciplined veterans. It was a decisive victory and Saladin pursued the routed army to the walls of Aleppo. Deciding against a time-consuming and wasteful siege, Saladin opted for a political settlement.

By sparing many of his defeated foes and releasing prisoners, he gained considerable favor among all but the ruling classes of Aleppo and Mosul. These he undermined with an unrelenting campaign to portray them as appeasers of the crusaders. Saladin continually preached the necessity to unify Islam against the Franks (the Muslim term for all crusaders), but this was disingenuous at best; Saladin also had made truces with the crusaders, and the only unified Islam he favored was one with him at its head. Still, by the middle of 1175 the rulers of both Mosul and Aleppo, defeated in battle and facing growing discontent at home, were forced to recognize Saladin's rights in much of Syria and promised to send soldiers to support his jihad against the Franks.

This turned out to be a short spell of peace. In the spring of 1176 Saladin was once more campaigning and, though he won another pitched battle and seized several fortresses, he could not take Aleppo. After coming to terms with the Assassins Sect—who had made at least one major attempt on his life—Saladin broke off military operations and returned to Egypt. It was not until Nur al-Din's son died unexpectedly in late 1181 that Saladin was able to enforce his rule on all of Syria and unify the Muslim armies against the Franks.

While in Egypt, Saladin faced another crusader invasion and mobilized his forces to meet it. When the threatening Latins instead marched north, Saladin seized the opportunity for a lightning assault on the Latin kingdom. Leading twenty thousand cavalry into Palestine, he faced only a small force of five to six hundred knights and a few thousand men-at-arms. These crusaders, led by the sickly "Leper King," Baldwin IV, made a brief stand but were heavily outnumbered and retreated behind Ascalon. Saladin, believing his enemy would never dare emerge from the protection of the walls, allowed his army to break up into small raiding packets as they raced toward an undefended Jerusalem. He and his army paid heavily for their overconfidence; he had not even left a covering force at Ascalon to alert him if the Latin force stirred.

Baldwin, reinforced by nearly a hundred Templars, did emerge, and on November 25, 1177, he reached Saladin's army. Caught by surprise, Saladin tried to rally his scattered forces. He was never given the chance, as Baldwin's military commander—Raynald of Châtillon—led an immediate charge at the center of the Muslim army. The thundering charge of the Latin heavy cavalry proved irresistible—as it almost always did—and Saladin's force broke. Baldwin's forces pursued the routed foe until darkness fell over the land. Latin losses at the Battle of Montgisard were heavy, but Saladin's army was destroyed and he had only barely escaped. This severely tarnished Saladin's image as a great commander, and he expended tremendous efforts in rebuilding it, in addition to spending many of his treasure reserves to form a new army. Fighting went on in the form of raids and counterraids until a truce was agreed to in 1180.

The truce allowed Saladin to once again turn his full attention on Aleppo and Mosul. Saladin took advantage of the deaths of the Abbasid caliph in Baghdad, Nur ad-Din's heir, and the emir of Mosul to push his claims on all of northern Syria. Throughout 1182 and 1183, Saladin maneuvered to capture castles, cities, and outposts, aiming to isolate his two primary targets—Aleppo and Mosul—from each other. The war stalemated, as Saladin could not capture the two cities, and his foes dared not meet his army in the open field. In June 1183, Saladin approached Aleppo once again. This time its ruler, Imad ad-Din Zengi, decided that, as Saladin's hold over northern Syria was unbreakable, he would make the best terms he could. On June 12, Imad opened Aleppo's city gates and Saladin, much to the astonishment of the inhabitants, entered the city unmolested. Saladin gave Imad other lands to control, and Imad became one of Saladin's most trusted commanders. Syria was now Saladin's to command, as Mosul without Aleppo's support was no longer a threat. He still had much to do to fully consolidate his control, but he now had the opportunity to turn the unified might of Islam against the crusader kingdom. As the general truce would last until 1187, Saladin had considerable time to prepare.

Unfortunately for the Crusaders' cause, although they could clearly see the danger on the near horizon, their preparations to meet the coming storm were negligible. Instead they gave themselves over to internecine political warfare, as varying factions jostled for power in a realm where a terminally ill king was followed by Baldwin V—a child in need of a regency to govern affairs. When he, too, died in 1186, at age eight, factions coalesced around Guy of Lusignan, who was married to Sibylla (sister of Baldwin IV and mother of Baldwin V), and Raymond III of Tripoli, Amalric's first cousin.

Most of the nobles declared their support for Sibylla if she put aside her marriage to Guy and married another who would rule as king. The leading nobles despised Guy, as several years before, he had refused battle with Saladin. Although Saladin's army subsequently broke up without consequences for the crusaders, the kingdom's warriors considered him a coward. After consenting to divorce Guy on the condition that she could choose her new husband, Sibylla double-crossed the stunned nobles at her coronation and called Guy forward to rule the kingdom. An incensed Raymond departed for Tripoli. The two factions only patched up relations in the weeks just before the Islamic assault.

Such problems only added to what had always been a precarious strategic position. From the very beginning the crusader kingdom was embroiled in expensive wars that could not be supported by Palestine's economic infrastructure. To stay afloat the crusaders depended on a constant flow of funds from Byzantium and the West. By 1187 this flow had slowed to a trickle, as European kings increasingly retained their revenues for domestic use. The constant struggle between France and England—repeated by many states throughout Europe—was expensive and severely limited the funds Western rulers had available to support a far-off crusader army. Moreover, Byzantine support waxed and waned according to political and economic relations between the Byzantine ruler, the crusaders, and Western commercial enterprises. In 1187 these relations had reached a low point.

In the past, lack of funds to pay for mercenaries had been embarrassing but not fatal, as the crusaders could maintain their fighting strength through a steady stream of new warriors taking the cross and making their way to the Holy Land. But by the middle of the twelfth century this flow reduced to a trickle. In addition to the nearly constant warfare in Europe, many knights found it easier to join the *Reconquista* in Spain or slaughter Slavs in the Teutonic *Drang nach Osten* than to make the long, perilous journey to the Latin East. The organization of the quasi crusading orders of religious knights—Templars and Hospitallers—had helped, but their numbers and the unquestioned fighting ability of their members were never sufficient to make up for the kingdom's chronic manpower shortage.

By the time Saladin invaded the kingdom of Jerusalem in 1187, this manpower deficit presented crusader leaders with a stark choice: They could either place an army in the field or man their strongholds, but they could not do both. If the knights remained behind their walls until the Muslim army faded away at the end of the campaign season, they would likely see their fields wrecked, further reducing their resources for the following year. However, if the leaders fielded a large army and lost, their weakened strongholds would surely fall in rapid succession. They could lose everything.

While the crusaders patched up their differences and begged Rome and Europe's rulers for assistance, Saladin assembled an army of at least thirty thousand men. Using an 1186 crusader attack on a major caravan as a pretext for ending the truce with the kingdom of Jerusalem, he launched his army in the decisive struggle for Palestine—the core of the Latin kingdom. King Guy, also realizing that the upcoming battle would decide the fate of the Latin states, mustered the full strength of the kingdom. By the end of June, he had massed approximately twelve hundred knights and eighteen to twenty thousand other troops of widely varying quality at the Springs of Sephoria. He had also ordered the True Cross—reportedly fashioned from remnants of the cross on which Jesus was crucified—be brought along to inspire the crusaders.

Toward the end of June, Saladin tried to lure the crusaders away from their water supply at Sephoria. Failing to do this, he besieged the city of Tiberias, where Raymond's wife, Eschiva, had taken shelter. Unsure how to proceed, Guy called a meeting with his leading nobles on July 2. Despite his wife's plight, Raymond strongly advocated for the abandonment of Tiberias and recommended that Guy bide his time until the Muslim army broke up at the onset of the dry season. Guy agreed, but he was uneasy with his choice. He had employed the same tactic four years earlier, and doing so had resulted in his being branded a coward. Other nobles pointed out that aggressive action had served the crusaders well in the past and recommended an immediate advance. During their conversation a message arrived from Raymond's wife, urgently pleading for rescue. Although Raymond still advocated leaving Tiberias to its fate, the rest of the knights took up a call to go forth and "save the Lady of Tiberias." Guy was swept forward on a tide of emotion and issued marching orders.

The crusaders advanced in three groups: King Guy commanded the center, with Raymond in the van and Balian of Ibelin and the Templars in the rear. On July 3, the crusaders set out from Sephoria. Saladin immediately broke off the siege of Tiberias and led his forces to confront the advancing crusaders. Scorched by the sun—these were the hottest days of summer—the armored crusaders advanced toward Tiberias. Saladin's skirmishers harassed the vanguard and flanks of Guy's army, while Muslim horse archers kept up a continual fire as they looked for weak points where they might be able to split the crusader column.

Saladin directed his main force against the crusaders' rear guard. He also sent the wings of his army around the crusader column to sit astride the crusaders' escape route. By 9:00 A.M., with the temperature rapidly rising, the crusaders were surrounded and effectively cut off from water.

For long hours Guy pushed his compact formations up the hills overlooking Lake Tiberias, but incessant Muslim attacks were stringing out his column. In the early afternoon, messengers from Balian and the Templars told the king the rear guard was in danger of being overwhelmed. Guy, once again unsure of what to do, sought Raymond's advice. His recommendation was to halt the column and pitch tents in order to mass his forces for a big push toward Tiberias in the morning. This was spectacularly bad counsel for an army in the desert without water.

On the western end of a plateau overlooking Tiberias and its freshwater lake, the exhausted and thirsty crusaders drew together and made camp for the night. Morale was low, and many of the infantry had already deserted or ceased fighting. As the crusaders suffered, Saladin resupplied his army with arrows and water. The exultant Muslim soldiers quenched their thirst at Saladin's order, and they began stacking brush upwind of the crusader camp. In the morning they set alight the great piles of tinder, enshrouding the demoralized crusaders in choking clouds of smoke.

At dawn the Muslims closed in on the crusaders, firing arrows by the thousands as they advanced. According to a Muslim chronicler:

> The Muslim archers sent up clouds of arrows like thick swarms of locusts, killing many of the Frankish horses. The Franks, surrounding themselves with their infantry, tried to fight their way to Tiberias in the hope of reaching water, but Saladin realized their objective and forestalled them by planting himself and his army in the way.

On the advice of leading nobles, Guy ordered his brother, Aimery, constable of the kingdom, to assemble enough knights for a concerted charge, to be led by Raymond. For almost a century the furor of a Frankish charge had turned the tide of many a desperate battle. But this time Saladin had drilled his army well. As Raymond's mailed fist of armored knights thundered forward, the Muslim line opened. Raymond and his men "rode away" and the Muslim "ranks were closed again, dooming the Crusader army." Raymond and his sons escaped the Muslim trap, and for many this was proof of his treachery. The fact that he died within months of the battle was seen as evidence of God's justice.

Guy's position was desperate. Under a storm of arrows and incessant skirmishes his battered force inched toward an extinct volcano known as the Horns of Hattin. There the knights sheltered amid Iron Age walled ruins, erected the royal red tent, and, presumably, placed the True Cross within it. But they remained surrounded, without food or water, and were apparently too exhausted to break through Saladin's army. As another Muslim chronicler relates:

> No matter how hard they fought, they were repulsed; no matter how often they rallied, each time they were encircled. Not even

an ant crawled out from among them, nor could they defend themselves against the onslaught. They retreated to Mount Hattin to escape the storm of destruction; but on Hattin itself they found themselves encompassed by fatal thunderbolts. Arrowheads transfixed them; the peaks laid them low; bows pinned them down; fate tore at them; calamity chewed them up; and disaster tainted them.

Only Balian managed to lead one desperate charge clear of the encirclement. But the rest of the army was trapped. Throughout the fight Saladin moved along the Muslim lines, encouraging his troops to greater efforts and at times physically restraining them when their courage wavered.

Despite their dismal predicament, the crusaders maintained discipline and continued fighting. At some point Guy spotted Saladin on the battlefield and gathered a force of mounted knights to assault his position in an attempt to turn the crusaders' fortunes. Twice they charged. Both attacks failed, although from the Muslim perspective they came perilously close to success. Muslim chronicler Ibn al-Athir recorded an eyewitness account from Saladin's son, al-Afdal:

> The Frankish king had retreated to the hill with his band, and from there he led a furious charge against the Muslims facing him, forcing them back upon my father. I saw that he was alarmed and distraught, and he tugged at his beard as he went forward crying, "Away with the devils!" The Muslims turned to counterattack and drove the Franks back up the hill. . . . But they returned to the charge with undiminished ardor and again drove the Muslims back upon my father. His response was the same as before, and the Muslims again counterattacked. . . . I cried, "We have beaten them!" My father turned to me and said: "Be quiet. We will not have beaten them until that tent falls."

No sooner had these words escaped Saladin's lips than the Muslims swept over the hill, collapsed the tent, captured the True Cross, and began rounding up prisoners. Saladin fell to the ground and wept with joy. He killed one crusader whom he had sworn to personally execute and then adjourned to a pavilion to enjoy some shaved ice and witness the execution of hundreds of Christian nobles and knights. He did, however, order the release of some of the crusaders in exchange for their ceding towns or castles, the cumulative effect of which was to hugely increase the pace of Saladin's reconquest of most of Palestine. But the true magnitude of the disaster can be gauged by the fate of the common soldiers. Contemporary chroniclers reported that their sale created a glut in Arab slave markets that took many months to clear.

Saladin's victorious army swept through the crusader territories almost unopposed. By early September most of the major ports (Sidon, Acre, Ascalon) were in Muslim hands. Only Tyre was saved by the timely arrival of Conrad of Montferrat from Europe, which put a new zeal in the remaining defenders. In the interior only the great fortresses (Montréal, Belvoir, Kerak, Safed, and Belfort) remained in crusader hands. On September 20, Saladin invaded Jerusalem, which was handed over to him on October 2, 1177. The Muslim population celebrated Saladin as the restorer of the world.

Western reaction was far different. Upon hearing of the defeat at Hattin, Pope Urban III died of grief and shock. His successor, Gregory VIII, immediately issued a papal bull—*Audita Tremendi*—calling for a new Crusade. The response, including Richard and Philip, was overwhelming. The two greatest military commanders of the medieval period were now on a collision course.

The Third Crusade

The Crusade to reclaim Palestine got off to an inauspicious start. On May 11, 1189, the Holy Roman emperor Frederick Barbarossa departed Regensburg with a powerful army using the overland route through Hungary and Anatolia. One month into the march, on June 10, the emperor, after seeing his army safely into Anatolia, drowned during the crossing of the Saleph River. His son Frederick II, Duke of Swabia, led the army into Antioch less than a fortnight later. But that was as far as the bulk of the army would go. Exhausted by the long march and hard fighting and further pruned by fever in Antioch, the army broke up. By the time Frederick of Swabia entered the Latin kingdom he probably had fewer than three hundred mounted knights. That was enough to defend a single fortress, but hardly sufficient for a war of conquest.

In the meantime, Saladin released King Guy in return for handing over Ascalon and a promise not to bear arms against Saladin ever again. He kept his promise for a year and then marshaled a small force in Antioch and marched down the coast. There were rumors at the time that Saladin released him from his promise, as he feared a superior general replacing Guy. Upon his release Guy ordered Tyre to open its gates to him. Conrad of Montferrat, fancying himself as contender of Jerusalem's throne and in no hurry to hand over power to the man who had lost the Latin army and the kingdom, refused him access. Conrad did resupply Guy's small army, which then continued down the coast. Arriving at Acre in late August, Guy opened a siege of the city despite his pitifully small force lacking the capacity to invest even a small portion of the walls. It would be nearly a year before the forces of Richard and Philip arrived in sufficient numbers to commence an effective siege.

Dynastic squabbles delayed both Richard and Philip in Sicily, and as the delay lengthened, tensions between locals and the visiting armies grew. When rioters in Messina attacked Richard's troops, he took the opportunity to seize the city by storm and then gave it over to his men to sack. Richard and Philip maintained a strained peace throughout their stay in Sicily and even found time to settle a longstanding point of tension—Alice, the French king's sister. Alice had been used as a pawn by Henry II for two decades, betrothed to Richard when she was eight years old, and Henry's ward from 1169 until his death. She may have become Henry's mistress and possibly bore him a son, which is likely the reason Richard refused to marry her, and instead took for his bride Berengaria of Navarre in May 1191. To make this marriage possible, Philip released Richard from his betrothal to his sister in return for 10,000 marks (likely never paid) and certain territorial concessions.

Richard I Charging the Enemy
(*Collection of the British Museum*)

Having spent more than half a year in Sicily, the two kings departed—Philip on March 30 and Richard on April 10. By stages the respective fleets inched their way toward Palestine. While in Cyprus, Richard fought two engagements against the local leader, Isaac Comnenus, the self-styled ruler of Byzantium. These engagements netted Richard many fine warhorses, a sizable treasure, and Isaac's promise to lead five hundred troops to Palestine with Richard. When, on the same day he made them, Isaac reneged on his many promises, Richard took the time to conquer the entire island, gaining him substantial booty to add to what he had already taken. More crucially, Cyprus provided him a local tax base and fertile fields from which to supply his army. When he departed Cyprus, Richard had secured all of the resources required to maintain a prolonged struggle. Whether this was an example of Richard's strategic brilliance or the result of on-the-spot improvisation is still a matter of historical debate.

The one cloud on the horizon was a result of continued political maneuvering. While in Cyprus, Richard was visited by King Guy, who hoped to gain his support in his ongoing struggle for political domination of Tyre and the ouster of Conrad of Montferrat—his scheming rival for the throne. As Guy had come to the Holy Land only after being driven from Poitou by Richard, the approach was not without some risk. But Richard, likely having heard that Philip had backed Conrad, greeted Guy with open arms. As a result, even before Richard had set foot in Palestine he had cast further fuel on a situation that would lead to a political rupture and destroy the crusader coalition.

Upon his arrival, Richard discovered firsthand how debilitating intra-Latin rivalries were. He was refused admittance to Tyre by a subordinate of Conrad's, who as the commander of Tyre had eventually felt obliged to join the crusader force around Acre. With no other choice Richard headed south and joined his army with the forces of Philip, Guy, and Conrad in the siege of Acre. His arrival sent a shock wave through the Muslim army that came close to breaking it up without a battle. As one chronicler wrote: "He was wise and experienced in warfare and coming had a dread and frightening effect on the hearts of Muslims."

They all promptly fell out. As per their agreement to share all conquests, Philip demanded half of Cyprus. Richard countered by demanding half of Flanders when, as a result of Philip of Alsace's death at Acre, the fief had temporarily reverted to Philip's control. Guy then formally accused Conrad of being a disloyal vassal and had his brother challenge him to a trial by combat. A furious Conrad retreated back to Tyre, taking his army with him. So it went with claim and counterclaim, ripping the fragile crusader unity asunder.

Throughout these political squabbles the crusader army continued to pound Acre. Crossbowmen swept the walls, and siege engines battered them day and night. When the Genoese fleet arrived, giving the crusaders total naval supremacy, it became impossible for Saladin to resupply or reinforce the defenders. The garrison resisted fiercely, and its sorties did substantial damage to the crusaders' siege engines. In a desperate attempt to give all possible aid, Saladin brought his army close to Acre. Whenever the crusaders attacked the walls Saladin would launch his army against the crusaders' base. In each instance the steady Frankish infantry drove off Saladin's force, without having any effect on the course of the siege. When he realized that nothing more was to be done, Saladin drew his army away, ravaging the countryside as he retreated to ensure that there was nothing in the surrounding area to sustain the crusaders once the city had fallen.

On July 12, after a particularly heavy English-Pisan assault, Acre's garrison sued for peace. The terms of the surrender are still disputed, but it certainly included the turning over of Acre's fleet (most of Saladin's naval power) to the crusaders, along with Saladin paying a huge ransom for the lives of Acre's defenders and releasing a large number of Christian prisoners. The kingdom of Jerusalem would also be split: Guy would continue to rule Acre and all points south, while Conrad received Tyre and the north as his domain. Finally, the mosques were converted back into churches and purified. When that was complete, Acre was once again declared a Christian city.

On July 31, 1192, Philip, who in the English view was tired of being humiliated and outshone by his vassal Richard, declared he had accomplished all that was expected of him and took ship for France. He did, however, leave the bulk of his army in Palestine, in effect making Richard the sole commander of the entire crusader force. Soon afterward negotiations between Richard and Saladin broke down. When Saladin refused to make the first installment on the agreed payment for the prisoners held at Acre, an exasperated Richard, after reserving a few of the most important, had the rest marched out of the city. An Arab chronicler reports on what happened:

> The enemy brought out the Muslim prisoners for whom God had decreed martyrdom, about 3,000 in ropes. Then as one man they charged them and with stabbings and blows with the sword they slew them in very cold blood as the Muslim advanced guard watched, not knowing what to do.

Encounter Between Richard and Saladin
(*The Collection of the British Library*)

The reasons for this mass slaughter are still hotly debated. But what to the modern reader appears a murderous crime against humanity was not viewed as such at the time. In fact, Richard was widely congratulated for having killed so many dangerous infidels. Examining the event in practical terms, it is clear that the prisoners were a huge drain on Richard's resources and were of little material worth, since Saladin would not pay a ransom. Moreover, such a huge host, even if disarmed, presented a formidable threat in Richard's rear, particularly with Saladin's army camped nearby. Convinced that Saladin was dragging out the negotiations in order to improve his own position, Richard ended them in a manner that would add further dread to his already ferocious reputation. Not to be outdone, Saladin ordered the execution of the crusaders he held prisoner.

After his victory at Acre, Richard had several options. The first, to march on Jerusalem, had the greatest emotional appeal, but it meant marching his army over wasteland and trying to secure an extremely vulnerable supply line. He might get to Jerusalem only to see his army perish for want of necessities. Moreover, if he did take the city, he did not have the manpower to keep it supplied. His next most appealing option was to follow in Philip's footsteps and declare his part in the Crusade done and sail for home. Richard was only too well aware that the longer he tarried in Palestine, the greater the danger to his Continental holdings, which would soon come under attack by Philip. But Richard apparently did not deem his part done. Given his known warlike character, he likely thirsted to bring Saladin to battle and reverse the damage done at Hattin—or at least avenge it.

As Saladin was clearly in no great hurry to launch his army into a suicidal assault on Richard's fortified camps at Acre, Richard took the only real course open to him. On August 22, he led his army down the coast toward the port of Jaffa, whose capture would widen his base of operations and possibly make an inland advance possible. Richard arranged his army in three divisions, with Guy's brother Geoffrey leading the van, Richard commanding the center, and the Duke of Burgundy leading the rear. Each division consisted of cavalry and infantry. As they marched, archers and bowmen stayed on the inland side. Beside them marched the steady spearmen who would hastily form to ward off any sudden cavalry charge. Between them and the sea were the Frankish heavy cavalry, and along the coast rolled the baggage train. As long as these divisions stayed close to each other and maintained their integrity, they were invulnerable to anything Saladin could throw at them.

Not that Saladin did not try. Every day he sent his cavalry and archers against the Latin ranks, hoping to cut off or somehow disrupt the cohesion of one of the divisions. The same Arab chronicler describes a typical engagement:

> He [Saladin] sent skirmishers forward and the arrows on both sides were like rain. The enemy was already in formation with the infantry surrounding it like a wall, wearing the iron corslets and full-length well made chain mail, so that the arrows were falling on them with no effect. They were shooting with crossbows and wounding the Muslims' horses, their cavalry and infantry. I saw various individuals amongst the Franks with ten arrows fixed in their backs pressing on in this fashion quite unconcerned.

Such was the march for more than two weeks. There was fighting on most days, but Saladin was never able to bring on a decisive engagement. In early September, Saladin gave up on trying to force the crusaders to do something rash and began scouting Richard's route for a place to launch a massed assault. He chose a section of the road near Arsuf, where a forest would hide his army until the crusaders had moved into the trap. Richard, an experienced soldier with as good an eye for the ground as anyone, also realized that the chokepoint near Arsuf provided a perfect place for a massive ambush—similar to Hannibal's at Lake Trasimene. Richard halted his army just short of Arsuf and prepared for battle.

At this point, Richard's army likely mustered close to fifteen thousand troops, of whom fewer than two thousand were mounted knights. Richard placed the Templars in the vanguard, while the Hospitallers supported the rear. Once again, Richard protected his cavalry with an outer screen of infantry, in which he placed Henry of Champagne, nephew to both Richard and Philip, in command. The center and wings each had four squadrons of cavalry as well as a complement of well-armored infantry. The center, consisting of Englishmen, Normans, and soldiers from Poitou and Guienne, was led by Guy and his brother Geoffrey. The right wing consisted mostly of the French force left behind by Philip and was commanded by James d'Avesnes. On the right with the Templars were the Bretons and soldiers from Anjou—the heart of the Angevin Empire—commanded by Templar Grand Master Robert de Sablé. Richard and the Duke of Burgundy kept a contingent of picked knights with them to ride along the line and keep the formation tight.

Richard I in Battle
(The Collection of the British Library)

Saladin's battle array is uncertain. The center was likely under the command of his young son al-Afdal, though, given his son's relative inexperience, this may have been a nominal command. There was a Damascus contingent under Sarim al-Din Quaymaz either attached to the center or held back by Saladin as a reserve. The right wing was commanded by Saladin's brother, al-Adil, while the left wing, consisting of soldiers drawn from northern Iraq, was commanded by a general out of Mosul. Saladin's forces probably outnumbered the crusaders by a wide margin, but contemporary claims of as many as three hundred thousand Muslim soldiers are easily discredited. It is, however, quite possible that given the reinforcements Saladin had received since the fall of Acre, he had at least thirty thousand soldiers, or a two-to-one advantage in manpower.

Richard's troops moved quickly through the forest in a formation so tight that it was said it was impossible to "throw an apple into the ranks without hitting man or horse." Though the sources make this uncertain, it appears that the rapid Christian movement caught Saladin by surprise, and it took him much of the early morning to get his army organized. By the time he did, most if not all of the Latin army had passed through the woods and was approaching Arsuf across a large plain and through the orchards that surrounded the city.

When his army was fully arrayed, Saladin sent forward masses of skirmishers from each of his divisions. After these skirmishers had loosed their arrows, the massed divisions of Saladin's army began pressing against the Frankish force. According to the chronicler Ambroise, thirty thousand Turkish troops in well-ordered groups charged. They were led by drummers whose clamor "drowned out the thunder of the Lord." The initial charge may have numbered ten thousand horsemen who, as Ambroise relates, "swept rapidly down upon our men, hurling darts and arrow, and making a terrible din with their confused war cries." As the Arab chronicler saw it:

The Sultan made them engage closely. . . . The enemy was tightly beset and the fighting was fierce and blazed into flame on both sides. . . . The situation became serious and the noose about them tightened, while the Sultan [Saladin] was moving between the left wing and the right, urging the men on in

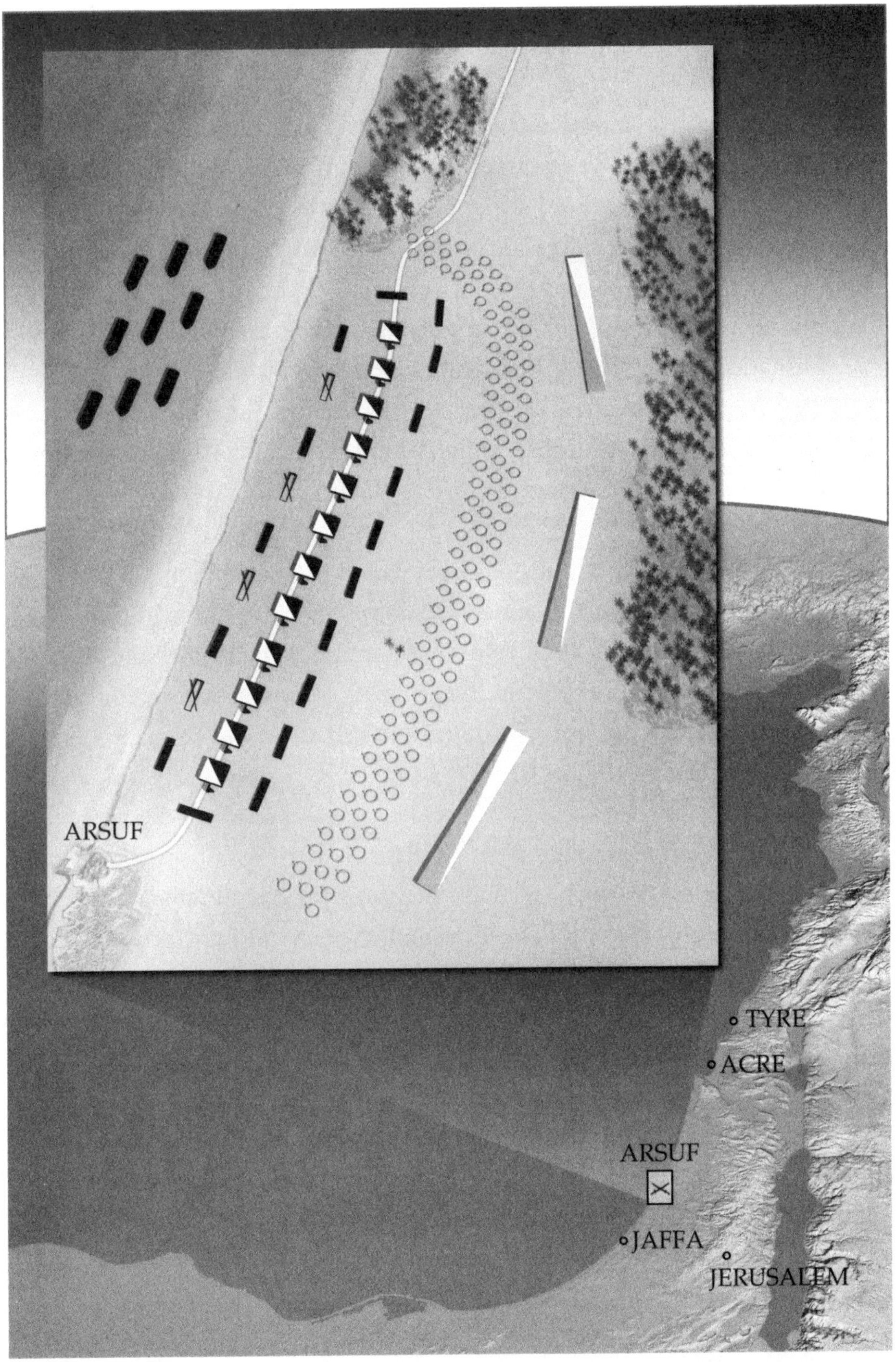

ARSUF

TYRE

ACRE

ARSUF
⊠

JAFFA

JERUSALEM

Jihad. . . . The enemy's situation worsened still more and the Muslims thought they had them in their power.

This was the moment Richard had been waiting for. For the first time, Saladin had committed the bulk of his army, and Richard forced his knights to remain in place until the Muslims were so embroiled that they could not retreat. Then, and only then, would he launch the decisive and always irresistible Frankish countercharge. But waiting so long meant running a great risk that some part of his formation might break before Richard ordered the charge. If that happened his army would be scattered and annihilated. It was a matter of fine, even exquisite, timing, and it would take a great general to call the moment. It was a close-run thing. As Ambroise relates:

> [The Franks] thought their lines would be broken and did not expect to survive one hour or to come out alive; know in truth that cowards could not help throwing down their bows and arrows and taking refuge in the army. . . . No man was so confident that he did not wish in his heart that he had finished his pilgrimage.

Saladin's forces seemed to concentrate their assaults on the rear guard, hoping to cut it off from the van that was already approaching the safety of Arsuf. The Hospitallers were so hard-pressed that their grand master, Granier de Napes, personally rode to Richard and begged him to order a general assault. Richard still did not deem the moment right and ordered the Hospitallers to hold on just a bit longer. The grand master returned but the Hospitallers could not hold much longer. Although they had not lost any knights, horses were falling at a frightful rate. Ambroise tells us that many Hospitallers feared they would be branded cowards if they endured such relentless attacks without striking back:

> So the Master returned to find the Turks pressing on and dealing death in the rear, while there was no chief or count who did

not blush for the very shame, saying to one another, "Why do we not give reins to our horse? Alas! Alas! We shall be convicted of cowardly sloth evermore, and deservedly too. To whom has such a thing ever happened before? . . . Unless we charge them speedily we shall earn ourselves everlasting ignominy; and the longer we delay the greater will be our disgrace."

Just as Richard was about to give the signal for the grand countercharge, the Hospitallers could take it no longer. Two of their number charged, carrying the rest of the Hospitaller knights with them. Richard, with no other choice, ordered a general advance, which his army carried out in perfect order. As al-Din relates:

I saw them grouped together in the middle of the foot-soldiers. They took their lances and gave a shout as one man. Their infantry opened gaps for them and they appeared in unison along the whole line. One group charged the right wing, another on our left, and a third our center. Our men gave way before them.

Now, nearly a thousand years after the event, one must work hard to picture the full frightfulness of the crusader heavy cavalry bearing down. Their horses were bred for war and of considerable size and strength. They were pampered and rested animals, as a knight usually rode a smaller horse throughout the day and only mounted his charger in the moments before a charge. Each horse weighed about 1,200 pounds and probably carried 100 pounds of armor, plus a fully armored and armed knight who probably added 250 pounds. Build a visual picture of two thousand nearly invincible killers charging knee to knee and closing at incredible speed. They were a wall of steel proceeded by the tips of deadly lances, and when those were broken, the men, trained for battle since childhood, would begin swinging giant broadswords, maces, axes, and other deadly instruments of war. It was not a brave man who stood and waited for a Frankish charge; it was a suicidal one.

Into the midst of the mêlée charged Richard. Ambroise relates:

Then King Richard, fierce and alone, pressed on the Turks, laying them low; none whom his sword touched might escape; for wherever he went he made a wide path for himself, brandishing his sword on every side.

It was little wonder that the shocked Muslim army ran. But the other crusaders had routed Muslim armies before, only to see them rally and counterattack the tired and scattered knights. This time Richard kept his knights well in hand and pressed his advantage. After the pursuit had gone a short distance, he ordered a halt, and the Latin knights re-formed and let their winded horses recover. When the inevitable Muslim counterattack came, it did not find a disordered force to run down. Rather, Richard's knights were again in a solid mass and immediately pressed home their assaults. This was repeated two more times, but a fourth Latin charge was unnecessary. Saladin's defeated army was scattered and demoralized.

Saladin's Siege of Jerusalem
(The Collection of the British Library)

Saladin would face Richard only one more time in open battle. This was for the control of Jaffa, which Saladin captured in a surprise attack. He then lost it to an equally surprising attack made by Richard, who came in from the sea with two thousand warriors, most of them crossbowmen. Saladin still had numerical superiority, so he launched an immediate counterattack to take the city. Richard's crossbows cut the Muslim attacking force to ribbons. Prior to this combat, which came toward the end of Richard's stay in Palestine, Saladin had conducted a scorched-earth strategy, as his army refused to meet the crusaders in open battle.

His first target was Ascalon, the greatest port in southern Palestine. If Richard held Ascalon, the crusader army could strike either at Egypt or at Jerusalem. In short, they could strike where Saladin and his army were not, inflicting a crushing and demoralizing blow at whichever target they chose. Recognizing the danger, Saladin force-marched his exhausted army to Ascalon and, working day and night, razed it to its foundations. Richard knew what was going on and implored the crusaders to march immediately on Ascalon. He recognized the crucial strategic importance of the city and port, but his leading knights, particularly the French, could not resist the lure of Jerusalem. In battle Richard was second to none, but as a leader who had to convince as well as command, he left something to be desired.

Richard accepted the advice of his war council and began rebuilding the fortifications of Jaffa, so it could be used as a base when his army struck inland toward Jerusalem. From this point the war became a guerrilla struggle, and Richard tried to build fortified posts to guard his supply lines from Jaffa to Jerusalem, while Saladin's forces constantly harassed the Latin army without bringing on a major battle. All through this period Richard, Saladin, Guy, and Conrad continued to conduct negotiations. In this area, if not on the battlefield, Saladin was easily the equal of Richard—and probably his superior.

In the end, Conrad was murdered, conceivably on Richard's orders, and Guy sold the island of Cyprus. To cut off another round of destructive internecine warfare, the Latin nobles selected Henry of Champagne as ruler. Throughout this period Richard was receiving messages that his brother John was plotting to take control of all or a substantial portion of his kingdom. More followed, warning Richard that John was in league with Philip. Downcast by these reports, Richard still managed to twice bring the crusader army within sight of Jerusalem. Both times the city was probably his for the taking, particularly on the first approach. But taking Jerusalem and holding it were very different propositions. The loss of Jerusalem would rally troops from throughout the Muslim world, while Richard could expect little assistance from Christendom. The Holy City was just as much a trap as a prize, and Richard refused to walk into it.

With his European kingdom at risk, Richard could not afford to tarry in Palestine. The summer of 1192 was given over to protracted negotiations. In these, Saladin should easily have had the upper hand. Richard was in a hurry to depart, and while he and his army were nearly invincible along the coast, any attempt by the crusaders to venture far inland was fraught with peril. But Richard established a new bargaining position by negotiating with various emirs who had grown wary of Saladin's growing power. To Saladin's chagrin many of the emirs visiting Richard's tent were from his inner circle, including members of his family. Richard may have been in a hurry to depart, but it was clear that most of Saladin's leaders were just as ready to see the endless warfare concluded.

In the end, both sides agreed to a three-year truce. Saladin retained control of Jerusalem, but Christians were permitted unfettered rights to access their holy sites. Moreover, the crusaders confirmed their control of the coastal cities, which meant there was a true Latin kingdom in Palestine. It would not be extinguished for another century, until Acre fell in 1291. Despite his best efforts, Richard could not save Ascalon for the crusader kingdom. Muslim armies again destroyed its walls, which Richard had rebuilt, and the city receded into obscurity.

Conclusion

So, who won? By any fair measure Richard proved himself the better battlefield commander. But one is again faced by the fact that for all of his tactical brilliance, Richard was unable to translate his battlefield victories into a lasting settlement that would have ensured the survival of the Latin kingdom. Some of this is a consequence of never having possessed the resources to capture and hold Jerusalem, or even to press advantages hard-won on the battlefield. But he was well aware of his constrained circumstances from the start and can be rightfully faulted for not designing his plans based on his paucity of means. His greatly outnumbered army could win great battles and multitudes of minor ones, but it was incapable of altering geopolitical reality—the European armies were too far from home to adequately sustain a major military effort against a united Islamic state.

Richard did manage to reestablish a small but powerful Latin state. In the wake of the Hattin disaster, this was no small feat. Moreover, these states became hugely prosperous over the next several decades. One cannot fault him for Europe's failure to support the Latin kingdom nearly a century after his death. Richard had accomplished everything that could be reasonably expected of him given the resources at his command. He proved himself a capable battlefield leader and demonstrated a high degree of operational brilliance and strategic nuance. Could he have accomplished more if he stayed? Possibly, but only at the margins. Richard never had the forces required to retake all of what had been lost—from current southern Turkey to the border with Egypt—and any attempt to do so with the meager resources at his disposal would have placed all of the Third Crusade's gains in great jeopardy, as the loss of Jerusalem would surely reunite the Muslims to one final jihad.

Saladin proved himself a great commander at the Battle of Hattin and during his conquests in the succeeding year—culminating with the capture of Jerusalem. On the battlefield, he was never a match for Richard, although, in the year after his devastating defeat at Arsuf, he demonstrated considerable operational adaptability. Though he was unable to stop the Latins from improving their fortunes, he did hold on to the interior of Palestine, particularly Jerusalem. It is possible that with Richard's departure, the rump state along the coast would have been easy pickings for Saladin as soon as the truce ended. But we will never know, as he died of yellow fever the following year.

As for Richard, his return to the Angevin Empire was delayed by his capture by an old enemy—Leopold V, Duke of Austria—who accused Richard of arranging the murder of his cousin, Conrad of Montferrat. He was transferred to the custody of the Holy Roman emperor, Henry VI, who had his own reasons for disliking Richard. Henry demanded 150,000 marks (65,000 pounds of silver), or almost three times the English crown's annual revenues. It took until early 1194 to raise the ransom. Henry released Richard in February, despite Philip and John offering Henry 80,000 marks if he would hold on to Richard until Michaelmas (September 29) 1194. Upon hearing of Richard's release, Philip sent a note to John: "Look to yourself; the devil is loose."

The last several years of Richard's life were spent in nearly constant warfare with Philip. He was finally brought down in 1199 by a young crossbowman during a siege of an insignificant castle, an unremarkable end for a remarkable general.

Napoléon and Wellington

In retrospect it is difficult to determine any purpose for the Napoleonic Wars except to serve the greater aggrandizement and glory of one man: Napoléon Bonaparte. By the time he seized power in 1800, the revolutionary fervor that had propelled hundreds of thousands of French citizens to defend *la patrie* and the revolution against the great European powers had waned. It finally died as a consequence of Napoléon's unceasing wars, which left the Grande Armée a shadow of its former glory. For all the brilliant reforms that Napoléon brought to France, he spurned numerous opportunities for a lasting peace, much preferring the glory of the battlefield to the dreary task of governing the fractious French and the other assorted nationalities that his ever-expanding empire had conquered. His search for absolute security and, even more fundamentally, his quest for glory led him to wage campaigns that in the end broke French power.

Napoléon's reputation largely rests on his brilliant operational maneuvering during his early campaigns. As the years went by, his army paid the price for his successes in battle, as the sharp cutting edge it possessed in 1805 was dulled and then finally ground out of existence. Moreover, as his enemies learned and adapted to his methods, Napoléon began eschewing maneuver in favor of increasingly bloody affairs where victory largely resulted from big battalions, massed cannons, and a willingness to accept massive casualties to retain control of the battlefield.

Foremost among Napoléon's faults was that he never recognized the limits of what was possible. France in the nineteenth century was a rich and powerful nation. It had sufficient industry and personnel reserves to engage in wars on a majestic scale. And in Napoléon, France had a battlefield genius on a par with—or greater than—any military commander in history. But France's wealth and military might were not inexhaustible, and they were certainly no match for the demands of sustaining multiple conflicts against successive coalitions of European powers—financed by Great Britain's massive financial wherewithal. This was certainly obvious to Napoléon as early as 1809, and it was unmissable in the wake of his 1812 Russian disaster. Still, rather than formulate a strategy that would have brought at least a temporary peace, Napoléon was determined to suck the last reserves of energy out of country and people. In the end, he brought both to ruin. There were, particularly after 1807, choices and strategic options available that could have brought a lasting peace and maintained France's position in the front rank of European powers, but Napoléon eschewed them in favor of glories his exhausted nation would no longer underwrite.

On the other hand, the British Wellington, Napoléon's final adversary at the Battle of Waterloo, was the product of a nation that relied on its navy for security and bought its continental influence by subsidizing the armies of its allies rather than fielding massive ground forces on the Continent. Consequently, Wellington always commanded relatively small armies and learned to make do with meager resources and the limited reinforcements the War Office in London provided. Wellington could never expend blood and treasure as lavishly as Napoléon. Thus, his battles were masterpieces of the rapier-like counterstroke, and his strategic plans were of necessity always aligned with his means.

It is ironic, therefore, that the ultimate confrontation between the two generals at Waterloo presented each with a tactical situation that demanded an approach quite different from what he had employed in the recent past. In 1815, because his army consisted largely of veterans, Napoléon possessed the best-trained force he had possessed since 1806. To win a war against the great coalition of European powers ranged against him, Napoléon would need to maneuver, strike, and maneuver again. Above all, his main field army had to remain nimble, and he had to win quickly and decisively against those forces closest to Paris—the British and Prussian armies—before turning to meet the great Russian armies already marching through central Europe. The one thing he could not afford was a slugging match that would decimate his rebuilt army.

Wellington's position was the obverse. For the most part, his army was poorly trained and far below the quality of his Peninsula army. Moreover, more than half of his army was not even British, and he had to maneuver closely with a Prussian army of unknown quality. He thus had to accept battle on terms where firepower and the capacity to accept horrendous losses were more important than maneuvering for advantage.

Napoléon

Napoléone di Buonaparte was born into a family of minor nobility in Corsica in 1769. As Corsica, formerly controlled by Genoa, only became part of France that year, Napoléon's first languages were Italian and a local Corsican dialect. He probably did not begin learning French until he was ten, and then only enough for enrollment in the French military academy at Brienne-le-Château in 1779. Throughout his life he spoke French with an Italian accent. Though an outsider, Napoléon received an excellent education and excelled in math. During his time at Brienne, others also began noting his extraordinary memory. After Brienne he attended the École Militaire in Paris, a school founded in 1750 to train poorer members of the nobility for military service. There, he trained as an artilleryman, and when his father's death reduced his circumstances, he completed the two-year course in a single year.

Napoléon received his commission as a second lieutenant in

1785. As the army of the ancien régime was enjoying a spate of peace, Napoléon was allowed the luxury of spending two of the next four years away from his regiment, mostly trying to settle his father's estate. At the beginning of the French Revolution he was in Corsica. At first he identified himself with groups calling for Corsican independence, but squabbles within the Corsican nobility led the locals to sack the Bonaparte home, forcing Napoléon to flee into the mountains. In 1793 the Corsican Assembly declared the entire Bonaparte family "condemned to perpetual execration and infamy." Desiring to live and fight another day, Napoléon and his immediate family departed for France—exiles and refugees.

As a result of the Revolution and its attacks on the nobility, most of the senior French officers had fled. Thus, in a real sense the French army became an army open to the talented and ambitious. Napoléon first secured a commission organizing convoys to support the Jacobin siege of Avignon. Soon after his arrival he also established his political bona fides by publishing, with the support of Augustin Robespierre (brother of the Revolution's leader Maximilien Robespierre), *Le souper de Beaucaire*. This highly political pamphlet marked him as an officer of undoubted political loyalty to the Revolution. Soon thereafter Napoléon received command of the Republican artillery besieging Toulon, where a British fleet had occupied the port. Working tirelessly, Napoléon built up a siege train of more than a hundred guns, almost all of them employed in reducing Fort Mulgrave—the Little Gibraltar—which dominated the hill overlooking the harbor. Throughout the siege Napoléon displayed great courage and competence, being stabbed with a British pike and having a horse shot out from under him in the final assault on the fort. Immediately on Fort Mulgrave's capture, Napoléon advanced his guns and fired hot shot on the Royal Navy's ships in the harbor. The British vacated.

Napoléon was the hero of the moment, and in early 1794 he received a promotion to general and command of the artillery in the Army of Italy. He distinguished himself in a short campaign and then returned to Nice. At that point, Robespierre's overthrow placed Napoléon in personal jeopardy. For two weeks he found himself under house arrest but managed to rally sufficient supporters to secure his release. Nevertheless, the Directory—the new régime— removed him from the active list when he refused an infantry commission. He viewed that assignment as a demotion, especially since it was to fight against a Royalist uprising in the Vendée. Through his political connections he managed to secure a position within the army's historical and topographical bureau, which, despite its title, was the coordinating staff for France's strategic planning. In reality, it was a nascent "general staff," and in that position Napoléon found himself at the nexus of military and political power. During his time there Napoléon received a graduate education in strategy and learned the ins and outs of all the many ingredients that made arrows on a map a practical reality on the ground.

Napoléon
(*The Collection of the British Library*)

In the wake of Robespierre's execution, the National Assembly tried to reform the government. But until it could create a new political structure, the republic was vulnerable, and the Royalists were stirring. The Assembly's leaders, viewing Napoléon as the most politically reliable of the generals in Paris, placed him in command of its forces and ordered him to put down the counterrevolutionaries. Napoléon sent a certain Captain Joachim Murat to secure artillery, which he placed at key intersections near the Tuileries. When approximately thirty thousand protesters marched, Napoléon allowed them to approach and even fire the first musket shots before unleashing a thunderous blast of canister that ripped the approaching protesters to shreds. Though some fighting continued, those first artillery blasts silenced the mob.

Having saved the Directory, Napoléon received command of the Army of Italy, which was opposed by France's key Continental enemy, Austria. Immediately taking charge of its five divisions, he radiated such energy and spirit that he convinced his older senior commanders that a general only twenty-six years in age was the right man for the job. Using experience gained from the Topographical Bureau, Napoléon laid out a campaign plan in which his army's speed, coupled with deception, would more than make up for its inferior numbers. Starting at Montenotte in April 1796, Napoléon knocked the Piedmontese out of the war in less than two weeks and then turned on the Austrians. In a lightning campaign, where he learned to appreciate the benefits of having his army live off the land for as long as possible, he outmaneuvered and outfought the Austrian army. During this campaign the Napoleonic legend burst into flame, not to be extinguished until the end of the "Hundred Days" in 1815.

In a rapid movement toward Milan, the French caught up with the Austrian rear guard at Lodi. To continue their pursuit, the French needed to cross a long, narrow bridge covered by fourteen guns and nine infantry battalions. It represented a daunting challenge, one Napoléon decided to meet by storming the bridge. Throughout the afternoon he assembled artillery to sweep the bridge, thus preventing its destruction, and to damage and demoralize its defenders on the far bank. As the guns went into action, Napoléon organized a column of thirty-five hundred men who were to charge the bridge under the cover of the artillery. After delivering an emotional appeal, Napoléon ordered the cannonade doubled and sent the infantry forward. It was a mad rush across the bridge, and the Austrian guns unleashed a hail of canister into the oncoming French, literally tearing the leading French ranks apart. For a few tense moments the assault wavered, but then French generals André Masséna, Louis-Alexandre Berthier, and Jean Lannes—all soon to number among Napoléon's greatest marshals—led the column forward. *La furia francese,* "the French Fury," burst on the demoralized Austrians, who promptly abandoned their positions. It was a minor victory with small losses on both sides, but this was where the Army of Italy truly became Napoléon's army. To the troops he would be from this point until the end *le petit caporal*—the little corporal—a sobriquet of which Napoléon approved.

The Austrians retreated into their great fortress of Mantua. There, Napoléon conducted a siege from early July until February. It was a long, hard struggle in which Napoléon fought eight major battles to defeat three determined relief attempts. In mid-January 1797 he destroyed the final attempt at the Battle of Rivoli. Even before Mantua surrendered, Napoléon turned on the Papal States to punish them for supporting the Austrians. He followed that move with an assault on Venice, which, after eleven hundred years, lost its independence. These actions ended the campaign. In approximately a year, Napoléon had taken over a demoralized army, marched it across northern Italy, and defeated more than a half-dozen enemy armies, all equal to or greater than his own. His men had killed or captured 120,000 Austrian soldiers.

No sooner had the campaign ended than Napoléon turned to protect his political flank. For several months the Royalists in the Directory had maneuvered to overthrow the government and place the Bourbons back on the throne. In the process they attacked Napoléon, who they believed was harboring dictatorial ambitions.

Worried about apparent Directory passivity, Napoléon dispatched a future marshal of France, Pierre Augereau, to lead a coup, the Coup of 18 Fructidor, which deposed the Royalists and put the Directory in complete control of France. This was the second time the army had saved the Directory. After Napoléon had negotiated a settlement with Austria, Continental Europe was at peace. But Napoléon still needed to keep his name before the public. Despite the acclaim he received on returning to Paris, Napoléon understood that the mob was fickle, commenting, "The people would crowd around me just as eagerly if I were going to the scaffold." Deciding that France did not possess the naval power to attack England, he set his sights on the Middle East, where he hoped to destroy Britain's trade with the region and threaten India. He had no trouble in persuading the Directory to support his adventure, since its members were happy to see him out of France.

On May 19, 1798, Napoléon, taking advantage of a gale that drove off the watching British frigates, sailed from Toulon with thirteen ships of the lines, a number of smaller vessels, and four hundred transports. After a pause to seize Malta and its treasury, he continued on to Egypt, having barely missed a nighttime collision with a pursuing British fleet commanded by Admiral Horatio Nelson. After seizing Alexandria, Napoléon marched on Cairo. Although harassed on the march, his troops did not meet significant opposition until outside of Cairo. There he found twenty-five thousand of Murad Bey's Mamluks waiting. Spotting the Great Pyramid of Giza some miles distant, Napoléon declaimed for the benefit of his troops: "Forty centuries are looking down on you from the tops of these monuments."

Advancing in five divisional squares with baggage in the center and artillery at the corners, the thirsty French, suffering greatly in the heat, slowly closed on Murad's position. In mid-afternoon, Murad threw his six thousand cavalry against the French. Thundering forward in proper order, the Mamluk horsemen, who had no experience against a disciplined European army, believed they would rout and then run down the French. But at the last moment their horses shied away or bucked to a halt. The French had not wavered in their disciplined ranks and the horses instinctively refused to charge into the mass of bayonets. The Mamluks could make no impression on the ordered French, while the continuous crash of artillery and disciplined musket volleys brought the Mamluks down by the hundreds. At the same time, an infantry assault broke into Murad's fortified camp at Embabeh and slaughtered the defenders. Napoléon had won a decisive victory. At the cost of only twenty-nine dead and fewer than three hundred wounded, he had killed more than two thousand irreplaceable Mamluks and more than four thousand infantry. For all intents and purposes, Napoléon was master of Egypt.

Then everything started to go wrong. Horatio Nelson finally caught up with the French fleet anchored at Aboukir Bay, where he slipped half his fleet between the French vessels and the land. As the French thought this was impossible, they had not bothered to load their guns on that side. Sandwiching the French line between ships sailing on both sides, the British massacred their opponents. Napoléon had conquered Egypt, but with the British now unchallenged masters of the Mediterranean, he found himself trapped on the wrong side of that great inland sea. One of his generals advised that he should wait to see how the Directory would help him, to which Napoléon savagely replied: "The Directory consists of a set of scoundrels. They envy and hate me, and will be glad to let me perish here." After blaming the fleet's commander, Admiral Brueys, whose "glorious" death had left him unable to defend himself, Napoléon turned to an attempt to salvage the operation and his reputation.

The Ottomans, greatly heartened by Nelson's victory and believing the French ripe for destruction, began preparing their own offensive. Before they could act, Napoléon marched with thirteen thousand soldiers into Palestine. In a bloody assault he took Jaffa, and in an act reminiscent of Richard I outside of Acre, he ordered forty-five hundred prisoners slaughtered. But Napoléon did not repeat Richard I's success at Acre. The French siege, which began on March 18, 1799, lasted two months, and the Ottomans beat back each major assault. The final French assault, which breached the walls, failed due to the combination of trench lines behind the breach and Admiral Sidney Smith's landing of British marines and sailors to assist in the defense. Smith then launched a short but decisive information campaign by sending Napoléon the most recent papers from Europe.

When Napoléon learned about the defeat that French arms had suffered in Europe, he understood he would receive no further reinforcements and that he needed to return to France as soon as possible because of the tenuous political situation in which the Directory found itself. Harassed during the retreat to Egypt, Napoléon ordered his remaining prisoners executed and many of his own sick men, victims of the plague, killed. After losing four thousand men, Napoléon reached Cairo, where he rested his army, and then defeated an invading Ottoman army at Aboukir. But this was all he could accomplish in Egypt, and there were pressing problems in France. In late August 1800, Napoléon abandoned his army and sailed for home. That army, besieged in Alexandria, held out until early September 1801, when it surrendered to the British.

By the time Napoléon arrived in France, a series of battlefield victories had relieved the country's military pressure and left him free to concentrate on political affairs. Despite the reverses in Egypt, he had returned to a hero's welcome at a time when the nation was bankrupt and the Directory hugely unpopular. Through a coup, the Eighteenth Brumaire, Napoléon had himself appointed first consul and rapidly established himself as dictator. To solidify his position Napoléon took command of the army in Italy and eked out a victory at Marengo. Soon thereafter an exhausted Europe opted for peace, and even the British signed the Treaty of Amiens. Nevertheless, from its signing, the peace was a weak reed. By 1803 Britain and France were again at war, and Napoléon began assembling an invasion force at Boulogne. In return, the British, using their financial resources to subsidize their allies, formed the Third Coalition.

Nelson's crushing victory at the Battle of Trafalgar made Napoléon's planned invasion of Britain impossible. But the newly crowned emperor benefited from his preparations. For more than two years he had trained more than two hundred thousand soldiers organized in seven corps into the finest fighting force in the world. This force formed the core of the Grande Armée and was immediately available to meet the growing Continental threat. Britain had brought Russia, Austria, and Sweden into the new coalition, and though Prussia hesitated to join, the combination already presented a serious threat to France. In August 1805, Napoléon decided on a preemptive strike.

The Austrians, foolishly not waiting for the arrival of the Russians, pushed much of their army deep into Bavaria. In September 1805 Napoléon launched his seven corps under Marshals Bernadotte, Murat, Davout, Ney, Lannes, Marmont, and Soult, racing east. These corps formations were Napoléon's major contribution to the art and science of war. Each represented a self-contained unit, consisting of infantry, cavalry, and artillery, able to fight as a combined-arms team and large enough (thirty to forty thousand men) to engage a larger enemy army, fix it in place, and hold the line until help arrived. In his scheme of maneuver, Napoléon spread these corps out and approached the enemy along several lines, thus increasing the speed his army advanced, compared to the dawdling pace of armies of the ancien régime. Each corps lived off the land to the extent possible and did away with cumbersome baggage trains, and all marched within supporting distance of the others. When one corps made contact, Napoléon expected other corps to march to the sound of the guns. It was this organization that allowed the Grande Armée to advance in sweeping maneuvers that other armies could neither contemplate nor adequately confront. But it represented a system, as with his battlefield tactics, that only superbly trained troops could execute. As attrition ate away at the Grande Armée and his enemies put larger and better-trained armies in the field, Napoléon had to stop employing his army as a rapier and to use it increasingly as a broadsword, to smash his opponents with massed artillery and infantry.

By September 25, the Grande Armée was on the Rhine, with the Austrians under General Karl Mack von Leiberich deployed forward at Ulm. Napoléon had met Mack at Marengo and described him as "a man of the lowest mediocrity I ever saw in my life; he is full of self-sufficiency and conceit, and believes himself equal to anything. He has no talent. I should like to see him opposed someday to one of our good generals." That "good general" was now Napoléon himself. During the Ulm campaign, Mack lived down to Napoléon's expectations. On October 6 and 7, as the French corps were crossing the Danube and racing around Mack's flank, the Austrian general remained focused to the west, blissfully unaware of the jaws closing upon him from the north and east. At the last moment he realized the danger, but rather than retreat to Munich or Vienna, he concentrated his army at Ulm to hold out there until the Russians arrived. For a time Napoléon thought the Austrians were retreating, causing him to deploy the Grande Armée toward the east in the direction of Augsburg and Munich, but on October 12 he realized his error and ordered his forces back on Ulm. After beating off one major Austrian counterattack, Napoléon demanded that Mack surrender his army, which the Austrian promptly did on October 19, 1805. Napoléon had removed an entire army from the military chessboard and cleared the way to Vienna, and the entire campaign had lasted a few weeks. As Napoléon noted later, "I have destroyed the Austrian army by sheer marching."

But the Third Coalition still existed, Austria had other field armies, and the Russians were advancing. Napoléon would not achieve future victories by hard marching but only by hard fighting. After allowing five days to rest and restore the army, Napoléon resumed the march east. The Russian commander, General Mikhail Kutuzov, valuing his army over Vienna, ignored Austrian pleas to defend the city and therefore denied Napoléon his hoped-for decisive victory before the gates of the Austrian capital. Instead, his entry into the capital was hugely assisted through the actions of two of his marshals, Lannes and Murat, who together approached a strongly guarded bridge over the Danube in full dress uniform. Under the watchful eye of the enemy's artillery and hundreds of muskets, the marshals marched onto the bridge and announced that

Napoléon had concluded an armistice with the Austrian govern-ment. Believing it impossible for marshals of France to lie, the Aus-trian commander failed to give any orders as a column of French grenadiers burst forward and rushed to the far side.

After replenishing their food and ammunition from Vienna's de-pots, the French took off in pursuit of the Russians and battered Austrian forces toward Olmütz. This time it was Murat's turn to be bamboozled. When one of the czar's aides approached with a truce offer, the marshal halted the advance guard to send a message to Napoléon. In the meantime, Kutuzov and the Austro-Russian army escaped. A furious Napoléon replied to Murat: "It is impossible for me to find words with which to express my displeasure to you. . . . You are causing me to lose the fruits of a campaign. Break the armi-stice at once and march on the enemy."

Stung, Murat pushed his troops hard in pursuit and fought a sharp battle with Kutusov's rear guard at Schöngrabern. On the same day, Kutuzov's exhausted army settled into Olmütz, forty miles to the northwest. Here he met with reinforcements from Gali-cia accompanied by ten thousand soldiers of the Russian Imperial Guard. Napoléon now began a deception campaign aimed at con-vincing the Russians that they outnumbered the Grande Armée, that the French were at the end of their supply tether, and that he desired a negotiated peace. At the same time, Napoléon hurried his corps toward what he hoped would be the decisive battle of the war. Not all of this deception plan was false. Months of attrition had dwindled the Grande Armée, and it being late in the year, Na-poléon's troops were rapidly exhausting local food as forage for the horses also disappeared. Thus, Napoléon desperately needed a con-clusive battle. The Austro-Russian army obliged.

The two forces met at Austerlitz. The Russians and Austrians brought nearly ninety thousand soldiers to the battlefield, greatly outnumbering Napoléon's slightly more than fifty thousand, al-though forces within supporting distance brought French strength up to seventy-five thousand. To further encourage the coalition army to attack, Napoléon voluntarily surrendered the dominant terrain feature, the Pratzen Heights, and denuded his left flank so as to tempt the coalition, as success there would let the Russians roll up the French flank and place them astride the road to Vienna. That meant the Grande Armée would have no avenue to retreat and would likely disintegrate from cold and starvation. Despite these apparent advantages, Kutuzov remained apprehensive about a major battle that would lose the war in a day. He counseled further retreat, but young Czar Alexander, not quite thirty and with his blood up, overruled his sage advice. The allies formed most of their forces into four columns on the left to attack the apparent French weakness on the right, while General Peter Bagration's smaller force guarded their other flank with the Imperial Guard held in reserve.

Napoléon, who counted on just such a move, concentrated much of his army in concealed positions behind the Pratzen Heights. Here he planned to wait until the allies had committed themselves before launching his forces up the heights to smash the allied center and trap their attack columns in a pincer. The night before the battle Napoléon anxiously wandered through the bitter cold from bivouac to bivouac before snatching a short nap. On the morning of December 2, 1805—the first anniversary of his coronation as emperor— Napoléon rose for battle. A heavy mist hung over the battlefield, hiding Napoléon's sixteen thousand assault troops under Marshal Soult, but making it equally difficult for him to determine when the allies had vacated the Pratzen Heights to assault his right flank. At eight o'clock Napoléon heard the rumble of artillery coming from Telnitz, a small town on his right, and ordered Soult to bring his columns up to the edge of the slopes leading to the heights. There, Soult was to await orders.

In the meantime, the battle raged on the French right, where an overwhelming attack threw the French out of Telnitz and threatened their positions in and around Sokolintz Castle. For a brief moment, the allies were on the edge of victory as the French right threatened to collapse before Napoléon could launch his decisive assault. But salvation came when Marshal Davout with his III Corps arrived to bolster the French right. He had driven his corps hard from Vienna, force-marching seventy-eight miles in forty-six hours. Telnitz fell to the allies at eight-thirty, and by eight forty-five a furious counterattack by Davout had retaken it. The battle to secure Napoléon's right flank remained desperate throughout the morning, but Davout held, while Napoléon was winning the battle elsewhere. Just after eight-thirty the red glow of the sun became visible, the famous *beau soleil d'Austerlitz* (beautiful sun of Austerlitz), and began burning off the mist, first on the Pratzen Heights and then in the valley below. While his own troops remained hidden in the fog, Napoléon watched as a torrent of allied troops marched off the Pratzen and toward his right. Success was now a matter of timing. He asked Soult, "How long will it take you to reach the heights of Pratzen?" Soult replied that he could do it in less than twenty minutes. Satisfied, Napoléon announced: "In that case we can wait another quarter of an hour."

Then with officers and sergeants shouting orders and more than two hundred drums beating the *pass de charge*, the French divisions, under Generals Louis-Vincent-Joseph Le Blond de Saint-Hilaire and Dominique Vandamme, began their ascent. Czar Alexander, now on the Pratzen, had been watching his army's attack on the French right, when his foreign minister pointed at a French force scaling the plateau. The czar asked if he placed their number at two or three battalions and was shocked by the reply: "Several regiments at least, Sire, if not several divisions," and a moment later: "It is an attack by an entire army corps." Alexander exclaimed, "But they came out of a clear sky!" His dejected foreign minister replied: "Your majesty should say rather that they came from hell."

Saint-Hilaire met scant resistance, and on reaching the heights, he wheeled his men, fortified by a triple ration of brandy, to the right, launching them into the rear of the forces attacking Davout. Vandamme met stiffer resistance, but he was one of Napoléon's more brutal and violent generals. Napoléon had supposedly once said that if he had two Vandammes the only solution would be to have one hang the other. He threw his men in with the bayonet and routed the Russians.

Unable to deftly maneuver the ponderous columns still marching toward Davout's hard-pressed troops, Kutuzov began assembling the few remaining troops on the Pratzen for a vicious counterattack. In the meantime, Napoléon sent the corps of Bernadotte, Lannes, and Murat toward the Russian right flank to support Soult and dislodge Bagration. This force proceeded nearly unchecked until it encountered two battalions of the Russian Imperial Guard at the village of Blasowiz. For more than an hour the French attacked at the point of the bayonet, and advanced slowly against Bagration's stubborn troops. The Russians collapsed only when Murat ordered his heavy cavalry to charge double their number. When the opposing lines crashed together, the sound of the impact rose over the din of artillery and musketry. After several minutes of close combat, the allied cavalry gave way and Bagration began an orderly withdrawal.

Back on the Pratzen, Kutuzov had finally mustered enough troops to launch a formidable counterattack. The Russians were no longer fighting for victory but for survival, and it was then that they were at their fiercest. For a considerable time Saint-Hilaire's division bore the brunt of the allied counterattack. At one point, he proposed retiring the division to a more defensible spot, but his subordinates disagreed, one exclaiming: "If we take one pace to the rear, we are done for. . . . We must put our heads down and go at everything in front of us." For nearly two hours successive French volleys held back the Russian counterattacks, until, short of ammunition, Saint-Hilaire sent them forward with the bayonet. This attack routed the Russians on their front, but many more were turning away from Davout and heading back up the Pratzen.

By this time, either Napoléon or Soult had ordered several batteries of artillery forward. These deployed at the edges of the French lines, where infantry masked them. A commander on the scene ordered the cannons filled with both round and grape, and, when informed that this would ruin the guns, he replied, "It will be all right if they last ten minutes." Waiting until the enemy columns were barely a dozen yards away, the French simultaneously unleashed a murderous musket volley and unmasked their cannons, which promptly fired a withering storm into the advancing Russians. "In those terrible shocks whole battalions of them were killed without one man leaving his rank, and their corpses lay in lines in which the battalions had stood."

Before noon Napoléon ordered Soult to turn his corps' advance toward the southwest, directly into the rear of the forces facing Davout. Kutuzov threw in his last reserves, the bulk of the Imperial Guard, but Bernadotte's corps was already moving up to support Vandamme's hard-pressed division on the Pratzen. The guard advanced bravely but uselessly, though at one point their advance appeared threatening enough for Napoléon to order his own guard cavalry forward. Later, when Napoléon viewed the mangled heaps of Russian aristocracy, he remarked, "Many fine ladies will weep tomorrow in St. Petersburg." Witnesses claimed to have seen the czar weep as the center of the Russian line completely collapsed. Napoléon was exultant: "It only remains to reap the rewards of our plans. . . . Forward against the enemy left."

The campaign of 1805 displays Napoléon at the height of his powers and his army at its greatest effectiveness. The emperor had not just won; he had fought a battle of annihilation that battlefield commanders have attempted to replicate for two hundred years. In a hundred days Napoléon had marched his army a thousand miles to defeat the combined forces of Austria and Russia. Entire German provinces were now under French sway, the Holy Roman Empire had finally died, and a cowed Austria agreed to a humiliating peace. France, teetering again on revolution and bankruptcy, greeted the news with delirious celebration, while the Third Coalition's architect, William Pitt, told his niece to "roll up that map; it will not be wanted these ten years."

Napoléon still had hard fighting ahead of him, as the Russians, though battered, were retreating north and determined to continue the struggle. More immediately, though, Prussia, which had sat out the war until now, became sufficiently alarmed by Napoléon's creation of the Confederation of the Rhine (to replace the defunct

Holy Roman Empire) that by July it had joined a Fourth Coalition with Russia, Saxony, and Sweden and then declared war. There have been few strategic blunders in history of such magnitude. By waiting until one ally (Austria) had left the war and another (Russia) was still recoiling and licking its wounds, Prussia had to face Napoléon and the Grande Armée alone. It would do so with an antiquated military system that had not been updated since Frederick the Great's death and a large number of senior generals who should have been put out to pasture decades before.

Caught by surprise by Prussia's ill-thought-out action, Napoléon moved with his customary speed. Gathering his corps deployed throughout the German states, Napoléon caught the Prussians unaware and fatally exposed over a sixty-mile front. On October 14, Napoléon encountered what he thought was the main Prussian army and immediately attacked even though he had fewer than fifty thousand soldiers on the battlefield. By 1:00 P.M. Napoléon could see that the Prussians were staggering and ordered an all-out assault on both flanks. The Prussians crumbled, and their center desperately tried to escape before the French surrounded them.

But the real action occurred to the north at Auerstädt. Here Davout, Napoléon's most competent corps commander, and his III Corps encountered the larger half of the Prussian army. Acting on instinct, Davout attacked. Outnumbered two to one, Davout's well-trained veterans grimly smashed their way through ill-managed Prussian attacks, while inflicting huge losses on their opponents. By 11:00 A.M., Davout's experienced eye could see that the Prussians were wavering, and he ordered his entire corps to switch to the attack. Seeing that all was lost, the indecisive king Frederick William II ordered his army to withdraw. At first Napoléon did not believe Davout had faced and defeated such a large force, telling the first messenger to deliver the news, "Your general must be seeing double." But when he was more fully apprised, he published a bulletin to the entire army saying that Davout and his corps "worked miracles." He also bestowed on Davout the title of Duke of Auerstädt, and throughout the army he became the "Iron Marshal."

The next morning Napoléon launched the Grande Armée in headlong pursuit of the retreating Prussians, who were never given a chance to regroup or stand. On October 25, 1806, Davout marched his exhausted corps into Berlin, and the rest of the scattered Prussian army was run to the ground by the middle of November. Murat reported to the emperor that his pursuit had ended for lack of an enemy. But Napoléon had little opportunity to enjoy his success, as he had to immediately turn to face the Russians. In two bloody battles at Eylau and Friedland the Russians were brought to heel, but at terrible cost to the Grande Armée, which was never qualitatively the same again.

Now Napoléon began to overreach, and by the end of 1807 the French made their first tentative forays into Spain. In early 1808 Murat led 120,000 soldiers to seize Madrid and place Napoléon's brother Joseph on the Spanish throne. Much of Spain then revolted, forcing Napoléon to personally lead an army into Spain in November 1808. By early December he had defeated the Spanish field army and retaken Madrid, and by January he had forced a British army, led by General Sir John Moore, to evacuate Spain by sea. For the moment Napoléon was master of the peninsula. It would not last long, as Wellington was soon on his way to Portugal, and the Spanish insurrection would flare into a brutal guerrilla war that would tie down three hundred thousand French soldiers, at a time when Napoléon was in dire need of their services elsewhere.

More immediately, Napoléon had to deal with a reconstituted Austrian army, which had learned many of the lessons of Ulm and Austerlitz. On April 10, 1809, the Austrians marched into Bavaria. Napoléon reacted quickly and, at the Battle of Eckmühl, heavily defeated the Austrian field army. Napoléon's pursuit soon gained him Vienna for the second time in four years, but the Austrian army remained a potent force on the other side of the Danube. On May 21, the French made their first attempt to cross the river and were roughly handled at the Battle of Aspern-Essling. Both sides suffered more than twenty thousand casualties, but the increasingly effective Austrian artillery made Napoléon's position untenable, and he withdrew his advance guard to Lobau Island in mid-river. For the first time, Napoléon had been defeated in a set-piece battle. The Grande Armée was losing its edge and its opponents were figuring out how to fight in classic Napoleonic style.

Six weeks later, Napoléon tried again. At the Battle of Wagram he won a clear victory, but only after two days of heavy fighting that left the battlefield littered with thirty-seven thousand French dead and wounded and forty thousand Austrian casualties. This time victory was won by the establishment of a "grand battery" of nearly one hundred guns to pound the advancing Austrians on Napoléon's left and center, while Davout's III Corps launched a costly grinding assault on the right. Gone were the days of sweeping operational moves and brilliant battlefield ripostes. In their place were huge columns and massed artillery. Maneuver had been replaced by hard slogging. Napoléon would still win victories, but there would never again be an Austerlitz.

After Wagram there was peace on the European Continent, with the exception of the Iberian Peninsula, for nearly three years. But there was still Britain—the "nation of shopkeepers"—which had not given up the fight, while the "Spanish ulcer" had become an increasing drain on French resources. But by far Napoléon's biggest concern was that the economic blockade he had decreed against Britain—the Continental System—was breaking down, while at the same time the British counterblockade of Europe—the Orders in Council—was causing increasing hardship throughout Europe and particularly France. When Russia abandoned the Continental System, ending its practical usefulness, Napoléon warned the czar that there would be serious consequences if he allowed himself to be drawn any closer to "Perfidious Albion."

Throughout 1811 both Russia and France made preparations for war and by January 1812 they knew it was inevitable. Czar Alexander made good use of the time. After debating various strategies, he decided the best course would be to avoid battle until the Grande Armée had exhausted its strength in Russia's vast expanse. Napoléon, on the other hand, had but one strategic concept: to win another Austerlitz in the first month of the invasion. But this was not the Grande Armée of 1805, capable of rapid movement and marching long distances with only the bare bones of a logistical tail. Moreover, there was not enough food along the road to Moscow to feed the army, a condition exacerbated by the Russians' destruction of everything along the French route of march.

All of this should have been foreseen by a general of Napoléon's ability. The logistical imperatives were clear: If the French failed to catch and destroy the Russian army by the time they reached Vitebsk (one-third of the distance to Moscow), there were two options: turn back or stop and build a massive supply depot at Vitebsk to use for operations the following year. But by now Napoléon was in the grip of megalomania. As Marshal Lannes, mortally wounded in the 1809 campaign, had warned him from his deathbed: "Your ambition is insatiable, it will destroy you; you sacrifice without scruple, without necessity, the men who serve you most faithfully." Lannes's plea fell on deaf ears, as did the protests of his senior officers who advised stopping at Vitebsk.

The Russians made a temporary stand at Smolensk but then resumed their retreat. By this point Alexander was under considerable pressure from his nobles not to surrender any more of "holy Russia" and reappoint General Kutuzov to command. Two weeks later, Kutuzov decided that the French army had exhausted enough of its strength to offer battle at Borodino, seventy miles from Moscow. Napoléon's numbers were down to barely 130,000 effectives and he had fewer guns at his disposal than the Russians (547). The Russians were well dug in, with two great redoubts centering their positions. Napoléon needed to employ all of his tactical genius to overcome the Russian army's stubbornness on the battlefield. Instead, he directed his generals to prepare for a direct frontal assault on the enemy's right and center. This was madness, and a furious Davout begged to take 40,000 men on a night march around the Russian left flank. Napoléon replied: "No! It is too extensive a movement; it would put me too much out of my way." When Davout persisted, Napoléon halted his arguments. A disbelieving Davout muttered about unreasonable prudence from a general who had always gambled.

The resulting battle was a savage affair, as a quarter of a million men bludgeoned themselves into bloody pulps. The French gradually began to overwhelm the Russians, but they gave ground slowly, causing General Armand-Augustin-Louis de Caulaincourt to exclaim to Napoléon's chief of staff: "These Russians let themselves be killed as if they were not human beings at all but machines. . . . They are citadels which only cannonballs can demolish." When cannonball splinters mortally wounded Bagration, Russian morale collapsed and their line gave way. An aide reached Napoléon at this crucial moment, telling him that the Imperial Guard was needed to finish this business. Napoléon exclaimed: "No! I will take good care of that; I will not have that destroyed. I will gain the battle without it." So far from France, Napoléon was loath to risk the one force he would need to get back home in the event of disaster. And it was this caution that finally cost him everything.

The rest of the battle was a confused mêlée, most of it centered on the great redoubt at the Russian center. In furious fighting the redoubt changed hands as whole battalions went forward, only to be torn to pieces within moments. One Russian general, bringing soldiers forward, described the fighting as a "walk into hell." But by 4:00 P.M. Napoléon was master of the battlefield. However, he had not broken the Russian army; it merely retreated to the next ridgeline. The Russians were in disarray, but Napoléon's marshals could see their officers re-forming their lines. Napoléon had by this time come forward, and Napoléon's stepson, Prince Eugène, Ney, and Murat again pleaded with him to send in the guard. Likely appalled by the carnage he had just passed through, Napoléon once more refused.

With that, the battle drew to a close with a long-range artillery bombardment. Napoléon had lost almost thirty-five thousand soldiers, and though the Russians had lost more (forty-four thousand), it was the French who were sixteen hundred miles from home and succor. It was a French victory, but a Pyrrhic one. When the Russians refused to surrender even after the French had entered Moscow, even Napoléon had to accept defeat and begin the trek home. During the long retreat what was left of the Grande Armée was exterminated. Only twenty thousand of the hundreds of thousands of men Napoléon had brought into Russia marched out.

For the next two years Napoléon worked furiously to hold his empire together. He raised new armies that were huge but far inferior in quality to those he previously commanded. At the end he was facing the combined forces of Russia, Austria, Prussia, and Great Britain. Despite the odds Napoléon fought on. He managed to gain some tactical success in Germany, particularly at the Battle of Dresden. But the allied armies had learned all of the lessons Napoléon had imparted over the past decade, and this, coupled with their huge numerical and material superiority, left little doubt of the end result. Wisely, the allies also avoided battle with any force with Napoléon at its head, while they sought out the detached corps of his marshals and began decimating the French army in detail. Finally at Leipzig the allies, with a two-to-one superiority, closed in on Napoléon. In the three-day battle Napoléon lost more than ninety thousand irreplaceable men and was forced to retreat to the French frontier.

In the winter campaign of 1814, Napoléon conducted with just seventy thousand soldiers what many judge as his most brilliant and hopeless campaign. In just six days he fought and won four battles, without making any impression on the strategic outlook. Moreover, he rejected several peace overtures from the allies that would have allowed him to rule a much expanded France. The invading armies took their losses in stride and continued their relentless advance on Paris, which fell in late March. When Napoléon proposed retaking Paris, his army, led by Marshal Ney, mutinied. Bowing to the inevitable, the emperor abdicated, and the allies exiled him to the isle of Elba. Here the former emperor watched developments on the Continent and bided his time. In late February 1815, he escaped and sailed for France with 607 grenadiers of the Old Guard. As he force-marched on Paris, he found the route blocked by the Fifth Line Regiment, sent to arrest him. Approaching the soldiers, Napoléon supposedly threw back his cloak, exposing his chest, and asked, "If there be among you a soldier who desires to kill his general—his Emperor—let him do it now. Here I am!" The soldiers burst into cheers: *"Vive l'Empereur!"* Ney, who had promised his new master, Louis XVIII, that he would bring Napoléon back in a cage, returned his loyalty to Napoléon. The road to both Paris and Waterloo was open.

Wellesley

Unlike Napoléon, Arthur Wellesley gave few early hints that he would become one of the foremost military commanders in history. The fourth son of the First Earl of Mornington, Wellesley was born in 1769 in Dublin, a member of the British aristocracy. Similar to Napoléon's defensiveness about his Corsican origins, Wellesley was self-conscious about his birthplace, supposedly once remarking, "Being born in a stable does not make one a horse." His earliest education was at the Diocesan School at Trim in County Meath. When his father died in 1781, Wellesley and one of his brothers were sent to Eton, while his oldest brother, not yet twenty-one, assumed the role of earl. His three years at Eton were a miserable time, and Wellesley never spoke well of that institution. As the family finances were strained after his father's death, Wellesley was taken out of Eton and moved to the Continent with his mother. As a result of idleness and disinterest, his studies suffered and he had few career prospects. His mother quipped that he was an ugly boy and only "food for the powder." In 1786 he was sent to Pignerol's military academy at Angers, where he mastered French and learned to ride well, but little else.

In contrast, Wellesley's brother Richard, Lord Mornington, was a brilliant scholar, and many marked him as a rising star in British politics. He secured Wellesley's first commission as an ensign in the Seventy-fifth Foot. In an army where officers bought their promotions, Wellesley's rise was meteoric: "Few soldiers have been more favored by fortune. . . . With no opportunity for the display of any kind of talent, he, after entering the army as an ensign at seventeen, became a captain and aide-de-camp to the Lord Lieutenant at twenty-one; Lieutenant Colonel at twenty-four; and Colonel at twenty-six." Wellesley served in several regiments, but only for short periods. Then from late 1787 to early 1793 he was a lieutenant in Ireland. In June 1794 he commanded a regiment and, despite having almost no experience as a proper soldier, he took his troops, the Thirty-third Foot, to join British forces fighting in Belgium. Arriving in Antwerp, the regiment joined the Duke of York's army as it retreated after a stinging defeat at Oudenarde. It was during the retreat that Wellesley had his first taste of combat. Near Boxtel he saw British forces pulling back with the French in close pursuit. He swung the Thirty-third into line across the road and allowed the retreating British to pass through a gap. When they had gone by, he calmly wheeled one of his companies into the gap and halted the pursuit with several well-aimed volleys.

Arthur Wellesley, First Duke of Wellington (*The Collection of the British Library*)

Greatly outnumbered, York continued his retreat until finally re-called to England to become the army's commander in chief. In the field the duke was incompetent, but in his new administrative role he instituted and oversaw the reforms that provided Wellesley with the trained manpower that would ultimately lead to victory in Spain, France, and Belgium. In the meantime, Wellesley endured a retreat of nightmarish proportions. To the end of his days he considered the army's survival a miracle. But seeing firsthand how poor plan-ning, incompetent leadership, and inept management quickly ru-ined an army changed Wellesley. He at least learned "what not to do," and after a brief flirtation with leaving the military, he dedi-cated himself to mastering the intricacies of his profession.

Wellesley did not have a long stay in Britain, as his regiment was ordered to India, arriving in February 1797. It was here that he began to make his military reputation, serving under his brother Richard, Lord Mornington, the new governor-general of India. By this time Wellesley had given up most of what he now saw as frivo-lous pursuits in favor of a regimen that included several hours of study a day. By the time his brother arrived, the Tipu Sultan, "the Tiger of Mysore," in concert with the French, was causing major problems for British rule and trade. Mornington advocated an im-mediate strike at the Tipu's capital and stronghold at Seringapatam. Local army commanders resisted, as they had vivid memories of two appalling campaigns led by Lord Cornwallis that had defeated the Tipu in a previous war. It was Wellesley who finally convinced his brother to postpone an immediate campaign until the proper prepa-rations had been made.

In August 1797, the Thirty-third was transferred to the Madras establishment, where Wellesley assumed preparations for war. He remained in command until February 1799 when General George Harris arrived and assumed control. Harris publicly commented on the excellent state of the army and Wellesley's logistical arrange-ments. Wellesley, as a result of his experiences in the Duke of York's army, had taken to heart the old military adage: "Amateurs talk tactics, professionals talk logistics." The so-called Army of the

Carnatic—some twenty-four thousand strong—marched on February 11, with Wellesley commanding the Indian Nizam auxiliaries to which the Thirty-third was attached. The army first went into action about twenty miles from Seringapatam. Wellesley acquitted himself well, and the Tipu's forces were seen off by steady British musket volleys.

The army arrived outside Seringapatam on April 5 and immediately attacked the enemy's outposts, planning to continue throughout the night. But they had conducted no proper reconnaissance of the route or enemy positions, and as Wellesley led the Thirty-third forward, he was met by a volley and rockets fired by forces waiting behind a ditch. The infantry advanced across the ditch but soon fell into a state of utter disorganization as they blundered through a small forest in the dark. Unable to find his reserves, Wellesley rode back to Harris's headquarters seeking reinforcements. He feared the worst for his regiment but was much heartened to find that, in his absence, the lead battalion had rallied and fallen back on the reserves. Losses were relatively light, though eight soldiers were captured and brutally executed, nails driven into their heads.

Wellesley still had much to learn about battlefield command, and one wonders if he could have remained in command, after making so many elementary mistakes, if his brother had not been the governor-general. The next day, Harris gave him another chance, and Wellesley's soldiers stormed the objective in textbook fashion. For the rest of his career he was to place great emphasis on intelligence and proper reconnaissance. He also learned that just as much thought and effort had to be placed on battlefield preparation as on logistics. This time he had been saved by the training and steadiness of the British soldiers and the ability of his junior officers, but in the future he would have to add his own planning and preparation to that mix.

The British stormed Seringapatam after an extensive artillery bombardment on May 4, 1799. Approximately one hundred men of the "forlorn hopes," fortified by an extra ration of whiskey, led the assault on the breach, which quickly fell. Following columns poured through the breach, making unsparing use of the bayonet. Finding retreat impossible, the Tipu died valiantly near the breach. Wellesley took no part in the assault, as the Thirty-third was in reserve. When Harris departed on May 6, Wellesley remained behind as governor of the newly conquered territories. He would hold this position until November 1802, receiving promotion to brigadier and then major general. His performance in this largely civil rule convinced his brother that Wellesley could make something of himself in the political realm. But Wellesley decided his destiny led elsewhere.

After the fall of the Tipu, only the Maratha Confederacy remained to contest British control of southern India. This confederacy consisted of five major groups that rarely missed an opportunity to fight among themselves, a weakness the British delightedly took advantage of. In June, Wellesley received full control of political affairs in central India as well as military command of all British forces in the region. Peace broke down in the early summer and Britain went to war on August 6, 1803. While Lieutenant General Gerard Lake conducted operations in the north, Wellesley, noting to his second in command, Colonel James Stevenson, that "a long defensive war would ruin us," immediately attacked. His first task was to take one of the great fortresses of India, Ahmednagar. Despite its fearsome appearance and reputation, the fort fell shortly after Wellesley's artillery opened fire. For the Marathas this was a wholly unexpected result, causing one Maratha chief to complain: "These English are strange people. They came here in the morning, surveyed the wall, walked over it, killed the garrison and returned for breakfast."

Wellesley did not tarry at Ahmednagar. As soon as he had gathered whatever supplies the fortress had to offer, he resumed his march. The Maratha armies, commanded by Scindia and the Raja of Berar, awaited him. On paper their numbers were imposing, but their true power lay in a European-trained core of fifteen thousand infantry supported by approximately 120 cannon and a small number of professional cavalry. If this force was defeated, the nearly twenty thousand infantry of lesser quality and thirty to sixty thousand light cavalry were likely to collapse. After two days marching, Wellesley's army was about to make camp, when scouts reported the enemy was a mere six miles away. This was far closer than Wellesley had supposed, and their proximity severely limited the options open to him. He later admitted that the sight of the tens of thousands of warriors spread out on a plain and protected by the Kaitna River gave him a moment's trepidation. But as he considered retreat as perilous as an advance and was loath to surrender the initiative, he attacked with his seven thousand regular infantry, fewer than fifteen hundred of them British, supported by five thousand irregular Mysore and Maratha cavalry. Unwilling to accept the losses he would incur by fording the Kaitna River in the face of the enemy, he used a ford downriver from the enemy encampment.

The Maratha artillery opened a long-range fire as the British approached, but Wellesley at first was unalarmed: "Well! They are making a lot of noise but I do not see anyone hit." That changed as the army began fording the river and the enemy guns found the range. Wellesley had a foretaste of what was coming when a cannonball took off the head of a nearby aide. He had hoped that his sudden move to the left would catch the Maratha army unawares and allow him to strike at an exposed flank, but he and the rest of his officers were shocked to see the enemy force rapidly change face with the same speed and precision as a European force. The Marathas formed with their elite infantry on the right, anchored on the Kaitna, and their lesser infantry and most of their cavalry on the left, anchored on the town of Assaye. The formidable Maratha artillery deployed along the line with a strong concentration of guns around Assaye.

Under heavy fire the British formed two lines of infantry and a third line of cavalry. One British officer remembered the moment: "In the space of less than a mile 100 guns, worked with skill and rapidity, vomited forth death into our feeble ranks." Even as fire wracked their lines the British continued to form: "Not a whisper was heard through the ranks; our nerves were wound up to a proper pitch and everyone seemed to know there was no alternative but death or victory . . . fear would make a man brave." As soon as the British battalions were on line Wellesley ordered the advance, with the Seventy-eighth Highlander Regiment leading the way on the British left. As the highlanders advanced, the Maratha artillery redoubled its fire, blasting large gaps in the advancing line. The British guns fired in support of the infantry, but they were buried under a hail of Maratha fire and quickly silenced. At fifty paces the Seventy-eighth halted, delivered a single devastating volley, leveled their bayonets, and charged. It takes thorough training to instill the discipline required for soldiers to stand and receive a bayonet charge, and the Maratha infantry had yet to achieve that level. Shaken by the volley, the Maratha lines dissolved and headed to the rear before the Seventy-eighth could close with them. For a brief moment the highlanders pursued, but their officers soon got them in hand and reformed them to meet an inevitable counterattack.

At this point, Wellesley, who was in the midst of the fighting, probably considered the day his, but a glance to the north revealed an unfolding disaster for British arms. He had issued orders to the commander of the pickets, leading the Seventy-fourth Regiment under Lieutenant Colonel William Orrok, to move alongside the Seventy-eighth, but to angle his attack so as to avoid the gun concentration around Assaye. Somehow, Orrok had misinterpreted his orders and moved to directly assault and seize Assaye. He marched straight at the massed guns and suffered a terrible slaughter. As the Seventy-fourth reeled, the Maratha light cavalry charged its flanks, inflicting substantial destruction. Only the center managed to form a ragged square behind mounds of dead bodies, but even here the British were shaken. This was the crisis of the battle, and Wellesley galloped north to salvage the situation. But Lieutenant Colonel Patrick Maxwell, waiting with the British cavalry, had seen what Wellesley saw and, on his own initiative, charged with the Nineteenth Light Dragoons, supported by the Fourth Native Cavalry.

Maxwell broke the enemy cavalry and pursued them to the banks of the Juah River, to the left and rear of the Maratha lines. A participant in the battle later remembered: "This was a noble sight, and to the persons in our situation, a most gratifying one. The whole of our line hailed it with a shout of triumph, and, advancing at the double-quick time, charged the enemy reserve, and drove it across the Juah." The remainder of the enemy infantry formed for a last stand along the Juah, but without artillery and with their cavalry fleeing they could not long stand. Maxwell led a cavalry charge into the Indian formation, but when a canister round took off most of his face, the charging dragoons lost heart and fell back. But by this time the Seventy-eighth had re-formed and turned ninety degrees to the north and was grimly approaching the Maratha line. Once again the enemy displayed little interest in meeting the leveled bayonets of the highlanders and broke.

Wellesley had his victory, one gained as much through his leadership and actions as through the courage of his troops. As one officer later commented, "The general was in the thick of the action the whole time, and had a horse killed under him. No man could have shown a better example to the troops than he did. I never saw a man so cool and collected as he was the whole time." In fact, Wellesley actually had three horses killed, one by a pike thrust.

There remained some hard marching and one more lopsided victory at Arguam before the campaign ended. At this point, his brother's time as governor-general was nearly over, and Wellesley realized that without high-level cover he was likely to find his prerogatives severely curtailed. Consequently, in March 1805, Wellesley boarded the HMS *Trident* and sailed for home. He arrived in September of that year, just as Napoléon was cinching the noose around the hapless Austrian army at Ulm.

Within two days of arriving, Wellesley met with an old Dublin acquaintance, Lord Castlereagh, newly appointed secretary of state for War and the Colonies. While waiting in an outside office he met Lord Horatio Nelson, who also had an appointment. Castlereagh was running late, so Nelson entered into a conversation with Wellesley, as he noted: "If I can call it a conversation, for it was almost all on his side, and all about himself, and, really in a style so vain and silly as to surprise and disgust me." When Wellesley hinted that he, too, was a man of repute, Nelson made an excuse and left the room. On discovering with whom he was conversing, Nelson returned a changed man: "All that I thought a charlatan style had vanished and he talked . . . with good sense, and a knowledge of subjects at home and abroad, that surprised me equally and more agreeably than the first part of our interview had done. . . . I don't know that I ever had a conversation that interested me more." The next morning Nelson boarded HMS *Victory* and departed for his own rendezvous with destiny at Trafalgar.

Wellesley did find time, at age thirty-seven, to get married, but the arrangement was never a happy affair. He also entered into politics and was elected to the House of Commons, where he spent much of his time defending brother Richard's performance as governor-general in India. He was appointed chief secretary for Ireland and a privy councillor. Despite his success in politics, Wellesley sought a field command with the army. A fleeting opportunity presented itself to command a brigade as part of an expedition to the Continent in 1806, in support of the Prussians. But Napoléon's victory at Jena–Auerstädt followed by the complete collapse of the Prussian state brought that initiative to a rapid close, and Wellesley returned to politics.

When, in 1807, he learned of an expedition being sent to Denmark, Wellesley stepped down from his positions and assumed command of a brigade. His unit was the first in that country and took part in the siege of Copenhagen, which surrendered after a three-day bombardment. Wellesley's brigade fought only one major action, at Køge on August 29, where it handily defeated an ill-trained Danish relief force and took fifteen hundred prisoners. On September 5, 1807, the Danes sued for peace, giving up their navy stores and navy. The British departed within six weeks, taking with them eighteen ships of the line.

Wellesley, promoted to lieutenant general after the Denmark invasion in April 1808, was given command of nearly ten thousand men formed in the Irish port of Cork. His original orders had been to raid Spanish colonies in South America. But when Napoléon moved to seize the Portuguese fleet as a replacement for what was lost in Denmark, the government decided to intervene against Napoléon in Portugal. It was an easy matter for Wellesley to convince them that his force was the best prepared for the task. After handing over his Irish duties, he discussed the trials ahead with his replacement:

> I [was] thinking of the French that I am going to fight. I have not seen them since the campaign in Flanders, when they were capital soldiers, and a dozen years of victories under Bonaparte must have made them better still. They have besides, it seems a new system of strategy, which has out-maneuvered and overwhelmed all of the armies of Europe. 'Tis enough to make one thoughtful; but no matter: my die is cast, they may overwhelm me, but I don't think they will out-maneuver me. First, because I am not afraid of them, as everyone else seems to be; and secondly, because if what I hear of their system of maneuvers be true, I think it a false one as against steady troops. I suspect the continental armies were more than half beaten before the battle was begun. I, at least, will not be frightened beforehand.

Wellesley sailed on July 12, 1808, and landed in La Coruña, where he began planning active operations. He was not there long when Castlereagh informed him that substantial reinforcements were on the way and that, as the Duke of York considered him too junior for such an important command, first Sir John Moore and then Sir Hew Dalrymple would supersede him when they joined the army. In a stroke Wellesley went from an independent command to third in the pecking order. He assured Castlereagh that he would serve whoever replaced him and would do nothing in the meantime to precipitate any personal quest for glory. In a more candid letter to the Duke of Richmond he wrote: "I hope that I will have beat [General Jean-Andoche] Junot before any of them can arrive and then they can do what they want with me."

Almost immediately he marched south and met a small French

force at Roliça. After a hard fight the French withdrew unmolested. Wellesley received a welcome four thousand reinforcements the next day, but that was a mixed blessing, as Lieutenant General Harry Burrard was on board one of the ships and outranked him. After hearing Wellesley's plan for a further advance, he advised caution and told Wellesley to await reinforcements arriving with Moore. That may have been the plan, but the French also had a vote, for at that moment Junot was already approaching the British camp at Vimeiro with fourteen thousand men. To say that Junot fought a poor battle is an understatement. Wellesley, on the other hand, fought an almost textbook battle that would become his hallmark on other fields in Portugal and Spain. Typical of a French assault, swarms of skirmishers, whose job was to make life miserable for the standing lines of enemy regiments, preceded the main attack. The idea was that they would shake the morale of the enemy regiments, which would then be easy prey for the massed columns of French infantry. Wellesley, however, countered this by sending out his own skirmishers, while keeping the bulk of his infantry on the reverse slopes of hills, protected from enemy fire. The rifle-armed British skirmishers, supported by artillery, made quick work of the French skirmishers, who broke to the rear. The thin British line then advanced, just as the French columns marched.

The "thin red line" of a battalion was only two deep, allowing all four to five hundred muskets to fire. As the British spent more training time on marksmanship than any other army, each volley was devastating. They had also perfected a platoon fire scheme that maintained a continuous fire on the enemy. As the French columns approached, they could hear the shouts of a British officer at the center of the line: "By platoons . . . FIRE!" On the far right a platoon would fire its deadly projectiles and a fraction of a second later the second platoon would fire. And so it went in succession as the command to fire and the deadly blasts rippled down the line. By the time the last platoon had fired the first had reloaded, and the entire process began again. As the French columns advanced, the long British lines were able to drive ahead on the flanks and envelop the

French in a concave formation that poured fire from three sides. Three times the French came on, and three times British fire destroyed their assault in the same manner. After the second attack General Burrard arrived. Taking in the action and results so far, he told Wellesley to finish the fight and did not assume command. It was only after his infantry routed the fourth assault that Wellesley experienced some tense moments. Hoping to completely break the shaken French force, he ordered the Twentieth Light Dragoons to charge. The Twentieth cut their way through the retreating French but exhibited a trait that Wellesley was never able to train out of the British cavalry: overzealousness. When they were checked by fresh infantry and two regiments of French cavalry, their horses were already blown. All they could do was run for safety behind the solid lines of advancing British infantry, leaving a quarter of their troopers dead.

The battle ended when British fire devastated a final French column. By midday the fighting was over and victory complete. Wellesley, claiming the French would not stand, pleaded with Burrard to start an immediate pursuit, saying the British could be in Lisbon in three days. Again the old general demurred and ordered Wellesley to wait for Moore and his reinforcements. Disgusted, Wellesley told his officers that they might as well go hunt partridges. When Dalrymple arrived the next day, August 21, 1808, he also took counsel of his fears and proposed that the army pause and build a supply base. As Wellesley urged offensive action, scouts reported that the French were again advancing. Wellesley's superiors ordered him to the defenses, but the French army turned out to be a general with a small escort carrying a truce offer. Junot, shaken by the severe handling of his army and believing he was now in an impossible position, was offering to surrender. Dalrymple not only welcomed the surrender; he went a step further and offered to evacuate the entire French army back to France on British ships and allowed them to take what they looted from the Portuguese with them.

Wellesley, who took no part in the negotiations, signed the document "The Convention of Cintra," but did so without reading it.

When it was made public in Britain, the backlash was vicious. Luckily for Wellesley, he had written Castlereagh the day after the agreement was signed that he was not at fault and thought the terms overly generous. Still, in November he was recalled along with Dalrymple to face a board of inquiry. Wellesley found himself cleared of all charges and his conduct of operations declared "highly honorable and successful and such as might be expected of a distinguished general at the head of a British army." Neither Dalrymple nor Burrard came off as well, but they were not censured. The army closed ranks to protect its own, while the government withstood the political attacks.

While Wellesley cooled his heels in Britain, the British efforts in Spain collapsed. At first in the months after his departure there was considerable success. A British army under Moore invaded Spain, and Spanish forces followed up their capture of an entire French corps at Bailén with a general offensive that pushed the French back to a few tenuous strongholds near the Pyrenees. But then things fell apart. The Spanish leadership fell out, while British logistics collapsed, stranding the army deep in the Spanish interior. And to ensure that the enemies of France would suffer a proper chastisement, Napoléon arrived with two hundred thousand veterans of the Grande Armée. The poorly trained Spanish army disintegrated under what Churchill called an "avalanche of fire and steel." Madrid soon fell, and Napoléon moved to finish off the British. Moore realized that he did not have the numbers to match the French and on Christmas Day began an epic 250-mile retreat to the coast, where the Royal Navy could carry his army to safety. After a week of hard marching, it became clear that the British could not be forced into battle, and Napoléon returned to Madrid with forty-five thousand soldiers, leaving Soult and Ney to finish the British off. Napoléon then left for France to prepare for war with Austria, while the pursuit continued. Soult caught up to the British in their defensive positions around Corunna, where they were screening the embarkation of the wounded and stores. In the ensuing battle Moore was killed, but the embarkation continued, and by January 18, 1809, the British had made good their escape. The flight to and from Corunna might be judged a necessity and a tactical victory, but strategically it was a disaster. British policy was in ruins.

In Britain, Wellesley sent Castlereagh a memorandum on how, with thirty thousand men, he could reverse the setback, hold Portugal, and support the Spanish. The government, no longer concerned about seniority, approved and sent his nomination as the expedition's commander to the king. It helped that the Duke of York had temporarily resigned from his position as the army's commander in chief over a scandal involving his former mistress and was not in a position to block the assignment.

Wellesley arrived in Lisbon on April 22, 1809, and immediately faced two military problems: Soult was to his north at Porto and Marshal Claude Victor was to his south at Medellín. As the British lacked an effective logistical base, Wellesley decided to attack Soult, the closer of the two, rather than Victor, whose army was in a more threatening position. Leaving twelve thousand men behind to protect Lisbon, Wellesley in early May sent six thousand Portuguese troops, commanded by General William Beresford, on a flanking march to establish a blocking position that would prevent Soult from retreating back upon Victor's force. He then took eighteen thousand British and another eleven thousand Portuguese soldiers to face Soult. Finding his force outnumbered, on the night of May 11, Soult pulled his men across the Douro River, blowing up the bridge and seizing all of the local boats as he crossed.

As Wellesley pondered his next action, he received two pieces of welcome news. His scouts reported a sunken ferry two miles away that could be refloated, and another officer discovered four small boats hidden in the immediate vicinity capable of carrying thirty men each. Wellesley sent two battalions of the King's German Legion to cross at the ferry point. While they marched, he started sending the Third Foot to the far side of the river in the smaller boats, a daring and risky daylight crossing. The first soldiers of the Third Foot to cross occupied an unguarded stone seminary and began fortifying it. More than an hour went by before the French counterattacked, and by that time more than six hundred soldiers had crossed. The British beat off two assaults easily, before anyone thought to awaken Soult and alert him. Rushing to the scene, Soult ordered the nearest brigade to attack the seminary, but this was the unit securing the town of Porto. As soon as the French left the town, the residents rushed every available boat over to Wellesley. Within minutes this makeshift flotilla was ferrying the British into an undefended Porto. With the British across the river in large numbers to his front and the King's German Legion moving onto his flanks, Soult's position became untenable. But with his escape route blocked by Beresford's force, the retreat turned into a rout. The French made their way along goat tracks, where many fell prey to irregulars who nailed the unfortunates to barns. Soult's army eventually made its way to Galicia, but it had lost four thousand men, all of its guns, and its baggage train.

Wellesley now planned to fall on Victor, but lack of funds and supplies forced a halt. While seeing to the efficient running of his logistical system and begging Parliament for funds, he reorganized the brigades into divisions, attached more riflemen to each brigade (for better skirmishing), and integrated a brigade of Portuguese soldiers into each division. In fact, Wellesley, who originally did not expect much from the Portuguese, found himself impressed by their courage and discipline on the battlefield. The time and expense the British put into building up the Portuguese army proved a sound investment and became a determining, if little noted, factor in Britain's ultimate victory.

When ready, Wellesley marched south to face Victor, who had taken up a defensive position behind the Alberche River. Wellesley had made arrangements to conduct this offensive in coordination with General Gregorio García de la Cuesta, who had received his commission before Wellesley was born. He was the embodiment of what was wrong with a decrepit Spanish army: "old, proud, incompetent, and ailing." In fact, he was an invalid and had to be hoisted onto his horse before battle. Both had agreed to meet near Talavera, where they hoped to engage Victor's army. After the allied advance guard had pushed Victor's screening force back past Talavera, Wellesley and Cuesta agreed to attack the next morning. Dawn found the British standing to, but no movement on the Spanish side of the line. When Wellesley went to investigate, Cuesta calmly explained that the Spanish were too tired to fight that day. A furious Wellesley held his temper and persuaded the Spaniard to attack the next day.

Victor slipped away during the night, and in the morning Cuesta took off in pursuit. Wellesley did not follow, as the Spanish had delivered none of the supplies promised to him and his army was in want of everything. He was considering retreating into Portugal, when Cuesta's army came running back, as the reinforced French, now with King Joseph in command, had attacked. Wellesley was forced to throw two divisions forward to cover the Spanish retreat. As the French approached on July 27, the Anglo-Portuguese force held strong defensive positions on the left (north) side of the line, while the Spanish held wooded ground on the right with their flank anchored on the Talavera and the Tagus River. Napoleon's brother Jérôme and Victor had forty-six thousand troops, most of them facing the British.

Victor decided on a night attack, before his entire force had come up and pushed a division onto Medellín Hill, which dominated the British position. In the darkness, General Rowland Hill had placed his division in the wrong position and left the hill practically undefended. Hill saw the French massing on the hill, and, believing they were British troops, he rode over to greet their commander. A French soldier greeted the British general and attempted to drag him from his horse. As Hill spun away, one of his aides was killed and his own horse wounded. Hill raced back, formed a brigade into assault columns, and charged the hill, which they retook in a confused fight. Wellesley arrived in the midst of the fighting, congratulated Hill on his initiative, and went to sleep wrapped only in his riding cloak. The next morning he rose to meet the entire French army.

At 5:00 A.M. the French began an eighty-gun bombardment.

Where the fire was heaviest, Wellesley had his men march to the reverse slope of the hills and lie down, allowing most of the cannon fire to pass harmlessly overhead. As his skirmishers fell back, Wellesley could see three huge divisional columns, sixty men across and twenty-four deep, emerging out of the smoke. It was a grand and terrifying spectacle that greeted Wellesley's regiments as they rose and marched back over the ridgeline. Silently the British waited, letting the enemy approach to a point where their volleys would be most effective. Once again the commands were shouted out all along the British line: "Raise! . . . Level! . . . Fire!" The leading French soldiers fell . . . those behind them fell . . . and the columns began to fall apart. French officers tried to deploy their men on line, but it proved futile as thousands of musket rounds smashed into the reeling French. The British went forward with the bayonet, and the French ran in disorder.

Only on the far left of the line was there trouble. Here Wellesley had to throw his cavalry against a flanking column. Though the cavalry halted the French advance, their losses were grievous, largely because they, once again, pursued the French too far and ran into French reserves. By dusk it was clear that the French assault had failed, and Joseph led the defeated army away during the night. Wellesley had won a major victory against superior numbers, but his losses had been heavy, approximately five thousand for the British and more than seven thousand for the French. After the battle his intent was to march on Madrid, but intelligence warned that Soult, with a large force, was in his rear. As Cuesta was uncooperative and his supplies had dwindled to nearly nonexistent, Wellesley had no choice but to retreat back into Portugal.

By the time he returned to Lisbon, Wellesley knew that Napoléon had been victorious at Wagram and the Austrians had left the war. That meant that in the following year the French would dedicate their substantial military resources to Iberia. Wellesley also knew that political squabbling in Britain meant few reinforcements and that he would have to beg for the bare minimum of resources and money. Thus, he redoubled efforts to enlarge and improve the Portuguese army, while ordering construction of a series of fortified lines to protect Lisbon—the Lines of Torres Vedras. These three fortified lines took advantage of every natural terrain feature—a series of trenches, redoubts, and forts that controlled the avenues of approach on Lisbon. He further strengthened these positions by placing strongpoints close enough together to provide supporting and interlocked fires. Almost a year in the making, the Lines of Torres Vedras were as close to impregnable as possible. Wellesley, to hinder the French advance, also stripped the countryside to the north bare of sustenance.

The French came in the spring of 1810 with almost 140,000 troops under the command of one of Napoléon's best marshals, André Masséna. In July they seized the fortresses of Ciudad Rodrigo in Spain and Almeida in Portugal and proceeded to advance on the Torres Vedras lines. Wellesley delayed them with heavy losses to the French at Busaco, but Masséna slipped around his flanks, forcing a British retreat. On October 7, 1810, the British and their Portuguese allies took positions behind the first line of Torres Vedras. A long stalemate ensued, as Masséna managed to feed more than sixty thousand men where Wellesley thought five thousand could not long survive. Though reinforced by a full corps, Masséna was never strong enough to attack the lines. Only through sheer obstinacy did he hold his army in place as long as he did. But plagued by hunger and disease and losing hundreds of men each week to Portuguese and Spanish irregulars, he finally had no choice but to retreat.

By the time they returned to Almeida, the French had lost thirty thousand men, and Wellesley was again on the offensive. After Wellesley defeated him in two more battles, Napoléon replaced the disgraced Masséna with Marshal Auguste de Marmont, about whom the army whispered that his promotion had resulted from friendship and not battlefield performance.

After two long and bloody sieges at Ciudad Rodrigo and Badajoz, where Wellesley cried upon viewing the carnage at the main breach, he was by early June 1812 on the march again. After severing the communications between Soult and Marmont, he marched into Salamanca. He was not there long when Marmont approached. Both armies prepared for battle, but neither opted to close with the other. When Wellesley received criticism for not forcing a fight on the outnumbered French, he forwarded a reply to the government: "The superiority was not so great as to render an action decisive of the result of the campaign in which we should sustain great loss." Later in the same letter he explained further: "Marmont will not risk an action unless he could have an advantage; and I shall certainly not risk one unless I should have an advantage; and matters therefore don't appear likely to be brought to that criterion very soon." What followed was six weeks of maneuvering, where Marmont's superior mobility, thanks to having no supply train, gave him a distinct advantage. Wellesley soon realized he was being placed in a position where he had to either fight or leave Spain.

But then, just a few miles from Salamanca, Marmont made a fatal error. As the French attempted to outflank Wellesley, their lead units marched too fast and opened a gap between themselves and those behind. Marmont was about to give orders to close the gap when a cannon shot mangled his left arm. Wellesley did not miss the error, shouting, "By God, they are extending their line; order my horses." He rode straight to his brother-in-law, General Edward "Ned" Pakenham, and, pointing at the gap, exclaimed: "Ned d'ye see those fellows there on the hill. Throw your division into column; at them, and drive them to the devil." Wellesley then rode along the line, ordering each division in succession to advance, aiming at the exposed flank of the French line. The French left wing collapsed under the fire of six thousand muskets and a bayonet charge. The British assault rolled on, striking another French division that had formed a square because of the presence of British cavalry. A square had its purposes on the battlefield, but fighting off an infantry assault was not among them. Another French division was soon wrecked. As they fled, the British cavalry rode them down. The French commander tried to restore his flank with one division while ordering another to counterattack. The counterattack failed for the same reasons the French so often failed against Wellesley's troops. A French column advanced against an unshaken double line of redcoats and was blasted into oblivion. After this the French retreated, leaving fourteen thousand men and twenty guns on the battlefield, a loss that could have been much greater if the force sent to cut off their retreat had not abandoned its position.

Wellesley, whom the French already viewed as an excellent defensive general, had demonstrated his capacity in attacking, as well. General Maximilien Foy, a French division commander at Salamanca, noted in his diary six days after the battle: "This battle is the most cleverly fought, the largest in scale, the most important in results, of any that the English have won in recent times. It brings up [Wellesley's] reputation almost to the level of Marlborough. Up to this day we knew his prudence, his eye for choosing a position, and his skill with which he used them. But at Salamanca he had shown himself a great and able master of maneuvering. He kept his dispositions hidden nearly the whole day; he allowed us to develop our movement before he pronounced his own; he played a close game: he utilized the 'oblique order' in the style of Frederick the Great." After the battle, Wellesley entered Madrid and briefly held the city. But when Marmont and Soult unified their commands, he found himself so greatly outnumbered that he had to retreat back almost to the Portuguese border.

In 1813, taking advantage of the weakening of the French army in Spain to make up for the catastrophic losses in Russia, Wellesley was once again on the offensive. This time he had more than 120,000 troops, nearly 54,000 of whom were British, a truly formidable force. After moving his supply base from Portugal to Spain's northern coast, he struck at the French lines of communications. As he advanced, the French abandoned Madrid and made for the Franco-Spanish frontier. After a hard march, Wellesley cut them off at Vitoria on June 21, 1813. He divided his army into four columns. Two he directed at the French lines, while he sent the other two marching to the north through what the French considered impassable terrain, to fall on their exposed flank. At first the French fought well, inflicting heavy losses on the allies. But then General Picton's Third

Division struck the French center just as Wellesley's flanking columns were descending on their exposed flank. The French collapsed. Only a stubborn rearguard action prevented a French catastrophe—that and the fact that many of Wellesley's soldiers broke off from the action to loot the treasures of Spain that the French were removing. Wellesley was to complain of their behavior to Lord Bathurst: "We have in the service the scum of the earth as common soldiers."

The battle earned Wellesley a promotion to field marshal and broke French power in Spain. He also received the title of the Duke of Wellington in 1814 in recognition of his accomplishment. Soult, now back in command, managed to hold off the inevitable, but as French fortunes fell everywhere, their battered army streamed back into France with Wellesley on its heels. Soult made a number of defensive stands and even severely mauled several British divisions at Toulouse, but when news arrived of Napoléon's abdication, Soult gave up the fight.

Wellington's long war was over. He had entered Portugal only a "Sepoy general" in 1809, but he was by the end of 1814 the foremost general on the European continent. Only Napoléon's reputation outshone his own. When Napoléon escaped from Elba, Wellington was participating in the Congress of Vienna. When offered command of the forces in the Netherlands, he jumped at the opportunity. Before he departed, the czar told him: "It is for you to save the world again." On April 4, 1815, Wellington arrived in Brussels to prepare his army for the test ahead.

The Waterloo Campaign

As Napoléon began what would be his final campaign, he was faced with one serious problem—his forces were few and his enemies many. A victorious Russian army halted its march home in Poland and reversed course back toward France; the Austrian army was on the march and mobilizing more forces; the Prussians were mobilizing even as their standing forces moved into the Low Countries, where they joined Wellington's forces in Belgium. If he was to have any hope, Napoléon had to defeat both the British and the Prussians before turning his attention to the threat posed by Austria and Russia. By winning a crushing victory against these forces, he would shake the allied coalition's will at its core and remove its British paymaster from the Continent. Such an event would make it possible to negotiate an armistice that would provide at least a temporary breathing space to prepare for further actions. Victory would also rally wavering Frenchmen to his cause, allowing him to consolidate his shaky hold on power.

To accomplish this task, Napoléon assembled a striking army whose quality was on a par with the Grande Armée of 1805. This was accomplished by recruiting tens of thousands of former prisoners of war who were repatriated after the Bourbon restoration. To a degree not seen in a Napoleonic army at least since 1809, the bulk of these soldiers were fanatical supporters of Napoléon and looked askance upon anyone whose loyalty they had reason to question. And that was the crucial weakness of Napoléon's army of 1815— most of its officers had switched their allegiance in 1814 to the Bourbons and then back to Napoléon when he entered Paris. With good reason, the rank and file of Napoléon's army suspected that many of their leaders would not hesitate to switch allegiances again at the first reverse, as many of them later did. The fact that a division commander and his entire staff deserted and joined the Prussians on the eve of battle did little to relieve the soldiers' misgivings. As it has always been, an army that does not have faith in its leadership is a brittle structure, likely to collapse when severely tested.

Still, Napoléon had at his disposal an army capable of maneuvering at speeds comparable to the great marches of the Grande Armée in its prime. Moreover, at forty-six, Napoléon was still mentally in his prime and quite capable of conceiving a military masterstroke— and now he had the instrument with which to execute it. By mid-May Napoléon had decided on his course of action, and by early June preparations were under way for a rapid march north into Belgium to confront the British and Prussians. As Wellington's headquarters in Brussels was a full forty-eight miles from General

Blücher's headquarters in Namur, Napoléon had his opportunity. If he could rapidly march his army in between the two allied forces, he could prevent their juncture and turn first on one and then the other, defeating them in detail. It was a bold plan, one that relied on secrecy, rapid marching, and his opponents reacting at a snail's pace. Napoléon got the first two, but it was the rapidity of Wellington and Blücher's response that brought all of his plans to ruin.

Napoléon began marching his forces toward Charleroi on June 6 and had concentrated five corps there by the fourteenth. Through stringent security measures he had kept this concentration secret until the Prussians of Lieutenant General von Zieten's I Corps could see the French campfires directly across the Sambre River. Zieten was ordered not to engage and to fall back on Fleurus, where Blücher had ordered his other three corps to form. Zieten promptly retreated but neglected to destroy the bridge over the Sambre before pulling back. By noon on the fourteenth Blücher was fully aware of where Napoléon's army was and of its intention. Unfortunately, this information did not reach Wellington until late the following day; though the exact time is much disputed, he surely knew something was up hours before attending the Duchess of Richmond's ball that night. Long before he went to the ball Wellington had issued orders preparing the army to march. What he could not tell them was *where* they were to march to—that answer came during the ball, when Wellington received confirmation that the French had crossed the Sambre and at least one wing of their army was approaching Quatre Bras. With the picture finally filled in, Wellington set his army in motion, and not a moment too soon.

Napoléon crossed the Sambre on the fifteenth and then, inexplicably, veered from his original intent of marching between the two allied armies in favor of a direct assault upon the rapidly concentrating Prussians. His approach was slowed by Zieten, who conducted a masterful rearguard action that continually brought Napoléon's columns to a halt. As Napoléon was no longer marching as he did in his earlier campaigns—with his columns distributed over a wide front— any stop at the head of the column brought his entire army to a halt.

By the time Napoléon's army reached Fleurus, Blücher was waiting just a short distance away at Ligny, with three of his four corps.

Napoléon, moving at a pace that was for him lethargic, spent most of the morning and early afternoon of the sixteenth placing his army on the battlefield. As at Wagram and other late Napoleonic battles, he eschewed maneuver in favor of a vicious and overwhelming assault in the teeth of the Prussian defense. Napoléon might win the day, but his approach ensured a butcher's bill that the fragile French army could no longer endure.

The Fight of Saint-Amand: The Opening Phase

As the church bell at Saint-Amand struck 2:30 P.M., Napoléon ordered a battery of the Imperial Guard to fire three rounds at intervals. Upon hearing the signal, General Vandamme, without reconnoitering his front or softening the Prussian line with artillery, ordered General Étienne Nicolas Lefol's Eighth Division to move on Saint-Amand. Preceded by a swarm of skirmishers and marching in three columns, the French division made slow progress. The men, sweltering in their greatcoats and carrying heavy packs, fought their way through fields of wheat, unable to see what was to their front. Driven by the harangues of their commander and encouraged by a regimental band playing *"La victoire en chantant,"* they stumbled forward. It was not long before Prussian artillery in Saint-Amand opened up on the densely packed French columns, with deadly blasts of chain and canister. Prussian guns on the ridge behind the town fired ball shot with deadly effect, but the French did not waver. Breaking free of the fields, they now met the point-blank fire of three battalions from General Friedrich Jagow's Third Brigade. But even this volley failed to check their charge. For the next quarter hour a vicious house-to-house fight ensued, until the Prussians broke and retreated north to reassemble behind the protection of the Ligny brook.

Lafol's division had already paid a fearful price but continued to press on. As the French debouched from the village, they met a storm of artillery fire from the Prussian grand battery stationed on the slopes to the east of Saint-Amand. Lefol's troops reeled back from the canister, just as the Prussians counterattacked. The shattered French infantry could not hold and the Prussians swept back into Saint-Amand, reoccupying the entire town except for the church. Chagrined, Vandamme ordered General Pierre Berthezène's division to deploy to Lefol's left and advance to his support, while he launched General Jean-Baptiste Girard's division against La Haye just north of Saint-Amand.

So opened the first of three battles that made up the Waterloo campaign. In this first fight, Napoléon, demonstrating a lack of respect for his enemies, aimed to bludgeon the Prussians out of existence. What he failed to consider was the fierce hatred the Prussians had for the French—who had humiliated them at Jena–Auerstädt—and the fighting spirit of their aged commander, Gebhard Leberecht von Blücher, nicknamed Marschall Vorwärts ("Marshal Forward") by his soldiers. Blücher had significantly improved his odds by concentrating his soldiers in the many small towns and villages that dotted the area. Thus, all they had to do was hold at every wall and inside every building, without trying to outmaneuver the French. If the Prussian dispositions had any weakness, it was the deployment of too many troops on the forward slopes of hills, where they were easy fodder for Napoléon's artillery. Blücher also felt General Friedrich Wilhelm Freiherr von Bülow's missing IV Corps, which—due to communications errors and Bülow's intentional obtuseness—was slow to arrive. If Bülow's corps had been at Ligny, there was a chance the Prussians would have had sufficient strength to hold Napoléon there, until Wellington and the British came to their aid.

Napoléon had delayed his assault until he heard the cannons at Quatre Bras, which informed him that Ney was attacking the British and his flank was secure. His basic plan was simple: He would either hold the Prussians in place until Ney sent the British reeling backward, whereupon he would turn his army ninety degrees east and march it into the Prussian rear; or, if the Prussians broke, Napoléon planned to sweep them aside before marching into the British rear, trapping Wellington between himself and Ney. In the actual event, the Prussians proved incredibly difficult to push aside and the British impossible.

At 3:00 P.M. three French divisions renewed their attack on Saint-Amand, just as Napoléon opened up a ferocious assault on the nearby town of Ligny, a mile northwest. The Prussians, outnumbered, fought like men possessed, but eventually the renowned "French fury" began to tell. The Prussians inched backward, incurring but also inflicting heavy losses for each yard they gave up. After an hour of bloody close-quarters combat, the Prussian force was nearing disintegration. When the French began moving past their flank into their rear, the Prussians gave up the town, leaving forty-six officers and twenty-six hundred men as a testament to their resistance. One brigade had held off Vandamme's corps for two hours—no small feat, considering Napoléon once said of his general that if he were attacking Lucifer's forces in hell, he would place Vandamme in the vanguard.

Blücher, who had been absorbed in the near-simultaneous fight in Ligny, now turned his attention to the mushrooming disaster on his right. Saint-Amand had fallen, along with La Haye. He could clearly see Vandamme's guns moving forward and the French lines re-forming. In a few more minutes the French would storm the Sombref–Bry Ridge and place themselves in the rear of the hard-pressed Prussian center. Vandamme, whose division had in 1805 led the French assault on the Pratzen Heights that smashed the Austro-Russian center at Austerlitz, was about to repeat that performance.

The Fight for Ligny

A quarter hour after Vandamme ordered the start of the attack on Saint-Amand, the mass of French artillery opened fire on Ligny and the exposed Prussians on the slope behind the town. Under cover of this fire General Etienne-Maurice Gérard's IV Corps assaulted Ligny. Approximately ten thousand French soldiers, with regimental bands blaring and the troops at a feverish pitch of excitement shouting *"Vive l'Empereur,"* went forward against well-prepared Prussian positions. The Prussians stood motionless, biding their time behind stone walls, inside stout buildings, and behind banked hedges. To their front, skirmishers were already taking a toll on the French columns. Still, the veteran French troops came on. When the French approached the Prussian main line, they were staggered by the impact of massed volleys. Only the demands of their officers got them moving again. But the hail of fire from Ligny and the Prussian artillery beyond proved too much, and the left and right columns recoiled. Only the center column, where the Thirtieth Regiment of the Line found a hollow road that afforded some protection, was able to form a line and charge into the town, getting as far as the church square. Here the Thirtieth halted, surrounded on three sides, and was virtually annihilated in a murderous cross fire.

The French re-formed and came on again, and then a third time. Napoléon, hoping to break the stalemate, sent forward several gun batteries from the Imperial Guard. Unlimbering less than four hundred paces from the Prussian positions, the guard artillery opened fire with devastating effect. Observing the fight from several hundred yards off, Carl von Clausewitz, the great theoretician of war, was certain from the volume of fire that every Prussian in Ligny had been hit: "Cannon balls shattered houses and ricocheted in the streets, the thatched roofs took fire and fell in; the conflagration burst out in ten different points at once." For the fourth time, the French stormed forward, as each side "slaughtered each other as if they were impelled by a deep personal hatred." A French officer recalled: "Prussian bullets swept us away by the dozen, but it was a thousand times worse in the houses." Each side fed battalions into the fight. The French even brought two guns into the church courtyard, where they "pulverized three battalions," before being lost. One French officer claimed, "The dead were piled in the streets three deep. In the main street the mud was red with blood and composed of crushed bones and flesh." Eventually, the Prussians gave way to superior French numbers and firepower. But they did not collapse. Rather, they fell back slowly, contesting every house and every room. By 5:00 P.M. the French held most of the town but could advance no farther. The Prussian center was holding, despite losses in the thousands.

Saint-Amand: The Closing Phase

Blücher understood that the situation at Saint-Amand could be relieved only by a powerful and immediate counterattack. Departing from Ligny, while that battle was still raging, he ordered a nearby brigade to attack. Advancing in eight concentrated columns in two lines, the Prussian brigade made a glorious spectacle as well as an inviting target for the French artillery. Saint-Amand changed hands again, leading to another French assault on the town. For the next three hours each side attacked and counterattacked, with Blücher himself leading one of the charges. At about five-thirty Napoléon decided it was time to finish the job and ordered the Imperial Guard forward. At that moment, the approach of an apparently large force on the French left appeared to destroy all of the emperor's calculations. Napoléon at first wondered if these forces were either Ney's from Quatre Bras or General Jean-Baptiste Drouet d'Erlon's corps finally arriving on the battlefield. But either of those forces should have been marching into the rear of the Prussian army and not into his own rear. He halted his own attack and sent an aide to determine the intent of the approaching troops.

In fact it was d'Erlon's I Corps, which had been marching to Ney's support at Quatre Bras when one of Napoléon's aides had ordered them to march to Ligny. D'Erlon sent a message to Ney that he would not be coming and turned his corps toward Ligny. He had almost arrived on the battlefield when one of Ney's messengers caught up to him with orders from Ney, explaining the critical situation Ney was facing and ordering his return to Quatre Bras. D'Erlon turned away and marched toward Ney's force, arriving after the fighting there had ceased. Remarkably, one of Napoléon's most powerful corps had marched and countermarched all day without affecting either battle.

At approximately the same time, Blücher received word from Wellington that he was heavily engaged at Quatre Bras and could not go to his assistance. Upon learning this, Blücher decided to launch his own counterattack upon the French left. The Prussians advanced bravely, but Napoléon still had fresh regiments, and as their repeated volleys struck home the attack faltered. Napoléon seized the moment and ordered the guard forward, supported by a corps of cavalry and a battery of sixty guns firing. The exhausted Prussians had no reserves and were running out of ammunition. Still, they put up a spirited fight, but the guard was soon through Ligny and forming to assault the Prussian artillery batteries on the hill beyond. In desperation Blücher ordered his last remaining cavalry to charge the advancing French. While personally leading one of the regiments forward, Blücher's horse was hit, pinning him to the ground. French cavalry stopped the Prussian attack and then rode right over Blücher without noticing the field marshal. In the gathering darkness a small Prussian assault stumbled upon their stunned commander, placed him on a horse, and led him to safety.

With the center pierced, the Prussians could no longer remain on the field. But instead of retreating toward the Rhine and Prussia, the three French corps slowly fell back toward Tilly, taking almost all of their guns and supply trains with them. By retreating north rather than east, Blücher's chief of staff and now temporary army commander, Lieutenant General August von Gneisenau, fatefully kept the Prussians within supporting distance of Wellington's army. As the army fell back, it came upon Bülow's IV Corps, which had prepared a strong position behind which the army could re-form and continue the struggle.

Napoléon had thrown the Prussians back, but, though severely damaged, the Prussian army had come off in good order. Given even a short recuperation period, it would be able to rejoin the fight. Napoléon's listlessness undoubtedly contributed to the mistakes that he now made. Worn out by the tension of battle and the heat, he retired to a nearby château to rest without giving any orders to his various corps commanders. He failed to send Marshal Grouchy with his thirty-three thousand men in pursuit of the Prussians until the next morning. Grouchy's mission was to either harry the Prussians to destruction or, failing that, to make sure they did not re-enter the fray as Napoléon marched to finish the British. He failed at both.

Quatre Bras

As Napoléon had formed his force to attack Ligny, he had dispatched Marshal Ney to the crucial crossroad town of Quatre Bras. If the French seized it, Ney would be free to march east and into the rear of the Prussian army, ensuring its destruction. Even by contesting it, Ney could keep the British and Prussian forces from concentrating and provide Napoléon time to defeat the Prussians. Similarly, if the British had an uncontested hold on the small crossroads town, they would have just as easily been able to march into Napoléon's rear, while he was locked in the deadly embrace of the Prussians. That the British held the town had much to do with the initiative of the local commander and little with Wellington. Once he discovered that the French were on the march, Wellington had issued orders for his scattered divisions to concentrate at Nivelles, west of Quatre Bras. If they had done so, Quatre Bras would have remained undefended, and Napoléon would have realized one of his primary objectives— splitting the Anglo-Prussian armies. Realizing the enormity of the error, Major General Jean Victor de Constant Rebecque, chief of staff to the Prince of Orange, on his own initiative, ordered the Second Dutch Division to reinforce the brigade commanded by Prince Bernhard of Saxe-Weimar-Eisenach and hold the crossroads at all hazards.

Wellington also received unexpected aid from Ney himself. Ney had caught up with the army only after the campaign was under way, and Napoléon had given him command of the left wing without fully informing him of his plan of operations. As such Ney had no idea of the importance Napoléon placed in seizing Quatre Bras as quickly as possible. Ney had joined his two corps while they were on the march, just as General Honoré Charles Reille's II Corps was approaching Quatre Bras. Finding the crossroads heavily posted and with darkness falling, Reille's vanguard pulled back and bivouacked for the night. With d'Erlon's I Corps still strung out on the road to the rear, Ney was content to let them sleep while he gathered divisional reports. In the morning Ney moved toward Quatre Bras, only to find that its defenders had multiplied to eight thousand infantry supported by sixteen guns. Still, with his twenty thousand men and close to sixty guns, he could have rapidly overrun the Prince of Orange's position. Inexplicably, Ney failed to give the order to immediately do so, allowing Wellington to reinforce the British position throughout the day faster than Ney could bring up fresh forces.

Wellington arrived at Quatre Bras at approximately 10:00 A.M., now fully comprehending the importance of the crossroads. He complimented the Prince of Orange on how well his troops were posted and then, as the French remained inactive, rode east to confer face-to-face with Blücher. Wellington believed he was facing only a few battalions and expected no major engagement at Quatre Bras.

As for the French, Ney did not receive clear orders until a note arrived at 11:00 A.M. from Soult, now acting as Napoléon's chief of staff, ordering him to advance immediately on Quatre Bras and push at elements at least two miles beyond the crossroads. It took another three hours before Reille formed his corps for the assault. His attack commenced at 2:00 P.M., and by 3:00 P.M. it had pushed within musket range of the crossroads. The Dutch troops on the other side were forming for a final stand, when a reinforcing cavalry brigade arrived with the lead elements of General Picton's British division after a twenty-mile force march from Brussels.

It was at this point that Wellington returned from his meeting with Blücher and assumed command. In an attempt to buy time for the British to deploy, the Prince of Orange led two battalions forward in a charge. They had just reached within musket range of the French when a sudden cavalry charge decimated both battalions before they could form a square. Then developed a series of cavalry mêlées of charge and countercharges, in which the French, due to their superior numbers, came off the better. As the Dutch and Belgians fell back, Picton's division went forward along with the Brunswick Corps. The Dutch and the Belgians were a spent force and played no role in the rest of the day's fighting. But they had done their job, holding long enough for Wellington to rush reinforcements forward. Wellington now recognized that he was facing a major French force, and by 3:00 P.M. he had ordered his divisions to concentrate on Quatre Bras. At the same time, his Prussian liaison, Baron von Müffling, warned Blücher that Wellington was in a major fight and could not provide aid to the hard-pressed Prussians.

Picton first advanced the Ninety-fifth Rifles and ordered them to take Thyle on the right of the British line. The British lost the race to the village, but their heavy and accurate fire checked the French advance on that flank. The Twenty-eighth Foot went forward next, but ran into superior French firepower. Behind them Kempt's battalions and Peck's brigades formed on line. Most of the British soldiers were ordered to lie down, making them immune from the worst of the French artillery fire. What galled them were the French skirmishers, who were taking a heavy toll on the officers. Wellington, who had seen much of this kind of fighting in the Peninsula, sent forward his own clouds of skirmishers to contest the ground between the two armies.

As the British received the French assault, Wellington ordered the Duke of Brunswick to take his troops into the Bossu Wood on the right of the line. The Belgian and Dutch troops that had been fighting there for several hours were done in and about to collapse. Brunswick sent several companies into the woods but formed up the mass of his troops just outside the wood line to the right of the British. As there was significant cavalry in the area, the Brunswickers were forced to remain in square formations and, as a result, had to endure grievous losses inflicted by artillery.

An increasingly desperate Marshal Ney threw in whatever formations of Reille's corps were at hand, but the advancing French columns ran right into the long lines of Kempt's and Peck's British brigades. Having learned nothing from six years of fighting in the

Peninsula, the French columns slowly advanced as the British waited patiently. All it took was one devastating volley to send the French columns reeling. Picton's two brigades went forward with the bayonet and routed the French, but the British advanced too far and found themselves in turn thrown back by a French counterattack.

Amid the smoke the fighting became confused. At one point the British Forty-fourth Foot was on line when its skirmishers started screaming, "Cavalry!" The charge was coming directly at the rear of the Forty-fourth, which was also threatened by forces to its front. It was too late to form square, so the Forty-fourth's commander took his only option, ordering the three hundred soldiers in the second rank to face about and bring their muskets to the ready. But their commander did not order them to fire. Rather, he waited for the cavalry to close. When the French were nearly upon them, the shout "Present" echoed across the line and three hundred muskets were leveled. And then, at the last possible moment before the crash . . . "Fire!" Almost the entire French cavalry formation went down.

The Forty-fourth and the Forty-second, known as the Black Watch, suffered serious losses as French artillery and musketry fire pounded them in their vulnerable square formations. Other British formations advanced to support the exposed regiments and inflicted a heavy toll on the French cavalry, who soon gave up the fight. As they did, the squares unfolded and the British regiments returned to the line. By 5:00 P.M. the addition of the Third Division had given the British bare numerical superiority.

It was at this time that Ney realized d'Erlon had marched off toward Ligny and would not be joining the French fight for Quatre Bras. In a final desperate bid to break the British line, Ney launched his last reserve of infantry and François Étienne de Kellermann's cuirassiers against the British right and into Bossu Wood. The Brunswick battalions stood for a while, but, at the end of their tether, they soon broke, their gallant duke killed as he tried to rally them. The French cavalry caught several battalions in line and severely mauled the Sixty-ninth, which became the only unit under Wellington's command ever to lose its colors.

The French, led by Napoléon's brother, Prince Jérôme, pushed past Quatre Bras, forcing Wellington to commit his last reserves, the Ninety-second Highlanders. The timely arrival of General George Cooke's First Division (the Guards) rebalanced the British position. Here also, another British commander employed his own initiative. The Guards had received orders to concentrate at Braine-le-Comte, almost ten miles west of Nivelles. But when Cooke saw other units march past toward Nivelles, he assumed his orders must have been lost and ordered his troops to head west. At Nivelles he received orders to hasten to Quatre Bras and learned he had made the right decision. He then force-marched his men six miles in brutal heat to the crossroads.

On Cooke's arrival, Wellington immediately sent his men into the fight. Moving rapidly from column to line, the Guards went forward to check the French advance and then grimly pushed through Quatre Bras and the Bossu Wood. The French either could not or would not stand, and the British rapidly reestablished their position at Quatre Bras. Massed French artillery and their re-forming infantry halted the British advance at the wood line, as the battle stalemated into skirmishing and long-range firing. A little after 9:00 P.M. the fighting ceased. It had cost the French four thousand casualties and Wellington nearly five thousand, but he had held the field. At approximately eight the next morning, Wellington received news of the Prussian defeat at Ligny. The Iron Duke immediately recognized that his position was untenable. It would have been easy for Ney to have pinned him in place, as Napoléon marched past his left flank and trapped the army. Still, Wellington considered himself secure enough to allow his men to eat breakfast before beginning the long march back to Mont-Saint-Jean, where they would await Napoléon's next move.

The Battle of Waterloo

Through the morning hours of June 17, neither Napoléon's nor Ney's force stirred. In all likelihood the emperor believed he had dealt the Prussians such a beating that they were no longer a concern.

He may have also thought that Wellington, after being beaten at
Quatre Bras and learning of the Prussian defeat, was running headlong for the Channel ports. After sending Grouchy after the Prussians, Napoléon waited for news. But on learning that the British had
made a firm stand at Quatre Bras and were still there, Napoléon
roused his troops for a hard march to swing into the British rear, assuming Ney would hold them in place so he could destroy them. But
in fact, Ney had done no such thing. The French did not get moving
until 2:00 P.M., by which time Wellington's troops had been on the
road for four hours. Napoléon was outraged when he arrived at Quatre Bras and discovered that Ney had neither pinned nor pursued the
retreating foe. Napoléon spurred his cavalry and infantry forward,
hoping to catch up to Wellington's forces on the march, but was
thwarted time and again by the superb handling of the rear guard by
Lord Uxbridge—Wellington's brother-in-law, who had eloped with
Wellington's wife's sister, to the family's disapproval.

Napoléon's pursuit was hampered by violent thunderstorms that
intensified throughout the day and continued until early the next
morning, making sure the soldiers of both armies endured a thoroughly miserable night. Napoléon's vanguard, approaching Mont-
Saint-Jean at about 6:30 P.M., saw Wellington's army arrayed before
it and was greeted by a heavy cannonade. Napoléon was delighted,
as he did not believe the British could long stand, and he was convinced that the Prussians were far off. Later that evening Grouchy
sent word that the Prussians may have sent a force of some thirty
thousand men to Wavre, but that Blücher and the main army were
marching toward Liège and away from Wellington. Grouchy was
wrong in every detail, as the main Prussian force was concentrating
near Wavre, within easy marching distance of Wellington's force.
But his report was sufficient to affirm Napoléon in his intention to
fight a major battle the next day. His adversary was just as determined. At nine-thirty Müffling sent a note to Blücher confirming
that Wellington was not going to retreat before Napoléon and
planned to remain and fight at Mont-Saint-Jean. By midnight

Blücher, fortified by a medicinal mix of garlic and gin, had issued the orders that sent his corps marching to Wellington's rescue at dawn.

Battle of Waterloo
(The Collection of the British Library)

The troops of both sides awakened before sunrise. All were soaked through and shaking with cold. Many of the French, strung out along the roads to the battlefield, were not yet in position, while the glutinous mud made it difficult to position artillery. Thus, despite Napoléon's order to make the first assault by nine o'clock, the battle did not commence until two hours later. Even then the Imperial Guard was just arriving on the battlefield as the first attack went forward. In the daylight Napoléon could see only a portion of Wellington's deployment. The British had positioned some troops and artillery along a low ridge to the front, but most of their troops were deployed behind the ridge where Napoléon's artillery could do them little damage. The British also had the benefit of two strong positions on the battlefield. The first, La Haye Sainte, was occupied by four hundred soldiers of the King's German Legion. They had broken down the wooden gates for use as firewood just hours before they received the order to fortify the position, a task made infinitely harder as they had no tools or materials with which to work. Still, this walled farm sitting just in front of the center of the British line represented a formidable obstacle. Surprisingly, Napoléon placed little importance on seizing this dagger aimed at the heart of Wellington's position until the day was well advanced.

The second position, Hougoumont Farm, stood a few hundred meters in front of the right side of the British line. It, too, was a walled farm complex and, while farther from Wellington's main line, a sunken lane connected it to the troops on the ridge. That allowed Wellington to funnel troops into the fight for Hougoumont throughout the day. It was also blessed with six-foot-thick walls and defended by the veteran soldiers of the Coldstream Guards, along with battalions from Nassau and Hanover, led by Colonel James Macdonell. When, despite these advantages, Müffling voiced doubts that the bastion could hold out, Wellington had a simple reply: "Ah, you don't know Macdonell."

Napoléon issued his final orders at approximately eleven o'clock, and they clearly showed that he had forgone any plans to win by maneuver in favor of bludgeoning his foe into submission. Given that he was commanding the best-quality army he had had since 1805, one can only wonder why he chose this approach to fighting at Waterloo, as if his army consisted primarily of barely trained conscripts. Quite possibly it was not the army he doubted, but its commanders. If so, he had only himself to blame, as he appears to have deliberately gone out of his way to sideline the best battlefield commanders available to him. In an attack reminiscent of the assault on the Pratzen Heights at Austerlitz, Napoléon planned to send d'Erlon's heavily reinforced corps to seize the ridgeline. D'Erlon was an adequate general if well supervised, but, in the person of Marshal Soult, Napoléon had with him one of his finest marshals. This was the man who had led the assault on the Pratzen Heights a decade before and had many times since then proven his worth. But at Waterloo Soult was not given a command. Instead, as Napoléon's chief of staff, he was managing the army's paperwork, a job he was particularly unsuited for. Napoléon had left Marshal Davout, argu- ably the best battlefield commander in the French army, in Paris handling the administrative duties of the empire. How different might the day have been if instead of Grouchy being sent to pursue the Prussians, Napoléon had sent Davout—the man who, with a single corps, wrecked an Austrian field army at Auerstädt. Late in the day, when a desperate Marshal Ney's massive cavalry attacks were failing to break even a single British square, one wonders if Napoléon regretted refusing the services of the dashing Marshal Murat, who had more experience breaking infantry squares than any living commander. Napoléon may have had the best-quality force he had possessed in a long time, but for reasons never adequately ex- plained, he selected the "B" team to lead it.

At 11:30 A.M. Reille's artillery opened fire on Hougoumont. The assault on the château was meant as a diversion but, unfortu- nately, Napoléon's brother Jérôme was commanding the division sent to assault the bastion. Blessed with none of his brother's mili- tary judgment, Jérôme adopted the view that taking Hougoumont was a matter of honor. He first sent in a brigade that rapidly cleared the orchards and woods around the château, but then found itself repulsed as it assaulted Hougoumont's walls. Another brigade went forward, and this one came within a hairbreadth of taking the bas- tion. Approaching the north gate, the French found it improperly secured. Sous-Lieutenant Legros, a giant of a man known through- out his regiment as L'Enfonceur (the Smasher), grabbed an aban- doned ax and smashed away the boards holding the door closed. A large force of French infantry followed him through the gate, and a desperate hand-to-hand struggle took place in the courtyard. The British began retreating into the safety of the farm buildings as more French poured through the open gate. As the British, shooting from windows, poured a deadly fire into the mass of Frenchmen, Macdonell gathered some troops and led them on a charge for the gate. Using rifle butts and bayonets, they forced their way through.

Several of the soldiers continued the hand-to-hand fight as the others pushed the two gate doors closed, holding them just long enough for Macdonell to slam the heavy crossbar into place. The thirty or so French soldiers who had burst into the courtyard, including Legros, were soon killed, and only a young drummer boy was taken prisoner. It had been close, but Hougoumont held. Throughout the day Jérôme would throw more and more of his division into the attack. Far from stopping this folly, Reille, who could easily have bypassed Hougoumont on either side, sent Foy's division and probably other elements of his corps to aid in the assault. Wellington, on the other hand, had employed a single brigade's worth of troops to defend the château. In return for this small expenditure, an entire French corps played no role in the outcome of Waterloo, other than to spend the day and all of its energies in a failed attempt to take a single farm complex.

By failing to put an end to the Hougoumont debacle, Napoléon demonstrated a failure in generalship explained only by the fact that his attention was elsewhere. For even as the fight for Hougoumont raged, Napoléon was overseeing the grand assault by the four divisions of d'Erlon's corps aimed at smashing into the British center and left and then rolling up the entire British line. The assault began with a massive cannonade fired from a small ridge just ahead of the main French line. At 1:30 P.M., sixty-two French guns opened fire. Napoléon counted on this hail of fire to demoralize and possibly even break the British line. Unfortunately for his plans, several factors caused the barrage to fall short of expectation. Most important was the fact that Wellington had placed many of his soldiers on the ridge's reverse slope, thus presenting few targets for the French artillery. Moreover, despite the late start, the ground remained sodden from the previous night's storms. Typically, a cannonball would strike the ground and continue to bounce and roll, destroying flesh and matériel as it traveled a considerable distance. But on this day most of the French cannonballs just dug into the wet earth upon impact. Finally, British leadership, from the noncommissioned officers through to the most senior generals—who displayed a casual

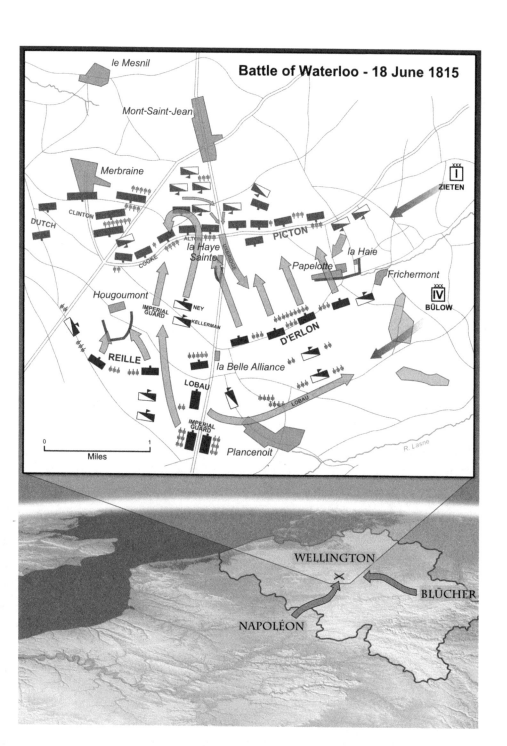

disregard for danger—set an example that did much to help morale, particularly as some cannonballs did find their mark, leaving torn and wrecked bodies in their wake.

As the French artillery pounded at the British line, d'Erlon's corps surged forward. The French troops were at first slowed by the necessity of threading their way through their own artillery. Once they had done so, the French divisions and battalions advanced in an antiquated formation last seen in the early days of the French Revolution. Each of the four divisions' eight battalions was placed on line, with one battalion behind the other. This created a division-sized column that was approximately 150 men wide and 24 deep. The effect of such a formation was to hugely slow the advance without gaining any commensurate firepower advantage at the front. By broadening the width of his columns, d'Erlon forfeited the single advantage of a narrow, deep column—the speed of its approach.

The French assault first hit a Belgian and Dutch brigade that had suffered grievously at Quatre Bras and was posted in front of a hedge that ran along the left half of the British main line. As such, the brigade endured significantly more damage from French artillery than other units, and having already been shaken before the French hit it, the brigade collapsed. But the French columns now veered to the right to avoid the intense fire of the King's German Legion and the deadly accuracy of the Ninety-fifth Rifles stationed at La Haye Sainte and a nearby sandpit. Despite the galling fire, the French columns came steadily on. Though the British had few batteries on the left, they made every shot count. It could hardly be otherwise given the density of the French columns; each discharge blew a gaping hole in the French lines, but the French soldiers merely filled in the space and kept marching. With d'Erlon leading them, drummers beating the *"Pas de Charge,"* and shouts of *"Vive l'Empereur"* rising above the din, the French neared the end of their nearly thousand-yard advance.

Overrunning the hastily abandoned British guns, the French fought their way through an intervening hedge. Seeing Kempt's and Pack's brigades in front of them, they tried to form in line, as Kempt ordered his three regiments to stand and advance. The lead French soldiers delivered a ragged volley, as the British halted . . . presented weapons . . . and fired a volley of their own. The British volley was devastating, dropping the leading French ranks almost to a man. General Picton, taking advantage of the chaos within the French columns, ordered a charge. The British let loose a loud shout and, with bayonets leveled, charged forward. At that instant, a musket ball shattered Picton's skull, and he fell dead from his horse. Farther to the right, other French division columns crested the ridge and ran into the same devastating British fire. Again, the leading ranks of the French columns went down, and the British followed with the bayonet. But this was an unequal struggle, as many of these British regiments had lost as much as a quarter of their numbers at Quatre Bras. Sheer weight of numbers was having an effect, and after the final British reserve—four hundred men of the Ninety-second Foot—made their charge, the British force on the left was spent. French shouts of *"Vive l'Empereur"* reached a crescendo as officers pushed their men forward. The British line was moments from disintegration, when salvation arrived.

From his position on the Heights of Rossomme, opposite Wellington's position, Napoléon could see only the white smoke enveloping the French columns, but it appeared that the smoke was heaviest on top of the ridge, meaning his columns were advancing over the ridge and the British were pulling back. Mounting his horse, Napoléon moved to a better vantage point near La Belle Alliance, where he commented that things were going as he predicted. At 2:00 P.M. the French appeared to be winning the Battle of Waterloo.

But visions of victory soon dissolved. Lord Uxbridge had positioned twenty-five hundred of the best heavy cavalry in the British army, General Edward Somerset's and General William Ponsonby's brigades, in a hollow a few hundred yards behind Picton's division. There they remained hidden from French view until they began their advance. As the French made their final surge, the British infantry opened their ranks to let their onrushing cavalry through.

Shocked at the cavalry bearing down on them, the French had no time to form square. Struck from front and flank, they went from jubilance to despair in an instant. Whole French battalions collapsed, many of the French throwing down their weapons in their rush to escape the slashing cavalry sabers. With horses kicking, the cavalry drove deep into French formation. An infantry soldier witnessing the fight later related:

> Horses' hooves sinking into men's breasts, breaking bones and pressing their bowels. Riders' swords streaming in blood, waving over their heads and descending in deadly vengeance. Stroke follows stroke, like the turning of a flail in the hand of a dexterous thresher; the living stream gushes red from the ghastly wound, spouts in the victor's face, and stains him with brains and blood. There the piercing shrieks and dying groans; here the loud cheering as an exulting army, animating the slayers to deeds of signal vengeance upon a daring foe. Such is the music of the field.

The British cavalry advanced without quarter, breaking each of the French columns in succession. In a matter of minutes the columns that had been on the verge of victory had become a mob with one thought: escape. But then, overcome by the bloodlust and the same lack of discipline that had plagued Wellington's cavalry throughout the Peninsula Campaign, the two brigades continued their charge long past the point where they should have halted and re-formed. Many rushed at the French artillery and began sabering the gunners, while ignoring the pleas of those few officers, including Lord Uxbridge, who knew they had to re-form and retreat. Disordered and flush with victory, the heavy brigade made too tempting a target to ignore, and Napoléon sent regiments of cuirassiers and lancers against them. Realizing they were now overmatched, the heavy cavalry turned to run, but their horses were blown. The French lancers taking advantage of the weariness of their opponent's mounts ran many British cavalrymen to the ground. When the remnants re-formed behind protecting British infantry, both brigades were useless. The cavalry again lived up to Wellington's expectations for both their bravery and their lack of discipline.

Still, they had done their job, as they had smashed d'Erlon's assault. D'Erlon's force would advance later in the day, but they no longer possessed the impetus they had demonstrated in that first attack. Moreover, in a short time they would face a new threat coming out of the woods to their east, for Blücher was as good as his word. Since daybreak the bulk of the Prussian army had been making its best possible time on the difficult march from Wavre. As they marched they heard again and again the voice of their commanding general shouting, "Forward! Forward my children!" As for Grouchy, who was supposed to be keeping the Prussians from joining Wellington, he could hear the cannons roar to the northwest but remained unsure of his course. To one of his corps commanders, General Étienne Maurice Gérard, the course was clear: "Monsieur le Maréchal, it is your duty to march toward the cannon." Grouchy retorted, "My duty is to execute the Emperor's orders, which direct me to follow the Prussians; it would be infringing his commands to follow your advice." Grouchy, by deciding to fight at Wavre and to ignore Napoléon's dictate to always march to the sound of the guns, ended Napoléon's chances for victory. By early afternoon Napoléon could see the lead Prussian columns three miles distant from his right flank. As a first reaction, he ordered Grouchy, who he was certain must be right behind the Prussians, to rejoin the army. Unfortunately, Soult's order to that effect failed to reach Grouchy until 8:00 P.M. By then it was too late.

With the cavalry fight over temporarily, the battle turned again to the artillery. Wellington moved General John Lambert's brigade over to reinforce his left and positioned it behind La Haye Sainte, as the depleted British line re-formed and prepared for d'Erlon to renew his assault. It took d'Erlon until after 4:00 P.M. to re-form his battered corps, and by then the leading Prussians were appearing on the field. To slow their advance Napoléon moved General Georges Mouton, Count of Lobau's VI Corps to his right flank. Napoléon,

Battle of Waterloo from Mont-Saint-Jean
(*The Collection of the British Library*)

demonstrating a rare disinterest in directing the battle, allowed Ney
to direct the next phase. Ney did not have much to work with.
D'Erlon's corps was too shaken to launch an immediate attack,
while on the other flank the assault on Hougoumont was fully absorbing Reille's corps. The only infantry remaining was that of the
Imperial Guard, and Napoléon refused to release it.

The intensity of the French cannonade increased, and Wellington ordered his regiments to pull back a farther hundred yards below
the ridge. This, along with the movement of numerous British ammunition wagons on the road toward Brussels to seek replenish-
ment, convinced Ney that the British were retreating. With no
infantry available, Ney decided he had no choice but to use cavalry
to break the British center. At Eylau, Marshal Murat had saved the
Grande Armée with a massive cavalry charge. But the cavalry available at Waterloo was not as numerous, or as well trained, or even as
well mounted as those at Eylau. Worse, Ney was no Murat. Opting
not to strike at the weakened British left, where the detritus of
d'Erlon's attack and the hedge that ran along the ridge would im-
pede the cavalry's momentum, Ney decided to strike at the center.

Here the French charge would find itself funneled between the strongpoints of Hougoumont and La Hay Sainte to strike at the freshest units Wellington had on the field. Moreover, Wellington could see the cavalry forming and took the opportunity to rush more battalions toward the center and order his units to form squares. He placed them in an almost checkerboard pattern so that each square could volley without putting other squares at risk.

The French cavalry, more than five thousand in number, charged, but the squares stood steady, and the French made little impression. In this kind of combat the bravery of the man counts little; it is the bravery of the horse that matters, and no horse will charge into an unbroken line of bayonets. Thus, the British squares beat off attack after attack. But the French came on again and again, swirling around the squares, looking for any opening through which they could charge. As they rushed past, each square unleashed repeated volleys into the French ranks. Ney was wasting the pride of the French cavalry in fruitless attempts to break the British squares. Why Napoléon allowed this carnage to continue is yet another major unexplained question of the battle. He failed to send his artillery or the fresh troops of the Imperial Old Guard forward to smash the vulnerable squares, even though if there were ever a time to send in the Guard, it was now. With the British infantry not daring to move out of their squares, they would have been easy prey for the grizzled veterans of the Old Guard. But through these crucial hours, the artillery remained impotent on the ridge, and the Guard waited in its serried ranks, menacing but unused.

The British squares were also suffering. For Wellington it was a moment of agony. No commander could enjoy watching his enemy continually pierce his lines. Many of his squares were close to collapse; if the French were to overrun just one, it might have started a cascade that would have led to the collapse of the entire British right flank. As the charges continued and British losses mounted, each casualty was dragged back from the line to the center of the squares, which soon resembled charnel houses. One Guardsman recounted:

During the battle our squares presented a shocking sight. Inside we were nearly suffocated by the smoke and smell of burnt cartridges. It was impossible to move a yard without treading upon a wounded comrade, or upon the bodies of the dead; and the loud groans of the wounded and dying were appalling. At four o'clock our square was a perfect hospital being full of dead, dying, and mutilated soldiers.

For two hours the battle remained at an impasse. The British squares were holding, but barely, while the French losses were mounting and the cavalry, mounts and men, were becoming progressively more exhausted. But then there was a long, thunderous cannonade on the British left. The Prussians had arrived. Two Prussian corps began their advance into the fight. Cheered, Wellington called in troops from both his flanks to strengthen his center. It was now a race against time. After two hours of incessant charges, the French cavalry had had enough. Reille's corps, d'Erlon's corps, and now the cavalry were spent forces. Since the VI Corps was trying to stem the Prussian tide, it, too, was unavailable, and there was still no sign of Grouchy.

By 5:00 P.M. Napoléon was losing the battle, and he had only one hope. The French must break the British center and open the road to Brussels. To accomplish this task Napoléon had only the weakened Imperial Guard, as he had been forced to rush the Young Guard to assist VI Corps in keeping the advancing Prussians out of Plancenoit. The Old Guard had never failed him, and its battalions would have to be enough. Napoléon had not yet made up his mind to release the Guard, when Ney's aide-de-camp came begging for infantry, telling Napoléon that the British center was wavering.

The time to break it was now. Hougoumont's defenders were low on ammunition and were saved only when a brave wagon driver rushed down the ridge and, at full gallop, made it through the gates. Still, it would take time to distribute the ammunition. At nearly the same time the defenders of La Haye Sainte ran out of ammunition, and despite a series of pleas for resupply, none was forthcoming. As elements of d'Erlon's corps burst through the makeshift barriers at the gate, the British abandoned La Haye Sainte. When several battalions advanced to retake it, in line rather than square, the French cavalry massacred them. As a result, French skirmishers gained the ridgeline, and at least one battery of artillery closed within a hundred yards of the vulnerable squares. Ney's practiced eye took it in and decided the British were on the verge of collapse, hence his request to Napoléon. But when the Prussians took Plancenoit, Napoléon's attention moved away from what was happening at the British center. As he rushed troops to face the Prussians, he denied help to Ney.

Bülow's Prussian IV Corps had first struck the French flank at approximately 4:00 P.M., and he steadily committed new regiments to the fight. The Franco-Prussian battle had stalemated in the vicious fight for Plancenoit, which until 8:00 P.M. remained in French hands. But Bülow's steadily reinforced corps was fanning out on the flanks, and its heavy artillery was rolling into position. A few minutes after the hour the hammer blow fell, as Prussian infantry swarmed forward. French courage counted little as overwhelming numbers swept them back. As this was happening, the greater part of Zieten's I Corps arrived on the field. Linking up with the left flank of the British line, they pushed through Frichermont and into d'Erlon's corps. The shaken French stood for a moment, but when they saw catastrophe unfolding in the center, they collapsed.

Napoléon now faced two choices. He could retreat, but his shaken army would likely rout if pressed hard; or, he could take a last desperate gamble for victory. He chose the latter, and the instrument of his intended salvation was the Guard. But by this point Napoléon had only twelve battalions of the Middle and Old Guard, the rest having deployed against the Prussians. He chose to employ ten of these in the attack, leaving a battalion of Grenadiers and one of Chasseurs (light infantry) in reserve. Supported by elements of Reille's and d'Erlon's corps and buoyed by rumors Napoléon had ordered circulated that Grouchy had arrived, the Middle and Old Guard battalions went forward at a steady cadence. Wellington was ready. A French deserter had alerted the British that Napoléon was preparing the Guard and Wellington had ordered more troops to his center, including a Dutch division not yet committed to the fight. As Wellington prepared, the Guard marched. At the start, Napoléon was at its head, but before the Guard crested the last small intervening ridge before the final approach to the British line, he moved aside and gave command of the advance to the intrepid Ney. As the Guard passed, the troops cheered him. The only disconcerted voice was his brother Jérôme's, who said to a nearby general: "Can it be possible that he will not seek death here? Never will he find a more glorious grave!"

Once again, the drummers beat out the *"Pas de Charge,"* the shouts of *"Vive l'Empereur"* echoed again, and the Middle Guard began its ascent of the ridge in four parallel battalion columns. The men overran the British guns, and all they could see were scattered remnants of half-beaten forces. This seemed to be the moment of victory. But British general Peregrine Maitland, who had previously had his brigade lie down, now gave his soldiers the order to stand. The French hesitated, as if seeing an apparition from hell. Where there had been a gap now stood eleven hundred British Guardsmen. Their first crashing volley devastated the Middle Guard's leading ranks. The bayonet followed, and the British charge broke the French columns and sent them reeling down the slope.

By this time, however, three more battalions of the Guard had formed up to the right of this first broken assault, and they now advanced up the ridge. After breaking General Colin Halkett's already heavily damaged brigade as well as several Brunswick and Dutch battalions, the French crested the ridge. The Prince of Orange, with a Nassau battalion and other scattered troops, launched a desperate counterattack, but when he fell wounded the attack disintegrated. It was another moment of crisis, and for the first time that day Wellington was not on the scene to direct events. For a short time General Hussey Vivian's cavalry, using their swords, forced the routed troops to re-form, but this line could not hold.

The moment called for a tested battlefield commander, and General David Hendrik Chassé rose to the occasion. His Third Division of Dutch troops had just formed behind the center and Chassé now ordered them to prepare to charge. Chassé and many of his soldiers had fought in Napoléon's armies for years. He had even fought against Wellington in Spain. They were not strangers to combat, and Napoléon had even nicknamed Chassé *"général baionette"* because of his fondness for closing with the bayonet. As his troops formed into assault columns, Chassé deployed an artillery battery forward. Its repeated volleys of canister at close range tore huge holes in the French columns and brought them to a halt. Chassé then ordered one of his brigades forward, telling it not to fire but to instead close with the bayonet. He then ordered his buglers to blow "storm charge" and the Dutch veterans went forward with a fury. It was too much for the remaining Guard battalions.

Napoléon had a single chance left. Maitland's First Guards had pursued too far, became disorganized, and ran headlong into the columns of the Old Guard coming forward to support the routed Middle Guard. Maitland's troops retreated in some disorder back up the hill from which they had just charged. Napoléon's Guardsmen came on in a steady pursuit that was just slow enough to allow the British to re-form. A prolonged firefight developed, and the British were losing it. They were beginning to step back—a dangerous sign—when Sir John Colborne took the initiative to march the 1,130 men of his Fifty-second Battalion out of line. He ordered his Peninsula veterans to forget their wounded and pivot as if they were a swinging gate to bring the entire battalion onto the flank of the Old Guard's assault. From this vantage point the Fifty-second unleashed a murderous volley and closed with the bayonet. Their charge routed the Guard.

All along the front, there was a pause as those witnessing the Guard's repulse stood in stark fascination, if British, and in horror, if French. Shouts of *"La Garde recule"*—"The Guard retreats"— echoed across the front and the French army began to disintegrate. Wellington waved his hat, the signal for a general advance, and the entire British line went forward. Few French units stood, and those that did died. There was no quarter asked nor given. Only the few reserve battalions of the Guard fell back in some semblance of order, covering Napoléon's escape and trading ground for lives. But sheer numbers eventually crushed them. Prior to their final destruction, British officers offered the commander of one of the Guard regiments, General Étienne Cambronne, the chance to surrender. His supposed response was: *"La garde meurt et ne se rend pas!"* ("The Guard dies and does not surrender!") It makes a fitting story for the end of Napoléon's empire, but witnesses claimed he actually just shouted *Merde!* Cambronne was shot in the face soon after his act of defiance, and the British annihilated his square.

For all practical purposes, though some hard fighting still continued, the Battle of Waterloo was over. While the British were in no condition to pursue until the next morning, the Prussian cavalry rode hard through the night, never allowing the French to stand or re-form, in effect harrying the broken force to death. The battle had been a costly affair, but it was a decisive allied victory that doomed the rebirth of Napoléon's empire. In the end Wellington provided the best summation of the great contest: "They came on in the same old way, and we sent them back in the same old way."

Conclusion

The Battle of Waterloo concluded historian Edward Creasy's list of the most decisive battles in history. It certainly deserved its inclusion, as the battle brought a final end to the Napoleonic Era. As Victor Hugo wrote in *Les Misérables:* "Waterloo is not a battle; it is the changing face of the universe," for nothing afterward was as it was before. Wellington's victory marked Great Britain's passage from one of many European powers to the greatest power of the Industrial Era. As 1815 closed, Great Britain was the world's mightiest economic and military power, bestriding a global empire upon which the "sun never set"—a geopolitical dominance it maintained for a hundred years. Further, the performance of the Prussian army at Ligny and then again at Waterloo sparked a nationalistic surge that was not completed until the close of the German wars of unifi-cation in 1871. As such, a direct line of causation can be drawn from Waterloo to the great world wars that racked the globe in the first half of the last century.

From a military standpoint, the decisive conclusion at Waterloo confirmed military strategists and policy makers in their belief that wars could still be won by a single battle. That is demonstrably true if the losing side has been physically exhausted by two decades of nearly unremitting warfare. This belief was sustained long past the point where it actually remained true. The resilience of modern nation-states would soon make it impossible to conceive of a single triumph, no matter the magnitude, collapsing a major power. But the Battle of Waterloo, having been studied by several generations of military officers, helped instill in Europe's militaries precisely the wrong lessons. Moreover, as Waterloo was won by dint of hard fighting, rather than the brilliant maneuvers witnessed at Austerlitz, future military leaders were convinced that great battles could yield decisive results as long as commanders were willing to endure heavy losses. As such, Waterloo was one stone of the mental edifice that led to the great slaughter in the trenches of World War I between 1914 and 1918.

Grant and Lee

The cannons have long since fallen silent and the armies dispersed, but the Civil War remains the greatest conflict in American history. It was a war dominated by two generals, Ulysses S. Grant and Robert E. Lee, who, between them, determined much of its course. During the century and a half that has passed, Lee has stood as the paradigm for great generalship, a noble cavalier who struggled against insurmountable odds. On the other hand, for much of the first half of the twentieth century, Grant's reputation was in eclipse. After all, he had the numbers and the weight of the North's industrial power and riches on his side. The Union victory was easily explainable: Grant's "bludgeoning tactics" and massive armies had finally overwhelmed Lee in the final great campaigns of the war. But over the past fifty years, Grant's reputation has risen while Lee's has declined, as historians have weighed more coherently and thoroughly the larger issues that the political, strategic, and operational conduct of the war brought in its wake.

The Civil War occurred at one of those crucial breaks in history's tortuous course. It followed two great revolutions that had changed the character of war during the eighteenth century: the French Revolution and the Industrial Revolution. Though having already happened at the time of the Napoleonic conflicts, these two revolutions had yet to make themselves felt on the battlefield, as they would later in the century. While it had been the industrial and financial explosion of the decades before the French Revolutions that had allowed Britain to finance the great coalitions that finally defeated Napoléon, that fact was not necessarily apparent to those alive at the time. Thus, Napoléon's extraordinary battlefield victories—rather than industrial and financial advancements—were what fired the imaginations of nineteenth-century military organizations as they thought about the conduct of future wars. It was the pursuit of decisive Napoleonic victory that in the end misled Lee, while Grant, ever the careful observer of events, followed a different trail that eventually led to the creation of the American way of war.

In the end, the Civil War heralded the emergence of a new form of war, one directly influenced by popular passions and at the same time energized by the extraordinary riches of the new industrialized, mechanized age. The products of that extraordinary revolution would allow the projection of military power over continental distances. The Civil War still brought about massive battles, but none of these would prove decisive by themselves. The era of decisive battles had ended, as the regenerative powers of societies and armies, even in the predominantly agricultural economy of the South, outstripped the damage that could be inflicted in any single battle. In these circumstances, battles served only to influence the course of strategic and political events to the final dénouement at Appomattox.

Background: The Making of a General

Both Grant and Lee descended from families of English immigrants who had arrived in the earliest colonial days. Lee's ancestors numbered among the tidewater aristocracy of Virginia. His father, "Light Horse Harry Lee," had been a hero of the Revolution but had fallen on bad days after the war, winding up in debtor's prison in 1809; his death in 1811 left the family close to destitution. Nevertheless, while his mother struggled in near poverty to raise the precocious boy, Lee was always considered a member of Virginia's aristocracy, which his eventual marriage to Washington's step-great-granddaughter, Mary Custis, solidified. Many viewed Lee's choice of a military career as a reflection of his desire to expunge the shame of his father's bankruptcy and restore the family honor. From Lee's earliest days as a cadet at West Point, he shined in his chosen profession.

Grant's ancestors were more plebeian. The first Grant to arrive in the colonies had emigrated to Massachusetts in the 1640s; thereafter, over the course of generations, the family had moved to Connecticut and onward, ever westward. Grant himself was born in Ohio, but his father eventually settled in Illinois. The owner of a prosperous tannery, Grant's father was relatively well-to-do. But Ulysses despised tanning, and his father responded by securing him an appointment to the military academy at West Point. Only the prospect of traveling across the country led Grant to the academy, an institution he would dislike throughout his four-year stay. In his memoirs he described a year at the military academy as equivalent to "five Ohio years."

Grant's academic performance was mediocre except in mathematics, at which he excelled, and he also had a reputation among his fellow cadets for exceptional horsemanship. During his last two years at the academy, he seems to have preferred reading novels in the library to concentrating on his studies. It was his intention to leave the army as soon as practicable. However, the Mexican War intervened, and that experience provided him with considerable insights into not only his own personality but also those of a number of his future opponents.

In almost every respect, the personalities of these two men could not have been more different. Such differences underline the fact that greatness is entirely idiosyncratic. Both were taciturn, but Lee was considered the brightest of the bright among the small but intimate circle of officers who made up the prewar officer corps of the army. In effect, from his earliest days as an officer, his persona dominated those of his comrades. In the Civil War, Lee would more than live up to his peacetime reputation as a great leader of men. Grant, on the other hand, exhibited little charisma, at least of the peacetime variety that military organizations so love. He was stolid and reserved. His peers respected him, but there was little in his personality that recommended him to his superiors. Lee does not appear to have possessed much of a sense of humor. Grant, at least based on his memoirs, possessed a dry wit. Both generals had outstanding memories and an ability to size up their opponents and subordinates. They were also willing to allow subordinates considerable latitude in following their instructions—what today would be termed mission-oriented orders—with the expectation ,that they would keep the larger goals in mind as they reacted to the unexpected.

In the Mexican War, Grant displayed extraordinary talents of discernment for a mere lieutenant. While his immediate superiors recognized his ability, including his capability as a quartermaster, it was his contemporaries who saw Grant's aptitude for war most clearly. The war, and particularly its commanders, General Zachary Taylor and General Winfield Scott—two extraordinarily different figures, as different as Grant and Lee were eventually to prove—left an indelible impression on the young lieutenant. Grant described Taylor, after whom he clearly modeled himself, in the following terms:

> General Taylor never made any great show or parade, either of uniform or retinue. In dress he was possibly too plain, rarely wearing anything in the field to indicate his rank, or even that he was an officer, but he was known to every soldier in his army, and was respected by all. . . . Taylor was not a conversationalist, but on paper he could put his meaning so plainly that there could be no mistaking it. He knew how to express what he wanted to say in the fewest well-chosen words, but would not sacrifice meaning to the construction of high-sounding words.

In effect that description perfectly fit Grant and his approach to generalship. Even more than Taylor, he possessed the ability to express himself on paper, an ability that makes his dispatches and orders a joy to read. It also explains the clarity and eloquence of his memoirs, which Mark Twain described as the finest piece of English literature in the nineteenth century.

But the postwar army was not to Grant's liking. Not only was its bureaucracy stifling, but Grant soon found himself shipped off to a post in Northern California without his wife, Julia, and young son. There, Grant used his free time trying his hand at a number of unsuccessful businesses, and it was probably at this time that he gained a reputation for not being able to handle alcohol. After leaving the army he continued his quest to become a successful businessman, but each attempt was met with failure. Interestingly, when his farm failed, Grant freed his one slave (who his wife had brought into the marriage) in spite of the considerable sum Grant would have received for selling the young man on the slave markets of Missouri. By 1860, Grant had ended up working as a clerk in his father's dry goods store, a dead-end job with few prospects.

For Lee, a military career had seemed foreordained from birth. He, too, fought with great distinction in the Mexican War, where his performance reflected a willingness to take risks, twice leading small patrols deep behind Mexican lines that enabled Winfield Scott's army commander to outflank the Mexican defenses. This personal risk taking put on display the qualities that Lee would repeatedly demonstrate in leading the Army of Northern Virginia. Lee's performance was so outstanding that he received brevet promotions to major, then lieutenant colonel, and finally colonel during the Mexican War. But in the regular army's peacetime hierarchy, Lee remained a captain of engineers. It was not his rank but his assignments leading up to the Civil War that underlined the trust his superiors placed in him. Such assignments included that of superintendent of the military academy at West Point and second in command of the Second Cavalry Regiment in Texas, commanded by another of the early Civil War's leading generals, Albert Sidney Johnston. In 1859 Lee was in Washington when news came of John Brown's raid on Harpers Ferry. Tasked by President James Buchanan to crush the raiders, Lee led the force of marines, soldiers, and militia that overwhelmed Brown and his followers in three minutes of fighting.

The War's Opening Year

With the election of Abraham Lincoln in the fall of 1860, a great crisis broke upon the United States. In the following months, Southern state after state seceded from the Union, while officers from those states confronted the choice of remaining with the Union and the army that had nurtured them or resigning and joining the new Confederacy's nascent military forces. A few remained, the most famous of whom was to be Major General "Pap" Thomas, a Virginian whose family promptly disowned him not only during the war but until his death. For Lee the choice was even more difficult, because it was clear that Lincoln, at the urging of General Scott, the army's commander, was willing to offer the Virginian a major command. When Virginia responded to the shelling of Fort Sumter by Confederate artillery by voting for secession, Lee decided to take his sword south to join the militia units the governor of Virginia was calling to the colors.

The new president of the Confederacy, Jefferson Davis, welcomed Lee with open arms. Davis was a graduate of West Point and had served as both a senator from Mississippi and secretary of war, so he knew the army's officers well—certainly an initial advantage compared to Lincoln, whose military experience was limited to a few months of service during the Black Hawk War of 1832. But the Confederacy enjoyed a more important advantage at the war's start: With no regular army, the officers who joined the Confederacy found themselves spread throughout the various state militias, where they were able to impart a modicum of training and discipline to the raw levies.

This happened more rarely in the North, because the regular army held on to its officer corps and rarely allowed junior officers to transfer to volunteer regiments. Those officers who had left the service before the war, such as Grant, were free to join the militia units, where their experience proved enormously useful to the few regiments lucky enough to gain them. Where there was no former officer, the chaotic, ill-disciplined regiments that sprang into being—Southern as well as Northern—proved almost unmanageable. In battle, surprisingly few ran away, but those who remained were forced to learn their trade in the unmerciful crucible of combat. Much of the problem lay in the fact that few in either the North or the South, especially the politicians, recognized how difficult it was to discipline and train raw levies straight off the farm or village. The expectation throughout the nation was that those on the other side of the Mason-Dixon Line would simply collapse at the first sight of the militia in blue or gray. But this war, as with all others, turned on more than machismo bravery. In the end, the outcome was determined by organization, discipline, training, and leadership.

Grant initially offered his services to the War Department and then George McClellan, but neither expressed the slightest interest. Eventually, the governor of Illinois offered him command of the Twenty-first Illinois, a particularly fractious and ill-disciplined lot. Their colonel had proven incapable of inculcating discipline and had returned home in disgrace. Grant took command and, as he later noted, "found it very hard work for a few days to bring all the men into anything like subordination; but the great majority favored discipline, and by the application of a little regular army punishment all were reduced to as good discipline as one could ask."

Grant's capacity to make do with what he had and not bother superiors with nonsensical reports and requests led to increasing responsibilities. In early July 1861 he received orders to march in command of several regiments against a small Confederate force under Colonel Thomas Harris, encamped to the south near the village of Florida, Missouri. Grant was anything but delighted with the prospects of his first command:

> As we approached the brow of the hill from which we expected
> we could see Harris' camp, and possibly find his men ready

formed to meet us, my heart kept getting higher and higher until it felt to me as though it was in my throat. I would have given anything then to have been back in Illinois, but I had not the moral courage to halt and consider what to do; I kept right on. When we had reached a point from which the valley below was in full view I halted. The place where Harris had been encamped a few days before was still there and the marks of a recent encampment were plainly visible, but the troops were gone. My heart resumed its place. It occurred to me at once that Harris had been as much afraid of me as I had been of him. This was a view of the question I had never taken before, but it was one that I never forgot afterwards. From that event to the close of the war, I never experienced trepidation upon confronting an enemy, although I always felt more or less anxiety. I never forgot that he had as much reason to fear my forces as I had to fear his. The lesson was valuable.

Thus, the war's first year was a learning experience for Grant. Lee, however, presents a different picture. There is no doubt that he was eager and ready, and he needed few lessons in the art of command, either tactical or operational. Yet, the year 1861 proved as much of a disappointment for him as it did a learning experience for Grant. Named as one of the Confederacy's full generals—the Union army would not even have a lieutenant general until Grant's appointment in February 1864—Lee's first assignment was to lead a group of ill-organized militia regiments and their incompetent commanders to regain the areas of West Virginia that had seceded from Virginia, when that state left the Union. Without proper logistical preparation and outnumbered by equally ill-prepared Union militia regiments, the expedition was a complete failure.

Lee's next assignment was to prepare the seaside defenses of South Carolina and Georgia to withstand Union naval attacks. In this effort, Lee's engineering skills magnified the effects of the Federal government's prewar program of constructing forts. His efforts here played a major strategic role throughout the war, as his strength-

Robert E. Lee
(*Civil War photographs,
1861–1865, Library of
Congress*)

ened fortifications hampered Union amphibious operations and
helped keep open several ports to blockade runners until January
1865. But the role of engineer officer on the Confederacy's coast
was hardly one that Lee had envisaged for himself. Upon returning
to Richmond, he was appointed President Davis's chief military adviser. In that position, Lee filled his time by organizing the construction of fortifications to defend the capital. Such work, however
crucial, did little to endear him to the populace or soldiers, the latter
of whom largely believed that digging was not for them but for
slaves.

1862: The Breakout Year

The new year of 1862 found Grant in command of a force at Pa-
ducah on the Ohio River, poised to move against the Tennessee and
Cumberland Rivers. Here the Confederates had deployed their

forces in a uniquely disadvantageous position. In September 1861, Leonidas Polk had broken a truce that had allowed Kentucky to remain neutral by invading the western portion of the state to seize the city of Columbus, the bluffs of which dominated the Mississippi. Focusing on securing this section of the Mississippi was a flawed approach, as control of Columbus would be useless if Union forces seized control of the rivers to the east that flowed into the Ohio and then into the Mississippi.

The Cumberland and Tennessee Rivers were in fact of far greater importance to the defense of the South's heartland than the Mississippi. By controlling the Cumberland, Union military forces could dominate most of the state of Kentucky as well as the important road and rail center at Nashville, Tennessee, while control of the Tennessee River provided Union gunboats with access deep into Tennessee and all the way through northern Mississippi to Muscle Shoals in northern Alabama. The crucial points that required defending were visible to anyone with a map, but the commander of Confederate troops in the west, Albert Sidney Johnston—who in his short stint in command before a Union bullet found him did little to justify his prewar reputation—had spread the defending forces across too wide an expanse for their numbers. By trying to defend everything, his thin lines proved incapable of defending anything.

The Tennessee and Cumberland Rivers flow parallel for a number of miles almost due north until they reach the Ohio River. Before Confederate troops moved into Kentucky in September 1861, local commanders had constructed two forts in the state of Tennessee: Fort Henry on the Tennessee River and Fort Donelson on the Cumberland. The two forts were supposed to be close enough to be within supporting distance of each other, but what appeared true on a map was not so in practice, as the ground in between them was close to impassable. The Confederates had also constructed Fort Henry in the dry season, so when the fall and winter rains came, it lay largely under water and defenseless. There was a better defensive position farther north in Kentucky, but with so much effort expended on the two forts, the Confederates failed to advance. This was to prove the most significant strategic miscalculation of the war.

Grant was now under Major General Henry Halleck, who in the prewar period had enjoyed a reputation as the army's leading intellectual, having translated the works of the Baron Antoine-Henri Jomini, the French theorist of Napoleonic warfare, into English. For a number of reasons, Halleck became Grant's nemesis throughout the early war. When Grant visited his superior in Saint Louis at the end of 1861, he requested permission to move against Forts Donelson and Henry but was met with a contemptuous dismissal. Several weeks later, however, Halleck received word that his rival in the west, Major General Don Carlos Buell, had begun to move forward against the Confederates in central Tennessee. Desperate not to be seen as falling behind, Halleck authorized Grant, with the support of the navy and its commander, Andrew H. Foote, to move.

Grant was off like a shot. He first moved against the weaker Fort Henry, where the Confederates put up little opposition in the flooded fort. Grant then sent a portion of his force with Foote's ships back down the Tennessee to the Ohio, and then up the Ohio and the Cumberland to strike Fort Donelson from the riverside. Meanwhile, Grant and the majority of what would soon be called the Army of the Tennessee struck across country. The combined force trapped a Confederate garrison of some fifteen thousand soldiers. A Confederate breakout attempt almost broke through, but Grant rallied his somewhat disorganized troops and pushed the rebels back into their starting positions. The next day Grant demanded and got the "unconditional surrender" of the Confederate army. Nearly thirteen thousand Confederate troops surrendered; Grant's losses were slightly more than twenty-five hundred.

Grant's victory was not just a tactical success; it represented the most important strategic success of the war. With one stroke, Grant had opened up the Tennessee and Cumberland Rivers to exploitation by Union naval and ground forces. Within a matter of weeks, Nashville had fallen; Union gunboats had cut the most important east-west railroad in the Confederacy, while ranging up and down both rivers;

and one of the South's most important agricultural areas was now largely under Union control. There was also a significant unintended effect. Thoroughly alarmed by the threat to Tennessee and the Mississippi River valley, Johnston concentrated much of the Confederate strength in the west for a counterblow at Shiloh. But by doing so, he denuded the major port city of New Orleans of its defenders.

One might have thought this success would raise Halleck's estimation of Grant's capabilities. It did, but only in the sense that he made every effort to remove Grant, now a potential rival, from command through a campaign of insinuation and outright lies. The last thing Halleck wanted was a highly competent subordinate who might pose a threat to his position. President Lincoln, however, would have none of it. Grant was the only Union commander who had won a major victory. Thus, when a group of visiting clergymen complained to Lincoln about Grant's supposed drinking problem, the president requested that they obtain the name of the whiskey the general drank so he could send it to his other generals.

Ulysses S. Grant
(*Library of Congress Prints and Photographs Division, Washington, D.C.*)

By late March 1862, Foote's naval craft and army transports had moved the Army of the Tennessee far up the Tennessee River to a hardscrabble farmland on its west side, near Shiloh Church, in preparation for a move against the rail center of Corinth, Mississippi. There, Grant and his division commanders continued whipping their raw volunteer regiments into something that resembled a military force. With perfect hindsight of the battle that was to come, historians have criticized Grant and his subordinates for not fortifying their position. In fact, the real problem was that Union commanders failed to aggressively scout the front of their positions. And when the few patrols that had been sent out reported back that there were strong Confederates to the west, the division commanders, especially William Tecumseh Sherman, refused to believe them until it was almost too late.

The Confederates were hardly better prepared for a major fight. At dawn on April 6, 1862, General Albert Sidney Johnston launched his army against Union forces that had only minutes to prepare for the onslaught. The Confederates came on in three corps, one behind another, so that once engaged they had no ability to redeploy. In a terrible, bloody battle, Grant's soldiers were steadily driven back toward the Tennessee River. In the fierce fighting, Johnston went down, mortally wounded, to die on the battlefield. Throughout combat that first day, Sherman distinguished himself along with Grant, who had initially been downriver consulting with Foote. Once on the field, Grant quickly sized up the situation and took command, bucking up wavering units and, most crucially, building a powerful artillery line along the last ridge before the river. Late in the day, Union troops along this ridge, supported by more than fifty guns and fire from nearby naval gunboats, repulsed the last Confederate attack with heavy loss. Sherman found Grant that night and was going to suggest a withdrawal, but he thought better of it and merely commented that it had indeed been a hard day of fighting. Grant's laconic reply was simply, "Yep, lick 'em tomorrow." And that is precisely what his tired troops, reinforced by soldiers from Buell's army, proceeded to do. When it was all over, the Confederates dragged themselves off the battlefield, but Grant's battered Army of the Tennessee was in no position to pursue. Union casualties were 1,754 killed, 8,408 wounded, and 2,885 captured or missing; Confederate losses were 1,728 killed, 8,012 wounded, and 959 captured. Shiloh was the first terrible killing battle of the Civil War, and it caused an uproar in the North, where the myth that Grant was a butcher of a general received its initial impetus.

In his memoirs Grant put Shiloh in its proper perspective:

> Up to the battle of Shiloh I, as well as thousands of other citizens, believed that the rebellion against the Government would collapse suddenly and soon, if a decisive victory could be gained over any of its armies. Donelson and Henry were such victories. An army of more than 21,000 men was captured or destroyed. . . . But when Confederate armies were collected which not only attempted to hold a line farther south . . . but assumed the offensive and made such a gallant effort to regain what had been lost, then, indeed, I gave up all idea of saving the Union except by complete conquest.

Shiloh was also important because it created the close bond between Grant and Sherman that endured to the end of their lives. Grant could easily have blamed Sherman for the lack of awareness he had displayed before Johnston's attack broke on the Union position. But Grant took full responsibility for allowing his army to be surprised. Sherman was never to forget Grant's loyalty and support, and the resulting partnership would play a crucial role in the war's outcome. In fact, Sherman credited Grant with making possible all of his own personal achievement in the war up to 1864, writing: "I knew wherever I was that you thought of me, and if I got in a tight place you would come if alive."

At this point, Halleck arrived to assume control of Grant's and Buell's armies. With more than one hundred thousand troops, outnumbering the Confederates by a huge margin, Halleck moved his host forward with excruciating slowness and entrenched every night.

Corinth eventually fell, but only after the Confederates had saved their army and pulled out all of the supplies they had concentrated in its depots. In every respect, Halleck had underlined his unsuitability for high command in his pusillanimous campaign. That did not stop him from making every effort to drive Grant from the army. He appointed Grant his second in command with no responsibilities. Disgusted by his treatment as well as the lack of drive Halleck displayed crawling to Corinth, Grant prepared to leave the army. However, Sherman talked him into remaining, at least long enough to see what developed within the Union command structure. Then chance intervened. Lincoln stepped in to appoint Halleck as the overall commander of the Union, with his headquarters in Washington, D.C. Distance made it considerably more difficult for Halleck to interfere with Grant's career. Nevertheless, he would continue to thwart Grant's far more perceptive understanding of the strategic road the Union needed to follow for the next year and a half.

While Grant was making his mark during the early months of 1862, Lee found himself in the uncomfortable position of being Jefferson Davis's military adviser. In that position he provided Thomas "Stonewall" Jackson with considerable support for his devastating campaign against badly led Union armies in the Shenandoah Valley in the spring of 1862. That campaign was to have a direct impact on Lee's operations in front of Richmond in June 1862, as it persuaded the Lincoln administration to prevent Major General Irvin McDowell's corps from moving south to join McClellan in front of Richmond. Nevertheless, Lee had to watch as General Joseph Johnston, rather than himself, contested the Union advance up the York Peninsula toward the Confederate capital. Lee's was an uncomfortable position because Davis was an extraordinarily difficult person, always ready to take umbrage, supremely confident that he was in the right, and rarely willing to take advice. In the honored traditions of American civil-military relations, Lee must be given his due for the forbearance with which he dealt with Davis throughout the war.

McClellan's advance on Richmond proceeded at a snail's pace in spite of the overwhelming strength his Army of the Potomac possessed. McClellan was an overly cautious general who believed his opponents always possessed larger forces, that the enemy was always ready to strike, and that the politicians in Washington, led by that "baboon" Lincoln, aimed to undermine him. In the advance up the York Peninsula, therefore, McClellan took extraordinary steps to ensure that what he believed to be the Confederate superiority in numbers would not result in catastrophe for the Union army—and for his reputation.

Perhaps most important for Grant's future, McClellan played a major role in setting the Army of the Potomac's command culture. The regular army in its worst bureaucratic aspects dominated the army's officer corps to an extent far greater than was true of the other Civil War armies. Thus, a bureaucratic mindset and an unwillingness to act aggressively or display initiative characterized its leadership from the war's beginning through to its end. McClellan did not initially select its corps commanders, whom the Lincoln administration imposed on him, but these old regular army officers soon died on the battlefield or disappeared into retirement. Their replacements came from division and brigade commands, who had been appointed by McClellan and then exhibited the faults and weaknesses of the man who had placed them in their first major commands.

Lee's chance came with the Army of the Potomac on Richmond's doorstep. At the Battle of Seven Pines, Johnston launched a major attack on two Union corps exposed south of the Chickahominy River. The Confederate attack collapsed in considerable confusion, but toward the end of the day, a Union bullet and then a piece of shrapnel struck Johnston, who had ridden forward to discern what was happening. Severely wounded, he would be out of action for nearly half a year. After a general mêlée the next day that added to the casualties, Davis had no choice but to name Lee the commander of the Army of Northern Virginia. Few Confederate officers, much less the rank and file, had much idea of what kind of commander Lee would be. The young Porter Alexander, who would soon rise to command General James Longstreet's artillery, asked one of his superiors whether Lee had the ability to conduct the war against the Northern invaders. The reply from a man who clearly knew Lee was: "If there is one man from either army, Confederate or Federal, head and shoulders above every other in audacity, it is General Lee! His name might be audacity."

Lee immediately prepared to take the offensive. First, he further strengthened Richmond's fortifications. With Jackson having thoroughly bamboozled Union commanders in the Shenandoah Valley, he ordered Stonewall to move his army as rapidly as possible to join up with the main army in front of Richmond. By June 26 everything appeared ready for a devastating Confederate attack. McClellan had divided his army, with one corps, Fitz John Porter's V, north of the Chickahominy, while his other four corps remained south of the river. McClellan's rationale was that Porter needed to be in position north of the river so that McDowell's corps could join it in the latter's move south. But instead of McDowell coming south, it was Jackson and his army who did. Jackson's arrival raised the number of effectives available to Lee to slightly more than 92,000, while McClellan's strength was more than 104,000.

Lee's plan appeared simple enough. His cavalry commander, J.E.B. Stuart, had ridden around the entire Army of the Potomac and discovered the crucial intelligence that only one Union corps was north of the Chickahominy with its flank up in the air. Lee proceeded then to concentrate sixty-five thousand troops north of the river, while leaving a mere twenty-five thousand south of the river to guard Richmond's approaches. His plan called for A. P. Hill's corps to fix General Porter's V Corps's attention to the front, while Jackson smashed into its right flank. Then, Longstreet and D. H. Hill were to follow up to destroy what was left of the Union force.

However bold and perceptive the plan, its execution was woeful. Jackson showed up four hours late, while A. P. Hill had gone ahead with his attack and suffered heavy casualties. Jackson then added to his error by proceeding to bivouac despite the sound of furious fighting to his south. Furthermore, Hill continued to launch attacks straight into the teeth of Porter's defenses, which added to the Confederate casualties. In a tactical sense, the fight at what became known as the Battle of Mechanicsville was a Union success, but the several small Confederate attacks south of the Chickahominy confirmed McClellan in his belief that he was facing overwhelming Confederate numbers. He reported to Washington that the Confederates had two hundred thousand men defending Richmond—a huge overestimation. At this point he decided to change his base of operations from the northern side of the York Peninsula to the southern side. McClellan's nerve was already cracking.

Nothing underlined McClellan's moral collapse better than the events surrounding the fighting at Gaines Mills the next day. Lee proceeded on the basis that his original plan would still work. And it should have. Astonishingly, McClellan, still firmly believing he was outnumbered south of the Chickahominy, provided no substantial reinforcements to Porter. But luckily for the V Corps, for inexplicable reasons, Jackson again failed to show up. Jackson, clearly exhausted from his campaigns in the Shenandoah, was having a few of his worst days of the war. Nevertheless, John Bell Hood's brigade of Texans was able to blow a hole in Porter's lines and drive the V Corps back in something resembling a rout. But darkness fell before the Confederates could destroy Porter's force. Under cover of night the badly shaken Union troops escaped to the southern side of the Chickahominy.

As McClellan began the process of shifting his army and its main logistical base to Harrison's Landing, Lee confronted the conundrum of discerning in which direction the Army of the Potomac would retreat. His initial supposition that McClellan would fall back to White Horse Landing, his current base, proved false. It was perhaps the first mistake Lee would make in the Seven Days Battles. Given that most of the Army of the Potomac was south of the Chickahominy, he should have known better, though, in his defense, he was under the pressure of two days of ferocious fighting. The next major flare-up between the two armies came on June 29 at Savage's Station, a major Union supply depot. McClellan, displaying a notable lack of moral courage, had already ridden south to Harrison's Landing, which was to be his new base. Because he did not trust the senior corps commander on the field, Major General "Bull" Sumner, McClellan had failed to appoint an officer to command in his absence. Thus, the Army of the Potomac would fight without any leadership at the top. Again, Jackson failed to show up when he was expected, but his failure was more than matched when a Union corps pulled out of the line without informing the other two corps commanders on the ground. Luckily, without the presence of Jackson's troops, what could have been a disastrous Union defeat turned into savage skirmishing.

The next day, the Battle of White Oak Swamp turned out much the same way. Jackson for the fourth time had a bad day, and only Longstreet launched a major attack on the disjointed Army of the Potomac, which again was without its commander. However, without support from the division commanders on his flank, Longstreet achieved little. Casualty figures on both sides were virtually the same, but the Army of the Potomac was able to continue its withdrawal to Harrison's Landing without significant disruption.

The final battle of the Seven Days occurred the next day. Finally, Union forces had been able to sort themselves out with a clear field of fire from the slopes of Malvern Hill. Some 250 guns dominated the landscape, all carefully deployed by McClellan's chief of artillery, Henry Hunt. Instead of attempting to outflank the Union, Lee determined to storm its position. The Confederate soldiers faced an impossible task under any circumstance, but sloppy deployments and Jackson's nonappearance led to an even greater slaughter of the attackers. General Hunt's artillery squashed the poorly deployed Southern artillery, while the rebel infantry attacks, sporadic at best, had no chance. Again, McClellan was not present, and when the battle was over, he ordered a retreat from Malvern Hill, to the outrage of a number of his subordinates. In the end, Lee's willingness to throw his troops across the killing ground in front of Malvern Hill reflected two factors: first, his frustration with the failure of his subordinates to act in accordance with his designs, and second—and perhaps most dangerous—a belief that the mere courage of the Confederate soldier could conquer firepower.

In terms of casualty figures, the Army of the Potomac seemed to have the better of the fighting over the Seven Days. Its losses were 15,854, or slightly more than 15 percent of its fighting strength at the outset. The Army of Northern Virginia had suffered 20,204 casualties, or over 22 percent of its force. But war is much more than a totaling up of casualties. At the beginning of June, when Lee assumed command of the Army of Northern Virginia, the Southern cause seemed on the brink of collapse: Forts Donelson and Henry had fallen to Grant, along with control of the Tennessee and Cumberland Rivers; New Orleans was in Union hands; and McClellan's massive Army of the Potomac was at the gates of Richmond. By the end of the Seven Days, Lee had achieved a stunning political and operational success and reversed perceptions in both the North and the South as to how the war was going. Moreover, he had saddled the Army of the Potomac with the belief that there was nothing it could do that would result in victory against Lee and the Army of Northern Virginia.

Some historians have criticized Lee for the heavy casualties his aggressive tactics inflicted on his troops. Yet, in the case of the Seven Days, those casualties were worth the cost, at least in terms of restoring Southern morale. The irony of Lee's success, however, was the fact that it inevitably pushed Lincoln to choose a harsher course in his effort to reunify the country, indirectly leading to the Emancipation Proclamation and a Northern approach to the war that aimed to destroy the Southern economy as well as its way of life.

Thwarted of the decisive, Napoleonic battle he had hoped to inflict on McClellan, Lee turned north. He sent Jackson heading toward Major General John Pope's Union Army of Virginia, which the administration had formed out of various units left behind by McClellan and some that had been withheld from the Peninsula. Lee was clearly thinking of a campaign into Maryland and perhaps even beyond, but he had to take care of Pope first. Jackson moved rapidly around the Army of Virginia's flank and then smashed up the main Union supply depot at Manassas Junction, before disappearing toward the northwest. Pope pursued and eventually found Jackson deployed not far from the old Bull Run battlefield. The Union commander focused entirely on Jackson and missed the increasing threat to his left flank from the just-arrived Longstreet's corps. When Longstreet was ready, Lee ordered him forward in a devastating attack that collapsed the Army of Virginia and ended its short-lived career. In the Second Battle of Bull Run, the Army of Northern Virginia came as close as it ever would to the destruction of a Union army. Pope's army streamed back to Washington, beaten and dispirited, the defeat magnified by the deliberate tardiness with which McClellan had pulled his Army of the Potomac out of the Peninsula.

Lee now overreached. Having won a significant victory at the gates of Washington, he was determined to achieve the decisive victory that would persuade the Northern public that it could not win the war against the South. He divided the Army of Northern Virginia, with Jackson taking half to attack Union troops guarding Harpers Ferry, while Lee took the remainder deep into Maryland on a raiding expedition. He expected that Marylanders would flock to the Confederate colors, while the Army of the Potomac would move with its usual sluggishness. He was wrong on both counts. Confederate sympathizers in Maryland took one look at the bedraggled soldiers of the Army of Northern Virginia and lost their enthusiasm for joining up. More dangerous was the fact that one of Lee's staff officers lost the plan of the campaign, and it found its way into Union hands. Thus McClellan, reconfirmed in command of Union forces defending Washington, moved with unusual dispatch, to foil Lee's plans.

Lee soon recognized that the Army of the Potomac was moving more quickly than he expected, but rather than retreat south he took the risk of concentrating the various pieces of his army at Sharpsburg, Maryland, along Antietam Creek. His decision represented an "audacious" gamble, and it almost resulted in disastrous defeat. On September 17, the Union army attacked, and only because he faced a commander as inept as McClellan did Lee escape. The Battle of Antietam was the worst day in American military history. By the time it was over, 22,717 Americans were killed, wounded, or captured/missing. Nevertheless, despite possessing 40,000 fresh troops, McClellan refused to launch further attacks the next day, and Lee's badly shaken army pulled back into northern Virginia.

At best the battle was a draw, but it had extraordinarily important strategic and political consequences. As it was not an outright defeat, Lincoln could claim a win and issue the Emancipation Proclamation without it looking like an act of desperation. With that act the president made the possibility of a European intervention in the conflict unlikely. He also assured the war would be fought to its bitter conclusion, because the proclamation represented a declaration of war against everything upon which Southern life was built.

1863

For Lee and Grant, 1863 was to see successes as well as disappointments. For Lee, the prelude to the new year had been his devastating victory at Fredericksburg in December 1862. There the Army of the Potomac had attacked the Army of Northern Virginia ensconced along the heights overlooking the town. The new commander of the Army of the Potomac was Ambrose Burnside, a thoroughly undistinguished general. Burnside decided that a sudden move against Fredericksburg would allow the Army of the Potomac to avoid the Wilderness and move into the more open areas north of Spotsylvania Courthouse. It might have worked, except that sloppy staff work had placed the bridging equipment at the rear of the advance. By the time it arrived, Lee had reacted and occupied Marye's Heights above Fredericksburg. Burnside then launched his troops in a series of hopeless attacks over open ground. It was not generalship, but murder. By the battle's end, Union troops had suffered 12,652 casualties, more than twice what their opponents lost.

Over the winter of 1863 both sides prepared for a renewal of op-

erations. Lincoln fired Burnside, not only for his incompetent handling of operations but also for his appallingly poor management of
the Army of the Potomac's administration and logistics. His replacement was Major General Joseph Hooker, one of the few aggressive
corps commanders in the army. Hooker put right the army's supply
situation and restored its morale. When he launched it south across
the Rapidan in early May 1863, the Army of the Potomac was at the
height of its power. Lee had been expecting the blow, but supply
problems throughout the winter had bedeviled preparations to the
extent that he had to dispatch Longstreet's corps to southeastern Virginia in the Norfolk–Suffolk area to feed it. Thus, when Hooker
crossed the Rapidan River, Lee had barely two-thirds of the Army of
Northern Virginia to parry the Union offensive. To make matters
worse, Hooker stole a march on the Confederates with a plan and
movement that should have allowed the Army of the Potomac to
cross the Wilderness entanglements before Lee could react. This while
John Sedgwick, with two corps, threatened the Confederate position
at Fredericksburg. But Lee was at his best in the ensuing campaign,
even if chance and luck contributed to Confederate success.

Having turned the Confederate position and placed the Army of
the Potomac in an excellent spot to deal a major blow to the Army
of Northern Virginia before it was ready, Hooker lost his nerve and
pulled back to what appeared to be a strong position near the Chancellorsville house. The position would have been stronger had the
XI Corps commander on the far right of the Union line, Major General O. O. Howard, obeyed his instructions and established a strong
defensive position on the Union flank. But Howard did not, and he
soon found his troops disastrously outflanked.

Given the opportunity, Lee struck. Leaving a single division to
watch Sedgwick, Lee moved against Hooker's main force deployed
around Chancellorsville. He then took the even more audacious
step of splitting his army. With two divisions and barely thirteen
thousand men, Lee faced off against Hooker's seventy thousand soldiers deployed to the southeast of the Chancellorsville house, while
he sent Jackson with twenty-eight thousand troops in a wide out-

flanking move to the west with the aim of hitting the Army of the Potomac's open flank. Any offensive move by the Union commander would have enabled Union forces to defeat Lee in detail, but Hooker remained quiescent. By late in the afternoon of May 2, Jackson was ready and launched his force against the flank of Howard's XI Corps. Caught by surprise, the XI Corps collapsed. For a time it appeared that Hooker's army was about to collapse with it. But Union commanders rallied, and in the gathering gloom of evening, Jackson's attack lost its cohesion and slowed to a stop. In the confusion of the battle Confederate troops fired on their commander and severely wounded Jackson.

Furious fighting followed over the next few days. For a period, Lee switched his emphasis to an attempt to destroy Sedgwick's corps near Fredericksburg, and then turned back to Hooker. Like McClellan at Antietam, the Union commander failed to heed Lincoln's advice to get all his troops into the fight. His two strongest and best corps, those of Major General George Meade and Major General John Reynolds, suffered hardly any casualties.

Over the battle's course, the Confederates had steadily hammered the Union forces, maintaining the pressure but at heavy cost. Toward the end of the battle, Lee came close to making the mistake he would later make at Gettysburg. By May 5, Hooker had retreated into a well-entrenched bridgehead just south of the Rapidan. It was a position from which dominant Union artillery could devastate the Confederate attackers. But before Lee could order the assault, Hooker overruled a council of his corps commanders and ordered a retreat that began early the next morning. The Army of the Potomac had once again been defeated, but interestingly, in spite of its humiliation, the Union force had inflicted almost as many casualties on its enemy as it suffered. The Union forces suffered 11,278 killed and wounded, while the Army of Northern Virginia lost 10,746.

The question that confronted the Confederate leadership was what to do with the victorious Army of Northern Virginia. With Longstreet's arrival from southeastern Virginia, Lee had his entire army concentrated along the Rapidan River. On May 16, Lee met with Davis and Secretary of War James Seddon. The two civilians urged Lee to consider detaching Longstreet and his corps to rescue what appeared to be a deteriorating situation in the west. Just how serious the situation there was they were yet to grasp, because Grant was at that moment defeating Major General John Pemberton's army at Champion Hill, which would place Vicksburg and Confederate control of the Mississippi River in mortal peril. But Lee demurred. He argued strongly and persuasively that the Army of Northern Virginia could win a decisive victory over the Army of the Potomac. Therefore he believed an invasion of the North was in order. In the end his political superiors agreed.

Lee's arguments rested on a number of dangerously false assumptions about reinforcing the west. The first was that the eastern theater of operations was more important than the west; second that whatever happened in the west, Union armies would not be able to seriously harm the Confederacy. Lee even suggested that Union soldiers from their Northern climate would not be able to handle the heat and humidity of high summer in the Southern portions of the Mississippi valley. Thus, for spurious reasons, he shrugged off the threat to Vicksburg and the possibility that Union forces would divide the western Confederacy from its eastern states. Lee also clearly believed in the innate superiority of his soldiers. For him the only thing that made sense was an invasion of the North, where he hoped to win a decisive Napoleonic victory. But as suggested earlier, even at the beginning of the nineteenth century such a success was no longer possible in a world where industrialized nations could mobilize their resources as well as their populations.

Thus, in mid-June 1863 Lee and his army advanced through northern Virginia on their way to Maryland and Pennsylvania. During the invasion, Lee divided his army in search of the sustenance and supplies that were always lacking due to an appallingly bad Confederate supply system. And again, as during the Antietam campaign, Lee substantially underestimated the speed with which the Army of the Potomac could move. What Lee missed until almost too late was that Lincoln had replaced the badly shaken Hooker with the much more competent Major General George Meade. In Meade the Union had a commander who, while lacking Hooker's aggressiveness, would not make any serious mistakes. Again, as in September 1862, Lee was warned in the nick of time and thus was able to concentrate his corps in time to meet the threat of the advancing Army of the Potomac.

The Battle of Gettysburg began on July 1, when Henry Heth took his division of A. P. Hill's corps across the ridge that lies between Chambersburg and Gettysburg to seize a supply of shoes supposedly available in the latter town. Paying no attention to Lee's orders that his subordinates were not to bring on a general engagement, Heth proceeded to do precisely that. Unexpectedly, the advance troops ran into a screen of Union cavalry. Heth immediately launched his troops against first the Union cavalry and then John Reynolds's I Corps deploying from the south. The result was a fierce encounter battle, in which the Confederates got much the worst of it. Arriving in the early afternoon, Lee could see General Richard Ewell's corps coming up on the Union right flank and decided to commit the Army of Northern Virginia to a full-scale assault. The onrushing Confederate reinforcements crushed the two exhausted Union corps on the field. Remarkably, even for the Army of the Potomac, Major General Henry Slocum and his corps sat five miles away at Two Taverns, refusing to move to the sound of guns, as they had no direct orders to do so. That night into the next morning, Lee had an extended argument with Longstreet, the latter strenuously urging a pullback to a defensible position that would force the Army of the Potomac to do the attacking.

But Lee's blood was up. The second day saw considerable indecision and muddle on the part of Confederate commanders. The major Confederate attack, launched late in the day on the southern portion of the Union line, achieved some tactical success but failed to drive Meade's troops from their strong defensive positions. On the third day Lee launched the mass attack on the Federal position that he had wanted to launch at Chancellorsville. It was a disaster. By the time it was over, General George Pickett's division was a division in name only, while the other two divisions were in scarcely better shape. Thus ended the second Confederate invasion of the North. It had achieved nothing at immense cost in casualties, casualties the South could not afford.

In the fall of 1863, Lee argued to again invade the North, but the disastrous situation in the west—with the fall of Vicksburg and the advance of Major General Rosecrans's Army of the Cumberland to Chattanooga and then on into northern Georgia—forced Davis to overrule Lee. In early September, Longstreet's corps of the Army of Northern Virginia began a long, tortuous journey over the broken-down Southern railroads to reach the murderous Chickamauga battlefield in mid-September, on the second day of the battle. Left with only two-thirds of his army, Lee engaged in skirmishing with George Meade's Army of the Potomac, but he was no longer in a position to consider striking northward. Lee's aggressiveness kept Meade and his army off balance, but never enough to win a victory. Moreover, Lee's lieutenants showed little competence. A. P. Hill even managed to get one of his divisions ambushed at Bristoe Station. When the fighting subsided, the Confederates had lost nearly fourteen hundred men, the Union slightly more than five hundred. Lee's laconic comment was, "Well, well, General, bury these men and let us say no more about it." But Hill's attack, for all its carelessness, merely reflected the Army of Northern Virginia's culture of aggressiveness, which Lee had done so much to create.

Meanwhile in the west, Grant had achieved an enormous success at Vicksburg through persistence, adaptation, imagination, and extraordinary leadership. His first move against Vicksburg had not turned out well. He had established his major logistical center at Holly Springs in the fall of 1862, so it could supply his forces when they moved in the winter. The bulk of his Army of the Tennessee moved overland in December 1862 toward Vicksburg, while Sherman with a smaller force was to carry out an amphibious landing north of the town. Unfortunately for Grant, a Confederate raiding force devastated the carefully prepared supply dump at Holly Springs. Grant then retreated, but he discovered that the area through which his troops marched was able to supply the army with the necessary sustenance. As he noted in his memoirs: "We could have subsisted off the country for two months instead of two weeks."

Over the winter's course, Grant and the Army of the Tennessee involved themselves in a number of overly ambitious projects, all of which expended much labor and energy, but none of which had much chance of success. Still, as Grant noted: "I let the work go on, believing employment was better than idleness for the men." As spring approached, Sherman urged Grant to pull back to Tennessee and repeat his advance through northern Mississippi to attack Vicksburg from the eastern side of the river. However, Grant recognized that such a retreat might have serious political consequences in the North, where Confederate successes in the last half of 1862 had had a serious impact on morale.

Moreover, Grant had considered a different—and riskier—approach to the Vicksburg problem. He determined to advance south on the western side of the Mississippi, cross the river below the Confederate citadel, and then either move north against Vicksburg or south to join up with the army of General Nathaniel Banks. The advance on the western side of the Mississippi depended on the cooperation of Admiral David Porter, commanding the navy's river flotilla. The admiral promised his full support. To kick off the campaign, Grant launched a major cavalry raid under Colonel Benjamin Grierson from northern Mississippi through to Union forces besieging Grand Gulf in Louisiana. In retrospect, Grierson's raid was the most successful cavalry raid of the war in terms of its strategic impact. By the time Union cavalry had reached Baton Rouge after causing havoc throughout Mississippi, Pemberton had focused his attention toward the east and central Mississippi. While Grierson was wrecking much of central Mississippi, Sherman, in command of the rearmost corps of Grant's army, was demonstrating across from Vicksburg on the river's western side. Meanwhile, Grant led his other two corps, soon to be followed by Sherman, south to the wonderfully named town of Hard Times. There they met up with Porter's gunboats and transports and crossed the river.

Grant had deliberately informed Washington of his intentions only after the Army of the Tennessee had crossed the Mississippi, knowing full well that the cautious Halleck would order him to link up with Banks. As he commented in his memoirs, given the time lag in communications, by the time Halleck ordered him to desist, his offensive would either have succeeded or failed. Banks was not yet ready, and Grant quickly determined to move inland. In what many consider the most brilliant campaign ever undertaken by an American general, Grant first advanced against Jackson, while feinting as if he were about to cross the Big Black River and attack Vicksburg directly. The fact that the Army of the Tennessee had cut its lines of communications and was living off the countryside further confused the Confederates. By cutting free of a lengthening supply line, Union forces moved into central Mississippi far more quickly than the Confederate commanders expected. Tactically, Grant's move to the northeast allowed him to split Pemberton from Joe Johnston, now the overall Confederate commander in the west. Grant's forces first drove Johnston and a force of Confederates out of Jackson. On the night of May 14, Grant stayed in the same hotel room Johnston had slept in the night before. In a nice piece of irony, the next day Charles Dana, the assistant secretary of war, paid the hotel bill for Grant and his party in increasingly worthless Confederate dollars.

Grant then turned the Army of the Tennessee west. In the Battle of Champion Hill, his troops came close to trapping and destroying Pemberton's entire army. Pemberton, following to the letter the orders that Davis had issued him, retreated into Vicksburg and allowed Grant to shut him and his army up in a hopeless position. Grant's stunning success led to a rapid flow of reinforcements from the North, so that he could replenish his supplies (particularly ammunition), besiege the Confederates, and fend off relieving forces. On July 4, 1863, Pemberton surrendered himself, the town of Vicksburg, and his entire army, at the same time that Lee began his retreat from Gettysburg.

Almost immediately Grant saw the strategic possibilities for operations that Vicksburg had opened up. He proposed to Halleck an immediate move against Mobile. Such a strike would carry with it three important advantages. First, it would cut off the flow of critical war-making supplies that Confederate blockade runners were bringing through that port. Second, it would allow the Army of the Tennessee to begin operations against central Alabama, a center of Southern industry. And third, it would support Rosecrans and his Army of the Cumberland's drive from central Tennessee by forcing the Confederate high command to pull troops away from the defense of Chattanooga and northern Georgia. Once again Halleck stepped in to diminish Grant by rejecting the suggestion, and at the same time he redeployed substantial portions of Grant's forces to other tasks. In effect, Halleck put the Union's most successful commander back on the shelf.

And there Grant remained for the next three months, without troops and with no significant task. But in mid-September 1863, Davis, over Lee's objections, had reinforced Bragg's army with Longstreet's corps. On the second day of the Battle of Chickamauga, Rosecrans mishandled his deployment by pulling one of his divisions out of the line to replace a gap that did not exist. Longstreet's corps struck the resulting opening, and the Army of the Cumberland collapsed, although most of it escaped, largely due to an impressive rearguard action by General Henry "Pap" Thomas. Nevertheless, Union forces in southeastern Tennessee soon found themselves in a serious position, besieged by Bragg's army and holding on desperately to Chattanooga.

In this distressing situation, Lincoln and Secretary of War Edwin Stanton stepped in to repair the damage. First, they shipped two corps of the Army of the Potomac from Virginia—a journey of well over a thousand miles—despite Halleck's pessimistic estimate that the transport would take three months. In fact, General Montgomery Meigs—the North's logistical genius—accomplished the herculean task in a mere eleven days, perhaps the most impressive troop movement of the Civil War. But most important, they placed Grant in command of the entire western theater of operations with orders to relieve Chattanooga. Grant moved with his usual dispatch. On the way from Vicksburg, he met with Stanton, who authorized him to assume control of all Union forces west of the Appalachians. He also met with Rosecrans, clearly devastated by his defeat. Lincoln had commented that the general was "confused and acting like a duck that had been hit on the head." Grant recorded the meeting in the following terms: "We held a brief interview, in which he described very clearly the situation at Chattanooga and made some excellent suggestions as to what should be done. My only wonder was that he had not carried them out."

Grant took charge of matters. Within days, he had opened up the supply line to Thomas's besieged army. Union forces now gathered from all over the western theater: Sherman's corps and other troops from the Mississippi River valley along with the two corps from the Army of the Potomac. In short order, Union troops stormed Missionary Ridge, as Bragg's fractious and badly led army collapsed. Southern incompetence contributed considerably to the Union victory. Bragg's artillery commanders had placed their artillery on the geographic rather than the military crest of Missionary Ridge, where it was virtually useless. But what was truly impressive was how quickly Grant had gathered the various threads of command together and articulated the whole force into a smoothly running organization.

1864–1865

Grant's stunning restoration of the Union position in southeastern Tennessee finally clarified what should have been obvious after the successful conclusion of the Vicksburg campaign. If ever there were a single general capable of providing the military guidance for the Union's overall strategic effort, it was Grant. Following the victory at Chattanooga, there was considerable pressure in Congress to resurrect the position of lieutenant general, which only George Washington had held, with Grant the obvious candidate. But the administration held back, perhaps because of fear that Grant might have presidential ambitions. Not until early March 1864 did Grant come east to accept the appointment Lincoln had finally tendered him. Until that point he and Sherman had focused on building up the rail and logistical infrastructure throughout their theater of operations, so that Union engineers could rapidly repair any damage inflicted by Confederate raiders. In addition, they had prepared the way for the rapid construction of a railroad from Chattanooga to supply Union forces as they moved south into Georgia toward Atlanta.

Grant's problem was that he had hardly any time to organize and develop his military strategy once he took command in early March 1864. Nevertheless, he aimed to place maximum pressure on all the fronts where the Confederate and Union armies were in contact. Lincoln had suggested something similar to McClellan in early 1862, only to have the pusillanimous commander express contempt for the president's stupidity. But, of course, Lincoln was right, and that was precisely what Grant articulated to his subordinate army commanders in the directives he issued in April 1864. To Sherman he stated directly: "It is my design, if the enemy keep quiet and allow me to take the initiative in the spring campaign, to work all parts of the army together, and somewhat toward a common centre. . . . You I propose to move against Johnston's army, to break it up and to get into the interior of the enemy's country as far as you can, inflicting all the damage you can against their war resources."

While the two main Union armies were attacking Lee's Army of Northern Virginia and Johnston's Army of Tennessee, Grant designed a series of subsidiary operations to increase the pressure on the Confederacy's failing resources and weaker military forces. Major General Ben Butler was to strike up the James River at Bermuda Hundred and thus threaten either Richmond or Petersburg, the latter the essential railroad link from the Confederate capital to the rest of the Confederacy. Banks was to finish up the Red River expedition—a militarily senseless operation that Lincoln, with Halleck's acquiescence, had pressed on Banks—and move against Mobile. Finally, Major General Franz Sigel was to move up the Shenandoah and wreck the granary of Lee's army. These efforts aimed at aiding the main offensive operations. Butler would distract Lee as the Army of the Potomac struck the Army of Northern Virginia; Banks would hold Polk's corps at Mobile, thus denying Johnston a substantial portion of his strength. Grant did not have much hope for Sigel's effort, but at least the German American politician "might hold a leg while some one else skins"—a phrase Grant got from Lincoln during the briefing of upcoming Union operations. Unfortunately for the possibility of Union victory in 1864, the subsidiary efforts utterly failed.

While Sherman was hammering Johnston's army, Grant, despite Sherman's urging that he return to the west, remained with Meade's Army of the Potomac. For Meade, Grant's instructions were much the same as he had given Sherman, except that he gave explicit orders as to the military object of the Army of the Potomac: "Lee's army will be your objective point. Wherever Lee goes, there you will go also." Grant interfered minimally with its command structure, except to bring the thirty-two-year-old Phil Sheridan from the west to command the eastern army's cavalry, which everyone agreed had had a miserable record of incompetence in its three years in existence.

What one sees in Grant's approach is a coherent military strategy aimed at making all of the pieces fit together into a whole. Across the Rapidan River, Lee displayed none of that larger strategic vision. Rather, with his focus on the northern Virginia theater of operations, Lee spent much of late winter urging Johnston to launch offensive operations against Sherman. Lee's reasoning appears to have been that, with reinforcements visibly strengthening the Army of the Potomac, the Union must be drawing down its forces in the west, particularly those facing Johnston. Thus, Lee supported Davis and his incompetent military adviser, Braxton Bragg, in their demands that Johnston not only attack Sherman but also march to regain Tennessee for the Confederacy.

Both commanders confronted considerable weaknesses and strengths in their armies. For Lee, it was a matter of numbers and resources. The Confederacy was simply losing the mobilization race. The Army of Northern Virginia was short of manpower, which Lee had all too often squandered, while everything else on which military organizations depend—from food to weapons to ammunition—was also in short supply. Yet, on the other hand, Lee still had Longstreet and Stuart, two of the greatest corps commanders in the war, and his other senior officers were for the most part competent.

The Army of the Potomac was almost the exact opposite. It lacked for little in terms of combat-tested soldiers and resources. The North's mobilization had reached full stride by this point. But its command culture was sorry indeed. Invariably, its corps commanders were rigid and unimaginative, rarely displayed initiative, and were sticklers for the worst aspects of regular army protocol and discipline. Grant admits in his memoirs that when he arrived to guide the Army of the Potomac's commander, George Meade, in the conduct of the campaign, he had little knowledge of the Army of the Potomac's senior officers. He appears to have believed that they were on a par with the subordinates he had commanded in the west. He was to find himself quickly disillusioned.

And so, the great contest began. On May 4, the Army of the Potomac crossed the Rapidan and Rappahannock Rivers and moved into the Wilderness. Like Hooker the year before, Meade aimed to outflank Lee's left flank, but this time there was no chance of catching Lee by surprise as had occurred in 1863. Lee intended to force the Army of the Potomac into an encounter battle in the Wilderness, where numbers would count for less than in the open fields lying to the east and southeast. He clearly hoped that a terrible killing battle would crack Grant's morale, just as it had that of previous Union commanders in the east.

Lee got the murderous battle he had hoped for, but in the largest sense the results were hardly what he desired. In percentage terms the two armies suffered equivalent casualties, but with its superior numbers, the Army of the Potomac lost more men. The difficulty for the Union was not that the Confederate soldiers were superior, but that the tactical framework within which the armies were fighting had altered entirely from 1861. In the first years of the war, both armies had often refused to fortify their positions, as many considered it unmanly or dishonorable to refuse to meet your opponent line against line in an open field. But by 1864, such quaint notions of honor had vanished. Now, when an army stopped, it dug, even when in the midst of combat. Soldiers had learned that the only way to survive on fields swept with industrial-strength firepower was to put a substantial amount of dirt between themselves and the enemy. Confederate and Union soldiers were extraordinarily quick to construct field fortifications, which provided those defending themselves a major advantage. Bullets hitting solid wood logs and dirt were capable of inflicting little damage on those sheltering behind even hastily constructed field fortifications.

By the end of the second day, Grant was beginning to pick up on just how much Lee had intimidated many of his senior subordinates. An officer rode up with his horse in a lather to Grant's headquarters, while shouting that the Confederates were about to outflank the Union position and destroy the Army of the Potomac. For one of the few times in the war, Grant lost his cool and turned on the officer: "Oh, I am heartily tired of hearing about what Lee is going to do. Some of you always seem to think he is suddenly going to turn a double somersault, and land in our rear and both of our flanks at the same time. Go back to your command, and try to think what we are going to do ourselves, instead of what Lee is going to do."

On the third day, no major fighting took place except for heavy skirmishing. Deciding the Army of the Potomac could achieve no more by battering at what were now well-prepared Confederate positions, Grant ordered the army to move southeast, around Lee's right flank toward Spotsylvania Courthouse. Should Union troops seize the road junction that ran through that village, the Army of the Potomac would be well on the way toward placing itself between Lee and Richmond, thus forcing the Confederates to do the attacking. The order to move went out to Union troops on the afternoon of May 7, but it did not specify the final destination. Many thought the order signaled another retreat back north. That night, as Major General Winfield Scott Hancock's corps prepared to move out, the troops spied Grant and his staff taking the right-hand turn in a fork

Grant in a Council of War
(Library of Congress Prints and Photographs Division, Washington, D.C.)

in the road leading south rather than north. They broke into spontaneous cheering, even though the road they now took led to more hardships and killing.

Lee was as uncertain as the Union troops as to what Grant was going to do, but he took the precaution of beginning a move to his right toward Spotsylvania Courthouse. Here the culture and typically bad luck of the Army of the Potomac intervened. Still unfamiliar with the army's corps commanders, Grant picked Gouverneur Warren's V Corps to lead the advance. Warren and his men dawdled on their way to Spotsylvania, at one point coming to a virtual halt because a portion of the road had flooded with several inches of water. Warren did little to push his men. Meanwhile, Lee had ordered Major Richard Anderson, Longstreet's temporary replacement after the latter's wounding the previous day, to move to the crossroads. Anderson had planned to halt and rest his troops on the way, but forest fires forced the Confederates to march through the night. Thus, even though they had farther to march, they beat the tardy Union troops to the crossroads. Warren's troops, reinforced by John Sedgwick's VI Corps, then spent most of the day getting ready to attack the Confederates, who were strenuously fortifying defensive positions. All in all the ensuing operation was typical of the Army of the Potomac. As one veteran recalled, "The dim impression of that afternoon is of things going wrong and of . . . much bloodshed and futility."

Further bloody fighting now continued on a par with what had taken place in the Wilderness. One of the bright spots in the fighting came when Colonel Emory Upton, class of 1861 at West Point, persuaded his corps commander to mount a surprise attack on a weak spot he had observed in the Confederate position, called "the Mule Shoe." With twelve regiments assigned to support his plan, Upton ordered his troops to hold their fire until approaching within two hundred yards of the Confederate positions and then, when the enemy fired, to charge with bayonets. The attack was a brilliant success, breaking into the Confederate position. However, Upton's division and corps commander, in spite of Grant's urging, dithered and failed to support the initial break-in. It was another case of senior Army of the Potomac commanders failing to display either initiative or drive. The Confederates, however, responded and quickly contained and then drove Upton's attacking force back.

Other attacks on May 10 failed dismally. But Grant was not dismayed. He commented on Upton's success: "A brigade today—we'll try a corps tomorrow." Thus, over the night of May 10–11 Hancock's corps moved into position immediately to the front of Confederate lines in preparation to attack directly south at the apex of the Mule Shoe—the Confederate defensive positions, so called because they were shaped like a mule shoe—while General Horatio Wright's VI Corps and Burnside's IX Corps would be in direct support. Before even the first glimmering of dawn reached the eastern horizon, they struck. Few Union commanders expected success, but for once luck aided the Army of the Potomac. A major thunderstorm covered the deployment, while at the same time the Confederates, at Lee's direction, began withdrawing their artillery from the Mule Shoe to support a shorter line across the salient's base. As a result of the surprise attack, the Confederate position at the position's apex collapsed.

But the Union troops fell into general confusion upon crossing the Confederate defensive positions. As was to occur innumerable times in the First World War, small unit leaders discovered it was one thing to break into an enemy position—and quite another to break out. As usual the Confederates reacted rapidly. Brigadier John Gordon sent one of his four brigades to hold the Yankees while gathering the other three for a concerted counterattack. His quick thinking drove Hancock's men back to the breastworks, where furious fighting continued throughout the day. That night Lee withdrew his troops to the base of the Mule Shoe. Casualties on both sides had been heavy: The Army of the Potomac, six thousand men killed or wounded; the Army of Northern Virginia, four thousand killed or wounded with a further four thousand captured.

As the Battle of Spotsylvania Courthouse fizzled to its dismal conclusion, there was one positive element to cheer Grant: Lee had largely lost the initiative. Unfortunately, Union commanders in the peripheral theaters—the Shenandoah (Sigel), Mobile (Banks), and Bermuda Hundred (Butler)—had dismally failed. Only Sherman's hard-driving advance on Atlanta continued with some success, although Johnston's brilliant defensive tactics slowed progress and increased the human cost for every yard gained. Having failed to break Lee's positions at Spotsylvania, Grant swung the Army of the Potomac around Lee's right flank and toward Richmond. As Hancock's II Corps marched out of line to move south, Lee launched Ewell's whole corps to attack its flank. But with only six thousand men Ewell was in no position to accomplish what Jackson's corps of twenty thousand soldiers had accomplished at Chancellorsville. At North Anna, the Confederates caught the Union forces divided but failed to act before Union forces had fortified their position.

General Grant,
Lieutenant Colonel
Bowers, and General
Rawlinson at Grant's
headquarters, Cold Harbor
*(Civil War photographs,
1861–1865, Library of
Congress)*

Several days later at Cold Harbor, Grant, perhaps disgusted by the Army of the Potomac's inability to execute his orders swiftly, launched a mass attack against well-posted Confederates that resulted in a slaughter of his own men. Flawed execution by the corps commanders worsened what would have been a dreadful situation in any case. Attacking a well-fortified position was a terrible miscalculation and one of two assaults that Grant, in his memoirs, said he regretted ordering.

Great generals do not, however, dwell on their mistakes. Rather than look back, Grant moved relentlessly forward. He now devised one of the more imaginative operational maneuvers of the war. He had the Army of the Potomac feint against Lee's right, threatening Richmond, while at the same time the bulk of the army moved across the James River to attack Petersburg, thereby cutting the crucial railroads that supplied the Confederate capital and the Army of Northern Virginia. For once everything ran like clockwork. Grant's move caught Lee by surprise, and the crossing of the James went smoothly. "Baldy" Smith's XVIII Corps crossed by boat to arrive in front of a defenseless Petersburg. But the Confederate commander on the scene, Lieutenant General Pierre Beauregard, put on a wonderful show of manning the city's defenses, while Smith hesitated

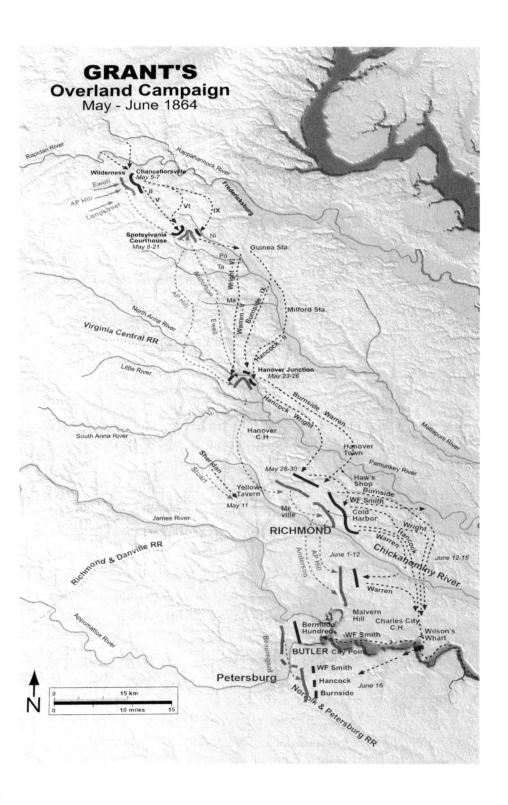

GRANT'S
Overland Campaign
May - June 1864

Rapidan River

Rappahannock River

Fredericksburg

Wilderness
Ewell
AP Hill
Longstreet

Chancellorsville
May 5-7

II
V
VI
IX

Ni

Spotsylvania Courthouse
May 8-21

Po
Ta
Guinea Sta.

Anderson
AP Hill
Ewell

Wright
Warren - V
Burnside - IX

Ma

Milford Sta.

North Anna River

Virginia Central RR

Little River

Hancock - II

Hanover Junction
May 23-26

Burnside
Hancock
Wright
Warren

South Anna River

Hanover C.H

Sheridan
Stuart

Yellow Tavern
May 11

James River

Mattaponi River

Hanover Town

May 28-30

Pamunkey River

Haw's Shop
Burnside
WF Smith

Me ville

Cold Harbor

RICHMOND

Wright
Hancock
Warren

June 1-12

Chickahominy River

June 12-15

Richmond & Danville RR

Anderson
AP Hill

Warren

Malvern Hill

Charles City C.H.

Appomattox River

Bermuda Hundred

WF Smith

Wilson's Wharf

BUTLER City Point

Petersburg

WF Smith
Hancock
Burnside

June 16

Beauregard

Norfolk & Petersburg RR

N

0   15 km
0   10 miles   15

and failed to launch a full-scale attack. Grant had nominated Smith for promotion before the campaign began, but as he acidly noted later: "I was not long in finding out that the objections to Smith's promotion were well founded."

After crossing the James, Hancock's corps dawdled in moving out and failed to arrive in front of Petersburg until June 16, a full day later than the XVIII Corps. Even then the Union commanders did not launch a concerted attack, which might have taken the city. By the seventeenth, Lee had awoken to the danger, and two of his divisions arrived to bolster the defenses. Again the Army of the Potomac had proven that it never missed an opportunity to miss an opportunity. By this time both armies had fought themselves to exhaustion. Lee's Army of Northern Virginia was a shadow of its former self. It could defend Richmond but little else; its offensive striking power was spent. And though Grant pushed the Army of the Potomac to keep up the pressure, it, too, was running out of steam and in dire need of a period of recuperation.

In August the Confederate defenses in the west finally broke. Admiral David Farragut's fleet crushed the Confederates at the Battle of Mobile Bay. Then Sherman took Atlanta in early September, as a result of Davis replacing Johnston with the inept but aggressive John Bell Hood, who quickly proved he had no conception of high command except to attack no matter the circumstances. Hood, with his overaggressiveness, did almost as much as any Union general to destroy the Confederate Army of Tennessee. Throughout the fall, while a Union army under General Thomas concentrated on defending central Tennessee from Hood's attempt to regain that state, Sherman—with Grant's blessing—cut loose from his supply lines and began his storied march through Georgia on the way to Savannah, taking the war to the heart of the Confederacy. Having smashed up much of Georgia and reached Savannah by Christmas 1864, Sherman then launched a destructive war aimed at the heart of secession, South Carolina. Sherman's forces left little of military or commercial utility standing as they moved into North Carolina in April, after one of history's most epic marches.

Robert E. Lee Leaves McLean House at Appomattox
(Morgan collection of Civil War drawings, Library of Congress)

By now Union armies were carrying their version of the "hard
war" to the people in the South. Unlike the wars of the twentieth
century, theirs was not aimed directly against civilians. But, by freeing the slaves, they destroyed the South's economic wealth; by
wrecking the South's railroads and infrastructure, they ensured that
the region's recovery would be slow and torturous; and by laying
waste to the countryside, they laid the foundation for an abiding
hatred of the North that would last for a century. But at the same
time, their ruthlessness ensured that Southerners would never again
attempt rebellion. The hard war was not only the province of Sherman and his armies. After general failure by Union commanders in
the Shenandoah, Grant persuaded Lincoln and Secretary of War
Edwin M. Stanton to appoint the youthful but fierce Phil Sheridan

to command Union forces in the valley. Sheridan's explicit orders from Grant were not only to destroy Confederate military forces in the valley but to lay waste to the rich agricultural lands that had supported Lee and his army throughout the war. As Grant noted to Halleck, he wanted the valley destroyed "so that crows flying over it . . . will have to carry their own provender."

The end finally came in April 1865. The Army of the Potomac maneuvered a bedraggled, weary, half-starved Army of Northern Virginia out of its positions defending Richmond and Petersburg. At the Battle of Five Forks, the Union army won only its second victory of the war—the other being Gettysburg—and drove ahead of the desperately retreating Confederates, who were forced to abandon their positions. Recognizing the impossible position of his army, Lee surrendered. It was the third army that soldiers under Grant's command had captured. The surrender did both men credit: Grant for the terms he offered Lee, and Lee for his willingness to accept reality and reject the possibility of the South's turning to guerrilla warfare.

Conclusion

In the end, Ulysses S. Grant stands as the greater general than his opponent, Robert E. Lee. In the strategic sense, Lee's audacious campaigns and battles carried with them a terrible irony; with the brilliance of his battlefield leadership, he clearly prolonged the conflict. And in doing so he ensured not only that the South's defeat would be more terrible but also that the war would destroy the fabric of the antebellum South's economic and political system. Moreover, one must note the unimaginative leadership of the generals that Lee faced in the Army of the Potomac. It is often easy for a general to appear a genius when he is facing incompetents.

Lee's greatest strength lay in his battlefield generalship. He was a superb judge of his subordinates, their strengths and weaknesses, those on whom he could rely, and those whom he had to watch carefully. In the early war years, he was served by two of the best corps commanders in the war: Jackson, who was capable of independent command, and Longstreet, who proved somewhat less capable on independent command but was fully up to commanding a corps on any battlefield. Equally important were a number of exceptional divisional commanders, such as Hood, the two Hills, and Jubal Early, among others. Lee's army also proved capable of developing extraordinary combat commanders who rose to the highest level. Here Gordon was a prime example. It was the symbiosis between Lee and his subordinates that made the eastern Confederate army such a lethal instrument of combat. For the most part, these were men who were willing to display initiative. Whatever Ewell's faults on the first day at Gettysburg, unlike Slocum, commander of the Army of the Potomac's XII Corps, the Confederate corps commander marched to the sound of guns, ignoring his orders to march to Chambersburg.

Lee rarely underestimated his opponents, except obviously Grant. Yet, that in turn led him to assume risks—such as Antietam—that came perilously close to destroying his army on a number of occasions. Both Antietam and Gettysburg underline Lee's willingness to take casualties in his quest for a decisive Napoleonic victory that his army, and particularly the Confederacy, could not afford. Even as the 1864 campaign in northern Virginia was winding down to its dismal conclusion after Cold Harbor, Lee could not avoid pointless—and hopeless—counterattacks. As the always-observant Porter Alexander, Longstreet's artillery chief, noted after the war about one of the aggressive attacks made by the Confederates during the Wilderness, it "ought *never, never* to have been made. . . . It was wasting good soldiers, whom we could not spare."

In terms of operations, Lee was a masterful general, the finest in the war alongside Grant. But in his grasp of the strategic issues that confronted the Confederacy, his record was less impressive. He never seems to have understood the crucial role that the western theater was going to play in the survival or defeat of the Confederacy. Thus, his advice to Davis and Seddon at the crucial meeting of May 16, 1863, was to launch an invasion of the North and not to reinforce the west. Nor did he perceive the threat that Grant and Sherman were preparing to launch from Chattanooga into northern Georgia over the winter of 1863–64. In fact, his expectations and advice to Johnston during that period were disastrously off target. He failed to recognize that, massively mobilized, the North was now capable of launching two great offensive operations, along with a number of subsidiary ones, in the spring of 1864. His belief further exacerbated Davis's misperceptions about the western theater— that with the swelling reinforcements reaching the Army of the Potomac, the Union armies in the west must be weak. He could not have been more wrong. In the end, Lee acted as a theater commander and by doing so lost it all.

How to judge Grant? Of all the generals in the Civil War, simple, straightforward Ulysses Grant recognized the war for what it was. As all military leaders have to do, he learned on the fly. But from his earliest days in command he recognized that his opponents had to fear him as much as he had to fear them. Moreover, as early as the Battle of Shiloh, Grant recognized that the Civil War was a war of people in which, in Clausewitzian terms, the North was going to have to break the will of the South. There was no road to a successful re-creation of the Union except by bloody conquest. In fact, the last major military operations in the west in March and April 1865 against central Alabama and Mississippi were aimed at ensuring that there remained no region of the South untouched by the hard hand of war.

Like Lee, Grant had the advantage in the west of fighting opponent generals who hardly represented the brightest lights. But unlike Lee, Grant had a far better sense of the geographic framework of the larger war. Thus, he recognized the strategic importance of the positions of Forts Henry and Donelson and, when finally allowed to move by Halleck, he not only captured the most important geographic area of the war but then recognized—in a fashion his superior did not—how much the opening of the Tennessee offered the Union in terms of strategic advantage.

As an operational commander, Grant was at least Lee's equal.

Unlike Lee, his campaigns resulted in the surrender of three Confederate armies: at Donelson, Vicksburg, and Appomattox. The Vicksburg campaign was undoubtedly his best, as it involved deception, supporting operations, and then a blinding movement that split his opponents, wrecked the transportation center of Jackson, and finally drove Pemberton's army back into Vicksburg. Equally impressive was his molding of the tactical, operational, and logistical factors together into a coherent whole that resulted in the lifting of the Army of Tennessee's siege of Chattanooga in the fall of 1863. In the largest sense, by 1864 Grant understood how operations over continental distances needed to be coordinated and how to manage the logistical requirements to support such a move.

Lee never had that option, but his advice to Davis about the situation in the west in May 1863 and then in the spring of 1864 suggests a general more concerned with the parochial concerns of the Virginia theater than with a broad strategic view. The failure of Banks, Butler, and Sigel to execute their operational and tactical responsibilities in 1864 in a competent fashion does nothing to minimize the brilliance of Grant's conception for the campaign. Meade's corps commanders also failed to move quickly or display initiative, robbing the Army of the Potomac of its chance to destroy the Army of Northern Virginia in 1864. But Grant was able to force the Army of the Potomac to fight well enough to ensure that none of Lee's army could be detached to help halt Sherman's devastating march.

The 1864 campaign in northern Virginia was brutal. As Warren noted in early June 1864, "For thirty days it has been one funeral procession past me, and it has been too much!" But in the end Grant robbed Lee of all chance to take the initiative, and eventually the cost of the terrible fighting wore the Army of Northern Virginia down to a shadow of its former self. That Grant's designs were so often thwarted was usually a consequence of the ineptness of his corps commanders. As Emory Upton, one of the young officers to rise high in the army because of his extraordinary competence, commented in a letter to his sister about the Army of the Potomac: "Some of our corps commanders are not fit to be corporals. Lazy and indolent, they will not even ride along the lines; yet without hesitancy, they will order an attack on the enemy no matter what their position or numbers." Even more than the British army of World War I, the Army of the Potomac was an army of "lions led by donkeys." In some cases, though, great generalship is a matter of making do with the material at hand. And Grant always made do.

This brings us to a larger point: Grant's understanding of the political and strategic framework within which the North was waging the war. In his memoirs, Grant makes no excuse for the fact that the Lincoln administration saddled him with "political" generals like Ben Butler, Nathaniel Banks, and Franz Sigel. What Grant understood was that competent generals in their positions might well have won the war in 1864, but the political generals were important democratic politicians who supported Lincoln's reelection. Had they returned home as disgruntled generals, now supporting McClellan's candidacy, Lincoln might well not have won what proved to be the surprisingly close election of 1864. Thus, Grant suffered through what proved to be a long, desperately fierce campaign in the east that resulted in a stalemate, which his forces eventually broke in 1865, largely because of the failure of such political generals to act with anything resembling military competence. But in so doing Grant pinned Lee and the Army of Northern Virginia down to the siege of Richmond, while Sherman, Sheridan, and others completed the job of wrecking the South and breaking the will of its people. The war's overriding political objective was the creation of a Union that would never again be threatened by the secession of a state or states. And that is precisely what Grant's generalship achieved in the terrible years of 1864 and 1865. However deep the bitterness in the hearts of Southerners in the war's aftermath, few, if any, were willing to consider taking up arms again to contest the issues that divided them from their brethren in the North.

Rommel, Montgomery, and Patton

I n terms of their personalities, it would seem that no three generals of the Second World War could have been more different than Erwin Rommel, Bernard Law Montgomery, and George Patton. Yet, in their own way, they set a standard that few military leaders in the history of war have matched. On one hand, George Patton was explosive, blasphemous, loud, boisterous, and nearly always boasting. He was admired by his soldiers, feared and scandalized by his colleagues, and loved by few whom he led. Almost his exact opposite, Montgomery appeared stolid and seemingly unwilling to take risks, and he had a reputation for arrogant disdain for his colleagues. One of his fellow officers during the interwar period described him as a "little shit." Yet, in spite of the disdain that many of his peers and superiors felt for him, he was deeply respected by his soldiers, because they knew he was never going to spend their lives needlessly—something he made clear from his first days in command in the desert in North Africa in 1942. And then there was the German master tactician Erwin Rommel, who led from the front, a risk taker par excellence, a general who for all his ruthless exploitation of his enemy's weaknesses possessed a sense of decency that few, if any, of his fellow German field marshals possessed. Moreover, of the three generals, Rommel appears to have been the only one whom those on the sharp end of battle genuinely loved. Only British field marshal Bill Slim, commander of the British Fourteenth Army in the Burma campaign, held similar affection among those he led.

These three generals set the standard for military excellence in the Second World War. And for all of their personality differences, Rommel, Montgomery, and Patton had similar approaches to the profession of arms. They were all consummate professionals. They read extensively, largely about military history. They were educators of their officers, whether in schools of professional military education or in the field. In peacetime they trained the units they commanded long and hard under the most trying of conditions. What marks all of them is their commitment to hard, unremitting work, whether in the study of their profession or in their willingness to engage in physical activity. Above all, they set standards for themselves that few of their contemporaries were capable of meeting. And none of them suffered incompetents. That was, of course, why all three possessed considerable enemies before, during, and after the war, not only among their colleagues, but among the historians who attempted to piece together the tangled web of their actions.

Formative Years: The First World War

Rommel

Erwin Rommel's parents were solidly middle-class Swabians, a subset of the German population known for their laconic disposition. His father was a principal, and young Erwin received an excellent education. While he was not a particularly outstanding student, he did graduate from a reasonably good gymnasium with an *arbitur*— a level of academic attainment easily superior to that achieved by 90 percent of the college graduates in the United States today. After graduation Rommel chose the military as a career. After a year's service in the enlisted ranks, he spent eight months in a cadet school and graduated in January 1912 as a newly minted lieutenant. While there, he met his future wife, Lucie Mollin, to whom he remained deeply attached until he died. He spent only thirty-one months in the peacetime 124th Infantry Regiment of the Württemberg Army before the First World War exploded. Some historians have puzzled why Rommel never received an assignment to Wehrmacht's primer staff school—the Kriegsakademie—but the simple explanation is that he was too junior to apply when the war began, and too senior at war's end.

Rommel's service in the war was spectacular. From his first moments in combat he proved not only a brilliant combat leader, but one who consistently pushed his subordinates to achieve their utmost. In August 1914 the Württemberg Twenty-sixth Division, to which the 124th was attached, formed a portion of the Fifth Army, commanded by the German crown prince. Its assignment was to advance through the southern portion of the Ardennes from Metz toward Verdun. From the start its commander singled Rommel out for the most dangerous reconnaissance tasks. Leading from the front in the battle of Longway, Rommel, whenever he was in combat, seemed to live a charmed life. In the midst of this ferocious fighting, the regiment lost 15 percent of its soldiers and 25 percent of its officers, but Rommel was untouched. His battlefield actions led to promotion to battalion adjutant, where he found himself used in innumerable combat-related tasks. But, on September 24, 1914, his luck ran out. Severely wounded in the thigh, he was evacuated back to Germany. He received the Iron Cross Second Class for his bravery and leadership—the first of many awards to come. Rommel did not return to his regiment until January 1915, probably too early, but typical of his willpower. By then the 124th was in the damp, cold, inadequately protected trenches of the western front. Despite his debilitated condition, Rommel found himself planning and leading trench raids, a task in which he reveled. On January 29 he received the Iron Cross First Class, for a spectacular raid. As his most impressive biographer in English noted: "Rommel, although adept beyond most men in battle in a fluid situation, was the reverse of slapdash. Where time allowed and the situation demanded method he was utterly methodical: but he never let method constrict his mind or slow his actions."

Rommel's time on the western front with the 124th ended after slightly more than a year. At the same time that he received promotion to Oberleutnant, he transferred to a new mountain battalion of the Württemberg army forming up. It proved to be an elite unit that would establish an outstanding combat record over the next three years. In retrospect, Rommel's assignment probably saved his life, because while his unit found itself in constant combat in the Vosges Mountains, Romania, and Italy, that fighting lacked the heavy concentrations of artillery that marked the great murderous battles of Verdun, the Somme, Passchendaele, and the Ludendorff offensives of 1918. Those battles were all dominated by huge artillery barrages, establishing artillery as the great killer in the First World War. It is unlikely that even Rommel with his phenomenal luck would have survived the catalog of horrors those battles unleashed.

After three months of intensive training, the Gebirgsbatallion was deployed to the western front in the Vosges Mountains, where, once again, Rommel distinguished himself. In late October 1916 the mountain troops were transferred to the campaign against Romania, which had entered the war on the Allied side. Here, Rommel again found himself in a war of movement. The mission was to reconnoiter terrain that forced his troops to carry ammunition and food up to heights of 6,000 feet. Conditions were appalling; their first attack came in the midst of pouring rain that turned to snow as they advanced against Romanian mountain positions.

Rommel was particularly lucky in that the battalion's commander, Major Theodor Sprösser, quickly displayed a deep trust in his aggressive subordinate. At times the major and the lieutenant acted as if they were co-commanders of the battalion, and rarely did Sprösser rein in Rommel during his advances into enemy positions. Despite the fact that Rommel was still only a lieutenant (Oberleutnant), Sprösser often placed the young officer in command of what the Germans termed a Kampfgruppe, two infantry companies and a machine gun company. It represented a command far larger than that normally held by a first lieutenant, but in the German armies of both world wars, officers often received command based on competence rather than rank.

In early 1917 the Württemberg mountain battalion returned to its familiar haunts in the Vosges, where it remained until August 1917, when it was shipped back to Romania. Here, Rommel participated in one of the final battles of that conflict—Mount Coşna. This was a heavily fortified position that took two weeks to clear. Initially, Rommel's advance went well, but eventually the forward push ran into serious trouble, trapped for a period by the Romanians, forcing Rommel to organize an all-around defense. Following the new German tactics, Sprösser fed in reinforcements, rations, and ammunition, while ensuring that Rommel received artillery support. Despite having been seriously wounded in the forearm, Rommel remained with his troops for a time, until, partially delirious and exhausted by loss of blood, he walked out under his own power. In the fighting, supposedly a mopping-up campaign, the battalion lost five hundred men killed or wounded, nearly a third of its strength.

In the fall of 1917, after several weeks of convalescent leave, Rommel returned to the battalion, which had received orders to report to the Italian theater. By this point, the Italians had been fighting for more than two years against Germany's ally, Austria-Hungary. The Italian chief of staff, General Luigi Cadorna, one of the most incompetent of World War I's generals, had ordered no less than eleven offensives along the Isonzo River. All had failed with heavy casualties, unsurprisingly, as much of the fighting took place in the Alpine foothills, perfect terrain for the defensive. By the summer of 1917, Italian morale had collapsed, exacerbated by the Catholic Church's attacks on Italy's participation in the war. Austro-Hungarian intelligence picked up on the weakened Italian morale and persuaded the Germans that a combined offensive could knock Italy out. The Germans agreed and supplied the Austrians with seven divisions including their elite Alpine corps. On October 24 the attack—the Battle of Caporetto—opened.

Not surprisingly, the Württemberg mountain battalion was in

the lead. At the onset, Rommel commanded his usual detachment. That force swiftly advanced through the first Italian defensive positions; in the second line the Italians had hunkered down behind formidable positions, ignorant of the fact that the Germans were already through their forward defenses. By mid-afternoon Rommel's detachment had rounded up the Italians in the second line and was advancing on the major enemy defenses on the Kolovrat Ridge. There, the Württembergers ran into their first serious opposition. They also encountered a detachment of the Royal Bavarian Infantry Lifeguards Regiment, whose unit commander ordered Rommel to support his Bavarians. Rommel, however, had no intention of following the orders of an officer from another unit. After conferring with Sprösser at dawn on the twenty-fifth, Rommel led his detachment well beyond the Bavarians' flank and moved up to and over the crest of the Kolovrat Ridge. Again, the Württembergers caught the Italians in their dugouts. But by advancing so far ahead of his support, Rommel was in serious trouble, under fire on the flanks as well as the front. Judging the situation well, Rommel enveloped the enemy that was holding up his advance, leading to the surrender of an entire Italian battalion. By now the Württembergers had captured more than fifteen hundred prisoners.

But Rommel was not through. Following a track down from the Italian positions, his detachment drove to the village of Luico, where after sweeping up large numbers of Italians, the Württembergers ran into a brigade of Bersaglieri. After a short firefight, fifty officers and two thousand more Italian soldiers surrendered. That evening the advance continued, yielding another thousand prisoners and seizing the heights of Mount Cragonza. Running into another strong force, Rommel, carrying only a white handkerchief, persuaded fifteen hundred soldiers of the Salerno Brigade to surrender. Disobeying Sprösser's orders to pause, Rommel continued the advance to the summit of Mount Matajur, the battalion's objective. Continuing forward, the Württembergers finally halted at the Piave River, stopped by the arrival of British reinforcements and exhaustion. By then Rommel's detachment had captured a long list of supposedly impregnable positions and approximately ten thousand Italians. Not surprisingly, those actions won him the coveted pour le mérite.

After this achievement, one might have expected Rommel to return to France to participate in the Ludendorff offensives. Instead, Rommel found himself transferred to a staff position in a second-rate division. Apparently the army's personnel system had identified him as an outstanding combat officer with the potential for higher command, and given the casualty rates for junior officers, the German Army appears to have given outstanding officers staff positions to ensure their survival in the postwar army. Thus, Rommel missed the catastrophe that the Ludendorff offensive inflicted on the German Army between March and July 1918—nearly one million casualties.

Montgomery

The First World War was not filled with such excitement for Montgomery, yet his experiences still prepared the young officer for the hard road ahead. His entrance into the army seems largely a result of his unruly and rebellious childhood—such a career seemed particularly appropriate to rein him in. Montgomery's father was an Anglican churchman and bishop who played little role in his son's youth. The problem was his mother, who beat the young rebel mercilessly to drum discipline into the boy. She apparently broke her other children, but Montgomery, to her chagrin, remained as willful as ever. As he commented later: "If my strong will and indiscipline had gone unchecked the result might have been even more intolerable than some people have found me. But I have often wondered whether my mother's treatment for me was not a bit too much of a good thing: whether, in fact, it was a good thing at all."

Montgomery's lack of discipline showed clearly when he came close to ending his army career before it began. At Sandhurst he was the ringleader of a prank that sent a cadet whom he and his accomplices disliked to the hospital. Only his mother's intervention with the commandant prevented termination of his military career. Montgomery then graduated from Sandhurst in January 1908 without sufficient distinction to gain admittance to his first choice, an Indian Army regiment. But he was assigned his second choice, the Royal Warwickshire Regiment in northwest India, south of the Khyber Pass. Once there, he quickly earned a reputation for taking soldiering too seriously. Already Montgomery was focusing on the soldiers in his platoon and demanding that they meet his high standards. In 1913 the regiment returned to Britain, where neither the army nor the people were prepared for war.

Only at the last moment—when it was clear that the war in Europe was about to begin, with a massive German invasion of Belgium and Luxembourg in contravention to treaties that guaranteed their neutrality—did a reluctant British cabinet commit a British Expeditionary Force (BEF) to Western Europe. British generals and several leading statesmen had already prepared the way in staff negotiations with the French. Thus, the BEF—including Montgomery's Fourth Division—arrived in northern France in early August 1914 to find itself on the left flank of the French armies in time to prevent the Germans from outflanking and then rolling up their opponents. After a series of encounter battles against a more numerous German opponent, the BEF retreated deep into France. But the Germans overreached, and when a slowly advancing BEF marched into the gap between the First and Second German Armies, it greatly assisted the French in winning the First Battle of the Marne and halting the German advance toward Paris. In November the BEF then moved to Flanders, where it was involved in fierce fighting that prevented the Germans from capturing the Channel ports, but only at the cost of the BEF's near extermination.

Montgomery's exposure to combat was short and horrific. His role, of course, was that of a small cog in massive battles. Nevertheless, unlike most of his fellow officers, he sensed the larger dimensions of what was to come. Even before the first fighting between the British and Germans occurred, he wrote his mother: "We are of course all looking forward very much to fighting the Germans; but this war will be no small thing & will demand all our endurance before it is over." For him the fighting that ensued hardly suggested much competence on the part of his superiors. In an attack during the Battle of Le Cateau, his battalion commander, Lieutenant Colonel Elkington, threw his soldiers against German positions without reconnaissance. The colonel then ran away. In the battalion's desperate retreat to catch up to the BEF's main body, Montgomery was one of the few who kept his head. The new battalion commander promoted the young officer to temporary captain with the command of a company.

After the German retreat halted on the Aisne, Montgomery mostly found himself involved in skirmishing, as both sides were exhausted. In October the BEF redeployed to Flanders, arriving precisely at the moment the Germans launched a major offensive to capture the Channel ports. After deploying his company in a position sheltered by a ditch and hedges, the young captain moved out one hundred yards "to see what the positions looked like from the enemy point of view—in accordance with the book!" The result almost ended his life. Hit by a bullet in one of his lungs, Montgomery lay in the open for the remainder of the day under sniper fire that also wounded him in the knee. He survived by taking shelter behind a dead body. Brought back that night, he was on death's door; as doctors operated, soldiers outside were digging his grave. Montgomery survived, but the first medical board to evaluate him characterized him as no longer fit for active service.

He proved the members of the board wrong. In less than two months, Montgomery was released from the hospital to go on convalescent leave. He received orders to serve in the vast effort to train the volunteers who had joined in August and September 1914. Since the War Office had sent nearly the army's whole establishment to France, there were few staff or training officers in Britain. Montgomery's first assignment came with the 104th Brigade. His commander was Brigadier G. M. MacKenzie, whose most recent experience had been in the Boer War. Montgomery was the brigade's only officer with recent combat experience. Like Sprösser with Rommel, MacKenzie gave his subordinate full rein to design and implement the brigade's training program. As a newly minted captain with no staff training, Montgomery nonetheless proved an exceptional trainer. In January 1916, the high command ordered the brigade to deploy to France. Given his age, MacKenzie was soon replaced; here again Montgomery's luck held. The new commander, Brigadier J. W. Sandilands, was an experienced combat veteran who not only provided the young captain latitude but acted as a mentor.

The first months in France saw the 104th deployed along a quiet sector. But in July the brigade moved to the Somme. Luckily its soldiers did not participate in the terrible first day, where the British Army suffered fifty-seven thousand casualties, nineteen thousand killed. Subsequent fighting resulted in a draw at the tactical level, with losses on both sides nearly equal, and since the BEF was doing the attacking, that fact represented a strategic success for the British. They could afford the losses and the Germans could not. German tactics, by cramming defending troops into frontline trenches and demanding that they hold every inch of territory, maximized the killing power of British artillery.

For the troops on the ground, however, the battle represented a nightmarish experience. During July and August, the 104th Brigade found itself involved in fighting that decimated its strength. The carelessness with which the British high command threw away its troops would remain in Montgomery's consciousness for the rest of his career. The year 1917 found Montgomery assigned as GSO 2 (general staff officer—training) to the IX Corps, part of the BEF's Second Army. The army's commander, General Herbert Plumer, was one of the more competent British generals, especially well known for his meticulous planning. In September, during one of the few bright spots in the Passchendaele offensive, the Second Army achieved a number of successes. Here, Montgomery's training directives played a significant role; by November he was signing the orders for the GSO 1 (general staff officer—operations).

The year 1918 saw the Germans deliver a series of body blows in their spring offensives. These attacks hit the British particularly hard, and Montgomery's IX Corps was in the midst of the heaviest fighting. In early April it joined the fighting around the Lys River, where for the second time that spring, the Germans broke through British front lines. For ten days the British held against savage German attacks along the Kemmel Ridge. Badly battered, the IX Corps was sent to a quiet sector on the Chemin des Dames, held by the French. Placed under a French commander who refused to allow British troops to deploy their defense in depth, the IX Corps suffered heavy losses when Ludendorff launched another massive offensive at the end of May. By the time the fighting was over, IX Corps found itself reduced to the strength of a single division. Montgomery, displaying his usual calm competence, came out of the fighting with a promotion to brevet major.

Montgomery's final assignment in the last months of the war was as chief of staff to the 47th (London) Division under an exceptional divisional commander. In his new position, Montgomery underlined how much he had learned. When possible, he planned division attacks by rehearsing movement over similar terrain in rear areas, and limiting attacks to what the division could effectively control. After each action, he ensured that all officers received a thorough lessons-learned brief. The BEF, with the help of the badly hurt French Army and the newly arriving Americans, broke a German Army that Ludendorff's manic offenses of the spring had exhausted. On the eleventh hour, of the eleventh day, of the eleventh month of 1918, the war officially ended. A British brigadier supposedly commented: "We can now get back to the real business of soldiering!" That was undoubtedly the attitude of many British officers, but not Montgomery.

Patton

Compared to Rommel and Montgomery, Patton's career in the Great War was relatively short—a reflection, of course, of how late the United States entered the war. He grew up in Southern California in a privileged family that had emigrated from Virginia after the Civil War and had then done very well. Unlike Rommel and Montgomery, Patton grew up wealthy. He did hear a constant barrage of family stories about the Civil War. His grandfather had been commander of the Twenty-second Virginia Infantry, killed in 1864 during the Third Battle of Winchester, while a great-uncle had died leading Confederate troops in Gettysburg in Pickett's Charge. This historical baggage poured into Patton's upbringing. Not surprising, he chose the military as a career. He was not an exceptional student but was an avid reader, particularly of military history.

After attending Virginia Military Institute for a year, Patton transferred to West Point. He initially had trouble with the academic curriculum—he had to repeat his plebe year—but eventually graduated in 1909 in the middle of his class. Nevertheless, he excelled in the military aspects, particularly in horsemanship and fencing. Commissioned in the cavalry, he did a short stint in Illinois before transferring to Fort Myer in Virginia, near Washington, D.C. There he demonstrated an ability to cultivate superiors and made friends with then secretary of war Henry Stimson, a friendship that was to save his career in 1943. He also received permission to participate in the pentathlon competition in the 1912 Olympics in Stockholm, where his aggressive, almost suicidal approach to fencing underlined his personality as much as any other competition. Two tours at the French cavalry school at Saumur followed, allowing Patton to stand out at the cavalry school at Fort Riley in Kansas, from which he graduated in 1915. By that point Patton had married an heiress, who provided a rock of support in spite of occasional infidelities and his bizarre behavior.

Patton's career took off after graduating from the cavalry school. He talked the personnel authorities into changing his assignment from the Philippines to the Eighth Cavalry Regiment at Fort Bliss, Texas. With revolutionary turmoil in Mexico bubbling up, the border appeared to be the obvious place for an eager, aggressive officer to make a name for himself. He suborned General "Black Jack" Pershing to allow him to accompany the punitive raid to Pancho Villa's attack on Columbus, New Mexico. When Pershing asked how long it would take him to get ready, Patton replied, "Tomorrow morning." Patton became Pershing's aide, and in that position he formed a deep and abiding bond with the general. In Mexico, Patton proved himself more than a boastful cavalryman. The pursuit of Villa crossed the forbidding deserts of northern Mexico, an area the Mexicans knew well. Ordered out on a foraging mission, Patton raided a Mexican ranch, which he believed was a hideout for Mexican leaders of the Villa gang. In a wild shootout, the Americans killed one of Villa's leading henchmen and several others, the corpses of whom they strapped to their automobiles. That exploit gained Patton his first notoriety, as a Boston newspaper proclaimed: MEXICAN BANDIT-KILLER WELL KNOWN IN BOSTON.

In April 1917 President Woodrow Wilson declared war on Imperial Germany and appointed Pershing to command the American Expeditionary Force (AEF). What he was going to command and how soon, however, was still open to some doubt. In early 1917, the U.S. Army numbered barely a hundred thousand soldiers, while Wilson had ordered America's military to undertake no planning or preparations for war. The result was a muddle that saw the United States strain to organize, equip, and train an army for war in Europe. Its forces barely made it into the fighting, arriving at the front only in the last months, but in time to decisively tip the scales in favor of the Allies.

General George Patton
(Library of Congress Prints and Photographs Division, Washington, D.C.)

Pershing, his staff, and his aide George Patton left the United States in late May 1917 to arrive to great fanfare in Britain and France. A desperate effort to prepare for the training facilities and logistical support the Americans would need followed their arrival. Although only an aide, Patton was noticed. After a visit by Pershing and Patton, Douglas Haig, commander of the BEF, noted in his diary: "The A.D.C. is a fire-eater! Longs for the fray!" While hospitalized with jaundice late in 1917, Patton received news that the AEF was establishing a tank school. He immediately wrote to Pershing and in November 1917 assumed command of a school that had no instructors, no troops, and no students. In this new job, he created not only the framework and organization for training the American tank forces but also the doctrine under which they would fight. As he proved in the next war, he was a rigid disciplinarian. It was that approach to discipline and his attention to detail that made Patton such an impressive trainer. Four months after assuming command, Patton and his soldiers received their first tanks; three weeks later he had already organized and run a complex and effective exercise. By now a lieutenant colonel, Patton earned command of the army's first light tank battalion, and by September 1918, he was in command of the army's 1st Tank Brigade. His soldiers would receive their baptism of fire in the Battle of Saint-Mihiel, the AEF's first major battle. Not surprisingly, Patton's tanks ran into war's normal frictions and uncertainties. Nevertheless, while suffering considerable losses in equipment and men, they achieved a substantial success. Once it was clear that his tanks had run into difficulty, Patton moved quickly forward and for the rest of the day led from the front.

The American attack on the Meuse-Argonne that followed was another matter. There, the Germans stood their ground, while the American lack of preparedness and rawness showed. Patton left his headquarters, "Bonehead," three and a half hours after the attack began, intent on pushing his force forward as rapidly as possible. The Americans initially caught the Germans by surprise, with fog helping the advance. But as the fog cleared, difficulties multiplied. The tanks outran the infantry and soon suffered heavy losses. Quickly organizing an ad hoc group of tanks and infantrymen, Patton got his force through two deep trenches to continue the advance. In the midst of heavy fighting, he was hit in his upper thigh. It took several hours before stretcher bearers could carry him to a field hospital. He returned to the tank school in October, but for him the war was over.

The Interwar Years

In the postwar period, vastly different circumstances formed the cultures of the officer corps in which the three generals rose to high command. For Rommel the German Army provided a clear framework for his talents in terms of leadership, doctrine, and tactical innovation. The Reichswehr and then the Wehrmacht were institutions that believed wholeheartedly that they would fight a major war in the future. As such, they prepared their officers for how that war would be fought based on a careful examination of the lessons from the last war. The author of the German Army's recovery was General Hans von Seeckt, who upon assuming command of the Reichswehr carried out two fundamental reforms. The first, forced on the Germans by the Treaty of Versailles, led to the reduction of the army to one hundred thousand soldiers with only four thousand officers. In reducing the officer corps, Seeckt placed the general staff in control while limiting the role of those with connections—the nobility. Rommel's claim to continuation lay in his performance in combat, but the fact that he had served in 1918 as a staff officer undoubtedly helped. The second major reform was the creation of a massive lessons-learned process. Seeckt ordered a major, realistic, tactical examination of what had actually happened in the war. Despite the officer corps' minuscule size, he created fifty-seven different committees for that purpose. As a result of Seeckt's efforts, the Germans evolved a combat doctrine emphasizing combined-arms, exploitation, speed, and mission-oriented tactics—the last with an emphasis on officers being provided general instructions on *what* they needed to accomplish, with the *how* left to their discretion.

Rommel fit in seamlessly with a culture in which the study of one's profession was the expected norm. His initial experience with the new army was as a company commander in an infantry regiment. By 1924, he was the commander of a machine-gun company. In September 1929 he received an appointment to the Infantry School in Dresden, with a promotion to major at the age of forty. His four years at Dresden underlined Rommel's enthusiasm for his profession. He was an outstanding instructor who loved teaching tactics; in turn he found himself admired by his students, colleagues, and superiors. It was during this period that he started work on what became his book, *Infanterie greift an* (*Infantry Attacks*), a deeply insightful memoir on leadership and psychology in war.

Rommel's next assignment was as a military adviser to the leader of the Hitler Youth, Baldur von Schirach. It was not an assignment he liked and he soon quarreled with the obnoxious Nazi, though Rommel impressed others in the Nazi hierarchy. Assigned to serve as Hitler's army escort at the 1936 Nuremberg Nazi Party rally, he made a deep impression upon the führer. When Hitler accompanied German troops in the occupation of the Sudetenland in October 1938 after the Munich Conference, Rommel commanded the führer's escort battalion. That November he was assigned to serve as the commandant of a new officer academy in Wiener Neustadt. In March 1939 he again served as the commander of Hitler's escort battalion during the occupation of the remainder of Czechoslovakia and then the invasion of Poland. Those attachments, which brought Rommel into close connection with Hitler, played a major role in his assignment to command the 7th Panzer Division in March 1940.

Montgomery's career in the interwar years was quite different from Rommel's. He was an outlier in the officer corps not only because of his personality but because of his approach to the profession of arms. Simply put, he was difficult to get along with. This was a consequence of his constant drive to change an army culture that avoided preparing for a future war. This, in fact, is the root cause for the army's failures, particularly in the early years of World War II. Unlike the high command of Germany, Britain's high command failed to institute a lessons-learned analysis of the war's tactical implications until 1932 and then whitewashed the final report as too critical. Its officers were more interested in foxhunting and polo than in studying their profession. Combined arms appeared occasionally in exercises at the staff college at Camberley, but rarely in practice. There were experiments with a tank force, but such efforts hardly disturbed the thought processes in the messes. Montgomery stood outside that culture. He took his profession seriously, never failing to point out the deficiencies of his subordinates and, on occasion, superiors. His reiterative emphasis on the need for serious study hardly made him a favorite among his peers.

Montgomery's first major assignment after the war came in Ireland during the Troubles, as the Irish fought a political and military insurgency to gain their independence. Here he displayed his ability to address a difficult situation realistically. He argued for a political rather than a military settlement, as he recognized that the latter would prove too costly, lead to further rebellions even if successful, and, most important, prove unacceptable to the British public.

Montgomery's career followed the pattern of assignments typical for his background and interests. His path slowly moved from command of a company, to a battalion, to a brigade in 1937. In all of these assignments, he excelled as a trainer who emphasized imaginative planning and realistic preparation. Nevertheless, his most important assignment had come in January 1926, with a three-year appointment to the staff college at Camberley, where he came under the influence of Colonel Alan Brooke, a man who was to exercise great influence over his career. The time spent teaching proved as valuable for Montgomery as it was for Rommel. It also brought him a wife, whom he deeply loved until her death in 1937.

Throughout his rise, Montgomery made innumerable enemies. One fellow officer commented that Montgomery would fail to rise to the highest level "because he could be so rude." He was not at all likeable, or, in British terms, clubbable. But his sheer competence as a trainer, planner, and commander prevented his being shunted off into the category of unpromotable. In June 1934, after battalion command with the Royal Warwickshires, Montgomery accepted a post as the chief instructor at the Indian Army's staff college at Quetta. He then returned to Britain in the summer of 1937 to assume command of the 9th Infantry Brigade. Devastated by the loss of his wife, while in command, he focused his attention on training the brigade to a pitch of readiness. Given how little funding the Chamberlain government was providing the army, hard training at the lowest levels of platoon and company was about all Montgomery could do. Nevertheless, in 1938 he organized an amphibious landing exercise, one that unfortunately had little impact on the army. Later that year he became commander of the 8th Infantry Division in Palestine, part of the force the British deployed to put down a major Arab rebellion. In July 1939 he returned to Britain, a nation desperately attempting to refurbish its army, to command the 3rd Division.

In many ways Patton fell between Rommel and Montgomery in his experiences during the interwar period. In fact, the U.S. Army was far more innovative and thoughtful an institution than the British one. In the war's aftermath, Pershing instituted a major lessons-learned analysis. But the continental expanse of American military posts, scattered across the United States, made it impossible to carry out major maneuvers during the interwar period. Starved of money and for the most part stationed in areas far away from the centers of American society, the army was a backwater. Although there was little money for exercises, the army did allow room and opportunities for its officers to think about war, in all of its dimensions. In particular, both the army and navy emphasized the study of strategic and logistic issues. Disgusted by the appalling American mobilization of 1917 and 1918, the army founded the Industrial College, which allowed the Americans to plan the nation's mobilization in the 1940s far more effectively than in 1917.

Patton's career in the interwar period represents a fascinating set of contradictions. On one hand he proved a major exponent of the tank. On the other, he paid his dues as a good cavalryman and advocate of his branch, while at the same time living the life of a polo-playing, socially well-connected officer. In the early 1920s, Patton and a young captain, Dwight Eisenhower, were strong proponents of using armor in ways similar to the Germans in their early blitz-kriegs through Poland and France. But both found themselves brought up short by their branch chiefs—infantry for Eisenhower and cavalry for Patton—who wanted to keep tanks spread out and in close support of the slow-moving infantry. Thereafter, Patton remained on the right side of his branch and eschewed writing or making suggestions that might annoy those above. But for those who knew him, he was an officer with serious intellectual roots in the history of his profession. In fact, of the three generals, Patton was the most widely read in military history. He took professional military education seriously, graduating with distinction in his class at Fort Leavenworth, Kansas.

Nevertheless, no matter how well Patton played the game, there was something manic about his behavior. He played polo with a frenzy and abandon, richly sprinkled with expletives. That penchant once got him a severe dressing-down from Major General Drum, superintendent of the Hawaiian Department. In the course of polo playing Patton suffered several concussions, which may well explain his less-than-disciplined behavior at higher levels. It is also clear that Patton at times drank too much; politically correct, he was not.

However, unlike many fellow officers, Patton smelled war on the horizon. His greatest fear seems to have been that because of age, he might miss out. Returning to the cavalry in 1927, Patton followed a number of command and staff assignments. None satisfied him fully; unlike most veteran officers of the last conflict, he had not had his fill of war. As he did throughout his life, Patton cultivated those who might help in advancing his career. When attached to the Cavalry Regiment at Fort Myer in the late 1930s, he made every attempt to present himself at the same time that General George C. Marshall went for his daily ride. Similarly, he kept up his close connections with Stimson. Over the 1931–32 academic year, Patton attended the Army War College; again he proved himself a serious student of his profession. The college's commandant forwarded his research paper comparing the advantages of conscripted versus professional armies to the War Department with the notation that it was one of "exceptional merit."

In July 1938 Patton finally regained the rank of full colonel, which he had held in 1918. That same month he assumed command of the 3rd Cavalry, only to find himself called to Washington to take command of the 5th Cavalry Regiment at Fort Myer. Patton's opportunity came at the beginning of September 1939: The Second World War broke out in Europe and, equally important, George C. Marshall became chief of staff. Because Marshall had a high estimation of the cavalry officer's ability, Patton was one of few over age fifty to survive Marshall's purge of old, infirm, and incompetent officers. But Patton still had to change with the times. The stunning German success in France in the spring of 1940 underlined that the day of the horse cavalry was over, and Patton abandoned his branch without looking back. In early August 1940 he assumed command of one of the armored brigades of the "Hell on Wheels" 2nd Armored Division; within a matter of days he found himself as the acting division commander, which became permanent at year's end. It was not an easy transition from cavalry to armor, but again Patton's attention to detail and discipline brought his gaggle of peacetime conscripts into something resembling military effectiveness.

In 1941 the army finally had the funds to conduct maneuvers on a giant scale. The resulting Tennessee (June) and Louisiana (September) Maneuvers represented the U.S. Army's first attempt to put together the pieces of its rapidly expanding forces and see how they all worked in coordination with one another. From a force that numbered barely one hundred thousand men in the summer of 1940, the army exploded to nearly 1.5 million men a year later. It was raw, its staff was inexperienced, its troops untrained, its commanders uncertain, and its tactics inadequate. The Tennessee Maneuvers displayed Patton's aggressiveness and self-confidence; his division already was earning a reputation as being exceptionally well-trained. During a briefing, he displayed a noodle on a plate and attempted to push it without noticeable success. He then announced: "Gentlemen, you don't push the noodle, you pull it. In other words, you lead." In the Louisiana Maneuvers, Patton's 2nd Armored Division was even more successful. Taking his division on an extended 350-mile march, Patton's blue force outflanked the opposing red army and swung in behind it to attack from the rear. So successful was his outflanking move that the maneuvers were halted five days early. No sooner had the Louisiana Maneuvers ended than the 2nd Armored Division moved into the Carolinas for a third exercise. Again Patton's division was impressive; this time he had the pleasure of capturing the opposing general, Hugh Drum, who had once chewed him out mercilessly in Hawaii in the 1930s. It was on the basis of their performance in these maneuvers that Marshall selected most of the army's commanders for the next war. Patton had certainly taken advantage of his opportunity.

Generalship in the Second World War

Rommel again became the commander of the führer's military escort in the 1939 Polish campaign—a campaign during which Hitler traveled extensively from one battle site to another. If Rommel had doubts about the potential of mechanized warfare, his observations made him a convert. Here the advantage the Germans enjoyed over their opponents in the war's first years lay in the fact that mechanization neatly fit the Wehrmacht's doctrine of combined-arms, decentralized tactics that aimed to create breakdowns in the enemy's defensive system at both the tactical and the operational level. It is not clear whether Hitler directly intervened to get Rommel command of one of the coveted panzer divisions, which would lead all future German offensive actions, but Rommel assumed command of the 7th Panzer Division in March 1940. The unit was still transitioning from a light division into a panzer division, and its equipment was somewhat unusual, since a substantial portion of its tanks were of Czech manufacture, part of the booty the Germans acquired as a result of Neville Chamberlain's surrender of Czechoslovakia at the

Munich conference in September 1938. During the "Phoney War" between the fall of Poland and the opening of the campaign in the west in May 1940, the Germans ruthlessly prepared their troops for the upcoming battle.

Rommel's 7th Panzer Division found itself attached to General Hermann Hoth's corps, which deployed on the right of the three panzer corps the Germans aimed to punch through the center of French lines in the supposedly impenetrable Ardennes. The crossing on the western edge of the Meuse was to create a breakthrough, the results of which would destroy the French Army. Of the six crossing attempts the panzer divisions made on May 13–14, four failed. Of the two that succeeded, Guderian's 1st Panzer Division has received most of the credit. However, the most thorough account of the campaign has noted that Rommel's 7th Division achieved the crucial success.

General Rommel in North Africa, 1942
(Library of Congress Prints and Photographs Division, Washington, D.C.)

Unlike Guderian's crossing of the Meuse, Rommel's effort received no close air support from the Luftwaffe. In effect it was a straight-out river crossing, in which artillery supported hard-pressed infantry under intense fire from the French. By the time Rommel arrived, the attempted crossing was on the brink of failure. Half a company had crossed, but only after suffering heavy casualties. At that point Rommel took matters into his own hands, jumping into the Meuse to help emplace an improvised bridge for the tanks to cross—an action that demanded that his infantry follow or die trying. He was, however, able to ferry some of his tanks across the river even before his engineers had completed the bridge's construction. Slowly the Germans pushed the French back. Without Rommel's leadership and drive, it is doubtful whether the division would have achieved a successful bridgehead.

But Rommel's saga in the campaign had hardly begun. The 7th Panzer Division's success opened the way for Hoth's other panzer division, the 5th, to cross. That division absorbed most of the French counterattacks, while Rommel struck deep into the French rear. The threat the 7th Panzer Division posed, along with Guderian's pressure farther south, led the French commander to order their fortress division defending Monthermé to retreat from its nearly impregnable position. This was a terrible mistake, as once in the open, the division had no chance against the 6th Panzer that was following behind Rommel and Guderian.

Once his armor was across, Rommel began an advance that quite literally ripped his French opponents to shreds. By the evening of May 14, the 7th Panzer Division had its full complement of tanks across. In its lead was the 25th Panzer Regiment, accompanied by Rommel, who led the division on a narrow thrust straight across the Franco-Belgian border and through the weakly held extension of the Maginot Line. Rommel said of the breakthrough into the open:

> The people in the houses were rudely awoken by the din of our tanks, the clatter and roar of engines. Troops lay bivouacked beside the road, military vehicles stood parked in farmyards and in some places in the road itself. Civilians and French troops, their faces distorted with terror, lay huddled in the ditches, alongside hedges and in every hollow beside the road. . . . On we went at a steady speed, towards our objective. . . . We were through the Maginot Line. Soon we began to meet refugee columns and detachments of French troops preparing for the

march. A chaos of guns, tanks and military vehicles of all kinds, inextricably entangled with horse-drawn refugee carts, covered the road and verges. . . . The French troops were completely overcome by surprise at our sudden appearance, laid down their arms, and marched off to the east beside our column.

As the German advance moved relentlessly forward, larger and larger groups of French troops surrendered after only weak resistance. To many commentators both at the time and afterward, Rommel was taking extraordinary chances with his drive along a single axis. But Rommel sensed, as did other German panzer commanders, that the French Army's command and control had collapsed. As the French aviator and author Antoine de Saint-Exupéry noted:

In every region through which [the German armor has] made [its] lightning sweep, a French army, even though it seems to be intact, has ceased to be an army. It has been transformed into clotted segments. It has, so to say, coagulated. The armored divisions play the part of a chemical agent precipitating a solution. Where once an organization existed they leave a mere sum of organs whose unity has been destroyed. Between the clots— however combative the clots may have remained—the enemy moves at will.

By May 18, Rommel was advancing through the open country of northern France on Cambrai. So far, the 7th Panzer Division had formed the most damaging of the German thrusts across the Meuse. In eight days, its tanks, infantry, and artillery had advanced 175 miles, captured more than ten thousand French soldiers, and destroyed nearly 150 tanks and armored cars. Its losses: thirty-five dead, fifty-nine wounded. It was perhaps the most impressive accomplishment by a single division in a week's time in the whole of the war, not only for its tactical accomplishments but also for its operational impact. On May 21, the 7th Panzer Division finally ran into significant resistance. In a counterattack near Arras, British tanks gave some of its lead elements a bloody nose. Though the British were repulsed, the failed counterattack had an effect on the German high command. Three days later Hitler issued the famous halt order, which stopped the panzers in their tracks and gave the British the breathing room they needed to evacuate their army through the port of Dunkirk.

The leading scholar on the German campaign commented on Rommel's performance: "There was probably nobody who practiced the principle of 'leading from up front' in a more extreme fashion than Rommel. In that way, he became a nightmare for his staff officers. On the other hand, Rommel had the intuitive talent for anticipating situation changes. Again and again, he turned up completely by surprise at the right time and right place and brought about the decisive turning point in the fighting through his intervention." It was indeed an extraordinary performance.

Even as the British were evacuating their army from the Continent, the 7th Panzer Division was redeployed toward the Seine River to take part in the assault that would finish off the French Army. It remained under Hoth's corps on the right flank of the offensive. This time the French put up stiff resistance, and the 7th Panzer, driving south to cross the Seine at Rouen, found the bridges blown. This necessitated a hard fight to cross the river, but once on the other side, the division broke the thin crust of French defenses. In the open Rommel, once again, moved so swiftly that he trapped the British 51st Highland Division on the coast. Thereafter, the 7th Panzer had an easy walk through Normandy to Cherbourg. It then turned south to reach for Bordeaux, but the armistice, signaling the final collapse of the French, halted the advance. All in all it had been a spectacular run, earning the division the sobriquet of the "ghost division."

By early July 1940 thoughts in the German high command—and not just Hitler—had already turned to a potential invasion of the Soviet Union. But fate had set a different course for Rommel. In early June, Benito Mussolini, Italy's dictator, sure Germany had won the war, declared war on Britain and France. The Italian services, however, were not ready for war despite the massive resources Mussolini had lavished on them. The problem lay with their incompetent officer corps, which had little interest in the study of its profession. As Marshal Rodolfo Graziani had proclaimed shortly before the Italian declaration of war: "When the cannon sounds, everything will fall into place automatically." In fact nothing fell into place. Beginning with the Italian invasion of Greece in October 1940, the Italians suffered a series of disastrous setbacks, culminating with the British destruction of an Italian invading army in Egypt's western desert in late 1940, followed by a rapid advance into Libya. At this point the Germans had to step in to rectify the collapsing strategic situation in the Mediterranean. Hitler detailed an expeditionary force of corps strength to deploy to North Africa, and he appointed Rommel to command the force, soon to become famous as the Afrika Korps.

Rommel arrived in North Africa in mid-February 1941. Since only the first major unit, the 5th Light Division, would not complete its deployment to North Africa until mid-March, the Oberkommando des Heeres (the OKH—the army high command) was explicit in its orders: Rommel was to remain on the defensive until May, when the 15th Panzer Division would complete its deployment. However, Rommel quickly recognized that a substantial opportunity existed in the western desert. The British had redeployed much of their North Africa–based army to Greece, while the units remaining in Egypt had little combat experience. Not only that, but the new crop of British division and corps commanders he would face had had little preparation to fight a mobile war. As soon as the tanks of the light division arrived in late March, Rommel, disregarding his orders, attacked. Ironically, British intelligence contributed to its own army's collapse. Ultra intelligence informed the British high command of the OKH's orders for Rommel to assume a defensive posture. They never guessed he would ignore his orders.

The speed of Rommel's attack scattered the British, and those not captured or killed hustled back toward the Egyptian frontier as fast as they could. By April 3, Rommel had captured Benghazi and his lead units were approaching Tobruk, which was held by a substantial number of Australians. Here, Rommel ran into his first setback. At the tactical level the Australians were among the toughest soldiers in the world. According to a German report, the Australians were "tough and hard opponents as individual fighters, highly skilled in defence . . . cold-blooded and skilled in in-fighting . . . and capable of hardships of all kind." Thus, attacks on Tobruk met dogged, effective resistance. In one attack the 15th Panzer Division, newly arrived, lost thirty-five out of seventy tanks; included in its casualties was its division commander.

The German high command was not at all happy with Rommel's deliberate disobedience. The chief of the army's general staff, Generaloberst Franz Halder, noted on April 23, 1941: "Rommel has not sent us a single clear-cut report all these days, but I have the feeling that things are in a mess. . . . All day long he rushes about between the widely scattered units; and stages reconnaissance raids in which he fritters away his forces. No one has a clear idea of their disposition or striking power. . . . Perhaps it is better to dispatch Major General Paulus. He has good personal relations with Rommel from way back, when they served together, and he is perhaps the only man with enough personal influence to head off this soldier gone stark mad."

Paulus, the future commander of the Sixth Army at Stalingrad, returned from his trip to North Africa to report that Rommel had gotten himself and the Afrika Korps into serious supply difficulties with the rapidity of their advance to the Egyptian border. In fact, Rommel was caught in a trap. His advance demanded a supply level the Italian and German logisticians could not meet as long as Tobruk remained in British hands, while the task of taking Tobruk would mean that the troops on the Egyptian frontier would remain vulnerable to a British offensive. The operational and logistical difficulties that Rommel confronted after his April offensive have led a number of historians to criticize his understanding of strategy and supply. What they miss is that Rommel's task was to restore Italy's strategic position in Libya and keep the British at bay. In one month of rapid mobile warfare he had achieved both goals.

One does have to admit that Rommel received considerable help from the British. Quite simply, the British Army was incapable in 1941 of waging combined-arms warfare. Many units were badly trained or trained within an entirely inadequate tactical framework. The different arms simply went their own way. The worst were the armored units, most of which had been horse cavalry in the interwar years and then converted to tanks just before the war. Their commanders and regimental officers seem to have regarded the battle in the desert as a large foxhunting expedition. Uninterested in the intellectual demands of their profession, they proved incapable of adapting to the speed and rapidity of Rommel's moves. A South African officer recorded his impression of new armored units arriving from Britain in the following terms: "Other officers told me they had seen the [8th] Hussars charging into the Jerry tanks, sitting on top of their turrets more or less with their whips out. 'It looked like the first run up to the first fence at a point-to-point,' the adjutant described it. This first action was very typical of those early encounters involving cavalry regiments. They had incredible enthusiasm and dash which was only curbed by the rapidly decreasing stock of dashing officers and tanks." The Germans, with their combined-arms tactics and an extraordinary battlefield leader, made mincemeat of such units. In the tight fighting around Tobruk in fortified positions, the British were more than capable of holding their own. But out in mobile war in the desert, they were hopeless.

The first British counteroffensive came in June 1941. Operation Battleaxe almost immediately underlined how far behind the Wehrmacht the British were. A well-laid screen of German 88mm anti-tank guns along the Halfaya Pass slaughtered the attackers. Then, Rommel's counterattack on the third day came close to putting the British Eighth Army in the bag. The Germans lost only nineteen tanks in the fighting, many repairable, while the British lost ninety-one. The speed with which Rommel moved from the siege of Tobruk to the battle on the Egyptian frontier underlines the mobility and flexibility of German doctrine, as well as his leadership. The defeat led Churchill to fire the Middle East's commander, General Archibald Wavell, and replace him with General Claude Auchinleck.

Five months later the British tried again. Both sides had built up their forces, although logistical difficulties placed considerable constraints as to what Rommel could do. Further, the fighting in Russia was already wearing down the Wehrmacht's ability to support the battle in North Africa, which the Germans regarded as a subsidiary theater. This time the British caught "the Desert Fox" by surprise, since he was on the brink of launching his own offensive to take Tobruk. In the Operation Crusader battles, the British possessed an enormous superiority in tanks—710, with 500 more in the pipeline—while the Afrika Korps had only 174. Moreover, Rommel was fighting on two fronts, as the garrison at Tobruk attempted a breakout. Both sides mismanaged the battle. A German attack near Sidi Rezegh cost Rommel half his tanks, and a wild drive by his armor into the British rear—a quintessential Rommel move—failed to disturb British efforts to break through to Tobruk. With his armor worn down and mounting supply problems, Rommel broke off the battle and retreated to El Agheila. Interestingly, Hitler failed to interfere with Rommel's decision to retreat, probably because the unfolding catastrophe in Russia, as the Wehrmacht's offensive on Moscow ground to a halt, was absorbing his attention.

In January 1942, with his logistical situation repaired and the arrival of a fresh supply of tanks, Rommel drove the British back to Gazala, where both sides went over to the defensive. The British built up a massive fortified line with a series of strongpoints that reached from the Mediterranean deep into the desert. However, none of these fortified positions were mutually supporting. Moreover, for unfathomable reasons, British commanders assumed that, were Rommel to attack, he would not attempt to outflank the Gazala position but rather would attack in the center of their defenses. Thus, they deployed British armor in the center rather than on the southern flank. And, given their enormous superiority in men and matériel, they did not believe Rommel would dare to take the initiative.

As usual, they were wrong. During the night of May 26–27, the Afrika Korps, with its German and Italian armor leading, began a massive outflanking move around British defenses. British reconnaissance armored cars picked up the move, but, secure in their assumptions, British commanders failed to respond. Within a matter of hours Rommel's attacking columns destroyed two motorized infantry brigades and an armored brigade. They also overran the headquarters of the 1st Armored Division and captured its commander, which rendered it incapable of fighting as a division. Rommel had hoped to drive through to the coast, thus trapping the British units within the Gazala line, but heavy British resistance in the center as well as increasing supply problems forced him to laager in the middle of British positions. There, a screen of the deadly 88mm antitank guns slaughtered uncoordinated counterattacks by British tanks, while on the western side of the German pocket, the Germans sought to break through and restore their supply lines. On June 5 the British lost nearly 250 tanks in these badly planned and executed attacks.

Nevertheless, not until June 10 did the Germans finally reestablish their supply lines. Two days later the Afrika Korps broke out. Again the British failed to coordinate their armor and thus wasted the advantage they still held in number of armored fighting vehicles. After overrunning two armored brigades, Rommel's screen of 88s then destroyed a third. At this point, British resistance collapsed, and dispirited British troops took off for Egypt. The question for the British high command was whether to continue holding Tobruk. The initial decision was to abandon the port, a decision that Churchill countermanded. However, while the number of soldiers available was reasonably large—a South African division, a brigade of Guards, and an armored brigade of seventy tanks—the British had made no preparations for a renewed defense of this crucial port. On June 19 the Afrika Korps drove past the port's defenses as if headed to Egypt. But during the night the Germans returned, and in the early morning hours they attacked. They caught the defenders completely by surprise, and in a matter of hours it was over. The South African division commander surrendered Tobruk with its thirty-three thousand defenders and massive booty. The success led Hitler to promote Rommel to field marshal.

The Axis leaders now confronted the question of whether to advance the Afrika Korps into Egypt—in spite of its severe debilitation during the Gazala battles—or launch an amphibious assault on Malta instead. Rommel persuaded Hitler that the former was the proper course, saying that an assault on Malta had a considerable chance of defeat, given that the Italian high command would be in charge. And so Rommel drove the Afrika Korps into Egypt. There, the Germans ran into well-sited British defenses at El Alamein, which held against Rommel's weakened forces. Both sides then turned to the processes of restoring and rebuilding their forces. For the British this also involved major changes not only in command but in their overall approach to the battle.

North Africa and Sicily

At the war's outset Montgomery found himself in command of a division. Unlike some of the other divisions in the BEF—and the French, for that matter—Montgomery trained his division with a thoroughness that made him infamous. The 3rd Division was ready for war, but its experience in May 1940 was much like that of the BEF in the first months of the last war: a rapid advance to contact with the Germans in Belgium and then an even swifter retreat.

Only here, Montgomery's division played a key role. As the retreat to the Channel gathered momentum, King Leopold of Belgium surrendered his army to the Germans. In a desperate night march, the 3rd Division covered the resulting gap on the Allied left flank, ensuring that the BEF and a substantial number of French soldiers could escape from Dunkirk. Montgomery's performance earned him justifiable praise, especially from Brooke. As a result, in the summer of 1940, Montgomery was promoted to acting lieuten-

ant general and given command of a corps defending the most exposed areas of southern England. By December 1941 he had
received promotion to South-Eastern Command.

However, it was not until the summer of 1942 that he received
his great opportunity. In July 1942 Winston Churchill and Brooke
arrived in Cairo to sort out the mess British generals had made of
the Middle East. After their deliberation, Auchinleck received his
walking papers, while General "Strafer" Gott received command of
the Eighth Army. Gott, however, never received his command, as on
his way to his new post a Bf 109 shot down the aircraft carrying him
and then strafed the wreckage. Gott died in the crash, and Brooke
persuaded Churchill to give Montgomery command of the Eighth
Army. The fact that it took the death of its newly appointed commander to finally provide Montgomery his chance suggests how
deeply he was disliked by his colleagues. The army that Montgomery inherited had just held off an Afrika Korps attack on the British
position at El Alamein. But British weaknesses still lay deep. Rommel perceptively pointed out in 1944: "[The Guards Brigade] was
almost a living embodiment of the virtues and faults of the British
soldier—tremendous courage and tenacity combined with a rigid
lack of mobility."

Montgomery set about to repair as many of the Eighth Army's
deficiencies as possible, given the constraints of time and the weaknesses of the army's leaders. Above all, he aimed to make himself
known to the soldiers at the sharp end. The one area where his efforts failed to gain the necessary results lay in the weaknesses of his
senior officers, particularly the commanders of his armored divisions, who seemed unable to adapt to the pace of modern armored
warfare. Because of this leadership failure, Montgomery was willing
to let Rommel have the first try at attacking. At the same time, he
made it clear to his officers and soldiers that there would be no retreat from El Alamein. As he informed the troops defending the
Alam Halfa Ridge, they would stay there alive, or they would stay
there dead. The El Alamein line had a significant advantage over
other positions in Egypt because of the Qattara Depression to the

south, a great morass of salt, impassable to heavy vehicles. Thus, the Afrika Korps could not make a flanking move to the south. Rommel would have to fight his way through the Eighth Army if he wanted to reach the Nile River valley.

Rommel attacked in early September, and the Eighth Army stopped the Afrika Korps cold. For the first time Rommel felt the full effect of the Royal Air Force, coordinated far better by Montgomery and his opposites in the air service than in the past. Nevertheless, in spite of the thrashing Montgomery's defenses inflicted on the Germans, he refused to allow his troops to engage in a mobile battle, in which the Germans were so superior. Instead, he built up his forces for an assault on the German positions, when ready. He ran into heavy pressure from Churchill to attack, the prime minister being influenced by Ultra intelligence indicating overwhelming British superiority in armor, infantry, and artillery. But Montgomery stuck to his guns. He would not attack until ready. By October's end the Eighth Army enjoyed a two-to-one advantage in soldiers and artillery and nearly three-to-one in tanks. But perhaps Montgomery's greatest advantage lay in the fact that Rommel was in Germany, recovering from a bad case of jaundice.

Montgomery's plan was straightforward: Diversionary attacks in the south would pin German attention there while infantry supported by heavy artillery bombardments created two passageways through the extensive defenses and minefields in the north. General Herbert Lumsden's X Armored Corps would then move rapidly through the lanes deep into German positions. Significantly, Rommel had built up a strong defensive position, because he knew that with the Afrika Korps' weaknesses in fuel and ammunition, he could not win a battle of maneuver. Operation Lightfoot began in the early evening hours of October 23 with a bombardment that lasted for over five hours and dumped half a million shells on the German and Italian positions. During the night British and dominion infantry reached half their objectives, but the armored units displayed little eagerness to close. On the other side of the hill, matters did not go well, either. Rommel's replacement in command of the Afrika Korps, General Georg

Stumme, died of a heart attack, which placed a great strain on the conduct of operations. Hitler ordered Rommel to fly back to North Africa, but the field marshal did not arrive back at his headquarters until late on the twenty-fifth. By then his subordinates had frittered away nearly 50 percent of the German tank strength, with the 15th Panzer Division losing nearly 75 percent of its armor, while losses in artillery and infantry were also heavy.

By the end of the second day Montgomery adapted; after a one-day pause to refit and redeploy his forces, he resumed the offensive. The British now launched an even heavier attack in the north. Over the next five days, through a steady process of attrition, the British, in Montgomery's words, "crumbled the German defenses." By October 31, Rommel was down to ninety tanks, while the British, with a constant flow of reinforcements, still had close to the eight hundred with which they had begun the offensive. Recognizing the game was up, Rommel ordered a retreat from El Alamein, which Hitler immediately countermanded. The next day the Afrika Korps finally slipped away, but the additional losses caused by Hitler's order to hold the line ended any chance of Axis forces making a stand in Libya.

El Alamein represented Britain's first significant offensive victory against the Germans during the war. Nevertheless, it was incomplete, because Montgomery and his division commanders botched the pursuit. Five days after Rommel's retreat from the battlefield, Anglo-American forces landed in Morocco and Algeria, fundamentally altering the strategic situation in North Africa. Rommel drew the correct conclusion from the landing: The Axis strategic position in North Africa was no longer tenable, given the enormous superiority the Allies enjoyed in air and naval power. The supposed strategic geniuses on the general staff, however, thought they knew better and advised Hitler to commit major forces to the defense of Tunisia. As a result, Rommel had to retreat as fast as possible back to Tunisia, as the logistical support and reinforcements were now flowing in there. By the time Rommel's retreat reached Tunisia, the Germans had covered fourteen hundred miles. On the other hand, Montgomery found his pursuit slowed by the steadily growing length of his supply tether. The Eighth Army barely made it to Tripoli before it had to halt to resupply and reinforce its exhausted divisions.

Interestingly, Patton and Montgomery met for the first time in Tripoli, when Montgomery held a study group on his experiences thus far in the North African campaign during the halt in the Eighth Army's advance to Tunisia. In spite of Montgomery's invitation to major Allied headquarters in the Mediterranean, few senior officers showed up. The only American present was Patton, whom Montgomery dismissed as "an old man of about 60." As he was leaving, Patton exclaimed: "I may be old, I may be slow, I may be stoopid, and I know I'm deaf, but it just don't mean a thing to me." However, an entry in his diary indicates that Montgomery had impressed him: "small, very alert, wonderfully conceited, and the best soldier—or so it seems—I have met in this war. My friend General Briggs says he is the best soldier and the most disagreeable man he knows."

While Montgomery reconstituted his lines of communication, Patton's chance came. Up to that point he had been serving largely as a diplomat in keeping the French and Moroccan leaders happy. But in mid-February, the roof fell in on the U.S. Army's II Corps. Its commander, Lloyd Fredendall, was the worst sort of general: arrogant, unwilling to listen to others, professionally inept, and a coward to boot. One historian, quoting a British general, described Fredendall as "a prime example of the traditional over-ripe, overbearing, and explosive senior officers in whom the caricaturists have always delighted." Fredendall had deployed his II Corps, consisting of green troops, over such an extended front that it invited a German attack.

By early February, Rommel was back behind defenses—the Mareth Line—the French had strung along the Tunisian–Libyan frontier, contemplating a major strike at the II Corps positions aimed at driving behind its lines, wrecking supply dumps, and perhaps inflicting on it the kind of humiliating defeat that had given the Eighth Army its deep-seated inferiority complex. The difficulty in making

Rommel's proposal work was the reality that Axis troops in North Africa had to strike quickly, before the Eighth Army arrived to assault the Mareth Line. But Rommel was no longer fully in charge of the North African theater. Holding the northern section of Tunisia, General Hans-Jürgen von Arnim had little interest in cooperating with Rommel, while Field Marshal Albert Kesselring, the overall Axis commander in the Mediterranean, failed to supervise the Tunisian theater closely. The result was that von Arnim frittered away his forces in a badly planned and executed attack against the British in the north, appropriately code-named Oxen Head. Thus, while Rommel's attack through the Kasserine Pass to the south achieved a considerable tactical success against the American II Corps, he had to break the attack off before it could inflict substantial operational damage on the Americans.

For senior British officers the American travails at the Kasserine Pass indicated that their ally was not up to the serious business of war, an estimation that persisted through to 1945. The British missed the fact that the Americans were steadily improving and would soon prove to be more tactically adept than comparable British units. In the period after his wounding in Normandy in July 1944, Rommel noted: "In Tunisia the Americans had to pay a stiff price for their experience, but it brought rich dividends. Even at that time, the American generals showed themselves to be very advanced in the tactical handling of their forces, although we had to wait until the Patton Army in France to see the most astonishing achievements in mobile warfare. The Americans it is fair to say, profited far more than the British from their experience in Africa."

Patton's job in the immediate period after he had relieved Fredendall was to clean up the mess his predecessor had created. The troops soon felt Patton's iron hand. They now had to wear their helmets at all times, salute their superiors, and pay attention to what some authors term "chicken shit," but which is essential if one wants to turn an armed mob into an army. Perhaps most important was the fact that the troops saw Patton often, especially those in combat; there he was inspecting, cajoling, threatening, and, more often than

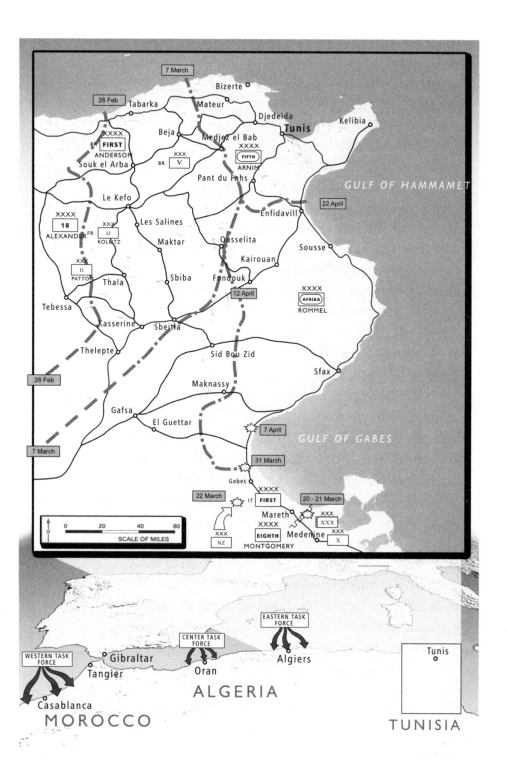

not, encouraging. Unlike Fredendall, there was no hiding in a head-quarters buried in a mountain.

While Patton was struggling to restore discipline to the II Corps, Rommel had turned south in an effort to catch the Eighth Army napping. But whatever his weaknesses in pursuing enemies in a mobile battle, Montgomery was always alert. In this case Ultra intelligence, based on the breaking of high-level German ciphers, provided him with a clear picture of Rommel's intentions. The result was a major defeat for Rommel and what little was left of the Afrika Korps. It proved to be Rommel's swan song in North Africa. Exhausted by two years of constant struggle against the British as well as his own high command, the field marshal was in no condition to command the coming battle of Tunisia. Soon after Rommel had returned to Germany, Patton turned the II Corps over to Omar Bradley and resumed his duties in North Africa, planning for the invasion of Sicily. By then, he had also made an enemy of Bradley, who had little understanding of Patton's style of leadership or his willingness to take risks. Bradley's jealousy was to simmer as a cancer and come close to destroying Patton's career. In April and early May, Montgomery, supported by the II Corps, completed the job of clearing Axis forces from the southern coasts of the Mediterranean.

With the collapse of the Axis pocket in Tunisia and the surrender of nearly 250,000 Axis troops (more than the Soviets had captured in Stalingrad three months earlier), Allied commanders turned to the invasion of Sicily. Harold Alexander, overall commander of Anglo-American ground forces in the Mediterranean, and his staff had made a hash of the planning for the proposed landings on Sicily, with differing-sized forces scattered over the southern and eastern portions of the island but no clear focus of effort. Montgomery, thoroughly dissatisfied with the proposed plans, stepped in and, in consultation with Eisenhower's chief of staff, General Bedell Smith, set out his conception of what the coming invasion should look like. By end-running his boss, Montgomery was putting himself in a dangerous political position, but his explanation for his action illuminates a great deal about the sharp edge that so many of his fellow countrymen found upsetting: "I have seen so many mistakes made in this war, and so many disasters happen, that I am desperately anxious to try and see that we have no more."

Montgomery's Eighth Army was to land on the southeastern corner of the island, while Patton, now a lieutenant general, would command the Seventh Army and protect the flank of British forces. The overall commander was Alexander, with the Fifteenth Army Group. Patton's army was activated shortly before the initial landing took place on July 9. In Operation Husky, the British and American landings went relatively well, although there were dicey moments in the landings at Gela, both within the city and in the beaches to the west, where the 1st Infantry Division had landed. The fact that Patton had lobbied hard with Eisenhower to ensure that he would have that experienced 1st Infantry Division in spite of Bradley's misgivings represented his major contribution to the landing's success. Bradley's opposition, which he later admitted had been wrong, rested on his dislike of the division's hard-charging, swearing commander, Terry de la Mesa Allen.

The campaign to drive the Germans and remnants of the Italian military out of Sicily demonstrated Alexander's lack of drive and competence. Anglo-American relations came close to the breaking point when, without informing his American subordinates, Alexander allowed Montgomery to take control of a key road leading north in the American sector. Then the fumbled replacement of forward units allowed the Germans to shore up their defenses and prepare the way for a slow-fighting withdrawal. While the British and many American units slogged north, Patton drove his forces on an end run to Palermo, gathering headlines in American newspapers but doing little operational damage to the Germans. And while Patton's troops barely reached Messina before the British, that, too, represented a flawed operational success, as the bulk of the German Army had escaped across the straits to Italy. The mistakes that led to the German escape were largely the fault of Eisenhower and Alexander— the former by failing to provide any substantive input to the ground campaign and the latter by failing to order his air and naval subordinates to close off the Strait of Messina, which they could have done at relatively little cost. The German troops' escape from Sicily led to a long and exhausting campaign on the Italian mainland, but those battles would involve other generals.

It was in the campaign in Sicily that Patton crossed the line between being a hard-nosed general and a tyrant who could not control his own feelings. His actions almost ended his career and certainly ended the possibility that he would become the chief American ground force commander in the campaign to liberate northwestern Europe. On August 3, while visiting a hospital, Patton came across a soldier who had no visible wounds. After slapping the soldier with his gloves, he then literally kicked him out of the hospital. One week later, while visiting another hospital, Patton acted in an even more abusive fashion, causing a huge scandal. Not surprisingly, Eisenhower was furious. His letter to Patton noted among other pointed criticisms: "I must so seriously question your good judgment and self-discipline, as to raise serious doubt in my mind as to your future usefulness." In the end Eisenhower still stood behind Patton and made clear to General Marshall how important he believed Patton to be for the upcoming invasion of northern France. For his behavior, Patton apologized in front of every unit in his Seventh Army. The incidents exploded back in the United States that fall, when the yellow journalist Drew Pearson attacked Patton. There were calls from many in Congress as well as the day's media that Patton return in disgrace. But both Marshall and Stimson, now the secretary of war, stood behind the general.

The Final Test: The Battle for France and Germany

At the end of 1943 Hitler ordered Rommel to inspect the defenses of northwestern Europe and assess their ability to withstand a major amphibious assault. Rommel's report was deeply pessimistic. The supposed "Atlantic Wall" existed only in the propaganda dreams of the clubfooted Dr. Joseph Goebbels; those who were to defend the beaches of France and the Low Countries were the tired veterans of the eastern front, as well as the sick, the lame, or those too old to be committed to a combat theater. For too long the western front had been not a place for training units to defend Fortress Europe, but rather a theater for rest and refit. Rommel's reward for his troubles was his appointment as commander of Army Group B, charged with the defense of the occupied territories from Denmark to Brittany.

Rommel's orders subordinated him to Field Marshal Gerd von Rundstedt, overall commander in the west, while the Oberkommando der Wehrmacht (OKW—the Wehrmacht's high command) oversaw the field commanders in the west. The setup allowed Hitler maximum chance to interfere with the disposition of military forces in the west, and in January 1944 he ordered that the defense of the west receive the highest priority. No longer would it be regarded as a holding tank from which forces would deploy to meet the next catastrophe in the east. Rommel took full advantage of that priority to ensure that the troops in the west trained ruthlessly; they and dragooned French workers laid masses of mines and obstructions along the coast; and his subordinate army, corps, and division commanders prepared themselves to fight under the conditions of Allied air superiority, which only Rommel understood fully.

Therein lay the rub. Rommel was one of the few senior commanders in the west who had experienced Allied air forces. That realization led him to the simple but realistic assumption that if the Germans failed to stop the Allies on the beaches, then with their air superiority and matériel, the Allies would inevitably win the battle of the buildup, and Germany would lose the war. Hitler, Rundstedt, and other senior commanders—especially the putative commander of the panzer army to be established after the invasion, General Leo Geyr von Schweppenburg—had not experienced those Anglo-American capabilities. The latter two generals argued for keeping the panzers back, away from the beaches, for a mobile defense. Their conception represented a conventional German response, one that paid little attention to the difficulties the Wehrmacht would con-

front once the Allies were ashore. Hitler, however, split the difference and declared that no panzer units could move without his
permission.

For Rommel the five months before D-day represented a hurri-
cane of action. He threw his efforts into building up the West Wall.
In two key areas, however, he found his judgment thwarted: one
by his superiors and one by his subordinate. In May he requested
permission to move the elite 12th SS Panzer Division, Hitler Jugend, from southwest of Paris to Carentan, where it could have
intervened—probably with disastrous results—in the American
landings on Omaha and Utah Beaches. However, he found himself
overruled, and the Hitler Jugend division remained where it was.
The second case, also in May, involved the 352nd Division, which
had just arrived in the area near Bayeux where the American landing
on Omaha Beach would occur. The commander of that division, following the dictates of German doctrine, held the bulk of his forces
back from the beaches to serve as a counterattack force. Rommel
ordered him to move those units up to the beaches, but the commander refused. The Omaha Beach defenses, manned by only two
battalions, still almost thwarted the American landing at that point.

For Montgomery and Patton, 1944 brought difficulties and
promises. Montgomery arrived back in England in early January
1944 with Eisenhower, the overall commander of the upcoming
landing. Montgomery's role was to be the ground commander who
would supervise the American First Army under General Omar
Bradley and the British Second Army under General Miles Dempsey.
Patton also returned to England early in 1944, but he remained
deep in his self-made doghouse. Bradley did not want to use Patton
at all and would have preferred to see him shipped back to the
United States. Eisenhower would have none of that. Instead, he
intended to use Patton after substantial U.S. forces had built up on
the Continent. In the meantime Patton received the task of preparing imaginary forces to make a second great landing on the Pas-de-
Calais—a grave misuse of the most capable Anglo-American general
in mobile operations. Moreover, given his travels through Nor-

mandy in 1912 and 1913, Patton was the only Allied senior commander with a grasp of the difficulties that the bocage country would present, with its heavy hedgerows, stone walls, and massive farmhouses.

Generals Patton (left), Bradley (center), and Montgomery (right)
(*Library of Congress Prints and Photographs Division, Washington, D.C.*)

Eisenhower and Montgomery immediately made it clear that the forces allocated for Operation Overlord—three infantry divisions and one airborne division—were completely inadequate. Montgomery warned that he would not be responsible for the invasion's success unless the total was upped to five divisions making the over-the-beach landings, supported by three airborne divisions. Much scrambling took place to ensure that the required amphibious capabilities were available. In many respects the Americans and the British approached the problems of the landing in a similar fashion, but with one important difference. With his prewar experience and that of the Sicilian landings, Montgomery understood the value of sustained naval gunfire support. Thus, the British landings received at a minimum one and a half hours of naval fires; Bradley, paying no attention to experiences in the Mediterranean or Pacific and characterizing the latter as "a bush-league theater," provided for only a twenty-minute naval bombardment on Omaha Beach, with an aerial bombardment to take its place. The aircraft, overshooting the target area, did no damage to the German beach defenses, while the naval fire was entirely inadequate for the job.

The Germans were, however, slow to react, as none of their senior commanders in France were willing to take the initiative to release either the mechanized or the motorized divisions to begin moving toward the Allied landings without Hitler's permission. The generals in the OKW were willing neither to wake Hitler up nor to release the mobile reserves on their own authority. The only individual who might have acted on his own was Rommel, but he was in southern Germany, visiting his wife on her birthday. The relatively slow German response in the first hours of the invasion proved of inestimable aid to the Allies, who by the end of "the longest day" were firmly ashore on all the beaches. Luckily for those landing at Omaha, the 352nd Division's commander moved his reserves off to defend against the British landings farther east.

Montgomery's plan for the ensuing battle appears to have been to break through to Caen on the first or second day and then wage a mobile battle of armor beyond, in which the British armored divisions would carry the bulk of the fighting. It did not work out that way. The 12th SS Panzer Division, with its highly trained soldiers, the murderous products of the Hitler Youth, smashed into the Canadians on the second day. They held on in the desperate struggle only with the support of naval gunfire. Thereafter, there was no chance of the British or Canadians reaching Caen on the first day or, for that matter, the second day. For the Germans, Allied air superiority proved a nightmare, just as Rommel had warned. On June 9 Ultra warned Allied intelligence that Geyr von Schweppenburg's Panzer Group was setting up for business and indicated its location. On the tenth, Allied fighter bombers wrecked Schweppenburg's headquarters, killing or wounding most of its staff officers.

For Rommel the problem was no longer launching a major counterattack against the beachhead but getting sufficient formations to
Normandy so that the defenders could hold the line against swelling
numbers of Allied forces. The SS Panzer division Das Reich was supposed to take only two days to arrive in Normandy from Limoges.
Instead, due to damaged rail and road networks, as well as interfer-
ence by the French resistance, it took nearly two weeks to move the
division's full complement of troops and equipment to the battlefield. Rommel spent the battle patching together a front in the face
of growing pressure from relentless Allied attacks, threatening to
break out into the open.

Yet Rommel was not the only one with difficulties. The British
Army continued to exhibit the weaknesses it had displayed thus far
in the conflict. On June 9 Montgomery and Dempsey recognized
that the German flank west of Caen was up in the air and ordered
the British 7th Armored Division to take advantage of the situation.
Driving past the German flank, a mechanized brigade of the division
reached deep behind enemy lines to Villers-Bocage. However, the
advance moved as if it were on peacetime maneuvers rather than
behind German territory. With no reconnaissance, the British failed
to recognize the presence of Tiger tanks to the east of the village.
Under the command of one of the Waffen SS's leading tank aces,
Michael Wittmann, the Germans attacked. Spread out over the very
long street of Villers-Bocage, the British found themselves out-
gunned and in a tactically hopeless position. By the time the battle
was over the Tigers had shredded the column, destroying twenty-
five tanks along with twenty-eight other armored vehicles. As
Dempsey admitted after the war, "The whole handling of the battle
was a disgrace."

But if the British were having troubles, so, too, were the Americans. One junior officer in the 90th Infantry Division, later to rise to
four-star rank, described the division as the finest organization ever
devised for the killing of young Americans. Bradley's First Army on
the western side of Normandy made only slow progress through the
bocage country. The problem was not just the easily defended coun-

tryside, but the fact that without a clear operational sense of how to deal with the tactical problems confronting him, Bradley frittered away American strength with division-sized attacks that bent, but never broke, the Germans.

Faced with unexpected difficulties on both flanks of the Normandy battlefield, Montgomery altered his strategy. The longer the stalemate lasted, the more pressure he found himself under not only from public opinion but from Allied military leaders as well. No longer thinking of a rapid breakout followed by an armored exploitation in eastern Normandy, Montgomery instead aimed to crack German resistance in a brutal battle of attrition—possibly, as he later claimed, to hold German attention on the eastern side of the lodgment to allow an American breakout in the west. Recognizing how brittle the British Army was and that Britain's manpower pool was rapidly drying up, Montgomery ensured that the British attacks rested heavily on tanks and heavy artillery support. Three major British attacks, code-named Epsom, Charnwood, and Goodwood, eventually resulted in the fall of Caen, but there was little left of the city, except shattered bricks, glass, and mortar. Yet, these failures worked to the Allied advantage. A breakthrough in late June or early July would have led to a battle of maneuver from Normandy to the German border, with the Germans enjoying not only tactical superiority but also the advantage of falling back on their supply dumps. As a consequence of the Germans holding their lines to the end, there were not enough of them to contest in any meaningful way the Allied race across France.

Although the British attacks failed to break through, they imposed a huge toll of casualties on the Germans. At the end of June, Rundstedt and Rommel met with Hitler to warn the führer how close the front in Normandy was to shattering. The resulting blowup led to Rundstedt's firing. Field Marshal Günther von Kluge, "clever Hans," became the new overall commander in the west. Enthused by the possibility for great victories at the führer's headquarters, Kluge dressed down Rommel for his supposed defeatism and unwillingness to obey orders. However, it did not take Kluge long to discover that Rommel's pessimism was fully justified. As the Germans desperately clung to their eroding position, a British Spitfire took Rommel out of the war on July 17. Thrown from his car with serious head wounds, the field marshal was hospitalized. In October, on the basis of his supposed complicity in the Twentieth of July Plot to kill Hitler, the führer ordered him to commit suicide.

Meanwhile the heavy fighting continued unabated. At the end of July, Bradley launched Operation Cobra, which finally broke the logjam in the west. After pushing the Germans back from the coast, American spearheads raced down the western coast of Normandy to seize the crucial town of Avranches at the base of the Norman and Breton Peninsulas. With possession of the town, the Americans broke out from the Normandy pocket, and the way lay open for a massive exploitation that should have resulted in the destruction of the German forces in the west. At this point on August 1, 1944, Eisenhower activated Patton's Third Army. Patton, for his part, recognized how tenuous his situation was with Bradley; he would do nothing to rock the boat. And Bradley for his part stuck religiously to the plan, drawn up before the invasion, which called for American forces to first move into Brittany to open up the Breton ports. But events had overtaken the plans, as both Montgomery and Eisenhower recognized. Nevertheless, Patton received orders from Bradley to send the first American divisions through Avranches into Brittany. Thus, the 4th and 6th Armored Divisions trundled off to the west, while the entire German front holding the Allies back in Normandy beckoned to the east. Major General John Wood argued strongly with Patton that his division was headed in the wrong direction, but no matter how much he might have agreed with Wood, Patton had his orders, and he was not about to upset Bradley.

At this critical point, Hitler added to German difficulties by ordering Kluge to launch a counterattack aimed at cutting off the coast road supporting the movement through Avranches. He was sacrificing his few remaining tanks in a forlorn hope. It also gave the Allies a glorious opportunity to trap all of the remaining German forces before they could retreat toward the safety of the Seine River.

Unfortunately, the Allied commanders fumbled it. Bradley eventually relented and allowed Patton to exploit the American breakthrough to the east. As Patton's Third Army began its swift advance, the question arose as to where Allied pincers might meet to seal off the German forces in the west. The decision, made without much consideration, was that Dempsey's Second Army would drive through Falaise and meet the Americans at Argentan. The choice made little sense, because the British were going to have to fight their way through fierce German resistance, while the Americans could easily have pushed farther north. On August 11, Montgomery made the serious mistake of reinforcing his order for the two armies to meet at Argentan. The next day Patton objected, but Bradley made clear the Third Army was not to advance beyond that stop line. Patton jokingly replied that Bradley should allow the Third Army to drive through to the Channel and push both the Germans and the British into the sea. More seriously, on August 17, Patton suggested that the Third Army advance to the northeast, into northern France, and then swing into the Channel ports, thus putting not only the German forces in Normandy but also the German Fifteenth Army guarding the Pas de Calais in the bag.

Montgomery and Dempsey failed to push the British advance to Falaise with sufficient vigor to close the gap through which the Germans were escaping. The destruction of German forces in the Falaise pocket was indeed impressive, but a significant number of the Wehrmacht's corps and division staffs escaped the wreckage, and upon them the Germans reknitted the defenses that held the Allies on the German frontiers for another half year. There is a fundamental point here: Both Montgomery and Bradley focused on gaining territory, while Patton, on the other hand, recognized that the primary purpose of operations should be the destruction of the Wehrmacht rather than simply seizing territory.

As the Allied armies surged through central and then northern France toward the Low Countries and the German frontier, a major argument broke out between Eisenhower and Montgomery as to the direction of Allied operations. Montgomery proposed that the

Americans give him twelve of their divisions and virtually all of the logistical support for a single powerful drive through southern Holland and then across the Rhine onto the north German plain. Eisenhower demurred and declared that the Allies would pursue a broad-front operational strategy, in which the American advance would receive equal emphasis with the British advance.

In the postwar period, British authors have argued that Montgomery's narrow-thrust drive represented the only chance to achieve a victory in 1944 and that Eisenhower's broad-front strategy resulted in the war lasting another six months. With some justification, the British pundit and military historian B. H. Liddell Hart, ever the contrarian, argued that a single, powerful thrust represented the best approach but that Montgomery was not the right general to lead it; rather Patton should have commanded it! What this postwar quibbling missed—and what Eisenhower understood—was that the political context within which the Allies were conducting the war demanded that British and American forces receive equal emphasis. This was important not only for the stability of the Anglo-American alliance during the war but for the postwar period.

At this point Eisenhower assumed direct command of Allied ground operations. Unfortunately, he did not grasp the reins firmly, and his subordinate commanders pursued their own immediate tactical goals without any clear strategic guidance from above. In the Allied campaign in September 1944, neither Montgomery nor Patton comes off well, but the former was to make the most serious mistakes, mistakes that resulted in a costly Allied defeat. As Allied forces rolled into Belgium, it appeared that the Germans were on the brink of collapse. While Eisenhower refused to turn the campaign over to Montgomery, he provided the newly promoted field marshal with substantial reinforcements. However, he also made clear that the first priority must be the opening of Antwerp to Allied logistics. On September 5, the British 11th Armored Division assaulted Antwerp and, by catching the Germans off guard, captured the port facilities in undamaged condition. The British XXX Corps, of which the 11th Armored was part, was now in position to move north, cut off Walcheren Island, clear up the north side of the Scheldt, and trap the remnants of the German Fifteenth Army, which had guarded the Pas de Calais.

Instead, Montgomery ordered a halt, which allowed the Germans to pull eighty thousand soldiers out and fortify both sides of the Scheldt, effectively sealing off Antwerp's port. After the war Montgomery's defenders argued that XXX Corps had run out of fuel, but, in fact, it had sufficient fuel for an advance of approximately sixty miles farther into Holland. Montgomery failed to prioritize the logistics that fighting on the western front was going to demand. Capturing Antwerp was not enough. The Scheldt Estuary had to be cleared if the city's port could not be opened. And without that base of support, Montgomery's planned lunge across the Rhine had every prospect of turning into a disastrous defeat. By halting his forces on September 5, Montgomery robbed British forces of their momentum and allowed the Germans to refit and reorganize their badly shaken units. And if there was one thing German units were still extraordinarily good at by this stage in the war, it was rapid recovery in the wake of a major defeat. What Montgomery wasted was time, perhaps the most important element in the calculus of war.

In the meantime he had garnered Eisenhower's support for a massive airborne operation—Market Garden. By laying a carpet of airborne troops for his armor to roll over, Montgomery was certain that his army could pierce the German front, cross the Rhine, and bring the war to an early conclusion. Based on flawed intelligence that ignored the evidence that there were strong German forces between Eindhoven and Arnhem, including the 9th and 10th SS Panzer Divisions, and beset by bad planning and leadership at the higher levels, Operation Market Garden never had a chance. Though the airborne attacks caught the Germans by surprise, the slow advance of the British XXX Corps left the airborne divisions, particularly the British 1st Airborne Division, exposed to crippling counterattacks. In the end, the attack failed in its primary objective of hurling British forces across the Rhine and cost the airborne divisions dearly. Confronted with defeat by the end of September, Montgomery called off the attack and switched his energies to his continuing crusade to control the Allied ground campaign and renew his thrust across the Rhine.

Astonishingly, Montgomery still ignored the problem of clearing the Scheldt to allow Antwerp's use. Instead, he wasted substantial resources in clearing the Channel ports, the lift capacity of which was minuscule compared to Antwerp's. In early October, Admiral Bertram Ramsay, commander of Allied naval forces, warned Eisenhower that Montgomery was still not placing the opening of the Scheldt among his highest priorities. In a meeting of senior Allied commanders, Ramsay recorded in his diary that "Monty made startling announcement that we could take the Ruhr without Antwerp. That afforded me the cue I needed to lambast him for not having made the [opening of the Scheldt] the immediate objective at highest priority and I let fly with all my guns at the faulty strategy we had allowed." It would not be until the end of November that the Canadians cleared the Scheldt, thus allowing the first supply ships to unload at Antwerp. The first ships docked at Antwerp on November 28, eighty-five days after the British had captured it. Even Montgomery's greatest supporter and loyal friend, Field Marshal Brooke, commented in his diary: "I feel that Monty's strategy for once is at fault, instead of carrying out the advance on Arnhem, he ought to have made certain of Antwerp in the first place."

In retrospect there was little chance that the Allies could have broken into the Reich, given the logistical desert that their air forces had created in destroying the French railroad and road network in preparation for Overlord, even had they opened up Antwerp earlier. Nevertheless, the September campaign put Montgomery in his worst light. His decision to halt the onrush of his forces on September 5 reflected a mentality, heavily influenced by his experiences of the First World War. He was not capable of thinking in terms of rapid, ruthless exploitation, because in his experience in the last war, such efforts had caused massive bloodlettings in innumerable offensives. Thus, his desire to tidy things up before resuming the advance against the Germans led him to miss a major opportunity: the fact

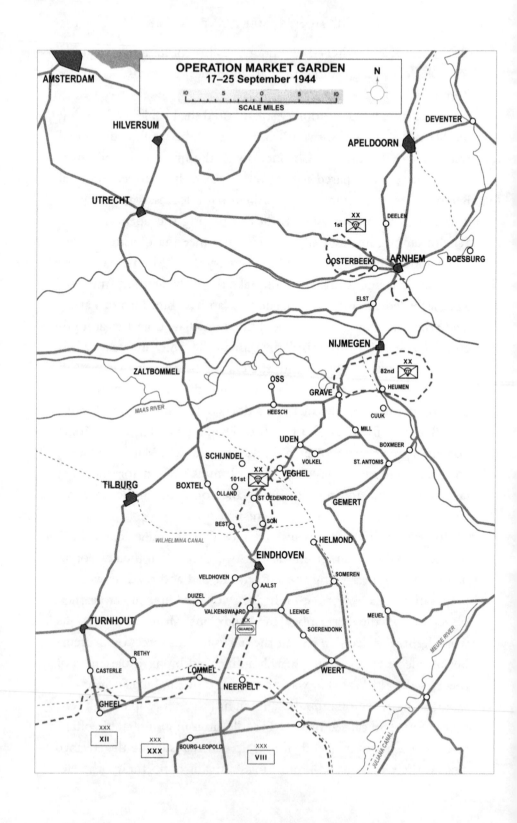

that while he was reorganizing and refitting, so, too, was the Wehrmacht. The period after the failure of Operation Market Garden was to prove one of great frustration for Montgomery. To his dying day he incorrectly believed that he had been robbed of a great victory by the decision to carry out a broad-front strategy. Thus, in the autumn gloom he whinged at everyone, but particularly Eisenhower. His behavior was so bad that at one point Eisenhower had to remind Montgomery who his superior was.

If September 1944 proved to be a bad month for Montgomery and the British, it proved no more successful for Patton and his Americans. Patton's drive across central France had been a brilliant piece of exploitation, but without any clear operational focus from above, it missed the opportunity to link up with American and French forces driving up the Rhône River valley and trapping a significant number of Germans, desperately escaping from southern France. Perhaps more important, Patton's superiors directed him to advance toward Metz, which offered no significant operational advantages. It would have been far better to push the Third Army into the Ardennes, where there would be no significant German formations until the end of October. But Patton offered no objections, apparently as entranced with Metz as were Eisenhower and Bradley. All three had been influenced by their staff college studies of the American campaign in World War I that had emphasized Metz, Pershing's objective in the Meuse-Argonne offensive. Pershing had believed Metz was the key transportation and logistical center for the Germans on the western front in 1918. It was not; rather the Liège Gap farther north had been the funnel through which all German logistics moved into Belgium. Thus, mistaken historical assumptions drove the Americans into the Lorraine campaign, which led nowhere of strategic significance. Moreover, the Metz region had been heavily fortified by the French and Germans during their various occupations. The Germans had even used the area to train their young combat officers and staffs throughout the war, meaning German officers and staffs were thoroughly familiar with Metz and its terrain.

Patton did not reach Metz in September as planned. Eisenhower's decision to place the emphasis on Montgomery's drive into southern Holland and onto the north German plain dried up the Third Army's logistical support, particularly its gasoline. Thus, its advance petered out well short of Metz and the Siegfried Line, during a period when it would have been possible to reach both objectives before the German defenses could consolidate. Patton's as well as Bradley's anger at that decision targeted both Montgomery and Eisenhower. In a meeting at the end of September with the press, Patton mimicked the field marshal and his clipped British accent to announce that the Germans "will be off their guard and I shall pop out at them like an angry rabbit."

Once stopped in September, the Allies found themselves foundering in the torrents of rain that normally occur in the European fall; the resulting mud exacerbated the logistical difficulties caused by Montgomery's failure to open up the Scheldt. Only the invasion of southern France by Operation Anvil and the rapid liberation of the Rhône River valley allowed sufficient supplies to reach the western front, so that the Allies could hold the German frontier without having to fall back into France. For the Third Army in the period of October and early November, the campaign to take Metz against tough German resistance added to the gloom of the rain and the mud. None of this helped Patton's humor or tamped down his belief that Eisenhower's favorable treatment of Montgomery was inexcusable.

But while the Allies were squabbling among themselves and wondering why they had not won the war in September, Hitler was preparing a nasty surprise. Unknown to Allied intelligence organizations, the Germans had prepared a massive blow through the Ardennes in a replay of their enormously successful thrust of May 1940. As with too many senior generals, those making the intelligence picture drew heavily on the belief that German defeat in Normandy meant that the Wehrmacht was finished and, while resistance might continue, the enemy was in no position to launch a major offensive—despite clear signs that the Germans were preparing to do precisely that. Patton's Third Army intelligence officer recognized early on that the Germans were up to something and that the target for a major effort on their part would probably come in the Ardennes. But there is no indication that he shared his prediction with higher headquarters.

On December 16 the Germans struck and almost immediately made considerable progress in spite of stiff American resistance. The Battle of the Bulge was to give Patton his most impressive moment as a general. After hearing the initial reports of heavy fighting to the north, Patton's initial instinct was to commit his divisions to combat so Bradley could transfer to First Army, which was already being hammered by the Germans. The next day he met with Bradley at the latter's headquarters in Luxembourg, and it was immediately apparent to Patton that the German attack was dangerous. Somewhat exaggerating what the Third Army could do, he indicated to Bradley that he could have two divisions moving toward Bastogne the next day and a third on the following day. On the nineteenth, Patton was summoned to a major meeting of senior American commanders at Verdun. Before he left, he had his staff sketch out several options with code words for each so that once the Verdun meeting had decided what the Third Army was to do, he could immediately telephone his headquarters to get matters rolling.

The Verdun meeting was vintage Patton. When Eisenhower asked how fast Patton could get divisions from the Third Army moving north, he replied that his divisions would be ready to move on December 21; the only question was where. Several British officers in the background snickered. For his part, Eisenhower testily demanded that Patton be serious, and it took several minutes before he realized that Patton was deadly so. Bradley remained silent through most of the discussion. Within a short period, the gloom at the meeting's start dissipated and the necessary decisions were made. One of Patton's staff officers present noted: "Within an hour everything had been thrashed out—the divisions to be employed, objectives, new army boundaries, the amount of our front to be taken over by Sixth Army Group [commander, General Jacob Devers], and other matters—and virtually all of them settled on General Patton's terms."

It was one thing to promise a massive move in a meeting of senior officers; it was another to actually execute such a move. But Patton's forces were ready and the Third Army delivered one of the most impressive maneuvers of the war. Its divisions turned over their fronts to relieving troops from Dever's Sixth Army Group, turned the axis of several frontline formations ninety degrees, redirected their logistical support structure, and then began a rapid advance north to gain contact with the advancing German spearheads—all of this in the midst of freezing weather, snow, and ice-covered roads. Over the course of the coming days, Patton spent his time on the road in an open jeep in brutally cold weather so that troops could see him. He badgered, praised, occasionally directed traffic, and even helped push a stuck vehicle out of a rut. Patton's leadership was in every respect as inspired and as inspiring as Rommel's had been in the crossing of the Meuse in May 1940.

In the midst of the fierce fighting, as Third Army troops attempted to break through to Bastogne to relieve the 101st Airborne Division, Patton took time out to ensure that all of his troops, including those in combat, received a warm turkey dinner on Christmas. (Whether they did or not is open to question, but the attempt was made.) On December 26 the lead tank battalion of the Third Army under Lieutenant Colonel Creighton Abrams, a future army chief of staff, broke through to relieve Bastogne and create a narrow corridor through which supplies and reinforcements could move to buttress the hard-pressed defenders.

While Patton was conducting the move to dam up the southern flank of the growing German salient, command on the northern portion of the salient had taken a surprising turn. The German breakthrough in the first days of the Battle of the Bulge caused Bradley to lose his composure. His communications with William Simpson's Ninth Army and Courtney Hodges's First Army had been cut, and without orders coming from Bradley, Hodges abandoned his headquarters to retreat to the rear in what some took to be panic. Instead of moving about as Patton had, Bradley remained hunkered down in his headquarters in Luxembourg. Eisenhower took matters into his own hands and turned the fight on the northern portion of the salient over to Montgomery. He left Bradley in the position of army group commander, but in command of only the Third Army. Bradley never forgave Eisenhower for this decision, but Ike's job was to win the war, not make his subordinate commanders feel good about themselves.

Alarmed by the events to his south, Montgomery had already taken the precaution of positioning the British XXX Corps so that its divisions could intervene if the Germans succeeded in breaking through to the Meuse. Once Eisenhower asked him to command the northern side of the salient, Montgomery took over with alacrity. To his credit, he handled his subordinate American commanders with tact. The Americans at the front were already fighting effectively when Montgomery assumed command. Only a portion of the 106th Infantry Division, newly committed from the United States, had fallen apart, and that was largely the fault of its commander. Moreover, American resistance along the Elsenborn Ridge channeled Sepp Dietrich's Sixth SS Panzer Army into a series of secondary roads that limited their ability to exploit their heavy armor. Only at the tip of the Bulge did the Germans come anywhere close to reaching the Meuse. There, "Fighting Joe" Collins, one of the best corps commanders in the army, whom Montgomery had explicitly asked Hodges to send south to the fight, used the 2nd Armored Division to crush the German spearheads.

By late December 1944, American defensive stands and counterattacks had brought the German advance to a halt well short of the Meuse. The question then became how to drive the Germans back from the territory they had gained. Patton argued for concentric attacks by the First Army at the northern base of the German salient and the Third Army from the southern base, with the aim of surrounding the Germans. That was seen as too risky by both Bradley and Montgomery, and it was ultimately their decision. For most of January the Americans pushed the Germans back out of their gains, bringing an end to the Battle of the Bulge. The casualty bill for the Americans was heavy: eighty-one thousand with nineteen thousand killed in action. The Germans lost more than one hundred thousand soldiers, and the battle had been a grievous defeat for them in the sense that it was their last shot.

Meanwhile, Montgomery had done his best to wreck the good-will that his handling of the First and Ninth Armies had garnered among the Americans. Holding a press conference in early January, he was at his most patronizing. His director of intelligence recorded: "He [Montgomery] said of course that he wanted to pay tribute to the American soldier and so on—but it came across as if he was, as if he had rescued the Americans—'of course they were jolly brave,' and so on and so forth, but he used that awful phrase 'a very interesting little battle,' or words to that effect." It did not go over well with the Americans.

The Ardennes offensive had been the last major effort by the Germans. They had no reserves left. Despite one of the coldest winters of the twentieth century to that point, the Allied advance picked up speed. With the Battle of the Bulge over, Eisenhower returned Hodges's First Army to Bradley but allowed Montgomery to keep Simpson's Ninth Army. In February a combined pincer movement by the Canadian First Army and Simpson's Ninth Army pushed the Germans back behind the Rhine. Simpson urged Montgomery to allow his Ninth Army to cross the Rhine at Uerdingen, but the British field marshal would have none of it. Instead, he delayed any such initiative in favor of waiting two weeks to launch his massively prepared airborne and amphibious assault across the Rhine, against the weak, dispirited German forces that were putting up little resistance.

The American approach was quite different. When soldiers of Hodges's First Army discovered the still-standing Ludendorff Bridge at Remagen, Bradley delightedly pushed American divisions across the opening as fast as they could arrive. Patton for his part pushed troops of the Third Army across the Rhine on March 22 at two points. The next evening, Bradley announced that Patton's troops had crossed the Rhine without an artillery bombardment, air support, or an airborne assault, a pointed comment on Montgomery's overprepared blow. For all intents and purposes, the war was over.

Montgomery returned to great honors in Britain and wrote a memoir that was economical with the truth, to put it mildly. Patton returned to the United States for a short visit but died that fall in an automobile accident in which he was not wearing a seatbelt—but not before causing a final furor by announcing that membership in the Nazi Party was no different than joining any other political party. And Rommel was, of course, dead.

Conclusion

How is one to compare and contrast these three great generals? Entirely different cultures, both national and military, formed their approach to leadership. Moreover, their personalities were extraordinarily different. Yet, they were all consummate professionals, who studied warfare as one would hope for in a true professional. Perhaps most important, they were outstanding trainers, who inculcated their professionalism and approach to the study of war in their subordinates. Therein lay much of their success both before and during the Second World War.

Rommel's performance shows that he was the most outstanding offensive tactician of the war. Yet, one must also give him his due for his conduct of the retreat from El Alamein and his conduct of the defense of Normandy after the successful Allied landings. In both cases Rommel was in an impossible situation, from which defeat was the only possibility. Rommel's presence in North Africa also ensured that the terrible crimes staining the reputations of most of the Wehrmacht's field marshals and generals on the eastern front and Balkans would not besmirch his persona. In addition, his understanding of the wider aspects of the military profession grew as his responsibilities in Africa and then Europe increased. After the war, a number of senior German generals criticized him as being no more than a good tactician with little understanding of strategy and operations. How-

ever, the wretched performance of the senior German military leaders in the operational conduct of the eastern front, where they paid
little attention to either logistics or intelligence in the planning or
executing of Operation Barbarossa, would suggest the opposite.

As for strategy, the best that his superiors—and not just Hitler—
could come up with was to dig in and fight the war through to the
bitter end. Immediately after the defeat at El Alamein and the Allied
landings in French North Africa, Rommel recommended that the
Wehrmacht abandon the southern side of the Mediterranean. Hitler, the OKW, and the Italian Commando Supremo all contemptu-
ously rejected that idea. The resulting defeat in Tunisia, entirely
unnecessary, made the defense of Sicily and eventually southern Italy
impossible and spelled the collapse of Fascist Italy in September
1943. Similarly, when charged with the defense of northern France
and the Low Countries, Rommel argued that the massive superiority
of Allied airpower and the inexhaustible quantities of supplies available to the Anglo-American powers would make it impossible for
the Wehrmacht to halt the Allies unless the Germans stopped the
Allies on the beaches. A successful Allied landing would lose Germany the war. Such clear strategic thinking was far beyond the realm
of Rundstedt and Geyr von Schweppenburg. In retrospect, "the
longest day" proved Rommel right and the so-called German strategists wrong. In the end, Rommel's tragedy was that, as a decent,
brilliant general, he served a criminal régime.

Montgomery's story was quite different. He was despised and
feared by his colleagues. Yet he understood that the "château" generalship of World War I had no place in a democracy's army. Thus,
he made every effort to create and encourage a bond with the soldiers, NCOs, and junior officers for whom he was responsible. His
greatest defect was his inability to get along with neither his superiors nor his colleagues, which caused him huge difficulty in his relations with not only British officers but his American partners as well.
Moreover, Montgomery proved to be his own worst enemy, with his
unwillingness to listen to others and his complete lack of tact.

Unlike Rommel, the instrument he led was deeply flawed in the culture of its officer corps. In effect, too many of its generals and colonels were regimental soldiers with neither the inclination nor the intellectual focus required for combined-arms warfare. In both the North African campaign and the operations in northwestern Europe, Montgomery led an army that proved dogged but unimaginative against a flexible, ruthless opponent. Unfortunately, Montgomery lacked the luxury of time to retrain and repair the defects in the various armies he commanded. Exacerbating his difficulties was the fact that the war stretched Britain's manpower to its limits. Thus, he had to be extraordinarily careful in husbanding the lives of his soldiers.

Montgomery's greatness as a general lay in his ability to understand the constraints of the forces he led. The care with which Montgomery commanded reflected a general who understood the limitations of his army and nation. He fought his battles in accordance with those realities.

Perhaps the most balanced and intelligent depiction of Montgomery's strengths and weaknesses came from Rommel, written in the last months of the German field marshal's life:

> Montgomery did not leave the slightest detail out of his calculations. He discounted all academic theorising and let himself be guided by experience alone. . . . His principle was to fight no battle unless he knew for certain that he would win it. Of course that is a method which will only work given material superiority; but he had that. He was cautious—to my mind excessively so—but then he could afford to be. . . . Montgomery was undoubtedly more of a strategist than a tactician. Command of a force in mobile battle was not his strong point, although, as far as he could see, he was fully alive to the fact that certain tactical principles must prevail. In the field of higher strategic planning he must be credited with outstanding achievements, not least during the invasion battle.

Patton is in some ways the most difficult to understand in terms of personality. Behind the blustering and boastfulness lay a man of considerable insecurities and sensitivity. At the same time, he was an individual of great bravery and real insight into the possibilities that mobile combined-arms warfare offered. His intuition in the early hours of the Bulge offensive allowed him to prepare and execute the relief of the 101st Airborne Division far earlier and more effectively than Eisenhower and certainly Bradley expected. Among the Allied senior leaders, Patton was the only one who understood that the goal was not the immediate seizure of ground but the destruction of the German Army.

Unfortunately, Patton's lack of self-discipline in the slapping incident in Sicily prevented him from having Bradley's job in Normandy, where he might well have created an earlier breakout with more devastating impact. Great generals can lead complex military organizations in the midst of man's most terrifying occupation—war. And Patton could certainly do that with insight, perception, and drive, buttressed by serious study. Of the three generals, only Patton appears to have been a real student of military history.

Patton's strengths, as with his flaws, were monumental. Of all the Anglo-American generals, he was the only one who perceived that the advantages of mobility, speed, and flexibility provided his forces the capability to destroy the Wehrmacht rather than simply gain territory. The persona that he presented to the external world was quite different from what lay behind the bombast. In private, when not acting, Patton was a thoughtful, intelligent professional. The fact that Patton and others emerged to build effective ground forces within a period of two years suggests the seriousness with which American officers had thought about the potential for another conflict, making them much more prepared than their British allies.

Conclusion

Modern Warfare and the System of Genius

I n military history, particularly in the case of the United States, one clearly sees the transition from war based on inspired battlefield leadership to an early form of the modern "system of genius," which reaches something of an apogee during the Second World War. This system has clear antecedents in earlier ages—such as ancient Rome—but its true character is a product of the modern era. For it is only recently that one can ask the question: Has war become so complex that there can never again be a solitary military genius capable of grasping all of its intricacies? One can go even further and wonder if the idea of the "master strategist" is more myth than reality. And within the current environment, does the lack of such a "God of War" much matter?

As this entire book is based on the idea that over the centuries some military leaders were far superior to others, we must first address the crucial question of whether the idea of a "master strategist" is a myth. In doing so we must differentiate between strategy and operations. In most of the cases in this book, we have focused on the capacity of various great commanders to master the battlefield. Only in two cases—Saladin and Grant—do we see leaders who possessed a clear strategic vision and saw it through to a positive outcome. There is no evidence that Hannibal had any long-range strategic plan beyond bringing Rome to the negotiating table, and he failed at that. Similarly, Scipio was a superior campaign planner; he clearly gave much thought beyond the operational battlefield and defeating his immediate enemy. The same is true of Pompey, and one must judge Caesar's strategic plan a failure, as it probably did not include being stabbed to death in Rome's Senate chambers. Though his successor, Augustus, did much better in the strategic realm, he was an inferior battlefield commander, often leaving that job to his talented subordinate, Agrippa. We have already addressed the strategic conceptions of Napoléon, and how they led to a series of blunders that ruined his army and left France a conquered nation. And while Wellington time and again proved himself a master of the battlefield, his strategic genius was never put to the test. Similarly, Lee clearly never conceptualized the war as anything much beyond the operational space between Washington and Richmond. Of all the modern generals covered in this book, only Grant displayed the capacity to consider, plan for, and direct the war's multiple theaters. Moreover, he was able to coordinate each of the theaters toward a single strategic goal—winning the war on terms that reunited the country into a single entity. We do not, however, see the same strategic mentality in Patton, Montgomery, or Rommel, who were never more than battlefield commanders, leaving the strategic direction of World War II to others.

In fact, considering the scale of the twentieth century's two world wars, it is remarkable that there were so few memorable masters of the battlefield. Few could name an American World War I general besides Pershing. Furthermore, most of the European World War I generals still discussed are remembered mostly for their failures to find an operational or strategic answer to bloody trench warfare. One may even wonder if Patton would be much remembered if not for the hit 1970 movie bearing his name. Certainly, his reputation has as much to do with his flamboyance as his battlefield achievements, which were closely matched by his peers.

It is worth noting that most of those whom we call "Gods of War" made their reputations at times when wars and battles were far less complex. Throughout most of history a commander could take in an entire battlefield from a single strategic vantage point. Even as late as the American Civil War, it was rare for any part of a battle to be fought greater than a short horse ride from the commander. Visitors to Waterloo today, standing upon the monumental Lion's Mound, are often shocked at how small the battlefield is. Similarly, from the top of Little Round Top one can take in the entire Gettysburg battlefield. This has not been true for well over a century, as by World War I a local battle covered hundreds of square miles, and other major battles were often being fought simultaneously hundreds of miles away.

This explosion in battlefield complexity was matched in the strategic realm. For most of history a state fielded one large army at a time, and often that state's ruler was with the army. Rome is one of the few long-term exceptions, as the empire maintained forces that stretched across continents. Still, except for periods of civil war, there was rarely more than one major Roman field army at a time, and the emperors could often be found with that army. Moreover, even Roman power and resources were severely stressed whenever Rome faced more than one military crisis at a time. By Napoléon's time this was no longer true. For instance, even as Napoléon led his major field army against Austria in 1809, he still had approximately 250,000 troops fighting in Spain, while the British navy was conducting a blockade of nearly the entire continent. As the pace of the Industrial Revolution picked up, the scope for military operations increased exponentially. Railroads reduced continental scale movements of armies from months to days, while steam-driven ships opened up the entire globe to military operations for many of the great powers.

If the advent of the "master strategist" had ever been possible, surely that day has now passed. The increased scope and complexity of the modern world—and the subset of that world embodied by military operations—has made it impossible for any one person to take on the role of "master strategist." As Lawrence Freedman has pointed out, the master strategist of today is counted on to "[be] a student of the present who must be aware of the past, sensitive to the possibilities of the future, conscious of the danger of bias, alert

to ambiguity, alive to chaos, ready to think through the consequences of alternative courses of action, and then able to articulate
all of this with sufficient precision for those who must execute its
prescriptions." Where today will one find this paragon of strategic
perfection, who is comfortable moving between the worlds of modern economics, politics, diplomacy, and military affairs? Where is the
strategist who can expertly discuss the economic fallout of the collapse of the euro in one meeting and in the next discuss with equal
expertise the threat China's new ballistic missiles present to U.S.
Pacific strategy? Even more crucially, where is the person who can
see how the two are interrelated and how they interact with hundreds of other events happening at the same instant?

For reasons beyond comprehension, in the United States the
president is often placed in this role, as citizens of other nations tend
to do with their own national leaders. Currently, Russian president
Vladimir Putin is garnering plaudits as a "master strategist" who is
playing a relatively weak hand with consummate skill. Maybe he is,
and history may one day render that verdict. But when he sent his
tanks into Georgia in 2008, he surely did not foresee that capital
flight would bring Russia to its financial knees within two short
weeks. One may also ask if the long-term benefit of taking the
Crimea is worth Ukraine's undying enmity, as it is likely to play the
same role that Alsace-Lorraine once did between Germany and
France. Certainly some would question the wisdom of actions that
threaten to reignite the Cold War, which brought the Soviet Union
to ruin. This is especially true when one looks east and sees an increasingly powerful China covetously eyeing the sparsely populated,
resource-rich Siberian provinces. Putin may be playing a masterful
game, but the long-term odds are stacked against him. It is much
more likely that he is an opportunist with no more capacity to pre-
dict second- and third-order effects than most other mortals.

The great truth that strategists of today and the future must accept is that no single person is capable of developing a holistic picture of the strategic universe that can even begin to comprehend all
of the factors impacting any strategic problem, much less the unpre-

dictable interaction of these problems. This is doubly impossible for the strategic practitioner who must make decisions while also heavily involved in the action. Presidents cannot step away from the action and examine the consequences of every decision, immune from the pressures of time, politics, and their own biases. Moreover, at the moment of crisis, expecting any leader to be able to peer decades into the future to examine the ultimate consequences of a decision is, as it has always been, a fool's errand. Is it conceivable that any British leader taking his country into World War I could have foreseen the four years of gruesome warfare that lay ahead, or that within a single generation the mighty British Empire's power would pale in comparison to the militarily puny United States, or that in one more generation the empire would cease to exist? How could a strategist, even one as capable as Winston Churchill, born at the height of Britain's power in the Victorian Age, a man who joined the last great cavalry charge of the British Empire, possibly have predicted that he would live to witness the dissolution of empire and Britain's decline to second-rate power status?

As we have previously stated, the advent of the modern era ended the idea of decisive victories. From the turn of the twentieth century onward, the belief that a great general could deliver a strategic outcome with one decisive blow was not only quaint but dangerous. It was this chimera that led the German General Staff to put all of its faith in blitzkrieg and the rapid conclusion of conflicts. Similarly, American strategists became enamored with ideas of "Rapid Decisive Operations" and "Shock and Awe," which were put to good effect in the 2003 "March to Baghdad," only to be befuddled when victory morphed into a new type of war Americans were unprepared to fight. In effect, the entire political-military strategic decision process became trapped in an illusion. The Pentagon's new visionary concepts—"Multi-Domain Operations" and "Globally Integrated Operations"—demonstrate that the U.S. military is trying to consider how operations impact a larger strategic picture, but the jury remains out. On a more positive note, the chances are very good that the system will eventually reset itself, as states have gotten it right in the past and those examples remain available for anyone willing to look.

In this regard, it is worth looking deeper into how strategy developed in World War II. It is crucial to understand that none of the three major allies trusted each other, nor did any of their leading politicians or military men think much of the strategic abilities of their counterparts. The Americans, with some justification, were convinced that the British were only interested in maintaining the empire in the postwar era and that fighting the main German armies was a secondary consideration. The British thought American strategic plans were foolhardy in the extreme, designed to kill as many Allied soldiers as possible in the shortest amount of time. As for the Russians, they were convinced that their allies were only too willing to fight to the very last Russian.

On a more personal level, Roosevelt got along with Churchill, but in late 1943, when he decided that the future would be dominated by the Soviet Union and the United States, the president did not hesitate to throw the prime minister over the side. In addition, Britain's chief of the imperial staff, Field Marshal Alan Brooke, wrote of army chief of staff George Marshall: "I liked what I saw of Marshall, a pleasant and easy man to get on with, rather overfilled with his own importance, but I should not put him down as a great man." As for Marshall, he told presidential adviser Harry Hopkins that he thought Brooke lacked brains. But this was a vast improvement over his fellow member of the American Joint Chiefs, Admiral Ernest King, whose dislike of the British bordered on the pathological.

The truth of the matter is that, at the highest levels of the Allied war effort, there were no great military strategists, though Roosevelt, Stalin, and Churchill proved political strategists of the highest order. This lack of genius military leadership was a fact that all of the participants recognized in each other, if not in themselves. Many current historians credit Chief of Naval Operations Ernest King with having the best mind on the American Joint Chiefs. But an examination of the record clearly demonstrates that King concerned himself with only a single facet of global strategy—the building up of a huge

American fleet in the Pacific. As for General "Hap" Arnold, his dominating concern centered on building huge bomber fleets capable of bombing Germany and Japan into submission. And Marshall, the renowned "architect of victory"? Let's say that some of his strategic notions bordered on the fantastical. When he persisted in his support for as early an invasion of northern Europe as possible, Brooke recorded: "His [Marshall's] strategic ability does not impress me at all! In fact, in many ways he is a very dangerous man whilst being a very charming one!" After further discussions with Marshall, Brooke wrote:

> I discovered that he had not studied any of the strategic implications of a cross Channel invasion. . . . I asked him to imagine that his landing had been safely carried out and asked him what his plans would then be. Would he move east towards Germany exposing his southern flank? Would he move south to liberate France and expose his left flank? Would he move east to secure some lodgment? I found that he had not begun to consider any form of plan of action, and had not even begun to visualize the problems that would face an army after landing.

More than seven decades later, what are we to make of this? Military officers today are taught to regard Marshall as the epitome of the "soldier-statesman" as well as the strategic thinker behind America's World War II victory. Marshall surely deserves most of the accolades that have been heaped upon him, but the truth is that Brooke got it right. For all of his great qualities, Marshall was a lousy strategist. If he had gotten his way on invading northern Europe, there is little doubt that the barely trained American divisions marked for a 1942 invasion of France (as exemplified by their dismal performance at Kasserine Pass) would have been massacred.

Marshall never seems to have considered the long-term negative effects of such a setback: the detriment of already fragile civilian (particularly British) morale, the morale uplift for the Germans, and the impetus it likely would have given the Russians to conclude a separate peace. Just as crucially, a setback in 1942—or even in 1943—would have sacrificed the best divisions in the growing American army, as well as exhausted the carefully husbanded reserves of the British Empire. It would certainly have been a long time before there was a second Anglo-American force ready to make another attempt, assuming the stomach remained for another try. In the meantime, Germany would have been free to ship dozens of divisions east, where they could have turned the tide in their struggle with Russia.

There is another truth: Marshall's inadequacies as a strategist simply did not matter. Nor did the particular strategic shortcomings of any other member of the Combined Chiefs of Staff. This was mainly a result of the fact that neither America nor Britain needed a military "master strategist" at the top of the decision ladder. For one, Roosevelt had firmly established himself as the nation's grand strategist, as is generally the case in democratic nations where the military serves its political masters. It was he who set the overall goals and the political direction of the war, and it was his job to keep the military focused on his priorities. As such he forced the military's hand in invading North Africa, knowing it was crucial to civilian morale that they see progress being made in the war, and leading Marshall to complain that he wished he had known from the start that, in wartime, politicians have to do something every year. Roosevelt also kept the Joint Chiefs focused on the ultimate objective, as when he squelched an attempt by Marshall and King, both annoyed by British intransigence, to move the nation's main effort from Europe to the Pacific.

What Roosevelt and Churchill required from their senior military commanders was the capacity to organize, train, and equip the massive forces each nation was raising. In short, they needed superb military technocrats, men who were expert at the conduct of war and could design and execute the plans that would ensure victory. But even as they bowed to political demands, the military chiefs took their responsibility to offer military advice seriously and pushed back hard whenever Roosevelt or Churchill advocated a course they deemed militarily unsound. In this capacity Marshall excelled, and Brooke's diaries are replete with anecdotes of him walking the prime minister back from some of his more nonsensical schemes.

There was another vital factor involved, as well. As was the case in ancient Rome, the American military had developed and continues to sustain a "system of genius" that prepares many hundreds of officers to operate at the strategic level. Rather than rely on one military genius coming to the fore and directing all operations, officers are encouraged to push their ideas into the open where they can be debated. Surviving plans and schemes flow up to senior commanders, where they are appraised and sometimes adopted, though more often thrown out. Even at the most senior levels, every plan is fought over until an optimal solution is reached. If one was to examine the minutes and other surviving records of the Joint and Combined Chiefs during World War II, they would be astounded by the ferocious debates that took place. Often more junior officers were excused from the room so that the chiefs could more properly yell and otherwise vent at each other. Throughout this process, ideas and plans came and went until a solution was arrived at. Rarely were such solutions to the liking of all concerned, but given the situation and positions of each of the participants, they reflected the optimal choice based on what could actually be achieved without splitting the alliance asunder. Marshall, for instance, was forced to give up his plans for a 1942 invasion, and then a 1943 invasion. Other priorities arose to replace them, and in hindsight the Allies hugely benefitted from the delays in conducting Marshall's scheme.

Compare this to the closed system that by 1942 pervaded Nazi Germany, where Hitler made almost every military decision of consequence and debate was either limited or, more often, completely stifled. This, as we have seen, is the common tendency whenever a military genius has gained both military and total political power in a state. It is almost always disastrous, and doubly so when that leader—like Hitler—demonstrates a huge amount of strategic incompetence. Although such leaders can lead armies and states to victory over a limited period of time, in the long run they almost invariably set both their military forces and nation along the road to ruin.

Will there be another military genius in our lifetime? Some, for a short while, elevated U.S. general David Petraeus onto that pedestal for his performance in Iraq. But as many senior officers have related, what they were doing before Petraeus arrived and what they were doing afterward changed little; they just had tens of thousands more troops to do it with. Besides, whatever magic he may have applied in Iraq totally failed him when he tried to apply it to Afghanistan. And finally, like Patton and most other modern generals, Petraeus was not acting on his own. In fact, he was part of a much larger system that maintained a constant and critical eye on his relevant political, military, and diplomatic actions. And it is that system that is crucial to military success in the modern world.

It is said that the last person capable of absorbing and comprehending the totality of human knowledge was Leonardo da Vinci. That was probably untrue even during the Renaissance, but no current or future polymath, even one of da Vinci's capacity, could absorb even an infinitesimal fraction of the world's current knowledge base, never mind comprehend it. The modern truth is that an effective world leader is probably better served by avoiding the complexities of any situation and instead focusing on a simple, easily explainable vision. This was the magic that made Presidents Reagan and Obama effective and is likely to work in the future. Successful strategists surround themselves with experts in a variety of fields who manage the day-to-day complexity of evolving situations, freeing them to focus on things only the president can do—make the big decisions. Senior leaders today make most major decisions based on fifteen-minute PowerPoint briefings. They have to apply their full attention for those few minutes, ask a few questions, and decide, counting on the fact that many dozens of others had spent hundreds or thousands of hours studying a problem and then distilling it down to a short decision brief.

Making all of this work does not require the rise of a "master strategist." Rather, it relies on producing many hundreds of "strategic operators" who can comprehend specific pieces of a complex and chaotic environment. Working together, these people create an adaptive system that will, in almost every case, present a better solution or set of solutions than any single person is capable of. As Professor Freedman has written: "We may do better, therefore, looking for good strategy rather than worrying about great strategists. What fascinates me about good strategy is not that it comes from people who are uniquely qualified, but that it can be generated by fallible human beings working through imperfect organizations operating in conditions of great uncertainty."

In the past, great "master strategists" have typically emerged in very particular situations where their specific talents gave them an edge over opponents. In every case, these situations were transitory, and their historic moment passed. A few had the grace and good sense to retire from the field before their inadequacies were on full display, but most pressed ahead until their fallibility was visible to all. Given the historic record of brutality and war that accompanies the advent of a military genius (real or imagined), one must ask why anyone would ever want to see another such genius arise.

Acknowledgments

The authors first and certainly foremost want to thank their wives, Sharon and Lee, who for years have put up with our cantankerous ways while stifling the urge to smother us in our sleep. For this we remain eternally thankful. We will always wonder how two troglodytes such as ourselves managed to convince such paragons of all womanly virtues to even give us a second glance, let alone join us on our great adventure of life. We thank the gods!

We must also thank our agent, Eric Lupfer, who encouraged this project from inception to completion. It has been said of Eric . . . well, everything has been said of Eric, but all the good stuff is true.

But the real heroes behind the publication of this book are the folks at Bantam Books and Penguin Random House. The first of these publishing giants we would like to thank is Jennifer Hershey, Bantam's editor in chief. This book manuscript had languished in someone's to-do pile for a long time after the authors delivered it. But Jennifer, whose eye for beautiful prose is second to none, rescued it from near oblivion. How she alone was able to recognize brilliance from just a glance at a title on a spreadsheet is a story for another time. But we assure you that her editorial colleagues remain in awe of her achievement that day. The authors would, however, like to quote the words she uttered as her hand, with one graceful finger extended, glided down the spreadsheet: "Hey, I think I have found the nonfiction equivalent of *Game of Thrones*."

But to truly appreciate what kind of person Jennifer is, you must meet her. One of the authors had the pleasure of joining her for breakfast in a quaint bistro ensconced somewhere between the Hudson and East Rivers, an area famous as the nonfiction equivalent of the Left Bank of the Seine. Fully expecting to encounter a stereotypical hard-bitten New York City editor, he was pleasantly surprised to discover that Jennifer was warm, giving, attentive, charming, gracious, and lovely both inside and out. I suppose some ungenerous person might say that these comments reflect the obsequious fawning of an author hoping to get a favorable reading of his next book proposal. Such a thought would indeed be uncharitable, as every word of this description is true.

To get the book though the publication process, Jennifer gave the book to a young superstar-in-the-making editor—Emily Hartley—known throughout the book world for her willingness to ruthlessly destroy anything and anyone that gets between her and a deadline, but with a smile. The authors found her delightful to work with, focused on her task, as well as possessing a keen wit, a gentle countenance, and a warm heart. And, if that same ungenerous soul, mentioned above, is still reading, the authors are not pandering to an editor that holds our future as writers in her hand. We would never do that.

Anyway, we discovered how much Jennifer and Emily thought of the book when they talked Carlos Beltran into quitting the Houston Astros, giving up on his quest for 3,000 career hits, and following his true passion—book cover design. After seeing the cover, the authors find it hard to believe he put aside his true genius to waste time playing major league baseball. Similarly, they somehow managed to get Ted Allen to take an extended leave from his hit TV show *Chopped* to work on the production of the book. The authors have never tasted his cooking, but if it is half as good as his production editorial work, our mouths are already watering in anticipation. Before someone sends us a nasty email on the above comments, others have pointed out that we may have confused Penguin's Carlos and Ted with two other people. But, keep in mind, we are trained historians, with decades of research experience. As such, the facts as we present them above are absolutely correct and will remain so until some evil revisionist historian comes along and changes them.

We also want to make sure we thank our copy editor, Muriel Jorgensen. Muriel—the great wordsmith of Teaneck, New Jersey—is famous throughout the publishing world for taking one manuscript a year and replacing all of the words with better words. The authors are eternally grateful that this year she selected our humble work. More seriously she made our writing much betterer (we threw that word in to see if she could resist changing it to "better"). We would also like to thank our publicist and marketer, but as this book goes to print, we have no idea who will be tasked with making sure this book becomes a bestseller. We, of course, hope they succeed, but plan to blame them for everything that is wrong with the world if book sales languish—no pressure, though.

Finally, the authors want to thank the publisher, Kara Welsh, and her deputy, Kim Hovey. Rumor has it that they cried together as they read aloud the chapter on Napoleon and Wellington. The authors have not met either publisher, but based on what we found online, we are supremely confident that they are not only erudite and passionate about great books, but also two of the kindest, most caring, and loving persons on earth!

Now, where was that next book proposal?

Notes

A Framework for War

3 **"No one starts a war"** Clausewitz, *On War*, ed. and trans. Michael Howard and Peter Paret (Princeton University Press, 1976), p. 579.

4 **In effect, that search has led them** Ibid., p. 87.

4 ***"Quel massacre!"*** David Chandler, *The Campaigns of Napoleon* (Macmillan, 1966), p. 555.

5 **"To the strongest"** Arrian, 7.24–7.27.

8 **"Indeed Themistocles was a man"** Thucydides, *History of the Peloponnesian War*, trans. Rex Warner (Penguin Classics, 1954), p. 117.

9 **"Janus also has a temple at Rome"** Plutarch, "Numa," 20.1.

16 **"But in 1793 a force appeared"** Clausewitz, *On War*, pp. 591–593.

26 **"We will punch a hole in their front"** John Keegan, *The First World War* (Hutchinson, 1998), p. 464.

27 **"It remains to me a mystery"** Churchill, *Hinge of Fate*, p. 120.

Hannibal and Scipio

33 **To assist in the planning effort** These and other studies were published in 1931 by the U.S. Army's Command and General Staff School Press. See https://www.armyupress.army.mil/Portals/7/combat-studies-institute/csi-books/cannae.pdf.

33 **No other army would approach the walls of Rome** Basil Henry Liddell Hart, *Greater than Napoleon: Scipio Africanus* (Biblio & Tannen, 1971).

35 **"If we are victorious"** Plutarch, *Pyrrhus* 21.9.

35   **"What a wrestling ground we are leaving"** Ibid., 23.6.

35   **"This conjecture was soon afterwards confirmed"** Ibid.

35   **Over sixteen years** Many would argue that he first met his match against Quintus Fabius Maximus Verrucosus—The Delayer (Cunctator). While Fabius should rightfully be credited with saving Rome at its nadir, and for creating the strategic conception that contained Hannibal, and which still bears his name, he never defeated him in a major battle.

35   **Because of this huge indemnity** Polybius 1.62. The text says 2,200, but another thousand talents were added before the Senate ratified the treaty (Polybius 1.63).

37   **According to Livy** Livy 21.1.

38   **Appian's account adds thirty-seven elephants** Polybius 3.35.

38   **Pressing on with fifty thousand infantry** Ibid., 5.40–47.

38   **After a torturous march** Ibid., 3.54–55.

39   **The exposed Gaelic cavalry** Ibid., 3.65.

39   **Polybius claimed** Ibid., 10.3.

40   **Hannibal started the engagement** The two main sources for this battle are Polybius 3.69–74 and Livy, bk. 21.

40   **Roman spirits further evaporated** Polybius 3.72.

41   **A ferocious hand-to-hand fight** Ibid., 3.73.

42   **Hannibal made a careful study** Ibid., 3.80.

44   **"most of them were cut down"** Ibid., 3.84.

46   **The Romans left** For a thorough discussion of the numbers of troops on the battlefield, see J. F. Lazenby, *Hannibal's War* (University of Oklahoma Press, 1998), pp. 75–80.

47   **Unusually, Varro had changed** Polybius 3.113.

48   **"As soon as the Iberian and Celtic cavalry got at the Romans"** Ibid., 3.115.

48   **"For a short time, the Iberian and Celtic lines stood"** Ibid., 2.115.

49   **"still they fought"** Ibid., 3.115.

49   **"By charging the Roman legions"** Ibid., 3.116.

49   **"As long as the Romans could keep an unbroken front"** Ibid., 3.116.

51   **"You know how to win a victory"** Livy 22.51.

53   **"I perceive the evil destiny of Carthage"** Florus, *Epitome of Roman History* 1.22.

53   **"No action was fought with Hannibal"** Livy 28.12.

56   **Only a few remnants of the army gathered** Ibid., 26.17.

56   **"they [the Roman voters] looked round"** Livy 26.18. A number of historians have thrown doubt on this event having taken place based on the idea that the Romans did not conduct themselves that way. In

this war, however, Rome did a number of things that broke with tradition. And while the decision for Scipio may have already been made based on his proven military skill and the effect that his name would have on wavering Spanish allies, there is no reason to doubt the events related by Livy took place, even if it was just a matter of political theater. At some point one has to trust the ancient sources, or just admit we truly know nothing of the period.

57   **And although Scipio probably counted on Roman discipline** Polybius 10.7.

58   **"knowing that if he destroyed those"** Ibid., 10.12.

58   **"Many of them fell in the actual battle"** Ibid.

59   **Alerted by local fishermen** This remains a matter of great discussion among historians, who note that the Mediterranean tides are nil, and wonder why this approach was unguarded if this lowering of the lagoon was a well-known phenomenon. My belief is that the water in the lagoon did ebb, through a combination of ebbing tides and a strong wind. But even if the lagoon had not fortuitously ebbed, Scipio still planned to launch this daring strike, as he had reason to believe the lagoon was fordable under any conditions, and he had procured guides for just this purpose. As Polybius relates: "he had learnt from some fishermen who plied their craft there that the whole lagoon was shallow and in most parts fordable, and that usually the water in it receded every day towards evening" (Polybius 10.8).

59   **"They entered the city"** Livy 26.46.

59   **"courage . . . redoubled"** Polybius 10.14.

59   **"Now that they had the enemy in front"** Livy 26.46.

59   **"They do this, I think, to inspire terror"** Polybius 10.15.

62   **Only a providential downpour** Ibid., 11.24.

62   **During the night** Livy 28.15.

63   **That allowed Scipio to enroll seven thousand veteran volunteers** Ibid., 28.46.

65   **Several of these centurions** Ibid., 30.4.

66   **Unobserved, Scipio's two columns** The ancient sources give various interpretations of these happenings. Appian says nothing about any negotiations or reconnaissance of the enemy camp. Rather, he claims that the attack was a result of a sudden decision by Scipio to move to the offensive. Others indicate that the Carthaginians were planning an attack for the following night, which Masinissa learned of. When he informed Scipio of the impending attack, the Roman decided to preempt with an immediate attack of his own. Dio claims that the event listed above took place but was not a ploy. In his version, Scipio broke off negotiations and attacked after a failed attempt to murder Mas-

inissa. I opt to believe Livy's account, as he clearly had the complete works of Polybius to refer to.

66   **"Scipio assigned a portion"** Ibid., 30.5.

66   **"All the rest hurried outside"** Ibid., 14.5.

67   **"For the fire spread with great rapidity"** Ibid.

68   **"[Scipio] went round the towns"** Ibid., 15.4.

69   **The knowledge that Scipio was without a cavalry** Livy reports that Masinissa's reinforcements came in before the scouts departed and that their report to Hannibal greatly distressed the Carthaginian commander (Livy 30.29).

69   **his opponent** Polybius 15.5.

69   **"No understanding was arrived at"** Livy 30.31.

69   **"At daybreak"** Polybius 15.9.

71   **"Keep before your eyes"** Ibid., 15.11.

72   **"Cast their eyes on the ranks of the enemy"** Ibid.

74   **"in their terror many of the elephants escaped"** Ibid., 15.12.

74   **"phalanxes slowly and in imposing array advanced"** Ibid.

74   **They then loosed their javelins** What follows is Polybius's version of the battle with my commentary interweaved; see Polybius 15.13–14.

75   **"greater number of the Carthaginians"** Ibid.

76   **The space between the two armies** Ibid., 15.4.

77   **"For there are times"** Here Polybius is quoting an unknown author, although some scholars believe it to be from a lost work of Theognis.

77   **The latter, we might say** Polybius 15.16.

77   **Moreover, Carthage had to pay** Livy 30.37. To put that 10,000 talents into perspective, one talent would pay all the cost of keeping a trireme at sea for approximately a month or pay twenty mercenaries for a year.

78   **"He was a an extraordinary man"** Livy 38.53.9–11.

78   *"Ingrata patria, ne ossa quidem habebis"* Valerius Maximus, Valeri Maximi Factorum et Dictorum Memorabilium Liber V. See http://www.thelatinlibrary.com/valmax5.html.

79   **"The first, the supreme, the most far-reaching act"** Clausewitz, *On War*, pp. 88–89.

79   *"Auferre, trucidare, rapere, falsis nominibus imperium"* Tacitus, *Agricola*, 30.

79   **on the other hand** Polybius 15.13.

Caesar and Pompey

85   **"They do not begin to use their weapons"** Flavius Josephus, *The Roman Jewish War*, ch. 5, para. 1.

86   The battlefront was not formed Julius Caesar, *The Conquest of Gaul*, trans. S. A. Handford (Penguin, 1951), p. 67.

87   The result was a competitive system William V. Harris, *War and Imperialism in Republican Rome, 327–70 B.C.* (Clarendon Press, 1979), p. 11.

89   "In his pleadings at Rome" Plutarch, *The Lives of the Noble Grecians and Romans*, trans. John Dryden and rev. Arthur Hugh Clough (New York, 1957), p. 850.

89   "I would rather be the first man here" Quoted in Philip Freeman, *Julius Caesar* (Simon & Schuster, 2008), p. 86.

92   "gave him absolute power" Plutarch, *The Lives of the Noble Grecians and Romans*, p. 756.

93   "Besides a great number of other vessels" Ibid., p. 759.

93   "And well had it been for him" Ibid., p. 772.

97   "Caesar . . . above all men" Ibid., p. 870.

97   "But he did not make the weakness of his constitution a pretext" Ibid., pp. 864–865.

100   "Attacking them encumbered with baggage" Julius Caesar, *The Gallic Wars*, 1.12.

101   It was not an easy fight Ibid., 1.26.

101   "the Germans should by degrees" Ibid., 1.33.

102   "surrounded their whole army with their chariots and wagons Ibid., 1.51.

104   When the Aduatuci saw the Romans Ibid., 2.29.

104   "the whole of Gaul was pacified" Ibid., 2.35

105   "[After an] eight-mile march was so speedily" Ibid., 4.14.

106   To the demand of the Nervii that he surrender Ibid., 5.41.

107   "Then Caesar, making a sally" Ibid., 5.41.

108   The Treveri made extensive overtures Ibid., 6.2.

113   "whenever I stamp with my foot" Plutarch, *The Lives of the Noble Grecians and Romans*, p. 781.

114   it would be easier to put the tribune to death Ibid., p. 644.

114   "The consuls at once fled" Ibid., p. 875.

117   "Caesar himself, on the other hand" Julius Caesar, *The Civil War*, 3.58.

118   "Fortune who exerts a powerful influence" Ibid., 3.68.

118   "If Pompey took the same route" Ibid., 3.76–3.80.

119   "Pompey's whole army talked of nothing but the honors" Ibid., 3.83.

122   "There is a certain impetuosity of spirit" Ibid., 3.92.

122   These new and fresh troops advanced rapidly Ibid., 3.93.

122   "It could readily be judged" Ibid., p. 154.

123 **"When Caesar's soldiers had taken the camp"** Plutarch, *The Lives of the Noble Grecians and Romans,* p. 792.

124 **"Caesar's daring, his impatience of the long game"** S. A. Cook, F. E. Adcock, and M. P. Charlesworth, *The Cambridge Ancient History,* vol. 9, *The Roman Republic, 133–44 B.C.* (Cambridge University Press, 1932), p. 646.

124 **"An excellent organizer"** Cook et al., Ibid., pp. 668–669.

Richard I and Saladin

125 **After months of destructive campaigning** Gilbert of Mons, *Chronicle of Hainaut,* trans. Laura Napran (The Boydell Press, 2005), p. 93. Rigord, *Deeds of Philip Augustus,* trans. Paul Hyams; see http://usna .edu/Users/history/abels/hh315/rigord_deeds_1179-1189.htm.

125 **Who would rule much of France** The decision was not tested in combat for another quarter century, at the Battle of Bouvines, in 1214. Here, Richard's brother and successor, King John, was decisively beaten by Philip. The defeat cost the English crown most of their holdings in France, and set John on the road to Runnymede and the signing of the Magna Carta in the following year.

126 **Their clash determined the final fate of the Holy Land** Writing about Saladin is fraught with difficulties. There are almost no contemporary archival records. Moreover, all of the contemporaneous biographies were written by persons within his inner circle, who self-admittedly wrote glowing panegyrics to their leader and patron. The most informative of these biographers was Bahā' al-Dīn Yusuf ibn Shaddād, whose work has been translated into English: Bahā' al-Dīn Yusuf ibn Shaddād, *The Rare and Excellent History of Saladin,* trans. D. S. Richards (Ashgate, 2002). This work was instrumental in the writing of this chapter. The authors were also informed by Stanley Lane-Poole's classic biography of Saladin (Stanley Lane-Poole, *Saladin and the Fall of Jerusalem* [G. P. Putnam's Sons, 1906]), as well as a brilliant new work by Anne-Marie Eddé, *Saladin* (Harvard University Press, 2011), and a valuable biography by Geoffrey Hindley, *Saladin: Hero of Islam* (Pen and Sword Books, 2011). For an excellent account of Saladin's wars also see Malcolm Cameron Lyons and D.E.P. Jackson, *Saladin: The Politics of the Holy Way* (Cambridge University Press, 1984). On the other hand, when it comes to Richard the archival record is voluminous. When coupled with later biographies it becomes almost overwhelming. Among the most important contemporary sources is *Itinerarium Peregrinorum et Gesta Regis Ricardi,* a narrative of the

Third Crusade composed in 1220 from two contemporary sources. A translation of the Bishop Stubb's Latin edition (1864) of this work was published by Helen Nicholson (Helen J. Nicholson, *The Chronicle of the Third Crusade: The Itinerarium Peregrinorum et Gesta Regis Ricardi* [Ashgate, 1997]). This work was also informed by the Annals of Roger of Hoveden (*The Annals of Roger de Hoveden: Comprising the History of England and of Other Countries of Europe from A.D. 732 to A.D. 1201*, trans. Henry T. Riley, 2 vols. (H. G. Bohn, 1853; rep. AMS, 1968), *The History of the Holy War: Ambroise's Estoire de la Guerre Sainte*, trans. Marianne Ailes (Boydell Press, 2003), and various translations of the works of Roger of Coggeshall and Roger of Howden. As for more current historians, the authors owe a debt to John Gillingham's biography, *Richard I* (Yale University Press, 1999). Though, Gillingham's biography remains unsurpassed, our work is also informed by the works of Jean Flori, Ralph Turner, Richard Hesier, David Miller, and Frank McLynn. See Jean Flori, *Richard the Lionheart: King and Knight* (Praeger, 2006); Ralph Turner and Richard Hesier, *The Reign of Richard the Lionheart: Ruler of the Angevin Empire 1189–1199* (Pearson Education, 2000); David Miller, *Richard the Lionheart: The Mighty Crusader* (Weidenfeld & Nicolson, 2003); Frank McLynn, *Richard and John: Kings at War* (De Capo Press, 2007).

126 **His father, Henry II, ruled the Angevin Empire** These counties and duchies were not part of the twelfth-century Île-de-France.

128 **"The mail clad Franks, now on foot"** Ralph V. Turner, *Eleanor of Aquitaine: Queen of France, Queen of England* (Yale University Press, 2009), p. 134.

128 **"Contrary to her royal dignity"** William of Tyre, *History*, XVI, 28: For a complete translation of this part of William's account, see J. Kelly Sowards, *Makers of the Western Tradition: Portraits from History*, vol. 1 (St. Martin's Press, 1997), pp. 169–172.

129 **After harrowing ordeals** Interestingly, Eleanor and her next husband, Henry, were even more closely related, as was Louis's previous wife (Constance of Castile), as well as his next (Adela of Champagne).

130–131 **Though there are many cases in English history** John Gillingham, *Richard I* (Yale University Press, 1999), p. 44.

131 **"All of your enemies"** *Chronicles of the Reigns of Stephen, Henry II, and Richard I*, trans. Richard Howlett, vol. 3 (Public Record Office, 1887), p. 217.

132 **"Richard, coming with tears, fell on his face"** "Medieval Sourcebook: Roger of Hoveden: The Revolt of 1173–74," from *The Chronicle*. See http://legacy.fordham.edu/halsall/source/1173hoveden.asp.

133 **"relieved their outraged feelings in an orgy of slaughter"** Gillingham, *Richard I*, p. 56.

134 **Richard was waiting for them** Though the national identity of France was really just forming during this period, and undoubtedly many of Taillebourg's defenders did not yet consider themselves Frenchmen, I use that nationality for the sake of simplicity throughout this account.

135 **"He carried off his subjects' wives, daughters"** As quoted in Gillingham, *Richard I*, p. 66.

136 **Immediately after looting the famous shrine** Then, as now, Rocamadour attracted pilgrims seeking miracles from the "uncorrupted" body of Saint Amadour or the statue of the Black Madonna. Others are attracted by the supposed "Sword of Roland" that sticks out of a crack in the rock-faced cliffs.

139 **"walk the path of righteousness"** Stanley Lane-Poole, *Saladin and the Fall of the Kingdom of Jerusalem* (G. P. Putnam's Sons, 1906), p. 73.

140 **"It was as though I was being driven to my death"** D. S. Richards, ed., *The Chronicle of Ibn al-Athir for the Crusading Period from al-Kamil fi'l-Ta'rikh* (Ashgate, 2010), p. 177.

142 **"My Lord need but send a courtier on a camel"** Geoffrey Hindley, *Saladin: Hero of Islam* (Pen and Sword, 2007), p. 67.

149 **"The Muslim archers sent up clouds of arrows"** Richards, *The Chronicle of Ibn al-Athir for the Crusading Period from al-Kamil fi'l-Ta'rikh*, p. 322.

149 **Raymond and his men "rode away"** Ibid.

150 **"They retreated to Mount Hattin"** Imad ad-Din al-Isfani (Saladin's personal secretary). See Elizabeth Hallam, *Chronicles of the Crusades: Eye-Witness Accounts of the Wars Between Christianity and Islam* (Weidenfeld & Nicolson, 1989), pp. 157–160.

150 **" 'Be quiet' "** Franscsco Gabrieli, *Arab Historians of the Crusades* (Routledge, 1984), p. 74.

154 **"He was wise and experienced in warfare"** Ibn Shaddād, *The Rare and Excellent History of Saladin*, p. 150.

156 **"Then as one man they charged them"** Ibid., p. 165.

158 **"I saw various individuals amongst the Franks"** Ibid.

160 **The right wing was commanded by Saladin's brother** David Nicolle, *The Third Crusade 1191: Richard the Lionheart, Saladin, and the Struggle for Jerusalem* (Osprey, 2005), p. 71.

160 **"throw an apple into the ranks"** Gillingham, *Richard I*, p. 176.

160 **"drowned out the thunder of the Lord"** Ambroise, *Itinerarium Regis Ricardi*, p. 149.

160 "swept rapidly down upon our men" Ibid.

160 "The Sultan made them engage closely" Ibn Shaddād, *The Rare and Excellent History of Saladin*, p. 177.

162 "No man was so confident" Ambroise, *Itinerarium Regis Ricardi*, p. 150.

163 "Unless we charge them speedily" Ibid., p. 154.

163 "Our men gave way before them" Ibn Shaddād, *The Rare and Excellent History of Saladin*, p. 151.

164 "Then King Richard, fierce and alone" Stanley Lane-Poole, *Saladin and the Kingdom of Jerusalem*, p. 318.

168 "Look to yourself; the devil is loose" Gillingham, *Richard I*, p. 44.

Napoléon and Wellington

172 "condemned to perpetual execration and infamy" Robert Asprey, *The Rise of Napoleon* (Basic Books, 2001), p. 67.

175 His men had killed or captured Andrew Roberts, *Napoleon: A Life* (Viking, 2014), p. 133.

176 "The people would crowd around me" August Fournier, *Napoleon the First* (Henry Holt, 1903), p. 116.

176 "Forty centuries are looking down on you" Antoine Henri Jomini, *Life of Napoleon*, vol. 1 (D. Van Nostrand, 1864), p. 220. Many modern historians question if any of the Pyramids were visible from the battlefield.

177 "They envy and hate me" A. Vieusseux, *Napoleon Bonaparte: His Sayings and Deeds* (Charles Knight, 1846), p. 185.

179 These corps formations Credit for these organizational developments is often given to Jacques Antoine Hypolite, Comte de Guibert, and Jean de Bourcet, and while these men and a few other post Fredrick the Great military thinkers may have been the intellectual fathers of the division and corps system, it was Napoléon who brought the system to its apogee on the battlefield.

179 Each corps lived off the land For an interesting summary of Napoléon's logistical arrangements for this campaign, see Martin Van Creveld, *Supplying War: Logistics from Wallenstein to Patton* (Cambridge University Press, 1977), pp. 42–61.

180 "I should like to see him opposed someday" Louis Antoine Fauvelet de Bourrienne, *Memoirs of Napoléon Bonaparte,* vol. 1 (Charles Scribner's Sons, 1891), p. 350.

180 "I have destroyed the Austrian army" Graf Maximilian Yorck von

Wartenburg, *Napoleon as a General,* vol. 1 (Kegan Paul, Trench, Trübner, 1902), p. 216.

181 **Believing it impossible for marshals of France to lie** Bourrienne, *Memoirs of Napoléon Bonaparte,* vol. 2, p. 160.

181 **"Break the armistice at once"** Alistair Horne, *How Far Austerlitz* (St. Martin's Press, 1996), p. 128.

183 **"In that case we can wait another quarter of an hour"** Yorck von Wartenburg, *Napoleon as a General,* vol. 1, p. 179.

183 **"Your majesty should say rather that they came from hell"** Horne, *How Far Austerlitz,* p. 156.

184 **"We must put our heads down"** Paul Charles Francois Adrien Henri Dieudonne Baron Thiebault, *The Memoirs of Baron Thiebault* (Smith, Elder, 1896), p. 164.

185 **"In those terrible shocks whole battalions of them were killed"** Ibid., p. 165.

185 **"Many fine ladies will weep tomorrow in St. Petersburg"** Horne, *How Far Austerlitz,* p. 175.

185 **"Forward against the enemy left"** Ibid.

185 **"roll up that map"** Earl Philip Henry Stanhope, *Life of the Right Honourable William Pitt,* vol. 4 (John Murray, 1867), p. 369.

186 **"Your general must be seeing double"** David Chandler, *The Campaigns of Napoleon* (Macmillan, 1966), p. 488.

187 **On April 10, 1809** For the best recent works on this campaign, see John H. Gill's three-volume *Thunder on the Danube* (Frontline Books, 2014).

189 **Moreover, there was not enough food** Andrew Roberts, *Napoleon: A Life* (Viking, 2014), p. 576.

189 **"Your ambition is insatiable"** Yorck von Wartenburg, *Napoleon as a General,* vol. 1, p. 108.

189 **"No! It is too extensive a movement"** Philippe-Paul Ségur, *History of the Expedition to Russia,* vol. 1 (H. L. Hunt and C. C. Clarke, 1826), p. 296.

190 **"They are citadels"** Michael Adams, *Napoleon in Russia* (Bloomsbury, 2006), p. 347.

190 **"I will not have that destroyed"** Roberts, *Napoleon: A Life,* p. 605.

192 **"Here I am!"** Montgomery B. Gibbs, *The Military Career of Napoleon the Great* (The Werner Company, 1895), p. 420.

192 **"food for the powder"** Christopher Hibbert, *Wellington: A Personal History* (Da Capo, 1999), p. 6.

192–193 **"With no opportunity for the display of any kind of talent"** Sir Edward Bruce Hamley, *Wellington's Career: A Military and Political Summary* (William Blackwood and Sons, 1860), p. 3.

194 **By this time Wellesley had given up** *The Quarterly Review,* vol. 158 (John Murray, 1884), p. 526.

196 **"a long defensive war would ruin us"** Arthur Wellesley of Wellington, John Gurwood, *The Despatches of Field Marshall, the Duke of Wellington,* vol. 1 (Parker, Furnivall, and Parker, 1843), p. 640.

196 **"They came here in the morning"** As quoted in Elizabeth Longford, *Wellington: The Years of the Sword* (Harper & Row, 1969), p. 88.

196 **If this force was defeated** The size and firepower of the Maratha army hugely varies in every consulted work. The numbers presented here are the authors' best estimate.

197 **"Well! They are making a lot of noise"** Rory Muir, *Wellington: The Path to Victory 1769–1814* (Yale University Press, 2013), p. 138.

197 **"In the space of less than a mile"** John Blakiston, *Twelve Years' Military Adventure in Three Quarters of the Globe,* vol. 1 (Henry Colburn, 1829), p. 165.

197 **"Not a whisper was heard through the ranks"** Ibid., p. 160.

199 **"The whole of our line hailed it with a shout of triumph"** Ibid., p. 168.

199 **"I never saw a man so cool and collected"** Wellesley, *Supplementary Despatches, Correspondence and Memoranda,* vol. 1, p. 186.

199 **"If I can call it a conversation"** *The Quarterly Review,* vol. 158, p. 552.

200 **I don't know that I ever had a conversation that interested me more"** Ibid.

201 **"I, at least, will not be frightened beforehand"** Ibid.

201 **"I hope that I will have beat [General Jean-Andoche] Junot"** Richard Holmes, *Wellington: The Iron Duke* (HarperCollins, 1996), p. 109.

204 **"highly honorable and successful"** Wellesley, *Supplementary Despatches, Correspondence and Memoranda,* vol. 3 (John Murray, 1859), p. 177.

204 **"avalanche of fire and steel"** Winston S. Churchill, *A History of English Speaking Peoples: The Age of Revolution,* vol. 3 (Dodd, Mead, 1957), p. 210.

206 **"old, proud, incompetent, and ailing"** Richard Holmes, *Wellington: The Iron Duke* (HarperCollins, 1996), p. 133.

209 **A long stalemate ensued** Wellesley, *Supplementary Despatches, Correspondence and Memoranda* (John Murray, 1851), p. 414.

210 **"The superiority was not so great"** Wellesley, *Supplementary Despatches, Correspondence and Memoranda* (John Murray, 1837), p. 255.

210 **"Marmont will not risk an action"** Ibid., p. 270.

210 **"By God, they are extending their line"** Huw J. Davies, *Wellington's*

Wars: The Making of a Military Genius (Yale University Press, 2012), p. 149.

210 **"Throw your division into column"** Ibid.

211 **"He kept his dispositions hidden"** Charles Oman, *Wellington's Army: 1809–1814* (Longmans, Green, 1913), p. 58.

212 **"We have in the service the scum of the earth"** Wellesley, *Supplementary Despatches, Correspondence and Memoranda,* vol. 6 (Parker, Furnivall, and Parker, 1845), p. 575.

212 **"It is for you to save the world again"** Longford, *Wellington: The Years of the Sword,* p. 389.

216 **Lefol's troops reeled back from the canister** These battalions made up the Twelfth and Twenty-fourth Prussian regiments.

217 **In the actual event, the Prussians proved incredibly difficult to push aside** In this battle narrative the term "British" is used for the purpose of simplicity. The British were joined on the battlefield by troops from Belgium, the Netherlands, and Germany (the King's German Legion), who all gave a good account of themselves throughout the campaign.

218 **"Cannon balls shattered houses and ricocheted in the streets"** Henry Houssaye, *Napoleon and the Campaign of 1815 Waterloo* (Adam & Charles Black, 1900), p. 94.

218 **"slaughtered each other"** Ibid., p. 95.

218 **"Prussian bullets swept us away by the dozen"** Roger Parkinson, *The Hussar General* (Purnell Book Services Limited, 1975), p. 222.

218 **"In the main street the mud was red with blood"** Ibid.

220 **Worn out by the tension of battle and the heat** Chandler, *Campaigns of Napoleon,* p. 149.

228 **"Ah, you don't know Macdonell"** Alessandro Barbero, *The Battle: A New History of Waterloo* (Walker Brothers, 2009), p. 97.

234 **"Such is the music of the field"** J. Anton, *Retrospect of a Military Life,* p. 210, as quoted in Garth Glover, *Waterloo: Myth and Reality* (Pen & Sword, 2014), p. 135.

235 **"My duty is to execute the Emperor's orders"** Houssaye, *Napoleon and the Campaign of 1815 Waterloo,* p. 169.

238 **"At four o'clock our square was a perfect hospital"** Rees Howell Gronow, *The Reminiscences and Recollections of Captain Gronow,* vol. 1 (John C. Nimmo, 1900), p. 190.

240 **"Never will he find a more glorious grave!"** John Booth, *The Battle of Waterloo: Circumstantial Details Relative to the Battle* (B. R. Howlett, 1816), p. 39.

242 **The Battle of Waterloo concluded** Sir Edward S. Creasy, *Fifteen Decisive Battles of the World: From Marathon to Waterloo* (Bentley, 1851).

Grant and Lee

244   **The Union victory was easily explainable** Douglas Southall Freeman, "The Sword of Robert E. Lee," in Gary Gallagher, ed., *Lee the Soldier* (University of Nebraska Press, 1996), p. 144.

247   **"He knew how to express what he wanted to say"** Ulysses S. Grant, *The Personal Memoirs of U.S. Grant* (J. J. Little & Co., 1885), vol. 1, chs. 7 and 8. (Hereafter *Memoirs.*)

250   **"found it very hard work for a few days"** *Memoirs,* vol. 1, ch. 18.

251   **"The lesson was valuable"** Ibid.

257   **"But when Confederate armies were collected"** Ibid., vol. 1, ch. 25.

257   **"I knew wherever I was that you thought of me"** Letter, Sherman to Grant, March 10, 1864. See Hamlin Garland, *Ulysses S. Grant: His Life and Character* (Doubleday & McClure, 1898), p. 254.

260   **"His name might be audacity"** Edward Porter Alexander, *Military Memoirs of a Confederate: A Critical Narrative* (C. Scribner's Sons, 1907), pp. 110–111.

270   **"Well, well, General, bury these men"** Douglas Southall Freeman, *Lee's Lieutenants: A Study in Command,* vol. 3 (C. Scribner's Sons, 1944), p. 327.

271   **"We could have subsisted off the country"** *Memoirs,* vol. 1, p. 163.

274   **"My only wonder"** Ibid., vol. 2, p. 28.

275   **"You I propose to move against Johnston's army"** Ibid., vol. 2, pp. 130–131.

276   **Grant did not have much hope for Sigel's effort** Ibid., vol. 2, p. 132.

276   **"Lee's army will be your objective point"** Ibid., vol. 2, p. 135.

278   **"Go back to your command, and try to think what we are going to do"** Horace Porter, *Campaigning with Grant* (Century, 1907), p. 70.

280   **"The dim impression of that afternoon"** Thomas W. Hyde, *Following the Greek Cross: Or, Memories of the Sixth Corps* (Houghton, Mifflin, 1894), p. 191.

280   **"A brigade today—we'll try a corps tomorrow"** Quoted in Mark Grimsley, *And Keep Moving On: The Virginia Campaign, May–June 1864* (University of Nebraska Press, 2002), p. 82.

284   **"I was not long in finding out that the objections to Smith's promotion"** *Memoirs,* vol. 2, p. 414.

287   **"It was wasting good soldiers"** Edward Porter Alexander, *Fighting for the Confederacy: The Personal Memoirs of General Edward Porter Alexander,* ed. Gary M. Gallagher (University of North Carolina Press, 1989), p. 363.

289   **"For thirty days it has been one funeral procession past me"** Quoted

in Shelby Foote, *The Civil War: A Narrative,* vol. 3, *Red River to Appomattox* (Random House, 1974), p. 295.

289–290 **"Lazy and indolent, they will not even ride along the lines"** Quoted in Bruce Catton, *A Stillness at Appomattox* (Doubleday, 1953), p. 171.

Rommel, Montgomery, and Patton

293 **"Where time allowed and the situation demanded"** General David Fraser, *Knight's Cross: A Life of Field Marshal Erwin Rommel* (HarperCollins, 1993), p. 45.

297 **"But I have often wondered"** Quoted in Nigel Hamilton, *The Full Monty,* vol. 1, *Montgomery of Alamein, 1887–1942* (Allen Lane, 2001), p. 17.

298 **"We are of course all looking forward"** Quoted in ibid., p. 49.

299 **"to see what the positions looked like"** Quoted in ibid., p. 67.

303 MEXICAN BANDIT-KILLER WELL KNOWN Carlo D'Este, *Patton, A Genius for War* (HarperCollins, 1995), p. 176.

304 **"The A.D.C. is a fire-eater!"** R. Blake, *The private papers of Douglas Haig 1914–1919, being selections from the private diary and correspondence of Field-Marshal the Earl Haig of Nemersyde* (Eyre & Spottiswoode, 1952).

307 **"because he could be so rude"** Quoted in Hamilton, *The Full Monty,* vol. 1, p. 218.

310 **The college's commandant forwarded his research paper** D'Este, *Patton,* p. 349.

311 **"Gentlemen, you don't push the noodle"** Ibid., p. 395.

314 **"The French troops were completely overcome"** Erwin Rommel, *The Rommel Papers,* ed. B. H. Liddell Hart (Harcourt, Brace, 1953), pp. 19, 21–22.

314 **"Between the clots"** Antoine de Saint-Exupéry, *Last Flight to Arras,* trans. Lewis Galantiè (Reynal & Hitchcock, 1942), p. 56.

315 **"Again and again, he turned up completely by surprise"** Karl-Heinz Frieser with John T. Greenwood, *The Blitzkrieg Legend: The 1940 Campaign in the West* (Naval Institute Press, 2005), pp. 338–339.

316 **"When the cannon sounds"** Quoted in MacGregor Knox, *Mussolini Unleashed, 1939–1941: Politics and Strategy in Fascist Italy's Last War* (Cambridge University Press, 1982), p. 121.

317 **"tough and hard opponents as individual fighters"** Quoted in Den-

nis Showalter, *Patton and Rommel: Men of War in the Twentieth Century* (Berkley Caliber, 2005), p. 236.

317   "**No one has a clear idea of their disposition**" Franz Halder, War Journal of Franz Halder, vol 1, p 80; See: https://archive.org /stream/HalderWarJournal/Halder%20War%20Journal_djvu.txt. Major General Friedrich Paulus, at that time the operations officer in the OKH and later to be the commander of the Sixth Army in the Battle of Stalingrad.

317   "**He has good personal relations with Rommel**" Franz Halder, *The Halder War Diary, 1939–1942*, ed. Charles Burdick and Hans-Adolph Jacobsen (Presidio Press, 1988), p. 374.

318   "**They had incredible enthusiasm and dash**" Major Robert Crisp, *Brazen Chariots; an Account of Tank Warfare in the Western Desert, November–December 1941* (Muller, 1959), p. 39.

322   "**[The Guards Brigade] was almost a living embodiment of the virtues and faults of the British soldier**" Rommel, *The Rommel Papers*, p. 222.

325   "**I may be old, I may be slow, I may be stoopid, and I know I'm deaf**" Quoted in Nigel Hamilton, *Monty: Master of the Battlefield, 1942–44*, vol. 2, *Life of Montgomery of Alamein* (McGraw-Hill, 1984), pp. 142–143.

325   "**My friend General Briggs says he is the best soldier**" Quoted in D'Este, *Patton*, p. 453.

325   "**A prime example of the traditional over-ripe, overbearing, and explosive senior officers**" Carlo D'Este, *Eisenhower, A Soldier's Life* (Henry Holt, 2002), p. 392.

326   "**The Americans it is fair to say, profited far more**" Rommel, *The Rommel Papers*, p. 523.

329   "**I have seen so many mistakes made in this war**" Quoted in D'Este, *Patton*, p. 493.

330   "**I must so seriously question your good judgment**" Quoted in ibid., p. 536.

335   "**The whole handling of the battle**" Quoted in Carlo D'Este, *Decision in Normandy: The Unwritten Story of Montgomery and the Allied Campaign* (Collins, 1983), p. 196.

341   "**That afforded me the cue I needed**" Quoted in Nigel Hamilton, *Monty: The Field Marshal, 1944–76*, vol. 3, *Life of Montgomery of Alamein* (David & Charles, 1986), p. 104.

341   "**I feel that Monty's strategy for once is at fault**" Field Marshal Lord Alan Brooke, *War Diaries, 1939–1945*, ed. Alex Danchev and Daniel Todman (Berkeley, CA, 2000), p. 600.

344 "will be off their guard and I shall pop out at them" Quoted in D'Este, *Patton*, p. 657.

345 "Within an hour everything had been thrashed out" Quoted in ibid., p. 681.

348 "He [Montgomery] said of course that he wanted to pay tribute" Quoted in Hamilton, *Monty*, vol. 3, *Life of Montgomery of Alamein*, p. 303.

351 "In the field of higher strategic planning" Rommel, *The Rommel Papers*, p. 521.

Conclusion: Modern Warfare and the System of Genius

355 **By Napoléon's time this was no longer true** Many historians would place the start of these changes with the Wars of Spanish and Austrian Succession or no later than the Seven Years' War, for which William Pitt the Elder made strategy and ordered the conduct of operations on a global scale.

355 **If the advent of the "master strategist"** The authors would claim that the period when a single "master strategist" was capable of grasping all of the complexities of a great conflict probably came to an end in the eighteenth century with the demise of Willian Pitt the Elder, who guided Great Britain through the Seven Years' War.

355 **"[be] a student of the present"** Lawrence Freedman, *Strategy: A History* (Oxford University Press, 2013), p. 238.

358 **"I liked what I saw of Marshall"** Alex Danchev and Daniel Todman, eds., *War Diaries 1939–1945: Field Marshall Lord Alan Brooke* (Weidenfeld & Nicolson, 2001), p. 246.

359 **"I found that he had not begun to consider any form of plan of action"** Ibid., p. 249.

363 **"What fascinates me about good strategy"** Lawrence Freedman, "The Master Strategist Is Still a Myth," War on the Rocks (October 14, 2014). See http://warontherocks.com/2014/10/the-master -strategist-is-still-a-myth/.

Index

Page numbers in *italics* indicate illustrations.

ABOUT THE AUTHORS

JAMES LACEY is the author most recently of *The Washington War: FDR's Inner Circle and the Politics of Power That Won World War II* and *The First Clash: The Miraculous Greek Victory at Marathon and Its Impact on Western Civilization,* as well as co-author with Williamson Murray of *Moment of Battle: The Twenty Clashes that Changed the World.* He is a widely published defense analyst who has written extensively on the war in Iraq and the global war on terrorism. He served more than a dozen years on active duty as an infantry officer. Lacey traveled with the 101st Airborne Division during the Iraq invasion as an embedded journalist for *Time* magazine, and his work has also appeared in *National Review, Foreign Affairs, The Journal of Military History,* and many other publications. He currently teaches at the Marine Corps War College and lives in Virginia.

WILLIAMSON MURRAY is the author of a wide selection of articles and books, including, with Allan Millett, the acclaimed *A War to Be Won: Fighting the Second World War.* He is professor emeritus of history from Ohio State, served for five years as an officer in the United States Air Force, and has taught at the Air War College and the United States Military Academy. He has also served as a Secretary of the Navy Fellow at the Naval War College, the Centennial Visiting Professor at the London School of Economics, the Matthew C. Horner Professor of Military Theory at the Marine Corps University, the Charles Lindbergh Chair at the Smithsonian National Air and Space Museum, the Harold K. Johnson Professor of Military History at the Army War College, and the Distinguished Visiting Professor of Naval Heritage and History at the U.S. Naval Academy at Annapolis. He is currently a defense analyst at the Potomac Institute for Policy Studies and teaches at the Naval War College.